THE ROLLING STONES

IT'S ONLY ROCK 'N' ROLL:
SONG BY SONG

dedication

This book is dedicated to Mares and Baby Nico

Text and design copyright © Carlton Books Limited 1997

1 2 3 4 5 6 7 8 9 10

This edition first published in Canada in 1997 by
Raincoast Books
8680 Camble Street
Vancouver, B.C. V6P 6M9
(604) 323-7100

Project Editors: Lorraine Dickey, Lucian Randall
Copy Editing: Terry Burrows, Mike Flynn
Project Art Direction: Zoë Maggs
Designer: Mary Ryan
Picture Research: Rachel Leach
Production: Sarah Schuman

All rights reserved. No part of this publication may be reproduced, stored in a retrieval system, or transmitted in any form or by any means, electronic, mechanical, photocopying, recording or otherwise, without the prior permission of the publishers.

Canadian Cataloguing in Publication Data
Appleford, Steve
The Rolling Stones
ISBN 1-55192-107-3

1. Rolling Stones. I. Title
ML421.R754A65 1997   782.42166'092'2   C97-910375-4

Printed in Italy

acknowledgements

Special thanks must go to the following people, who granted interviews specifically for this book: Marty Balin, Jim Barber, Rodney Bingenheimer, Hal Blaine, Ollie Brown, Lindsey Buckingham, George Chkiantz, Jim Dickinson, Marianne Faithfull, Mick Farren, Mick Fleetwood, Charlie Goodan, Dave Jerden, Andy Johns, Bobby Keys, Wayne Kramer, Harvey Kubernick, Tammi Lynn, Ray Manzarek, John Mayall, Roger McGuinn, Christine McVie, Jim Price, Mike Simpson (of the Dust Brothers) and Bobby Womack.

For their help and enthusiasm, I am also grateful to: Scott Becker, Bill Bentley, Chuck Crisafulli, Saul Davis, archivist extraordinaire Rebecca Esmerian and Jim Baltutis, Billy Groak & Leslie Rice, Linda Hasert, Jack Lancaster, John Mastro, Judy Miller, Chris Morris, Robert Pettersen of Shattered Music, Craig Rosen (for many reasons, including access to his taped interviews with Glyn Johns, Chris Kimsey and Andrew Loog Oldham) and Rob Seidenberg.

Finally, this book would not exist if not for the superhuman patience and stamina of the fine editors at Carlton Books: Lucian Randall, Julian Flanders, Terry Burrows and Lorraine Dickey. The nineteen nervous breakdowns of deadlines, uncertain e-mail, faxes, transcontinental phone calls, etc., resulted in the book safely in your hands, thanks to them.

THE ROLLING STONES

IT'S ONLY ROCK 'N' ROLL: SONG BY SONG

Steve Appleford

RAINCOAST BOOKS

Vancouver

contents

6   Preface
8   Introduction
12   Chronology

1960s

16   The Rolling Stones
22   The Rolling Stones No. 2
28   Out Of Our Heads
34   Aftermath
44   Between The Buttons
54   Their Satanic Majesties Request
68   Beggars Banquet
82   Let It Bleed

1970s

96   Sticky Fingers
108   Exile On Main Street
126   Goats Head Soup
136   It's Only Rock 'N' Roll
146   Black And Blue
154   Some Girls

contents

1980s

- 166 **Emotional Rescue**
- 174 **Tattoo You**
- 188 **Undercover**
- 202 **Dirty Work**
- 216 **Steel Wheels**

1990s

- 228 **Voodoo Lounge**
- 240 **Hot Stuff: Singles, EPs, B-sides And Other Oddities**
- 248 **Not Fade Away: The Rolling Stones In 1997**

- 252 **You Got Me Rocking: A Rolling Stones Discography**
- 256 **Index**

preface

Hit or miss? The Rolling Stones judge new releases on TV's Juke Box Jury.

he Rolling Stones were never bigger than Jesus. They didn't need to be, and not because of any pact with an overrated Prince of Darkness. Why call on Satan or the Messiah when the masses were already hailing you as "The World's Greatest Rock And Roll Band"? The Stones keep their own counsel. It's been a fast and furious journey from their days as teenage blues fanatics, cuddly Soho Bohemians and jet-setting decadents to their present role as elder statesmen of rock. Death and despair have touched them along the way, but the dirty work continues.

The last time I saw Mick Jagger in the flesh, the man seemed a bit agitated, hopping like a tick beneath the bright lights of the Los Angeles Memorial Coliseum. From where I sat, about as far back as possible, in virtually the last row, the massive *Steel Wheels* tour juggernaut of 1989 looked like a well-lit puppet show. Even the big screens at either side of the stage were like distant, flickering smudges of light. That's how big the Stones had become. That's maybe too big. But the music that night could not be denied, with a sound richer, crisper and more stirring than most things I've witnessed at homier venues like the Hollywood Palladium, where, to my everlasting envy and awe, my friend Billy Groak caught the Stones in 1972. But at the Coliseum, the Stones could still deliver.

To those who care deeply about rock and roll, the Rolling Stones have left an essential body of work. In the context of their peak years in the sixties and seventies, that music was as inventive in its own way as the Velvet Underground was with its tales of heroin and drag queens. Composers Jagger and Richards have explored a fair share of grim subject matter along the way, too, finding metaphors for their own tales of endless sex and salvation, of filth and fame, to fuel songs from the lustful charge of '(I Can't Get No) Satisfaction' to the defiant outlaw anthem 'Before They Make Me Run'. The fierce rock mixture of the Stones emerged from a passion for the deep blues, and its wisdom on the extremes of human

preface

emotion. What they discovered there was often enlightening, but not always pleasant.

Keith Richards forged a new pop standard, weaving the sounds of Chuck Berry and Muddy Waters into a dynamic brand of rhythmic, riff-based rock. Jagger never could quite reproduce the absolute lowdown timbre of the great bluesmen, nor the soulful transcendence of Sam Cooke or King Solomon Burke. But he didn't need to. There were certainly moments of breathless authenticity on the Stones version of Mississippi Fred McDowell's 'You Gotta Move' and other blues exercises. And yet by the time the Stones declared "It's the singer, not the song", Jagger had taken his art and message to a new plateau, one that reflected the fears of a new generation, with a powerful growl that was more about the coming darkness than the bad love of the old blues singers.

This book is not intended as the definitive telling (yet again) of the Stones' epic story. Look to Stanley Booth's *Dancing With the Devil/The True Adventures Of The Rolling Stones* and Bill Wyman's *Stone Alone* for that. Consider this instead a gathering of moments, of small vignettes that attempt to capture the endlessly ecstatic and horrible stories behind the making of the Rolling Stones' hits, near-misses and utter catastrophes. In short, it's a look at the music that makes the story worth telling at all.

It's a telling made more difficult by the jumbled release of the band's material in America, where fans found Stones albums very different from their counterparts in Europe. The Beatles suffered much the same fate early in their career, but that's all been sorted out for the digital age with the CD re-release of the Beatles catalogue in the original British versions, as the band always intended. No such luck with the Stones, whose early releases on Decca and London are controlled by ex-Stones manager Allen Klein and remain a jumble.

This book's title is taken from the Stones song and album of the same name, a slogan weighted with perhaps more meaning than even Jagger intended. Critic Dave Marsh once described 'It's Only Rock 'N' Roll' as "Mick Jagger at 32, desperately trying to explain himself to Bianca and her Studio 54 cronies". That's a harsh, but fair interpretation. During the 1980s, Jagger suffered a crisis of confidence in the Stones and a life dedicated to singing the devil's music. The Stones nearly broke apart as the singer embarked on a solo career bent on tapping into the fleeting pop fashions of the moment. Keith Richards described it as Jagger's "Peter Pan Complex".

Jagger regained his composure by the beginning of the 1990s to help lead a revitalized Stones to the end of the millennium. Which is where we find the Stones today. In 1997, the band completed their 21st studio album, and announced plans for another epic world tour, ignoring as best they can the suggestion that middle-aged men have no business playing rock and roll.

Bassist Bill Wyman was asking that question himself when he decided to retire from the Stones in 1993. No one has joined him yet. As veteran British bluesman John Mayall told me during the course of writing this book, "Creating music is an art...the years only make you more mature...you learn more and more as the years go by". And Keith Richards recently told *Rolling Stone* magazine, "We're the only band to make it this far, and if we trip and fall, you'll know that's how far it can be taken."

So this book is merely the story so far. Writing it has been a massive undertaking, requiring a careful look at the Stones' three decades of work through hundreds of old articles and new interviews with the band's closest associates and contemporaries. As I pieced the story together, the Stones were gathering across town in Hollywood to record their new album with producers Don Was, the Dust Brothers and Babyface. I found some comfort in that, knowing that as my writing chores drifted deep into the early morning hours, Keith Richards was not far away, and probably just getting tuned up.

> "We're the only band to make it this far, and if we trip and fall you'll know that's how far it can be taken"
> — Keith Richards

Steve Appleford
Los Angeles
June, 1997

introduction

Too young for the blues? The Stones pose for an early promotional shot.

The Thames ain't the Mississippi. And yet the blues descended on post-war London town like a prophetic message from another world – a place of moonshine, sharecroppers and bad, bad love. It was a sound fuelled by tragedy and inner strength. And it was played by men like Muddy Waters, who arrived at his first ever field recording session in July 1942 in bare feet and with a borrowed guitar, singing with profound sexual tension of getting no satisfaction at all. "I woke up this mornin', found my little baby gone."

The blues told the story of Black America, where the great singer Bessie Smith, the celebrated "Empress of the Blues", bled to death when she was denied entry into a white hospital after a car accident. It was a world where Waters (born McKinley Morganfield) was a field worker by the age of 10, making less than 75 cents a day; and where even a blues titan like the dignified Son House, the man who taught Robert Johnson himself, was caught under the indifferent thumb of a white boss and landowner.

In the early 1960s, their music of intense joy and pain made an unlikely connection with British youth, with the likes of Brian Jones and Mick Jagger and Keith Richards, who knew little of the trouble Waters had seen, but who understood that the folk blues of Mississippi was about something real and passionate.

Baby Mick had first heard those sounds as a 12-year-old, spinning race records mailed direct from America. Then in 1960, Jagger was travelling to his classes at the London School of Economics, carrying a precious stack of new vinyl by Chuck Berry, Little Walter, Muddy Waters and Mississippi Fred McDowell, when he was spotted on the train by Keith Richards. Both of these solidly middle-class urchins were born in Dartford in 1943, and had known each other as children at Wentworth County Primary School before losing touch after the age of 11. Now young Mr Richards was hungrily eyeing the records under Mick's arm: "You're into Chuck Berry, man, REALLY?"

Records were still a scarce luxury in those days, so Keith invited Mick up to tea. Together they studied every groove, every ragged moment of love, hate, desperation and euphoria. For Richards, the discovery of these three-minute dispatches transformed his black and white life in suburban London into glorious Technicolor. By this time, Keith was an art school misfit, more obsessed with learning guitar than any of his class work. Mick was already singing Buddy Holly tunes for his own amusement at weekends, and soon began jamming rock and blues tunes with Richards at a friend's house.

Mick and Keith dreamt of the monumental sounds they might make together, and often travelled to hear live music at local clubs. In 1962, they arrived at the Marquee Club in London in time to see Alexis Korner's Blues Incorporated, where they discovered a young blond guitarist sitting in, hunched like a madman over his instrument, playing slide guitar on 'Dust My Broom' not unlike the great Elmore James. Except that this cat – who called himself Elmo Lewis – wasn't from the Mississippi Delta country, but had come all the way from genteel

introduction

Cheltenham for his few moments of blues glory. His real name was Brian Jones, and he told Jagger and Richards of his plans to form his own blues unit, once he escaped to London.

Jones was fanatical in his quest to create the Rollin' Stones, a name taken from a Muddy Waters lyric. And he had soon recruited Jagger, Richards, bassist Bill Wyman (nee Perks), drummer Charlie Watts (another Blues Incorporated veteran) and pianist Ian Stewart. This was Brian Jones' band. Mick was just the singer then, Keith just another guitarist. But they all shared a deep love for the rock and blues of Mississippi and Chicago, from the likes of Jimmy Reed, T-Bone Walker, Big Bill Broonzy, Bo Diddley, John Lee Hooker and dozens of other American artists largely overlooked in their own country.

The Rollin' Stones quickly found themselves at the forefront of a new movement of young British blues players, committed to spreading the gospel according to Chess Records, home to many of the most distinctive bluesmen and rockers. It was an almost religious experience for the pious Stones, copying the old blues standards as if they were scripture, never pausing to seriously consider writing their own material as the Beatles had done from the very beginning. Anything else would have been SACRILEGE, or at least require an effort thus far beyond the band's reach. What could these London choirboys have to offer that hadn't already been said to greater effect by the original blues masters?

Jagger's voice was not yet the distinctive, seething growl that would emerge in the coming years, and was sometimes lost amidst the earnestness of the band's delivery. Likewise, Jones and Richards were hardly instrumental virtuosos, not in the manner that would have overheated graffiti artists declaring Eric Clapton as God. The duo instead locked together into a tight rhythmic juggernaut, working toward a rare mastery of rhythm guitar, the core element that would lead to the mature Stones sound later heard within 'Brown Sugar' and *Exile On Main Street*.

Soon, the Stones were joined on the stages of London by a crowd of new blues-based artists in search of their own musical voices. The Animals arrived from Newcastle. Spencer Davis and Stevie Winwood came from Birmingham. Any new band hoping to succeed had to come to London. "It was a fresh thing for most people because for ten years people had been listening to nothing but New Orleans jazz, then called Trad Jazz," says John Mayall, who arrived from Manchester in 1963, leaving his job in the graphics department of a hometown advertising agency. "That had been the reigning music in all the clubs. That same lineup of trumpet, trombone, clarinet and the rhythm section was all people really heard until this fresh Chicago sound came in. It appealed to the young generation. They'd had an audience in the coffee shops and the folk clubs at that time in London. They just took it a step further. They were heavily influenced by Muddy Waters' work with Little Walter and the amplifiers and so forth – they just got electrified. And in those same folk clubs they started to get an audience."

At the centre of that movement was Alexis Korner, whose Blues Incorporated launched the careers of many young blues players. He also arranged for bands such as the Stones and the Yardbirds to share bills with visiting American bluesmen. If Korner was not one of the scene's exceptional guitarists, his great enthusiasm for fellow players inspired many. Mayall remembers Korner's constant encouragement, and how the Hungarian-born guitarist personally introduced Mayall to London club-owners and musicians, essentially kick-starting Mayall's career as bandleader to the Bluesbreakers.

"It was Alexis' movement," recalls Mick Farren, a musician and writer who would later make his mark with the Deviants. "He was a great proselytizer. He was a really lovely guy. If he had it, he'd lend you money, and listen to your problems. He was everybody's godfather, rabbi, whatever. Alexis was an exceptional guy."

Alexis Korner, patron saint of the London blues scene.

introduction

Among the young blues acts travelling the back roads of England with visiting American bluesmen was Chicken Shack, a band that included singer and pianist Christine McVie (née Perfect), later of Fleetwood Mac. "We used to have B.B. King and Freddie Guy and all these characters come over from the States, and all these white English groups would support them and go on pub tours with them," McVie remembers fondly. "American blues became such a part of the English subculture back then. People were hunting around for these obscure 45 singles. It was wonderful."

Soon enough, the traditional jazz bands were being elbowed aside in London clubs to make room for increasingly popular British blues bands. "Brian was so pleased to see the last jazz band disband and us taking over the clubs," Richards told Stanley Booth in *Dancing With the Devil/The True Adventures Of The Rolling Stones*. "It was his happiest, proudest moment."

During these first years, Jones was the prime mover behind the Rollin' Stones. Playing the blues was now his life. He had been kicked out of college, drifted from one job to another, and he already fathered at least one son. Mick and Keith were still living at home, far from being

Tapping the source: Ronnie Wood trades licks with blues deity Muddy Waters.

the great hedonists the Glimmer Twins would later become. "Success never came into it," Richards told *Creem* magazine in 1975. "We never dreamed of it, never even thought we could turn the whole of London on to what we were doing, let alone the world. We didn't even think like that. We just thought, 'wouldn't it be great if we could play one night a week with a few people dancing?'"

The irony of their success was not lost on the Stones. Within a few years, their renditions of American R&B songs would climb high into the charts, while the music's black originators often couldn't get on US pop radio at all. "By the time we got here, you could've heard all this shit ten times better, five years before the Beatles or us arrived," Keith told *Spin* magazine in 1985. "It was here already."

Still, there was a growing authenticity in the Stones' delivery of these R&B experiments. "I thought it came off real," says Bobby Womack, co-author of 'It's All Over Now', which became the Stones' first UK chart-topper in 1964. "It was them being real with what they were about. Sometimes you can't be somebody else. You're going to be yourself, no matter what they do. So they put their English touch into it, and they introduced to white audiences all around the world how important singing from the heart and singing soul was. That caused the black music to be recognized. Think about it: B.B. King had been kicking for years, Tina Turner, a lot of artists. The Rolling Stones said it was OK to feel this music. Forget the politics. Music ain't about that. It made the music grow."

The early Rollin' Stones were devout followers of that soulful, blues-drenched sound. Eddie Cochran numbers were never part of the Stones repertoire. The beginning of the sixties was the fading era of melodramatic pop balladeers named Bobby and Ricky and Billy and Cliff, who sang of teen dreams and sugar plum fairies, beneath hair perfectly sculpted into greasy tidal waves, corkscrews and duck tails. This wasn't the image young Mr Jagger was cultivating for himself. Prior to one performance, he was famously quoted as saying, "I hope they don't think we're a rock and roll band".

But rock and roll was always part of the Stones' mix, guaranteed by the presence of Richards, who worshipped the flying riffs and wry minimalist poetry of Chuck Berry at least as much as the heavy blues of Muddy Waters. That meant poor Brian had to endure the occasional Chuck Berry rocker during their sets, never imagining that the Stones legacy would hinge less on blues devotion than to recreating rock and roll in their own image.

introduction

In March 1963, the Stones caught the attention of Andrew Loog Oldham, hipster impressario and a former publicist for the Beatles – a boost to any pop resumé. He convinced the band to sign him up as their manager, and had them in a studio a week later to record Chuck Berry's 'Come On', the band's first single. His influence on the Stones was dramatic. First, he convinced Jones to drop founding pianist Ian Stewart from the band, simply because he looked too square. He put the remaining quintet in matching checked suits with black velvet collars – like the Beatles – but quickly played up the bad-boy angle, ruining their reputations for good citizenship for the sake of newspaper headlines. Most profoundly, Oldham demanded that Jagger and Richards begin writing original material, a career move that made their continued survival possible.

If Oldham tended to guide the Rolling Stones with the most commercial pop aims in mind, the band never abandoned their love for American R&B. During their first tour of the United States, they immediately sought out the famed Harlem Apollo, where they watched Joe Tex, Wilson Picket and James Brown demonstrate the state of their art.

"We wanted to be a blues band, but then we gave it up because it was a complete waste of time," Jagger told *Creem* in 1978. "Keith kept saying we're a BLUES band. I didn't give a shit what they wanted to call it in the end. In the beginning we were very dedicated. We didn't want to be called a ROCK band. So we did something else 'cause we couldn't do R&B exactly right. And because we couldn't do it exactly the same way, we HAD to do it our own way."

The Stones sound had already changed by the time Lennon and McCartney offered them 'I Wanna Be Your Man'. In the Stones' hands, the song was more primal, more seething than the cleaned-up version later done by the Fab Four. The song was their big break on to the charts, but their greatest successes came only when the band stepped out of the purism that hobbled the earliest days of their contemporaries, and sought a new, darker voice. The hard-headed boogie-woogie absolutism of Ian Stewart would never have lasted in a world of 'Let It Bleed' and 'Wild Horses'.

"The Rolling Stones, starting with that blues base, they brought it up into a more modern sonic dimension," says guitarist Wayne Kramer of the MC5. "They started using the sounds that you can get out of electric guitars, and really finding the core of the power of that sound and those tones you can get from overdriving an amplifier a little bit. Some of the those songs were brilliant, masterful productions."

For their followers and contemporaries, every new Stones single, every new batch of tracks, were like a dispatch to the world. And more often than not during the 1960s, the Stones built on their history, singing and playing to ever greater effect on love, hate, faith, decadence, addiction and fame. For the MC5, those messages emerged with a harsh clarity. While on tour in the summer of 1969, the MC5 were travelling along some long-forgotten expressway when the radio DJ announced that he had the new Stones single, something called 'Honky Tonk Women'. "We cranked it up, and it just floored us all," Kramer remembers. "We just said, 'Man, the Stones did it again! Man, they did it, man! LISTEN TO THAT SHIT, MAN!!! THEY'RE FUCKING NAILING IT!!!' It was like winning the pennant: the beat, the guitar tone, the solo, the whole thing was brilliant."

By the 1970s, the Stones were calling themselves "The World's Greatest Rock And Roll Band". Newer acts like Led Zeppelin were already surpassing them in gross sales, but the Stones' history and influence could not be eclipsed. Even such epic pretenders to their throne as the Who, Zeppelin and the Clash have been and gone. More than three decades later, the Stones remain. Along the way, Brian Jones was found dead, Bill Wyman became a retired, elderly restauranteur, Mick Taylor walked away from the best and worst gig in rock, a bored Mick Jagger had a diamond embedded into his tooth, and Keith Richards continued a never-ending search for that perfect riff.

> "Success never came into it. We just thought, 'wouldn't it be great if we could play one night a week with a few people dancing?'"
>
> Keith Richards

chronology

1936
OCTOBER 24: Bill Wyman is born William Perks in Penge, Kent.

1941
JUNE 2: Charlie Watts is born Charles Robert Watts in Wembley, Middlesex.

1942
FEBRUARY 28: Brian Jones is born Lewis Brian Hopkins-Jones in Cheltenham, Gloucestershire.

1943
DECEMBER 18: Keith Richards is born in Dartford, Kent.

1944
JULY 26: Mick Jagger is born Michael Philip Jagger in Dartford, Kent.

1947
JUNE 1: Ron Wood is born in Hillingdon, Middlesex.

1948
JANUARY 17: Mick Taylor is born in Welwyn Garden City, Hertfordshire.

1960
OCTOBER: Childhood acquaintances Mick Jagger and Keith Richards accidentally meet on a train from Dartford. Jagger is carrying an armful of blues albums (including discs by Chuck Berry and Muddy Waters). The pair renew their friendship.

1962
APRIL: Mick and Keith see Alexis Korner's Blues Incorporated at the Ealing Marquee Club in London. They meet a slide guitarist who calls himself Elmo Lewis (aka Brian Jones).

MAY: Brian advertizes for musicians to audition for his band. Pianist Ian Stewart is the first to respond and joins. Meanwhile, Mick is singing with Blues Incorporated.

JUNE: Mick quits Blues Incorporated to join Brian's band. Keith also joins.

JULY 12: Brian names the band the Rollin' Stones, a name borrowed from the Muddy Waters song 'Rollin' Stone Blues'. They debut at the Marquee. The Stones rhythm section is bassist Dick Taylor and drummer Mike Avery – Bill Wyman and Charlie Watts have yet to join.

SEPTEMBER: Dick Taylor quits to focus on university studies.

OCTOBER 27: The Stones record their first demo at London's Curly Clayton Studios, and perform Bo Diddley's 'You Can't Judge A Book By The Cover', Muddy Waters' 'Soon Forgotten' and Jimmy Reed's 'Close Together'. Tony Chapman plays drums.

DECEMBER: Bassist Bill Wyman joins.

1963
JANUARY: Band changes name to the Rolling Stones.

JANUARY 9: Charlie Watts replaces Tony Chapman who has been fired.

JANUARY 14: Mick, Keith, Brian, Charlie, Bill and Ian play their first gig together at the Flamingo, in Soho.

FEBRUARY 2-28: The Stones record at IBC Studios, London, engineered by Glyn Johns. The tapes, owned by IBC, are later bought back by Eric Easton so that the group can sign a recording contract.

APRIL 28: Future manager Andrew Oldham, a 19-year-old former PR man for Beatles' manager Brian Epstein, sees the Rolling Stones perform for the first time in Richmond.

MAY 3: The Stones sign an exclusive management agreement with Oldham and Eric Easton. Days later, Oldham procures a recording contract for the band with Decca Records.

JUNE 7: Decca releases the Stones' first single, 'Come On'/'I Wanna Be Loved'. It reaches No. 21 on the UK chart.

JULY 7: The Stones make their first television appearance performing 'Come On' on ATV's *Thank Your Lucky Stars*.

SEPTEMBER: Oldham brings John Lennon and Paul McCartney to a Soho studio where the Stones are rehearsing. Once there, Lennon and McCartney finish writing 'I Wanna Be Your Man' and give the song to the band.

SEPTEMBER 29: The Stones begin their first major tour with Bo Diddley and The Everly Brothers.

NOVEMBER 1: The Stones second single, 'I Wanna Be Your Man'/'Stoned', reaches No. 9 on the UK chart.

1964
JANUARY 6: The Stones begin first tour as headline act, touring with the Ronettes.

JANUARY 10: The Stones release their first EP. It includes the songs 'Bye-Bye Johnny', 'Money', 'You Better Move On' and 'Poison Ivy'. It hits No. 15 on the UK chart.

FEBRUARY 21: The Stones release their third single, 'Not Fade Away'/'Little By Little', reaching No. 3 on the UK chart.

MARCH 6: 'Not Fade Away'/'I Wanna Be Your Man' becomes the Stones' first US single. It reaches No. 48.

APRIL 17: Debut album, *The Rolling Stones*, tops the UK chart for 11 weeks. A performance at the Cubi-Club in Rochdale is stopped when the audience riots.

MAY: *England's Newest Hitmakers – The Rolling Stones* is released as the band's first US album. It reaches No. 11 on the US album chart.

JUNE 1: More than 500 fans are waiting for the Stones when they arrive at Kennedy Airport to begin their first US tour. The band is mobbed.

JUNE 11: A press conference outside Chess Studios in Chicago is broken up by police after fans swarm members of the band, nearly stopping traffic.

JUNE 26: The Stones' first No. 1 single, 'It's All Over Now'/'Good Times, Bad Times' is released in UK. Over the coming months, the band's gigs are marked by hysteria, including one performance at Longleat House where 200 girls faint.

AUGUST 14: *Five-By-Five* EP released on Decca in UK. Songs are 'If You Need Me', 'Empty Heart', '2120 South Michigan Avenue', 'Confessin' The Blues' and 'Around And Around'. It reaches No. 7 on the UK chart.

AUGUST 9: 'Time Is On My Side' backed by 'Congratulations' is released in the US where it reaches No. 80 on the chart.

OCTOBER 24: The Stones second US album, *12 X 5* is released and reaches No. 3 on the US album chart.

NOVEMBER 13: Advance orders of 300,000 await the Stones' fifth UK single, 'Little Red Rooster'/'Off The Hook'. It goes straight to No. 1.

1965
JANUARY 15: *The Rolling Stones No. 2*, the band's second UK album, is released. Enters the album chart at No. 1.

JANUARY 22: Charlie Watts's illustrated children's book on saxophonist Charlie Parker's life is published.

FEBRUARY 13: *The Rolling Stones, Now!*, the band's third US album, is released and reaches No. 5 on the album charts.

FEBRUARY 26: The Stones' sixth UK single 'The Last Time'/'Play With Fire', is released and hits No. 1 on the chart. Released a few weeks later in the US, the single reaches No. 9.

MARCH 18: While returning to London from the last gig of a tour, the Rolling Stones are refused the use of toilet facilities at a petrol station in West Ham. Bill Wyman, Brian Jones and Mick Jagger then relieve themselves against a nearby wall and are soon arrested, charged with urinating in public.

MAY 10-13: In the US for their third North American tour, the Stones spend five days at Chess Studios in Chicago, where they record four tracks in 17 hours. The band then flies to Los Angeles, where three more tracks are recorded at RCA Studios in Hollywood, including '(I Can't Get No) Satisfaction'.

MAY 27: '(I Can't Get No) Satisfaction' backed by 'The Under Assistant West Coast Promotion Man' is released in the US and reaches No. 1.

JUNE 11: The Stones' third EP in the UK, *Got Live If You Want It*, reaches No. 7 on the chart. It reaches No. 6 in the US.

JULY 30: *Out Of Our Heads*, the Stones' fourth US album, is released. It hits No. 1 three weeks later. The same album, with a dramatically different track listing, is released in the UK on August 24. It reaches No. 2 on the chart.

AUGUST 4: Andrew Loog Oldham establishes his own record label, named Immediate Records.

AUGUST 20: '(I Can't Get No) Satisfaction' backed by 'The Spider And The Fly', the Stones' seventh single in the UK, is released. The single tops the charts for three weeks. Decca also releases *The Rolling Stones Songbook* by the Andrew Oldham Orchestra. Keith Richards plays on the album.

AUGUST 24: The Stones meet with businessman Allen Klein for the first time.

chronology

AUGUST 28: Allen Klein begins co-managing the Stones with Andrew Oldham. The band signs a new five-year recording contract with Decca for a huge advance. The following day, it is announced the Stones have signed a new contract with London Records in the US.

SEPTEMBER 11-15: The Stones tour Germany and Austria. Fans riot in Düsseldorf and Hamburg. In Berlin, fans damage 50 rows of seats and 400 police clash with audience after the concert.

SEPTEMBER 25: 'Get Off of My Cloud'/'I'm Free', the Stones' eighth US single, is released. The record tops the chart for two weeks. A month later, 'Get Off Of My Cloud'/ 'The Singer Not The Song' is released as the band's eighth UK single and spends three weeks at No. 1. Overzealous fans continue to riot at shows, including a gig in Dublin where 30 teens overrun the stage. Mick Jagger is thrown to the floor, Brian Jones wrestles with three youths, and Bill Wyman is pinned against a piano. Keith Richards escapes.

OCTOBER 3: During a melee by fans at a Manchester show, Keith Richards is knocked unconscious for five minutes by flying debris.

OCTOBER 27: The Stones begin another North American tour.

NOVEMBER 19: Chris Farlowe's EP, 'Farlowe In The Midnight Hour', is released by Immediate Records. It is the first release of We Three Producers, a new production company formed by Mick Jagger, Keith Richards and Andrew Oldham.

DECEMBER 4: The Stones release their fifth US album, *December's Children*. It reaches No. 2 on the album chart.

DECEMBER 5: At the Los Angeles Sports Arena, the Stones play to 14,000 fans.

DECEMBER 18: 'As Tears Go By'/'Gotta Get Away' is the band's 9th US single. It reaches No. 6 on the chart.

1966

FEBRUARY 4: The Stones release '19th Nervous Breakdown'/'As Tears Go By', their ninth UK single. It reaches No. 1. On Feb. 12, '19th Nervous Breakdown'/'Sad Day', the band's tenth US single, is released. It also reaches No. 1.

APRIL 2: *Big Hits (High Tide And Green Grass)*, the first Rolling Stones compilation LP and sixth US album, is released. It reaches No. 2 on the chart. In November, the album is released as the band's fifth album in the UK. It peaks at No. 4.

APRIL 15: The Stones release *Aftermath*, their fourth UK album. It spends seven weeks at No. 1. The following month, the album is released in the US with a different track selection. It also reaches the No. 1 position.

MAY 7: 'Paint It Black'/'Stupid Girl' is released as the band's 11th single in the US. It reaches No. 1. On May 13, 'Paint It Black'/'Long Long While', their tenth single in the UK, is released. It also reaches No. 1.

JULY 2: 'Mother's Little Helper'/'Lady Jane' is released as the band's twelfth US single. 'Mother's Little Helper' reaches No. 8 on the charts and 'Lady Jane' hits No. 24.

SEPTEMBER 23: The Stones release 'Have You Seen Your Mother, Baby, Standing In The Shadow?'/'Who's Driving Your Plane'. It is the band's eleventh single in the UK and thirteenth in the US. It reaches No. 5 in both countries.

1967

JANUARY 13-14: 'Let's Spend The Night Together'/'Ruby Tuesday', released as the band's 12th single in the UK, and 14th single in the US. 'Let's Spend The Night Together' reaches No. 2 in the UK, and 'Ruby Tuesday' goes to No. 1 in the US.

JANUARY 20: The Stones release *Between The Buttons*, their sixth UK album. It peaks at No. 3 on the album chart. A few weeks later, the album is released as the band's ninth album in the US, where it reaches No. 2.

FEBRUARY 12: Mick Jagger, girlfriend Marianne Faithfull and Keith Richards are detained during a police raid on Redlands, Richards' thatched palace in West Sussex. Police seize suspicious substances – including pep pills Jagger purchased legally in Italy. Faithfull is found naked and wrapped in a fur rug. Art dealer Robert Fraser also arrested.

MARCH: Mick, Marianne, Keith, Brian Jones and Anita Palenberg vacation together in Tangier. Along the way, Jones suffers an asthma attack and is briefly hospitalized. Keith and Anita begin their relationship. Brian returns to their hotel to find his girlfriend and bandmates have returned to London.

MAY 10: Mick Jagger, Keith Richards and Robert Fraser appear in court on drug charges. They are released on bail and ordered to trial in June. Brian Jones and a friend are arrested at Brian's home in South Kensington. The pair are charged with unlawful possession of drugs. Brian is released on bail.

JUNE 27-29: Mick Jagger found guilty of illegal possession of drugs – four tablets of amphetamine. Richards found guilty of allowing his West Sussex house to be used for smoking marijuana. Robert Fraser is judged guilty of possession of heroin. All are jailed. Jagger is sentenced to three months in jail, Richards one year, and Fraser six months. Jagger spends three days locked up, and Richards is held for two days before being released on bail on appeal. Fraser serves four miserable months.

JULY 7: *Flowers*, the Stones' tenth US album, is released and hits No. 2. The compilation album is only released in the US.

JULY 31: Mick and Keith's drug charge sentences are overturned by a court of appeals.

AUGUST 18: 'We Love You'/'Dandelion', the band's 13th and 15th single in the US and UK respectively, is released. 'We Love You' is intended as a thank you to fans for their support during drug trial.

SEPTEMBER 29: Stones announce that Andrew Oldham is no longer their manager or producer. Allen Klein is now their sole representative.

OCTOBER 30: In court, Brian Jones acknowledges possession of marijuana and allowing his home to be used for smoking. He pleads not guilty to possession of cocaine and methedrine, but is found guilty. He is sentenced to nine months in jail and spends one night in Wormwood Scrubs before being freed on bail pending appeal.

DECEMBER 2: 'In Another Land'/'The Lantern' is released in the US as the band's sixteenth single. 'In Another Land' is the first and last appearance of a Bill Wyman composition on a Stones LP.

DECEMBER 3: Brian Jones' drug sentence is set aside after psychiatrists portray him as a 'an extremely frightened young man' with suicidal tendencies. He is given three years probation.

DECEMBER 8-9: The Stones release *Their Satanic Majesties Request* in the UK and US. It reaches No. 3 on the UK chart, and No. 2 in the US.

DECEMBER 23: The single 'She's A Rainbow'/'2000 Light Years From Home' is released in the US.

1968

MARCH 15: Jimmy Miller becomes producer of forthcoming *Beggars Banquet* album. He remains the Stones' producer through 1973's *Goats Head Soup* album.

MAY 11: Mick Jagger announces he will write the soundtrack for, and star in a move called *Performance* directed by Nicholas Roeg and Donald Cammell. Co-starring is Anita Pallenberg.

MAY 21: Brian Jones arrested again at his home for marijuana possession.

MAY 24: 'Jumping Jack Flash'/'Child Of The Moon' is released in the UK and US. It hits No. 1 on both the UK and US charts.

JUNE 5: Jean-Luc Godard begins filming the Stones studio sessions of 'Sympathy For The Devil' for his film *One Plus One*. Godard's lighting crew later sets fire to the roof of Olympic Studios by accident.

JULY 26: A three-month battle between the Stones and their record company over the cover art for *Beggars Banquet* delays its release. Record company officials refuse to release a planned cover that shows a grafitti-covered bathroom wall. The Stones eventually back down.

AUGUST 31: 'Street Fighting Man'/'No Expectations' released in the US, and climbs to No. 48 on the chart. The single is not released in the UK until June 20, 1970.

SEPTEMBER 26: A London court fines Brian Jones for possession of marijuana.

DECEMBER 6-7: *Beggars Banquet* is finally released in the UK and US. The album reaches No. 3 in the UK and No. 2 on the US chart.

DECEMBER 12: The Stones shoot *The Rolling Stones' Rock And Roll Circus* television special at Wembley. Performers include John Lennon and Yoko Ono, Eric Clapton, The Who, Taj Mahal, Jethro Tull and Marianne Faithfull. Jagger is unhappy with the Stones' performance on-screen – the entire project is scrapped.

1969

MAY 28: Mick Jagger and Marianne Faithfull are arrested on drug charges at Mick's home at Cheyne Walk, Chelsea. They are released on bail.

JUNE 7: Keith Richards crashes his car near his home in Sussex. Anita, seven months pregnant, breaks her collar bone.

JUNE 8: Brian Jones is fired from the Stones. Four days later Mick Taylor, 20, is hired as his replacement.

JULY 3: Brian Jones, 25, drowns in the pool at his home in Hartfield Sussex.

JULY 4-5: 'Honky Tonk Woman'/'You Can't Always Get What You Want' is released. It tops the singles charts in both the UK and US.

JULY 5: The Stones perform a free concert at Hyde Park, London, which they dedicate to Brian Jones.

JULY 13: Mick Jagger begins filming *Ned Kelly* in Australia.

SEPTEMBER 12-13: The Stones release the compilation album *Through The Past Darkly (Big Hits Volume 2)* in the UK and US. It reaches No. 1 on the UK chart and No. 2 in the US.

DECEMBER 5-6: *Let It Bleed* is released in the US and UK. The album hits No. 2 in the US and goes to No. 1 on the UK chart.

DECEMBER 6: Death and despair greet the Stones at their free concert at the Altamont Speedway near Livermore, California. Mick Jagger is punched in the face by a fan backstage, and Marty Balin

13

chronology

from the Jefferson Airplane is knocked unconscious by Hell's Angels who have been hired to provide security at the concert. During the Stones' performance of 'Under My Thumb' 18-year-old Meredith Hunter is beaten and stabbed to death by the Angels. *Gimme Shelter*, a documentary film of the concert, is released in December 1970.

DECEMBER 18: Mick is fined for being found guilty of possession of marijuana resin. Marianne is acquitted.

1970

JULY 20: Allen Klein is dismissed as the Stones' business manager, though he retains the rights to their early recordings. Two days later, the band's contract with Decca Records expires.

AUGUST 1: *Performance*, starring Mick Jagger, James Fox, Anita Pallenberg and Michele Breton, is released by Warner Bros. Jagger sings 'Memo From Turner' in the film.

AUGUST 15: The Stones announce the formation of their new record label, Rolling Stones Records. Albums are to be distributed via licensing agreement with Atlantic Records.

SEPTEMBER 6: *Get Yer Ya-Ya's Out*, a live album of the Stones' 1969 US tour is released. It hits No. 1 in the UK, and No. 5 on the US chart.

1971

MARCH 30: The Stones hold a farewell Britain party before fleeing to France to avoid British taxes.

APRIL 16: 'Brown Sugar'/'Bitch'/'Let It Rock', a maxi-single, is released in the UK, where it reaches No.1 on the singles chart. In the US, 'Bitch' is on the B side. It also tops the chart there.

APRIL 23: The Stones release the *Sticky Fingers* album in the UK and US. It spends four weeks at No. 1 slot in the US. The cover by Andy Warhol includes a real zip on a bulging pair of jeans.

MAY 12: Mick Jagger marries Bianca Rose Perez Moreno de Macias in St Tropez.

JUNE 12: 'Wild Horses'/'Sway' is released in the US where it reaches No. 18.

OCTOBER 18: The album *Brian Jones Presents The Pipes Of Pan in Joujouka* is released on Rolling Stones Records. It was recorded in Morocco by Jones and engineer George Chkiantz in 1968.

1972

APRIL 14: The Stones release 'Tumbling Dice'/'Sweet Black Angel'. Hits No. 5 on the UK chart and stops at No. 10 in the US.

MAY 26: *Exile On Main Street*, the Stones' first double album is released. Hits No. 1 in both the UK and US.

JULY 15: 'Happy'/'All Down The Line' is released in the US and goes to No. 14.

1973

AUGUST 20: The Stones release 'Angie'/'Silver Train' in the UK and US. It hits No. 2 in the UK and tops the chart in the US.

AUGUST 31: *Goats Head Soup* is released. The album reaches No. 1 in both the UK and US.

OCTOBER 15: Keith Richards fined and given a one-year suspended sentence by a French court for hosting drug parties at Nellcote in 1971. He is also banned from France for two years.

DECEMBER 15: 'Doo Doo Doo Doo Doo (Heartbreaker)'/'Dancing with Mr D' is released in the US where it reaches No. 10.

1974

JULY 26: The Stones release 'It's Only Rock 'N' Roll'/'Through The Lonely Nights'. It goes to No. 10 on the UK charts and No. 18 in the US.

OCTOBER 18: Release date of *It's Only Rock 'N' Roll* album – the first to be credited to the Glimmer Twins (aka Jagger and Richards). Tops the US chart and reaches No. 4 in the UK.

OCTOBER 25: 'Ain't Too Proud To Beg'/'Dance Little Sister' released in the US. It reaches No. 15.

DECEMBER 12: Mick Taylor abruptly quits the Stones, and joins former Cream-bassist Jack Bruce and engineer Andy Johns for a never-completed project. Rather than replace him immediately, the Stones "audition" several guitar players during the making of *Black And Blue* in Munich.

1975

APRIL 14: The Stones' announce that Faces guitarist Ron Wood will play with the band during their US summer tour. Wood insists he will remain with the Faces.

JUNE 6: *Metamorphosis*, a compilation of previously unreleased outtakes is sold by Allen Klein, much to the chagrin of the band. It reaches No. 8 on the US chart, and enters the UK chart at No. 27.

JULY 4: Memphis police warn the Stones not to perform 'Star Star' (aka 'Starfucker') during a local concert. When Jagger performs the song, police back down from arresting the singer in the face of probable rioting and certain litigation.

1976

FEBRUARY 28: Ron Wood permanently joins the Stones.

APRIL 20: The Stones release *Black And Blue*. Hits No. 2 on the UK chart and No. 1 in the US. The single 'Fool To Cry'/'Crazy Mama' released in UK and goes to No. 4. In the US, with 'Hot Stuff' is the B-side, it reaches No. 9.

1977

FEBRUARY 16: The Stones announce a new recording contract with EMI, which will distribute records on The Rolling Stones Records label, except in North America. In April, the band renews their contract with Atlantic Records for North American distribution rights.

FEBRUARY 24: Keith and Anita arrive in Toronto, Canada, where Anita is arrested at the airport when marijuana and heroin are found in one of her suitcases. She is released on bail.

FEBRUARY 27: Canadian police raid Keith and Anita's rooms at the Harbour Castle Hotel. They are arrested for possession of heroin for sale, a charge that could bring a life sentence.

MARCH 14: In a Toronto court, Anita is fined on a charge of importing drugs. The court holds her passport and begins deportation proceedings. A few weeks later, Keith and Anita are allowed to leave Canada so Keith can undergo treatment for drug addiction in New York.

SEPTEMBER 16: *Love You Live*, a double album, is released. Hits No. 18 on the UK chart and No. 5 in the US. Andy Warhol-designed cover.

1978

MAY 14: Bianca files for divorce from Mick Jagger. Jagger is already living with Texan model Jerry Hall.

MAY 19: 'Miss You'/'Girl With The Faraway Eyes', is released. Hits No. 2 in the UK and goes to the top in the US.

JUNE 9: The Stones release *Some Girls*. Hits No. 2 in the UK and No. 1 in the US.

AUGUST 28: 'Beast Of Burden'/'When The Whip Comes Down' released in the US and goes to No. 7 on the singles chart.

SEPTEMBER 15: 'Respectable'/'When The Whip Comes Down' released in the UK where it reaches No. 22.

OCTOBER 3: Reverend Jesse Jackson launches campaign against the Rolling Stones over a lyric in the song 'Some Girls' that explicitly describes black women as sexually insatiable. Some black radio stations refuse to play it. Mick insists the song is a parody of stereotypes. "If they can't take a joke," he says, "fuck 'em".

OCTOBER 23: Keith pleads guilty to possession of heroin in Toronto. Charges of trafficking and possession of a large quantity of heroin are dropped. Richards is given one year probation, and is ordered to continue his drug rehabilitation in New York. He is also instructed to perform a benefit concert.

NOVEMBER 29: 'Shattered'/'Everything Is Turning To Gold' is released in the US, but only hits No. 27.

DECEMBER 12: Keith Richards releases a Christmas solo single – a cover of Chuck Berry's 'Run Rudolph Run' – on Rolling Stones Records.

DECEMBER 16: Mick Jagger appears with Peter Tosh in New York on TV's *Saturday Night Live*.

1979

JULY 20: At Keith and Anita's house in South Salem, Westchester County, a 17-year-old boy fatally shoots himself in the head. The boy and Anita had been in bed watching TV. Anita is arrested and questioned by police for 12 hours. Anita tells police the boy had talked of playing Russian roulette. In November, Keith and Anita end their relationship.

1980

JUNE 20: 'Emotional Rescue'/'Down In The Hole' released. It reaches No. 8 in the UK chart and No. 3 in the US.

JUNE 23: *Emotional Rescue* album is released. It tops the charts in both the UK and US.

SEPTEMBER 19: 'She's So Cold'/'Send It To Me' released. Hits No. 27 in the UK and No. 21 in the US.

1981

MARCH 4: *Sucking In The Seventies*, an anthology album, is released in the US. Hits No. 17 on the chart. It is released on April 13 in the UK.

AUGUST 17: 'Start Me Up'/'No Use In Crying' is released in the UK and reaches No. 4 on the singles chart.

AUGUST 31: *Tattoo You* album is released in the UK and US. The album hits No. 1 in both countries.

SEPTEMBER 1: The Stones announce their upcoming US tour will be sponsored by Jovan perfume.

NOVEMBER 20: 'Waiting On A Friend'/'Little T & A' single released in the US.

1982

JANUARY 11: 'Hang Fire'/'Neighbors' released in the US.

JUNE 1: *Still Life American Concert 1981*, a live album, is released. Hits No. 2 in the UK. 'Going To A-Go-Go'/'Beast Of Burden', a single, released. It goes to No. 19 in the UK and No. 20 in the US.

SEPTEMBER 1: 'Time Is On My Side'/'Twenty Flight Rock' is released in the US.

1983

JULY 25: The Stones sign with CBS Records for four albums. The band will get $6 million per album, making it the most lucrative deal ever in the record industry.

chronology

SEPTEMBER 31: 'Undercover Of The Night'/'All The Way Down' is released. Hits No. 8 in the UK and No. 9 in the US.

NOVEMBER 7: The Stones release the album *Undercover*. It tops the UK chart and hits No. 4 in the US.

NOVEMBER 10. The promotional video for 'Undercover' is banned by the BBC's *Top Of The Pops* for being too violent. It is also banned later by the Independent Broadcasting Authority. Mick Jagger insists the film by director Julien Temple depicts the real-life violence and repression in Argentina. The Stones edit the film to make it acceptable for broadcast.

DECEMBER 18: Keith marries model Patti Hansen on his 40th birthday in Cabo San Lucas.

1984

JANUARY 1: Alexis Korner dies at age 55.

JANUARY 23: 'She Was Hot'/'I Think I'm Going Mad' is released. Hits No. 40 on the UK chart and No. 44 in the US.

FEBRUARY 24: Bill Wyman meets 13-year-old Mandy Smith at a night club in London. Wyman begins dating the girl who will become his wife. The relationship causes a scandal in the press.

1985

FEBRUARY 4: Mick Jagger's solo single, 'Just Another Night'/'Turn The Girl Loose' is released. Hits No. 27 in the UK and No. 10 in the US.

MARCH 4: Jagger's first solo album *She's The Boss* is released. Hits hits No. 6 in the UK and No. 8 in the US.

APRIL 19: Jagger's solo single 'Lucky In Love' is released in the US. It hits No. 38.

JULY 13: Stones choose not to play *Live Aid* benefit concert. Instead, Jagger appears with Tina Turner. Keith Richards and Ron Wood back a muddled Bob Dylan. A video of Jagger and David Bowie performing 'Dancing In The Street' is shown.

AUGUST 23: Jagger and Bowie's recording of 'Dancing In The Street' is released. It tops the chart in the UK and reaches No. 7 in the US.

DECEMBER 12: Ian Stewart, the Stones' road manager and original pianist, dies of a heart attack at age 47. Two months later, the band plays a tribute to Stewart before invited guests at London's 100 Club.

1986

JANUARY 23: Keith Richards presents Chuck Berry with the first *Rock And Roll Hall Of Fame* Award.

MARCH 3: 'Harlem Shuffle'/'Had It With You' is released. It reaches No. 7 on the UK chart and No. 5 in the US.

MARCH 24: The Stones release 'Dirty Work'. Hits No. 3 in the UK and No. 4 in the US. The Glimmer Twins begin a public feud after Mick refuses to tour with the Stones, in part, to focus on his new solo career.

MAY 19: 'One Hit (To The Body)'/'Fight' is released in the UK and US.

JULY 21: Mick Jagger's solo single 'Ruthless People'/'I'm Raining', from *Ruthless People* film soundtrack is released in the US. Hits No. 51.

OCTOBER 16: Keith leads Chuck Berry's band for the rock pioneer's two 60th birthday concerts at the Fox Theater in St Louis. Guest performers include Eric Clapton, Etta James and Linda Rondstadt. The shows are filmed by director Taylor Hackford for a movie later released as *Hail! Hail! Rock 'N' Roll*.

DECEMBER 1: *Live At The Fullham Town Hall*, is released by the Charlie Watts Orchestra.

1987

AUGUST 31: Mick Jagger's 'Let's Work'/'Catch As Catch Can' is released. Hits No. 39 on the chart in the UK and No. 35 in the US.

SEPTEMBER 14: *Primitive Cool*, Jagger's second solo album, is released. It hits to No. 18 in the UK charts but stalls at No. 41 in the US.

NOVEMBER 9: 'Throw Away'/'Peace Of The Wicked', another Jagger solo single, is released.

1988

JANUARY 20: Mick Jagger introduces the Beatles at their induction into the *Rock 'N' Roll Hall Of Fame*.

SEPTEMBER 17: Mick launches his solo Australian tour.

SEPTEMBER 23: Keith Richards releases his solo single 'Take It So Hard'/'I Could Have Stood You Up'.

OCTOBER 4: Keith's first solo album, *Talk Is Cheap*, is released. It goes to No. 24 on the US charts.

NOVEMBER 24: Keith and his band – the X-Pensive Winos – perform in Atlanta to kick-off their first tour.

1989

JANUARY 18: The Stones are inducted into the *Rock 'N' Roll Hall Of Fame*. Mick Taylor attends; Bill and Charlie do not.

MARCH 15: The Stones sign a contract with Concert Productions International to perform 55 shows in the US and Canada. The Canadian promoter promises the band between $65 million and $70 million.

APRIL 24: 'Make No Mistake', a Keith Richards solo single, is released.

MAY 17: Wyman opens *Sticky Fingers* restaurant/nightclub in London.

JUNE 2: Bill Wyman, 52, announces he will marry Mandy Smith, 19.

AUGUST 17: 'Mixed Emotions'/'Fancyman' is released. Hits No. 33 in the UK and No. 5 in the US.

AUGUST 29: The Stones' album *Steel Wheels* is released in the US. Hits No. 1. It is released in the UK on September 11 and reaches No. 2.

AUGUST 31: The band launches its *Steel Wheels* tour in the US.

NOVEMBER 20: 'Rock And A Hard Place'/'Cook Cook Blues' is released in the UK.

1990

JANUARY : The Stones 'Almost Hear You Sigh'/'Break The Spell' is released in the US.

JUNE 16: 'Almost Hear You Sigh'/'Wish I'd Never Met You' is released in the the UK.

JULY 26: 'Terrifying'/'Rock And A Hard Place' is released.

OCTOBER 24: Bill Wyman's autobiography, *Stone Alone*, is published. It recounts in detail the career of the Stones up to 1969.

NOVEMBER 21: Mick Jagger and Jerry Hall are married in Bali, Indonesia.

NOVEMBER 22: Bill announces that his marriage to Mandy Smith is over.

1991

MARCH 4: The Stones' single 'Highwire'/'Sex Drive' released in the US.

MARCH 21: Release of the single 'Highwire' in the UK sparks protest from those who claim it is critical of the Gulf War. The first verse is edited out by BBC's *Top Of The Pops*.

APRIL 2: In the US, the Stones release *Flashpoint*, a live album. It includes two new studio tracks: 'Highwire' and 'Sex Drive'. Six days later it is released in the UK.

NOVEMBER 19: Virgin Records and the Stones sign a deal for three albums and distribution rights to the back catalogue of all Rolling Stones Records material.

NOVEMBER 26: Virgin Records releases *Keith Richards & The Expensive Winos Live At The Hollywood Paladium, December 15, 1988*.

1992

JANUARY 16: Mick attends the first screening of the film *Freejack*. He co-stars in the science-fiction film with Emilio Estevez.

MAY 19: *A Tribute To Charlie Parker, With Strings* is released by the Charlie Watts Quintet.

OCTOBER 20: Keith's *Main Offender* album is released.

1993

JANUARY 6: Bill Wyman officially leaves the Rolling Stones.

FEBRUARY 8: *Wandering Spirit*, Mick Jagger's third solo album, is released.

1994

Voodoo Lounge is released.

1995

Release of *Stripped*, a live album taken from club and theatre performances and rehearsals in Amsterdam, Paris, Tokyo and Lisbon. The band performs Bob Dylan's 'Like A Rolling Stone'.

The Rolling Stones' Rock And Roll Circus from 1968 is finally released both on video and on record. It receives largely enthusiastic reviews.

1996

OCTOBER 22: *Shared Vision II: The Songs Of The Rolling Stones* is released. It gathers songs of the Stones as performed by Johnny Cash, Rod Stewart, Joe Cocker, The Pogues, Tom Jones, the Feelies and others.

1997

FEBRUARY 20: Announcement that Madonna has signed with Mick Jagger's Jagged Films to star opposite Gabriel Byrne in an upcoming film about the 1930s photographer and political activist Tina Modotti.

SPRING: The Rolling Stones join producers Don Was, the Dust Brothers and Babyface in Los Angeles to record their 21st studio album. Working song titles that emerge from the sessions at Ocean Way Studios (formerly United Western) and the Dust Brothers' PCP Labs include: 'Thief in the Night', 'Out of Control', 'Juiced', 'Saint', 'Already Over Me', 'Always Suffering', 'Nobody's Seen My Baby', 'Gin Face', 'Too Tight', 'You Don't Have to Mean It', 'How Can I Stop', 'Flip the Switch' and 'Any Way You Look at It'. Among the guest players are Wayne Shorter (formerly of Weather Report), Lili Haydn, Waddy Wachtel, Jim Keltner and Bernard Fowler. An autumn tour is announced.

chapter one

1964 the rolling stones

The Stones arrive in America, finding nonsense, admirers and profound inspiration.

Route 66
(TROUP)

I Just Want To Make Love To You
(DIXON)

Honest I Do
(REED)

I Need You Baby
(McDANIELS)

Now I've Got A Witness (Like Uncle Phil And Uncle Gene)
(PHELGE)

Little By Little
(PHELGE/SPECTOR)

I'm a King Bee
(MOORE)

Carol
(BERRY)

Tell Me (You're Coming Back)

Can I Get A Witness
(HOLLAND/DOZIER/HOLLAND)

You Can Make It If You Try
(JARRETT)

Walking The Dog
(THOMAS)

the rolling stones

ity the young Rollin' Stones, trying so hard to get it right. Their love of the blues was real. Their commitment to the sound of Black America boundless, thanks largely to the fanaticism of little Brian Jones. Such innocence, and so worshipful of the great bluesmen of Chicago and the Deep South. And yet in the context of Britain in 1964 – a nation afloat on good vibes from the happy, shiny Beatles – these brooding boys from London looked like very bad news indeed.

But what were they really? THIEVES stealing the very soul of American R&B, little better than Pat Boone crooning whitebread renditions of Little Richard and Fats Domino tunes, helping to keep the segregated pop charts clean and bright. The difference, of course, was that the Stones at least seemed to understand the music they were playing, digging those crazy sounds for all they were worth.

Not that the Stones were out to clean up the blues. In their hands, it remained a potent force, a sound virtually unknown to polite middle-class England. They just wanted to be young R&B prophets, spreading the good news of the deeply passionate music of Muddy Waters, Elmore James and Howlin' Wolf. Pop wasn't their mission. At least not yet, even if manager Andrew Loog Oldham already had other ideas. His plan was to sell his Fab Five as the anti-Beatles, a quintet of surly bad boys ready to wreak havoc on society and its daughters. Their evil intent was quickly established with Oldham's well-publicized question: "Would you let your daughter marry a Rolling Stone?"

The answer seemed clear enough in the messages of seething manhood found within songs like Slim Harpo's 'I'm a King Bee' – "I can make honey, baby, let me come inside" – and revelations that Brian had already fathered two children by two separate lady friends.

Maybe the Rolling Stones just wanted to play their blues and rock and roll, but Oldham had noticed the beginning of Beatlemania in America just a few months earlier. It was clear that a British Invasion of the US was brewing, and he wanted the Stones to be part of it.

Thus the Rolling Stones' eponymous debut album would be better known to Americans by its subtitle, *England's Newest Hitmakers* – surely an indication of just which bandwagon Jagger and his cohorts were boarding. And yet a look at the track listing of *The Rolling Stones* shows a band still smitten with their beloved R&B and Chuck Berry-style rock, not a group of hooligans out to cash in on the next big pop thing.

"Being pop stars didn't even come into the realm of possibility," Keith Richards told journalist Lisa Robinson in 1989. "We saw no connection between us and the Beatles – we were playing blues, they were writing pop songs dressed in suits. We were too hip to be pop stars, it was like that was the only dignity we had left."

Their first single, released in the summer of 1963, had put the band's shared interests to work on Chuck Berry's 'Come On' and Willie Dixon's 'I Want To Be Loved'. It was a modest success, hitting No. 21 on the UK singles chart. The Stones pattern in those early days was to find worthy R&B songs that were virtually unknown in England, and had been unreasonably ignored back in the US. That formula took The *Rolling Stones* to the top of the UK album chart for 11 weeks, while reaching No. 11 in the US. Two months later, the Stones earned their first chart-topping single with a cover of the Valentinos' 'It's All Over Now'. This wasn't exactly welcome news to co-author Bobby Womack. He and his brothers in the Valentinos were an American R&B band struggling to cross over to lucrative white audiences, and just beginning to enjoy some success with 'It's All Over Now'. Soulman Sam Cooke, who signed the Valentinos to his Sar Records label, warned Womack about the upcoming version of his song by the Stones, and suggested that it could be a good thing.

"I was very angry about it," says Womack now. "That was the first song that I had written that became a big record and was going real big for me and my brothers. That's hard to understand

> **" Being pop stars didn't even come into the realm of possibility "**
> Keith Richards

the rolling stones

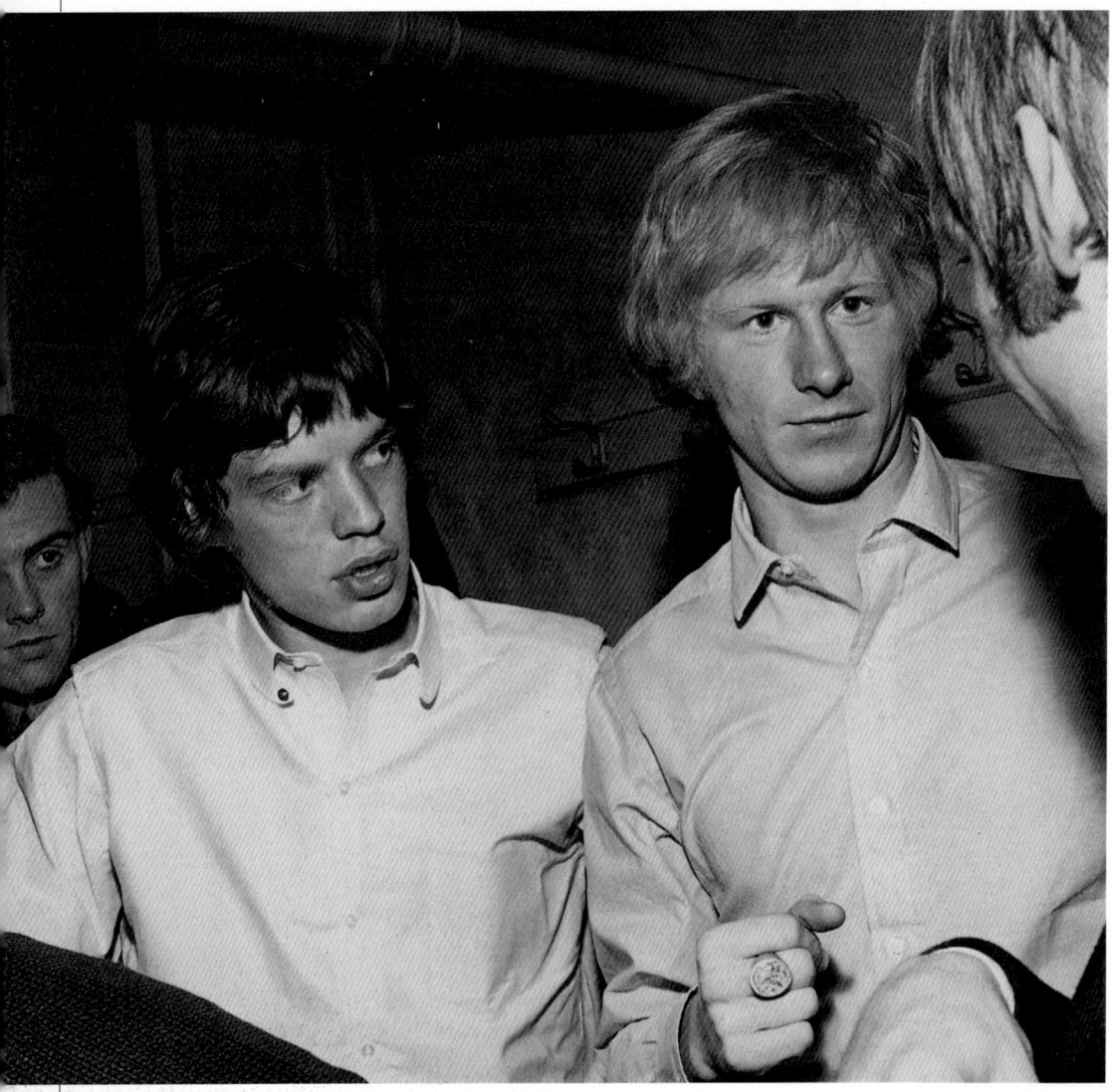

Mick Jagger with Andrew Loog Oldham, the band's manager, producer and maker of bad reputations.

when you come from the ghetto and you finally get a record and you know the importance of it. I knew their record was going to go so far, and ours was going to quit."

But Cooke turned out to be right, says Womack, now a longtime friend and occasional sideman to the Stones. "The record immediately took off and it carried us a long way. When I saw the first cheque I was shocked. It was huge." The song's success was a boost to Womack's career, and he's continued to receive fat royalty cheques ever since. "I said to the Stones after we met, 'I've been chasing you guys to get you to record another song.'"

Sessions for *The Rolling Stones* began in late January 1964 at Regent Sound in London. The Stones were by now a tight, toughened unit, fresh from their first major UK tour with the Everly Brothers,

Bo Diddley and the Ronnettes. But Jagger was still a boy, singing Willie Dixon's 'I Just Want To Make Love To You' more like a sloppy kid than with the fire and dread of a Muddy Waters. His voice was often thin, and uncertain during those first album sessions. The blues were not yet his own. But even as the Stones watered down the blues of Jimmy Reed's 'Honest I Do', their performance still carried an element of danger.

The album was produced on a simple two-track machine by the multi-talented Andrew Loog Oldham, who in fact had absolutely no experience in the studio at that time. He thought electric guitars were plugged directly into wall sockets and (fortunately for the band) that final mixing of the tapes was a boring inconvenience best left to the lowly sound engineer. Oldham largely stepped back and allowed for the simple documentation of the Stones sound: the clashing guitars, the euphoric moaning of harmonica, the rollicking keyboard work of the banished Ian Stewart. The result was an album of raw, primal force, pushing classic R&B toward the edgy rock terrain that the Stones would soon come to epitomize.

Oldham's main contribution to the Stones was his insistence that the band should begin writing original material. He was rightly convinced that the group's future would be limited if it depended on searching out obscure R&B gems to cover. Jagger and Richards knew it could be done. They had seen it with their own eyes the previous September when Lennon and McCartney visited their rehearsal space in Soho. The Beatle composers had been working on a song called 'I Wanna Be Your Man' for Ringo, but it was unfinished. As Jagger and Richards watched, the dynamic duo completed the song and offered it to the Stones. Within a month, the supercharged 'I Wanna Be Your Man' had become the Rolling Stones' first top-10 single.

"We thought it sounded pretty commercial, which is what we were looking for, so we did it like Elmore James or something," Jagger told *Rolling Stone* in 1968. "I haven't heard it for ages but it must be pretty freaky 'cause nobody really produced it...but it was a hit and sounded great on stage."

One day, Oldham pushed Jagger and Richards into a room with instructions not to leave until they had written at least one song. They did. So three songs on *The Rolling Stones* were credited to either the mysterious Nanker Phelge – a nonsensical *nom de plume* for group compositions – or to Jagger and Richards. The Glimmer Twins were born.

now i've got a witness (like uncle phil and uncle gene)

Motown gone wrong. This light-hearted instrumental jam was the first original song to appear on a Rolling Stones album. Credited to Nanker Phelge, the track rides a soft blues rhythm that emerged during their session covering the Marvin Gaye hit 'Can I Get a Witness'. 'Now I've Got A Witness' borrows the same central keyboard riff, replacing the revival-meeting piano melody with a swell of organ. Wistful blues harp cuts across Charlie Watts' rock steady beat before the track finally catches fire with a charged Keith guitar lead.

Nothing profound about their performance, just joyful playing. The Uncles Phil and Gene in the title refer to producer Phil Spector and pop singer Gene Pitney, who were frequent visitors to the sessions for *The Rolling Stones*. Spector was the mad studio genius whose "wall of sound" created a rich musical fabric for 1960s pop epics by the likes of the Crystals and the Ronnettes. His studio magic made for some visionary pop, although not exactly relevant to the blues and rock of the Stones. Spector's presence at Regent Sound was just for friendly encouragement and to keep a wary eye on his sex-pot wife, singer Ronnie Spector, who had just met the Stones while touring England. Crooner Pitney had often collaborated with Spector, crafting weepy epics memorable for their rich melodramatic arrangements. Though a songwriter himself – he had written 'Hello Mary Lou' for Ricky Nelson – Pitney scored another hit in January 1964 with the early Jagger/Richards song 'That Girl Belongs To Yesterday'. It was the first Glimmer Twins composition to hit the US charts.

'Now I've Got A Witness' was perhaps most notable for its clear view of the young players in the Rolling Stones. Uncluttered by Jagger's mush-mouthed approximation of the blues, the track captured the legendary rhythm section in its earliest glory.

"Bill and Charlie locked together," notes Bobby Womack, who would later witness the Stones at work many times on stage and in the studio. "Bill made Charlie a hell of a drummer, and vice versa – he made him a hell of a bass player. Being a musician is not how many notes you play, but what you don't play. Music is simplicity."

> **"Bill and Charlie locked together. Bill made Charlie a hell of a drummer, and vice versa – he made him a hell of a bass player"**
>
> Bobby Womack, co-composer of 'It's All Over Now'

the rolling stones

the rolling stones

little by little

Bad love is as timeless as the blues itself. It's sent men no less formidable than Willie Dixon, Muddy Waters and B.B. King into howls of joy and hate, crafting soul-searching music as mournful as it is strangely euphoric. Love gone wrong also provided the young Stones with an early successful attempt at blues authenticity.

'Little By Little' mixes a young man's pain and resignation with a frenetic blues-rock rhythm as foreboding as the album's shadowy cover photograph of five grim-faced young men, solemnly preparing for some unspeakably dirty work.

Co-credited to Nanker Phelge and Phil Spector, 'Little By Little' made its debut as the B-side to their hit single of Buddy Holly's 'Not Fade Away' (which was included on the US version of the album). While Spector plays maracas, Jagger portrays a man stalking his woman, watching from his car, afraid of the heartbreak he expects to find as he follows her to some unknown rendezvous.

Between flashes of harmonica, Jagger sings more about internal pain than the more suggestive contents of the blues originals featured on the album. He might as well have been a heartbroken teenager – he was still only 19 at the time of this session on February 4, 1964. And yet Jagger finds new depth within his voice, a grinding edge that would emerge as a key element in the classic Stones sound, finally turning the black man's rhythm and blues into something of his own.

"Nobody sounds like Mick," says Bobby Womack. "You can say you know artists that are much better, but if I tried to sing like Mick I would be totally out of league. When you're different, it's like Ray Charles. He's a stylist."

Phil Spector was a frequent visitor to the early Stones sessions in Los Angeles.

tell me (you're coming back)

This was a long way from the music the Stones had initially set out to play. But 'Tell Me (You're Coming Back To Me)' was an early indication that the new Jagger/Richards writing team was capable of crafting a song worthy of the band's time. It was only a first step for the Glimmer Twins, but the song's pleasant, if unspectacular, pop melody was a move toward undermining the dominance of Brian Jones.

Keith plays a jangly 12-string guitar and sings harmonies into the same microphone, as Jagger's vocals fall just short of pleading.

"It's a very POP song, as opposed to all the blues songs and the Motown covers, which everyone did at the time," Mick Jagger told *Rolling Stone* magazine in 1995.

Other new compositions that emerged at the same time included 'As Tears Go By' and 'That Girl Belongs To Yesterday'. They had little in common with the blues, or with the bare-knuckle rock the Stones would later create, but this early balladry was an important foundation for the melodic pop of their dynamic work of the mid-sixties.

"We were writing ballads, don't ask me why," Jagger said. "We didn't want to do blues forever, we just wanted to turn people on to other people who were very good and not carry on doing it ourselves," Jagger explained later. "So you could say that we did turn blues on to people, but why they should be turned on by us is unbelievably stupid. I mean, what's the point of listening to us doing 'I'm A King Bee' when you could listen to Slim Harpo doing it?"

21

chapter two

1965 rolling stones no. 2

Young Mick Jagger in mid-flight, lighting a fuse that would drive the little girls mad.

Everybody Needs Somebody To Love
(RUSSELL/BURKE/WEXLER)

Down Home Girl
(LEIBER/BUTLER)

You Can't Catch Me
(BERRY)

Time Is On My Side
(MEADE/NORMAN)

What A Shame

Grown Up Wrong

Down The Road Apiece
(RAYE)

Under The Boardwalk
(RESNICK/YOUNG)

I Can't Be Satisfied
(WATERS)

Pain In My Heart
(REDDING/WALDEN)

Off The Hook

Suzie Q
(BROADWATER/LEWIS/HAWKINS)

et the rioting begin. Maybe Andrew Oldham was a genius after all, selling the Rolling Stones as a pack of dangerous delinquents. It was driving the little girls mad, and had sent *The Rolling Stones* album to the top of the UK chart for 11 impossible weeks. Until then, their shows across Britain had taken place with little incident – just the occasional sad-eyed girl looking for idols. Now there were 4,000 gate-crashers with phony tickets rioting outside their performance in Aberdeen. And soon the halls of Europe would be aflame with the passion of teens erupting to the sounds of blues and soul, sending chairs and chandelier pieces through the air, with girls being carried out in straight jackets, boys spitting at Brian and Keith, ripping the clothes off young women. And police everywhere, hopelessly addled and confused.

This was the Stones legacy of 1964. And yet the master of this great rock and roll swindle was young Andrew – every bit to the early Rolling Stones what Malcolm McLaren would be to the Sex Pistols in 1976. He was not there to create, but to exploit. Both were impresarios in search of the worst publicity imaginable – taking any opportunity to create an alarming headline. Oldham also fancied himself as a producer in the epic Phil Spector mould, arriving at the studio in dark threads and shades. He even wrote liner notes to the albums in the cryptic hipster-speak of Anthony Burgess' novel *A Clockwork Orange* – "Here are your new groovies so please a-bound to the sound". "He was like a beatnik," remembers Mick Farren, writer and leader of the Deviants, "but a few years too late."

So the rioting rolled on. The Stones set out on a three-week tour of the US. It was the beginning of three years of almost constant travel and playing, a lifestyle that would have a profound effect on the frail Brian Jones.

As it turned out, there was little rioting in the States. The Stones had perhaps come too early, unlike the Beatles, who waited until 'I Want To Hold Your Hand' was a No. 1 hit in America before landing at Kennedy Airport to a greeting from thousands of screaming fans and Mr Ed Sullivan. Despite Andrew's evil brainstorming, the Stones' career was never quite so premeditated. If the Beatles seemed to live in a rock and roll fairy tale, the Rolling Stones' biography would never read quite so smoothly. In any case, why should the Stones have waited any longer? After all, as the 500 fans who greeted them well understood, these were "ENGLAND'S NEWEST HITMAKERS!"

The first Rolling Stones tour of the US – along with Bobby Vee, the Chiffons, Bobby Goldsboro and Bobby Comstock – did very well on the coasts, hitting New York and Los Angeles like visiting pop royalty. But the band had a tougher time travelling the great expanse of emptiness in between, enduring small crowds and Midwestern ambivalence. Even before the tour officially began, the Rolling Stones found themselves, their sound and their dress, the subject of ridicule.

In the days leading up to their first gig in nearby San Bernardino, the band appeared at a Los Angeles taping of Dean Martin's *Hollywood Palace Show*. Here they were seen on American television playing Willie Dixon's shuddering 'I Just Want To Make Love To You', Brian beneath his great helmet of yellow-blond hair, Keith twitching nervously through his riffs, Bill holding his bass like a shotgun, Mick clapping and kicking his heels politely and Charlie somehow oblivious on the drum seat and looking the most comfortable in his own skin. But Dino didn't much like their hair or their music. And he certainly didn't understand the blues – "Now something for the youngsters…"

Dino was a hipster from the old school, a wisecracking, crooning funnyman in greased hair, forever carrying a burning cigarette in one hand, a tumbler of booze in the other. He was a product of the World War II generation, whose cultural

> "We were blues purists who liked ever so commercial things but never did them on stage because we were so horrible and so aware of being blues purists, you know what I mean?"
>
> Mick Jagger

dominance was most threatened by the likes of the Beatles and the Stones. Even Elvis was worried.

"Some people have the impression that some of these new groups have long hair," Martin told the Palace audience with a roll of his eyes. "Naaaaaaaah, it's an optical illusion, they just have low foreheads and high eyebrows." Their parents, Dino went on, had even contemplated suicide at the very idea of the Stones and their music.

Insulting? Yes, but by the time the show was broadcast across the nation ten days later, it hardly mattered at all. The Stones had arrived at Chess Studios in Chicago, the "Holy Grail" of American blues and rock and roll, and the site of immortal recordings by Muddy Waters, Chuck Berry, Little Walter and Bo Diddley. While they were there, the band recorded 'It's All Over Now', 'Confessin' The Blues' and '2120 Michigan Avenue', encouraged by the masters – Chuck and Muddy – who visited the Stones sessions to see these young white R&B fanatics for themselves.

The early 1960s had been lean years for the Chess roster, and the Rolling Stones were bringing their music back into the spotlight. For years, Richards claimed that when the Stones arrived at Chess, they found Waters at work painting the ceiling, though Wyman disputes the memory. Either way, bands like the Stones and, later, the Yardbirds and the Animals, were helping to keep the music alive for a new generation.

Yet as each of those acts would quickly demonstrate, the irresistible attraction of POP was as real as the latest Beatles chart triumph. The Stones managed without trouble to stay true to their roots while recording within the hallowed halls of Chess, but it was just as inevitable that a change was gonna come. As Jagger explained to *Rolling Stone* in 1995, "We were blues purists who liked ever so commercial things but never did them on stage because we were so horrible and so aware of being blues purists, you know what I mean?"

On their return to England, the Stones found that local hysteria had only intensified in their absence. A concert in Belfast was halted after just 12 minutes as police grew increasingly alarmed at the sight of fainting girls and shouting boys. In Paris, more than 150 fans were arrested during rioting at the Olympia. It was the kind of bad press Andrew had fantasized about. Now the Stones found themselves banned from hotels and refused service in the best restaurants. His dream had come true.

What was behind all of this? The authorities only had to look at the Stones album covers to realize their worst fears. As on their debut, the sleeve of *The Rolling Stones No. 2* – photographed by David Bailey – presented the band as a gang of brooding young thugs. The music inside was dark and rumbling. It had been recorded during the band's second tour of the US at the end of 1964, shortly after Charlie's wedding to Shirley Ann Shepherd. If the first album owed its raw edge to the barebones setting of Regent Sound, *The Rolling Stones No. 2* found a new potency within the studios of Chess and RCA in Hollywood, home of Elvis Presley. "It is very soul influenced, which was the goal at the time – Otis Redding and Solomon Burke," Jagger said later of the album.

An immediate success, the new album entered the British chart at No. 1, turning the Rolling Stones into instant rivals for the Beatles' pop crown. In truth, however, *The Rolling Stones No. 2* was less impressive as a musical document. None of the three original compositions here were particularly memorable, and were easily overshadowed by the band's recording of 'Time Is On My Side'. Though faithful to the Irma Thomas original, the Rolling Stones made the song their own with Jagger's heartfelt reading and Richards' most dynamic guitar work to date. Also included was an unfortunate attempt by Jagger to recreate the wistful romance of 'Under The Boardwalk'.

Even amidst the erratic mix of hits and missteps, the Rolling Stones were slowly refining their role, and laying a foundation for the important work to come.

> "It is very soul influenced, which was the goal at the time – Otis Redding and Solomon Burke"
>
> Mick Jagger on 'The Rolling Stones No. 2'

rolling stones no. 2

what a shame

irst released in December 1964 as the B-side to the Jagger/Richards-penned single 'Heart Of Stone', 'What A Shame' reveals the Stones confidently creating some blues of their own. Jagger's pipes are deeper, gliding across searing blasts of harmonica, the spirited piano riffs of Ian Stewart at the edges, and the Wyman-Watts rhythm section snapping it all into place. By the time a lengthy instrumental jam closes the track, the Rolling Stones have nearly mastered a form they first encountered as boys studying Chess imports from America.

That confidence doesn't emerge everywhere on *The Rolling Stones No. 2*, but 'What A Shame' at least documents the Stones in command of a basic blues formula – nothing fancy, and nothing that Brian Jones hadn't already preached as the one true path. Jagger and Richards had – with the encouragement of their manager – now claimed for themselves the task of writing original material for the band. The sharing of songwriting credits as the mysterious "Nanker Phelge" was soon a thing of the past. The reality in 1965, though, was that the defining vision for the band hadn't yet been relinquished by the fanatical Elmo Lewis.

"The Rolling Stones that I joined were led by Brian Jones," Bill Wyman wrote in his autobiography, *Stone Alone*. "To the millions who figured it was Mick Jagger's band, it may come as a shock to record that in 1963 Mick was simply the singer. There was no doubt whatsoever who led the group in every way. Brian called the shots partly because he had pulled the musicians together, but mainly because what mattered most at that stage was music, and Brian was by far the most knowledgeable about what we were playing."

Jones would never be able to compete with the developing songwriting talents of Jagger and Richards, but he remained a key player in the sound of the Stones until creeping bad habits, failing health and paranoia slowly took it all away. His collapse in Chicago from physical exhaustion while on tour was an early signal that Jones might be unable to keep up with his creation.

Mick Jagger (centre) slowly found a voice that would emerge as a key element in the classic Stones sound.

rolling stones no. 2

grown up wrong

The Stones roadshow now rolled ever onward. During their second American tour, the band debuted on the influential *Ed Sullivan Show* on October 25, 1964. The result was a near riot of screaming young men and women in Sullivan's studio audience, leaving the host a shaken man. "I promise you they will never be back to our show," he told the assembled press. "They were recommended by my scouts in England. I was shocked when I saw them."

Rock and roll was becoming dangerous, as seen on TV. And yet the Stones would of course be back on Sullivan's stage within a year. Sullivan had seen this kind of hysteria twice before, first with Elvis Presley, whose offending pelvic thrusts and gyrations had to be cropped from the TV picture. But Sullivan had also taken Presley in his arms during the broadcast to declare him "a fine young man". Similarly, the Beatles had also come and gone with little real trouble.

How strange that Sullivan's early anxieties of the fearsome Stones emerged from a fittingly restrained reading of 'Time Is On My Side'. If anything, Mick performed the song as a classic romantic, politely tapping his feet. Jagger hadn't yet learned to chew the scenery from his first dose of live James Brown.

Likewise, Jagger's vocal chops were not fully developed at the time of *The Rolling Stones No. 2*. He sounds earnest enough on 'Grown Up Wrong', but his vocals lack the weight of his blues and soul models. Even with the accompaniment of Jones' testy slide guitar, Jagger in 1965 simply didn't sound like someone ready to offer meaningful advice about love. That wouldn't come until the deeply moving performances of raw blues and country on 1968's *Beggars Banquet*.

In America, 'Grown Up Wrong' appears on *12 x 5*, the Stones' second album release in the US, a typical bastardization of the UK releases. Material from *The Rolling Stones No. 2* was roughly divided in the States between *12 x 5* and *The Rolling Stones Now*, both of which are filled out with miscellaneous singles and EP tracks. Although the Beatles suffered a similar fate with their early albums, discrepancies were eventually resolved with the CD reissues. The early Stones catalogue, controlled by Allen Klein's ABKCO Records, still remains something of a mess.

> **" I promise you they will never be back to our show... I was shocked when I saw them "**
>
> Ed Sullivan

off the hook

The riffs of Chuck Berry (opposite) had a profound impact on Keith Richards.

This charmingly simple pop nugget was the first Jagger/Richards composition to suggest the pure pop-rock sensibility that would emerge with such impact on 1967's *Between The Buttons*. Recorded at London's Regent Sound on September 2, 1964, 'Off The Hook' first appeared just two months later as the B-side to the band's 'Little Red Rooster' single, which quickly topped the UK chart.

The song opens with a buoyant Chuck Berry-style guitar melody, as Jagger sings of calling his girlfriend late one night only to find her line constantly busy. He sounds ready to accept any explanation – she's asleep, she's ill, her line's been disconnected for an unpaid bill – except for the unmentioned possibility that she's found someone new. His tone is closer to irritation than worry, but still far from the bitter female trouble Jagger would regularly complain about in the Rolling Stones songs of the coming three decades.

rolling stones no. 2

chapter three

1965 out of our heads

At home in America: The Stones take a short cruise during the never-ending rock and roll roadshow.

She Said Yeah
(JACKSON/CHRISTY)

Mercy, Mercy
(COVAY/MILLER)

Hitch Hike
(GAYE/STEVENSON/PAUL)

That's How Strong My Love Is
(JAMISON)

Good Times
(COOKE)

Gotta Get Away

Talkin' 'Bout You
(BERRY)

Cry To Me
(RUSSELL)

Oh Baby (We Got A Good Thing Goin')
(OZEN)

Heart Of Stone

The Under Assistant West Coast Promotion Man
(PHELGE)

I'm Free

Keith Richards had a dream, and the dream was good. Another night on the road in the States in May 1965, and Keith was jarred awake in his Florida motel bed by a sound echoing in his skull. It was a fierce rumbling, with the words "can't get no satisfaction, can't get no satisfaction" mercilessly rolling between his ears. He played it immediately using his new Gibson Fuzzbox and taped it before passing out again. What was this? Not even Keith knew, so when the Stones twice attempted '(I Can't Get No) Satisfaction' at Chess and RCA Studios that same week, he rejected the song as virtually unreleasable, at least as a single. Too damn simple, with a riff dangerously close to Martha and the Vandellas' 'Dancing In The Street'. Andrew Oldham soon convinced him otherwise. 'Satisfaction' was released as a single that same month. It became the band's first American No. 1 hit. Everything had now changed – the Rolling Stones had experienced their first absolutely decisive moment.

'Satisfaction' was music designed to explode from a small transistor radio, that lo-fi conduit between pop culture and the adolescent masses. It was the sound of testosterone boiling over, Jagger demanding sexual healing, Richards' fuzzy guitar a fucking ball of nerves. No one had ever made a sound quite like this before, not Muddy or Chuck or Bo. If the implied raunch of the Stones' billion blues covers hadn't already transmitted the message, 'Satisfaction' made clear everything that parents feared for their children – SEX.

"When they assimilated the blues aspect INTO the band, that's when it really happened for me," says Ray Manzarek, keyboard player with the Doors, who had grown up hearing the blues in Chicago. Until then, he had found the British blues bands nice, but hardly definitive next to the originals. "The first time I heard 'Satisfaction' on the radio I couldn't believe it. The lyrics were so terrific, they were talking to all young American males. This guy is singing a song to US."

The song had emerged from a typically harried schedule of recording sessions, squeezed between concert dates: four tracks recorded in 17 hours at Chess in Chicago, followed immediately by three more tracks in two days at RCA in Hollywood. The result was *Out Of Our Heads*, which, like the 'Satisfaction' single, was first released in the US in July. This, rather ironically, made it the original version of the album, which had a significantly different, and diminished, track listing by the time it was released in the UK that September.

"I think it was because we were actually there," Andrew Oldham told journalist Craig Rosen in 1994, discussing the band's decision to release the album in the States first. "Once you make a record like 'Satisfaction' you basically just want to get it out. We weren't going to be back in England for quite a while, and you really couldn't put something out in England without being there. It was something you just don't do. It really would have been slighting people."

The Rolling Stones were rarely home now, except as another stop on their endless world tour. There were the occasional pit stops in England, long enough to find a new pad, buy a sports car or be fitted for a fur parka. Then it was back on the road. They were enjoying their accelerating success, even with the usual mishaps along the way. One afternoon in Odense, Denmark, Jagger was nearly fried from an electrical shock during rehearsals. Later, some 3,000 Australians rioted upon their arrival at the Sydney airport, and 40 fans charged the stage in Brisbane, ripping the clothes off whatever Stones they could reach. And back in the UK, a Manchester girl broke some teeth after falling from a balcony during a show.

Then, at the end of a UK tour, the Rolling Stones had their first brush with the law, an early warning of the strange days to come. The Stones were returning to London on March 18, 1965, when Ian Stewart pulled the car over at a filling station in East London. There, Wyman was denied use of the toilet by a cheeky mechanic named Charles Keely, who later referred to the Stones as "long-haired monsters".

> **" The first time I heard 'Satisfaction' on the radio I couldn't believe it. The lyrics were so terrific, they were talking to all young American males "**
>
> Ray Manzarek, the Doors

out of our heads

Wyman, Jones and Jagger then used a nearby wall instead, shouted a few insults at Keely and drove off. The incident was immediately reported in the press, and the Stones were charged with insulting behaviour by urinating in public. They were fined £5 each in July. The judge told them: "Because you have reached the exalted heights in your profession, it does not mean you have the right to act like this... You have been found guilty of behaviour not becoming young gentlemen."

Travelling across the US was difficult for other reasons. Celebrated in the major cities, the Stones found smaller audiences elsewhere. So their visits to Chess studios were partly designed by Oldham simply to raise the band's spirits.

"The touring was to get a body of fans under our belts everywhere because we weren't selling any plastic. And these tours were not very successful that had gone before," said Oldham. "So they've been very good boys, 'I've got a present for you: we're going to go to Chess!' It's like telling the Pope you can go to the Vatican. It was very good for them, but it wasn't totally productive for my commercial aims. It tended to get a little too bluesy and go in a different type of streak than I was trying to encourage their songwriting."

Just three recordings from Chess would make it on to *Out Of Our Heads* – 'That's How Strong My Love Is', 'Have Mercy' and 'The Under Assistant West Coast Promotion Man'. The majority of the album was recorded at RCA, where the Stones found inspiration in the work of engineer Dave Hassinger, who was able to capture sounds and nuances that had so far eluded them. Not that many of these early sessions resulted in crisp and shiny tracks, not like the Beatles and their deluxe producer George Martin, whose records still sound clean enough to sit alongside the latest puddle of syrup from Bryan Adams. True blues was still their aim. "We are recording in the US solely because we believe we can produce our best work there," Jagger said at the time. "We can record right through from 6 o'clock in the morning without so much as a tea break."

Out Of Our Heads spent three weeks as America's top-selling album, but stalled at No. 2 in England. In retrospect, the British version of *Out Of Our Heads* was clearly inferior to the original US release, which included the songs 'Play With Fire' and '(Can't Get No) Satisfaction'. Because both tracks had already been released as singles, they were left off the record, robbing UK listeners of what otherwise would have been cornerstone tracks on *Out Of Our Heads*. "You did not put singles on albums," Oldham said of the Stones' UK releases. "Remember, we'd won the war but we had lost it. Not many people had that much money. So it was considered ripping people off."

The Stones were also busy in other ways. Charlie Watts published *Ode To A Flying Bird*, an illustrated children's book on the life of Charlie Parker he had written in 1961. Oldham released a ridiculous album via Decca called *The Rolling Stones Songbook* and credited to the Andrew Oldham Orchestra, with guest Keith Richards. The Stones' impresario also launched the Immediate record label, which would ultimately earn resentment from the band. And the Rolling Stones kept playing and recording, with little restriction.

"You're dealing with a time when all acts were tied by their neck to recording companies, recording in Studio A or B somewhere with a house producer," said Oldham. "We were suddenly getting the rewards of a totally independent life. The only other one who was independent at that time was Dave Clark. This was the first album where we were seeing the results of being in control of our own lives."

> **" We were suddenly getting the rewards of a totally independent life. This was the first album where we were seeing the results of being in control of our own lives "**
>
> Andrew Loog Oldham, manager and producer of 'Out Of Our Heads'

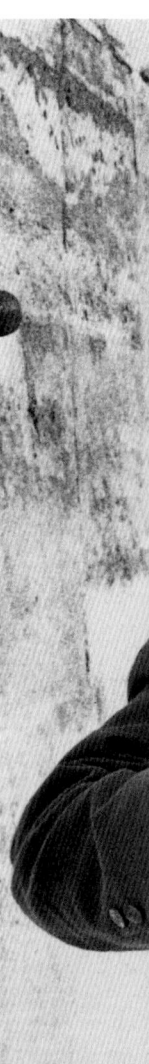

gotta get away

This is Mick Jagger's idea of a love song, or a love-gone-wrong song, to be more precise. Either way, 'Gotta Get Away' gave an early taste of the Glimmer Twins' habit of exploring romance as an endlessly bitter confrontation. The indelicate treatment of women would emerge repeatedly in their work – 1978's *Some Girls* even saw Jagger listing varieties of women like items in a supermarket. There would be poignant exceptions to this theme, such as the deeply felt 'I Got The Blues', a heartbreaker from 1971 – we can blame the exit of Marianne Faithfull for that one. But 'Gotta Get Away' established a recurring motif for the Stones, where Jagger is never left in a relationship without the upper hand.

Indeed, 'Gotta Get Away' has the singer ending a love affair with some faceless chick in a tone of self-righteousness, when not drifting into cruel indifference – "To think I believed all your lies". Jagger is at once soothing and mocking in his phrasing, while the band builds a blithe folk-pop rhythm out of a blend of driving acoustic and electric guitars. The recently wed Charlie Watts keeps a steady beat, as he has done ever since through three decades of marriage. 'Gotta Get Away' is the first of many two-minute bursts of glib manhood.

The early Stones were sold as "anti-Beatles", bad boys wreaking havoc on society.

out of our heads

heart of stone

Recorded at RCA Studios in Hollywood, this lumbering anti-love ballad is part old blues and part Elvis-style torch song, except that Jagger denies any feeling whatsoever. Romance is a game he's won by shutting himself off from any sign of vulnerability. The message of 'Heart Of Stone' is almost numbing, as Jagger confesses "There've been so many girls that I've known, I've made so many cry". It's a puzzled revelation the singer mentions here with only passing interest. His concern isn't in understanding women, only in conquering them. The track did not appear in the US until 1966 as part of the *Big Hits (High Tide And Green Grass)* compilation. But even then, the Stones' statement on bad love didn't seem to scare off the little girls.

the under assistant west coast promotion man

The Rolling Stones were a very special case for London Records, the American arm of Decca. Jagger and his cohorts were clearly more than just another "British Invasion" act designed to cash in on a passing fad. The Stones had something else to offer. With roots firmly in the great blues tradition, their own sound and vision went far deeper than 1960s pop. They were also Decca and London's last best hope of at least approaching the monumental success of the Beatles, who were then, as John Lennon would later famously quip, "bigger than Jesus" – at least to the young record-buying public. After all, Decca had passed on the Beatles, a decision that would later go down in A&R infamy. So now that the Stones were in their grasp, the label felt obliged to put their best men on the case.

In the US, that meant sending promotions man George Sherlock on the road with the Stones whenever they hit the West Coast. It actually got on the band's nerves at first – a chaperone was not what anyone had in mind, not with a full schedule of first-class debauchery ahead of them. And yet the presence of Mr Sherlock suggested that the label had actually made the Rolling Stones a top priority.

"There was a wonderful guy with a great wit called George Sherlock, who I think was THE West Coast promotion man for London Records," Andrew Oldham recalled. "In England promotion men never left their office, and we never saw a record. In America we saw both of these things, so we were slightly knocked out. To have a promotion man actually touring with you."

The band's reaction emerged via 'The Under Assistant West Coast Promotion Man', a biting satire on their experiences with poor Mr Sherlock. The last song to be credited to Nanker Phelge, the tune is an upbeat blues, with a twangy guitar melody mingling with heated harmonica lines. Jagger sings comically of a record company character with an inflated sense of importance – "Well, they laugh at my toupee, they sure put me down... I'm a necessary talent behind every rock and roll band".

> **" Yeah, but he didn't know anything about blues "**
>
> Mick Jagger on
> Andrew Loog Oldham

'The Under Assistant West Coast Promotion Man' was first released in the US as the B-side to the 'Satisfaction' single. It was recorded at Chess in Chicago, with Oldham producing.

"Yeah, but he didn't know anything about blues," Jagger said of Oldham in 1968. "The cat who really got it together was Ron Malo, the engineer for Chess. He had been on all the original sessions."

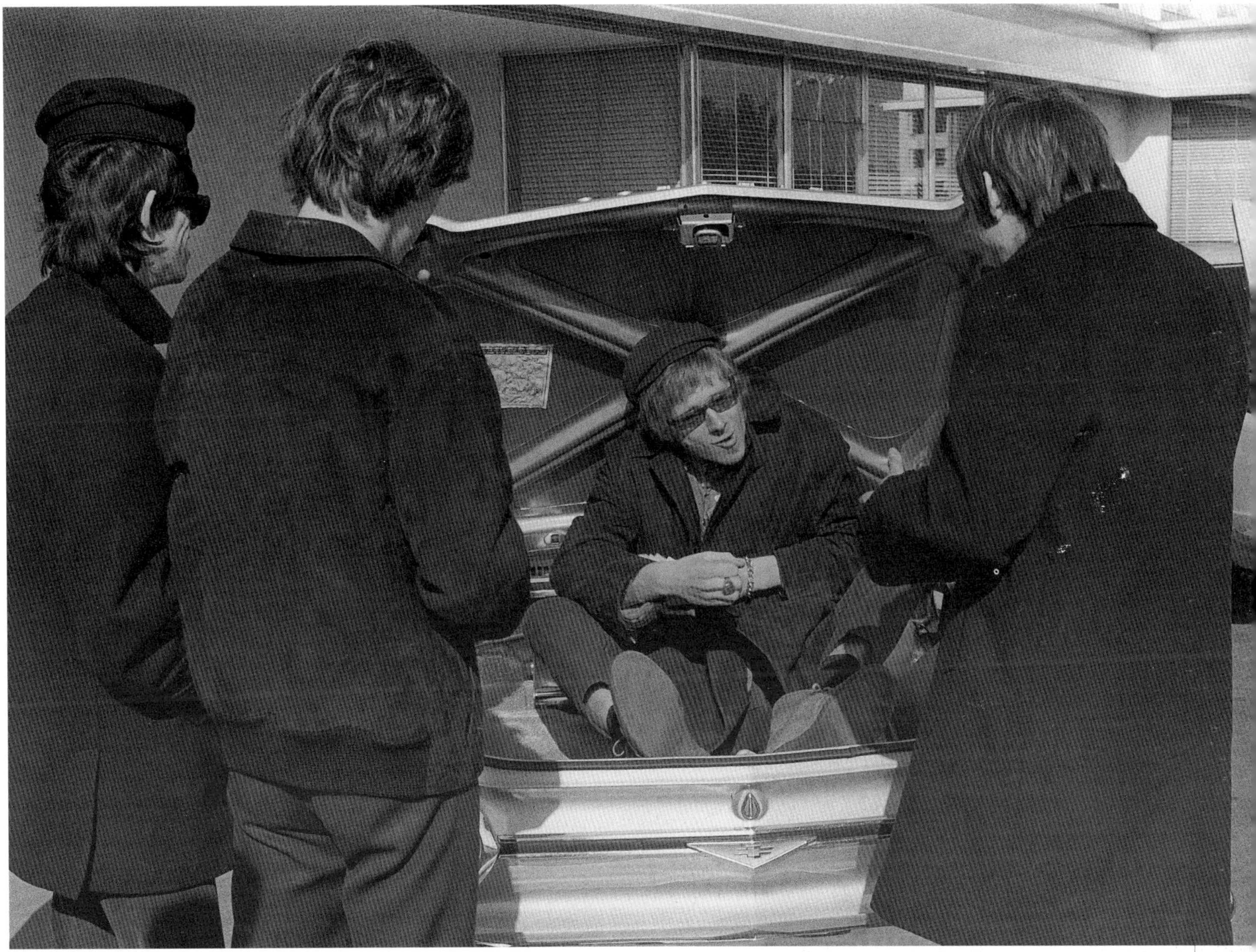

Andrew Loog Oldham (centre) demanded that Jagger and Richards begin writing original material.

i'm free

He really means it, man. It's as if Jagger and the boys had only just realized their unique place in society. By now it was clear that the Stones had somehow escaped the real-life limitations of working-class and middle-class Britain. They were now members of a new kind of royalty, where no whim was too ridiculous to be seriously considered. They were worshipped by young girls and Decca's accountants alike, celebrated in these innocent days before the drug raids, the divorces, the deaths and decay, and their fate as rootless tax exiles. For now, the band could happily weave a shimmering backdrop of blues-pop, while Jagger strutted to the very idea that he's "free to sing my song knowing it's out of trend". The singer further suggests that he's entitled to ANYTHING he wants, including the warmth and feminine comforts from the subject of his current affections. Not to celebrate, but to serve. It's all the same to him.

chapter four

1966 aftermath

He may have lost control of the Stones, but Brian Jones created a new role for himself as multi-instrumentalist extraordinaire.

Mother's Little Helper
Stupid Girl
Lady Jane
Under My Thumb
Doncha Bother Me
Goin' Home
Flight 505
High And Dry
Out Of Time
It's Not Easy
I Am Waiting
Take It Or Leave It
Think
What To Do

nd now, re-introducing the Rolling Stones, new and improved for 1966. Or at any rate, different. These were no longer teenage blues copyists out to worship their black elders. The Stones were now making music entirely of their own creation. Anyone could have seen the changes coming. During the previous year, the band had enjoyed international chart-topping singles with 'Get Off Of My Cloud', '19th Nervous Breakdown' and 'Paint It Black', all of them mixing a strange new pop dementia with the band's blissful aggression. Here were the Stones basking in the elegance of pop without abandoning the primal code of the blues. Thus, the release of *Aftermath* would have seemed anticlimactic had it not been a cocksure manifesto of purpose for the Stones and an important milestone for the rock era.

Aftermath was the first album written entirely by the suddenly thriving Jagger/Richards songwriting team. Not even Nanker Phelge was allowed to interfere with that monopoly — which of course meant that Jones, Watts and Wyman were now locked out of any publishing royalties. This was just as Andrew Loog Oldham had wanted, and of course he was right. Something new and dangerous was going on between the Glimmer Twins, who had discovered new ways to forge rich pop arrangements to their own dark ends. Tracks such as 'Mother's Little Helper' and 'Under My Thumb' were agitated tales, challenging an older generation while showing no mercy toward feminist notions of justice.

Brian Jones played no small part in this new development. Blues priest Elmo Lewis had become bored with his guitars, which were soon replaced in Brian's repertoire with a dazzling mix of sitar, dulcimer, marimbas and bells, as well as anything else picked up during his travels to the hills of North Africa. No instrument seemed too exotic or beyond his reach. Mick and Keith were quickly taking over the band he'd first imagined as a boy back in Cheltenham, but Jones remained a powerful musical force within the Rolling Stones.

These were developments that their friends back at Chess might have had trouble understanding. And yet the Stones were making an important statement with *Aftermath*, demonstrating to the pop masses and the blues purists alike that the blues were simply a beginning for them — a step on the road to creating a sound for their own age. They would ultimately return to the songs of Chicago and the Mississippi Delta in coming years, but then it would be by choice, not necessity.

The Rolling Stones were hardly the only band of young British blues purists to edge ever deeper into rock and pop. Just as the Yardbirds, the Animals, Them and others experimented in newer styles — even if they sometimes earned the wrath of hardcore fans — the Stones found themselves inevitably drawn to the exciting new musical possibilities in the air.

"I found it logical," says London blues devotee John Mayall, who has led his Bluesbreakers through three decades of blues devotion. "Everybody was very young and drawn to the electrification of the guitars and the music of Bo Diddley, Chuck Berry and Muddy Waters. That was a starting point really for them as musicians. They had to find their own way of expression. That kind of led them into the areas that just happened to make them very popular on the rock and roll pop scene. In all cases, everyone ended up finding their own identity. The blues was their starting point."

> "Everyone ended up finding their own identity. The blues was their starting point"
> John Mayall

The sounds of *Aftermath* emerged during two intense periods of work at RCA Studios in Hollywood: five days in December 1965, followed by two weeks the following March. Visitors from Phil Spector to Brian Wilson of the Beach Boys often stopped by, usually just to observe, but sometimes to participate.

The Stones were deep into their own creative revolution, but not everyone was happy with their share of the credit. "There was injustice in the way some songs came to be written and credited solely to Mick and Keith," Wyman noted in his autobiography. "Experimenting in the studio, Brian or I often contributed a riff or a suggestion that was adopted and became a vital part of the song."

aftermath

By the time *Aftermath* made its April debut in the UK (and June in the US) the entire band could bask in the afterglow of yet another No. 1 album, just as they embarked on a fifth American tour. So what if the unbeatable Beatles remained masters of the widest spectrum of pop culture? The Rolling Stones had their own music to make. They had their own destiny to chase.

"That was a big landmark record for me," Jagger told *Rolling Stone* magazine in 1995. "It was the first time we wrote the whole record and finally laid to rest the ghost of having to do these very nice and interesting, no doubt, but still cover versions of old R&B songs – which we really didn't feel we were doing justice, to be perfectly honest, particularly because we didn't have the maturity."

mother's little helper

"What a drag it is getting old". Mick's not kidding. And this was no accidental affront to his elders, but a jeering statement for a new generation whose time was fast approaching.

All of this undoubtedly came as alarming news to the Dean Martin generation, who had won the war and built the suburban dream for every middle-class family from Burbank to Bristol. Now the Rolling Stones were talking about things that were best left unsaid. 'Mother's Little Helper' is the diary of a mad housewife, designed to discredit that post-war, pre-fab existence while exposing a deep sadness just beneath the surface.

Jagger sings about a housewife who resorts to some mysterious pep pills (amphetamines? valium?) to get her through her days of instant cake and frozen dinners, serving an inattentive husband, whose presence is barely felt in her world. "The pursuit of happiness just seems a bore," Mick goes on, and mother's dose gets heavier with every passing day.

Dissatisfaction with society as it is, and the mundane life it encourages, is a recurring theme in the Jagger/Richards songbook – examine, for example, 'Have You Seen Your Mother, Baby, Standing in the Shadow?'. "Mick's always written a lot about it," Richards told *Rolling Stone* in 1971. "A lot of the stuff Chuck Berry and early rock writers did was putting down that other generation. We used to laugh at those people but they must have gotten the message right away because they tried to put rock and roll down, trying to get it off the radio, off records. Obviously they saw some destruction stemming from it…they felt it right away."

As recorded, the song is a muddy tangle of acoustic guitars, given jarring definition from a twangy sitar riff played by Brian Jones. The primitive sitar experiments of Jones and George Harrison initially alarmed the likes of master Ravi Shankar, but without them mid-sixties pop music would not have been the same.

The songwriting duties were fairly evenly divided between the Glimmer Twins. In most cases, Mick handled the writing of the words and Keith the music, although Richards would often come up with a single lyric or phrase that would act as a title or chorus. Most of the writing was also done on the road, and recorded between concert gigs. "An American tour meant you started writing another album," said Richards. "After three, four weeks, you had enough and then you went to LA and recorded it. We worked very fast that way and when you came off a tour you were shit hot playing, as hot as the band is gonna be."

> "An American tour meant you started writing another album. After three, four weeks, you had enough and then you went to LA and recorded it"
>
> Keith Richards

aftermath

stupid girl

T he increasing anti-female tenor of the Stones repertoire should have been a warning to Chrissie Shrimpton, Mick's long-suffering girlfriend. If women were frequently the obsessive subject of Jagger/Richards compositions, they were also depicted as being untrustworthy and disposable.

'Stupid Girl'? Just *who* was Mick talking about? Poor Chrissie may have got her answer the following year, when she attempted suicide after Jagger abruptly abandoned her for singer Marianne Faithfull. Of course, there was no shortage of female companionship in the world of the Rolling Stones. Young women wept at their very presence. Previously unapproachable royals and debutantes lined up to meet young Mick. He certainly obliged, but with an increasingly critical eye.

On 'Stupid Girl', Jagger turns bitter as he cruelly picks apart the deceptive facade he's perceived on the women he's met. Not even the finest makeup, shoes, hair and comely good looks can disguise their dubious intentions. "She's the worst thing in this world!" Jagger shouts across a bed of organ sounds and a flash of light guitar duelling at the bridge.

"Obviously, I was having a bit of trouble," Jagger explained in 1995. "I wasn't in a good relationship. Or I was in too many bad relationships. I had so many girlfriends at that point. None of them seemed to care they weren't pleasing me very much. I was obviously in with the wrong group."

Chrissie Shrimpton (right) endured the early anti-female lyrics of beau Jagger.

aftermath

lady jane

The true measure of any great mid-sixties pop band was an ability to shift gears, to move convincingly from one musical extreme to the next. Both the Beatles and Kinks drifted effortlessly from tough-guy rock to achingly sweet balladry. Now that the Rolling Stones were deep into their own pop period, they could do no less. So even if it was ludicrous to set the anti-chick diatribes of 'Under My Thumb' and 'Stupid Girl' around the suddenly romantic 'Lady Jane', the Stones pulled it off from the sheer force of their shared personality.

The band had already demonstrated a knack for this sort of thing just the previous December with 'As Tears Go By', originally written for Marianne Faithfull, and a top-10 hit in America for the Stones. Light pop balladry may have had nothing to do with the roaring gutbucket rock and blues that would constitute the band's greatest legacy, but it was a necessity for the mid-sixties Stones. ('Lady Jane' was, in fact, omitted from the US release of *Aftermath*, and would not appear until the US-only *Flowers* compilation.)

'Lady Jane' opens with Keith Richards picking quietly at an acoustic guitar and Brian Jones elegantly tapping at a dulcimer. They're joined by Jack Nitzsche on harpsichord as a strangely devotional Mick Jagger recites a love letter, declaring himself "your humble servant".

Chrissie Shrimpton assumed the song was for her, though early press accounts suggested it was based on the story of King Henry VIII and Jane Seymour, his third wife. Seymour was one of Henry's few wives to be spared the executioner's blade, although she died from complications of childbirth after bearing the king's only song, Edward, in 1537.

"I don't really know what that's all about, myself," Mick said in 1968. "All the names are historical but it was really unconscious that they should fit together from the same period." In 1971, Keith told Rolling Stone, "Brian was getting into dulcimer then… We were also listening to a lot of Appalachian music then, too. To me, 'Lady Jane' is very Elizabethan. There are a few places in England where people still speak that way, Chaucer English."

> " I don't really know what that's all about, myself "
>
> Mick Jagger on the lyrics for 'Lady Jane'

under my thumb

More good vibes from the chivalrous Mick Jagger. The songwriting of the Glimmer Twins had now progressed beyond the struggle to simply craft a commercial pop nugget. Rolling Stones songs now reflected the ideas and attitudes of the songwriters themselves. But what were they saying? The singer has said the driving rock assault of 'Under My Thumb' was simply a distasteful reply to one particularly unpleasant woman. Just a caricature, he insisted, not an anti-feminist diatribe – "It's a bit of a jokey number, really."

Whatever the inspiration may have been, 'Under My Thumb' was a powerful track, with Jagger emerging as a hypnotically self-righteous frontman. He sings in a rough, jeering tone, bragging about his power over a young woman who once dominated him. Now Jagger has her in a pathetically submissive role, even deciding for her what clothes she is to wear – "She's the sweetest pet in the world, she does just what she's told". His repetition of the song's title says it all.

Equally effective on the song is the spirited tapping of marimbas by Brian Jones, leading the Stones into some new musical territory. Yet the dark textures Jones and the band were extracting from otherwise pleasant pop owed something to the grim

38

blues hoodoo of their recent past. "That riff played on marimbas really makes it," Jagger said in 1995. "Plus the groove it gets in the end of the tune. It speeds up, actually. And it becomes this kind of groove tune at the end...and then it became a thing feminists fastened on."

The song took on a whole new meaning at the end of 1969, when it served as a horrific soundtrack to the murder of Meredith Hunter at Altamont. A song about the struggle between men and women, and between the classes, was now transformed into something darker than even Jagger had intended.

doncha bother me

Brian Jones creates a reasonable facsimile of the Mississippi Delta blues here with fiery bottleneck guitar, set against Keith's sharp riffing and a thumping heartbeat from Charlie Watts. It wasn't going to get them on the pop charts, but the Stones were still happy to drift back into a heavy blues mode.

'Doncha Bother Me' is a convincing version of the blues, and a precursor to the edgy decadence that would later emerge on *Exile On Main Street*. Not that the sentiment here cuts much deeper than the song's self-explanatory title. In 1966, Jagger's message was a simple rant, perhaps directed at the growing crowd of hangers-on surrounding the Stones.

goin' home

At just over 11 minutes, 'Goin' Home' was *Aftermath*'s strangest exercise. It was more a loose jam session than a finished song, and was at once an earthy throwback to the Stones' early blues days and a shimmering glimpse of the coming psychedelic era. The track's length and aimlessness also shattered any limits of sense, going well beyond the usual three-minute boundary. Still, 'Goin' Home' was finally more successful conceptually than as a worthwhile musical experience.

Singing across understated layers of harmonica, guitar and piano, Jagger huffs and puffs with conviction. He hadn't yet mastered the vocal improvisation that would become second nature by the 1970s, so he claps his hands to the bluesy, trance-like rhythm, repeating, "Well, come on! Come on!" What else was there to do?

"It was the first long rock and roll cut," Keith Richards said in 1971. "It broke that two-minute barrier. We tried to make singles as long as we could do them because we like to just let things roll on. No one sat down to make an 11 minute track. The song was written just the first two and a half minutes. We just happened to keep the tape rolling."

'Goin' Home' sounded much like the early Stones, if not for the echoing, almost psychedelic vibe at the edges. The track's all-night session was hosted by Andrew Oldham at RCA Studios in Hollywood. Brian Wilson was one visitor, along with the dancers Terri Garr (later a successful actress) and Toni Basil (later a choreographer and singer) from TV's *Shindig*. LA scene-maker Rodney Bingenheimer, once dubbed the mayor of the Sunset Strip, remembers seeing a white duck wandering the studio. There was also a young African American

> "They worshipped Phil Spector"
>
> Rodney Bingenheimer, LA scene-maker

aftermath

The Jefferson Airplane crossed paths with the Stones a number of times during the 1960s.

groupie wearing a long fur coat and, apparently, nothing else. Outside was a crowd of kids, all hoping desperately for a glimpse of some rock star, preferably one of the Stones.

Inside, Jagger sang 'Goin' Home' over and over again. "Mick Jagger had a hand-held mike and was on his knees, singing 'Goin' home, I'm goin' home'," says Bingenheimer, who remembers Mick as wearing a striped button-up shirt, and Keith in a leather coat and shades. "It was really long. The whole night was like one song."

Bingenheimer came across Jagger again that year at Phil Spector's session for Ike and Tina Turner's epic 'River Deep Mountain High' at Hollywood's Gold Star Studios. Brian Wilson was also visiting. And Bingenheimer noticed some similarities between the sessions. "They worshipped Phil Spector," says Bingenheimer, who later worked as a local club owner and a radio personality. "And whenever Phil Spector produces a record, he has an audience. He puts on a show. Maybe Mick got that idea."

flight 505

Recording in LA, touring Australia, wives and girlfriends back in Britain, Ed Sullivan in New York, Christmas with the folks at home... The Rolling Stones spent much of their youth in the air, crossing the Atlantic with the frequency of a cross-town commuter. How strange then that Jagger and the band could so happily describe the crashing of a passenger plane into the sea on 'Flight 505'.

Mick's morbid streak had the singer imagining a fate similar that of the Buddy Holly, Ritchie Valens and the Big Bopper, all killed when their small plane crashed into Clear Lake on February 3, 1959. Jagger sings to some glancing Chuck Berry-style chords and boogie-woogie piano, doubtless played by Ian Stewart. The band's later membership of the so-called "jet-set" suggests that if Jagger had any lingering fears of flying, they were quickly overcome.

high and dry

Here is an early blast of folk rock masquerading as country. Despite some spirited harmonica, 'High And Dry' comes closer to a kind of hillbilly skiffle sound, not unlike some of the Beatles' acoustic tracks of the period.

Accompanied by Bill Wyman's thumping bass lines and the crashing cymbals of Charlie Watts, Jagger sings of being dropped by a rich girl without much regret. At first glance, 'High And Dry' seems to depict the girl as being in control, far from a prisoner under Jagger's thumb. And yet the song's situation was almost certainly inspired by Jagger's own life as a Rolling Stone, where some women were certainly attracted less to young Michael Philip Jagger than to his fabulous fame and fortune.

aftermath

out of time

Although Brian again plays the marimbas to amusing effect, it's overwhelmingly Mick's performance – both intimate and seeped in attitude – that carries the moving 'Out Of Time'. The sound is pure Motown pop, with a casually sensuous Jagger snapping his fingers with utter self-confidence and pity, much like a punk prowling the streets of *West Side Story* and ignoring the girl at his heels.

"You're out of touch, my baby, my poor discarded baby," Jagger sings with an air of superiority as he tells of brushing off a girlfriend who had once abandoned him, much to her later regret. He's moved on, but even if he hadn't, this moment of revenge would be too sweet to let go. She must suffer as he did.

Though too often lost in the crowd of mid-sixties Jagger/Richards songs, 'Out Of Time' landed the Stones within their own cruel brand of soul music. There's nothing here to remind listeners of their unfortunate attempts at 'Under The Boardwalk' and 'My Girl'. And not even the few seconds of flat, nasal Bill Wyman singing backup can destroy the moment. Though Chris Farlowe's more compassionate reading the following year would hit No. 1 on the British singles chart, Jagger's typically self-absorbed performance is definitive.

'Out Of Time' was another song left off the American release of *Aftermath*, emerging later on the *Flowers* compilation.

Chris Farlowe (right) topped the UK charts with his version of 'Out Of Time'.

it's not easy

While *Aftermath* was an important step for the Stones, the album's second half inevitably lacked the impact of those first tracks. What could compete with the energy and social impact of 'Mother's Little Helper'? Indeed, most of these later songs would rarely emerge again even as part of the band's live playlist. This is not to say that *Aftermath's* final tracks are mere fillers, except in the context of their coming accomplishments. With its driving rhythm, Chuck Berry riffing, and Mick's moaning chorus about being abandoned by his woman, a song like 'It's Not Easy' holds up well in most other company. If his expression of loneliness is not entirely convincing, Jagger at least treats the female character in the song with affection and regret.

aftermath

i am waiting

It's a long journey from Elmore James to the innocence of 'I Am Waiting', but the Rolling Stones find the right mood here via folky acoustic guitars and Brian Jones' dulcimer. This is the young Stones at their most convincingly romantic, making pop that explodes into moments of yearning.

Jagger's lyrics are unusually obscure, erupting during the chorus to fine melodramatic effect – a method Bill Wyman would put to use for his 'In Another Land' on *Their Satanic Majesties Request*. Mick sings in embracing, soothing tones, and shows rare restraint during the quieter moments, followed with bursts of emotion.

The Searchers: What made them cover 'Take It Or Leave It'?

aftermath

take it or leave it

'Take It Or Leave It' sounds like any number of the early, easily forgotten Jagger/Richards originals written under orders from Andrew Oldham.

As recorded, the song is a shapeless misfire, a flat gathering of acoustic chords, accented with the delicate ring of finger cymbals. Although the song is admittedly performed with some conviction, it leads nowhere. *Aftermath* would have been a better album without it, a fact that must have occurred to London Records, who omitted the song from the album's US release – it would not emerge until the *Flowers* compilation came out in 1967.

Just why the Searchers would choose to cover *this* particular Jagger/Richards composition is one of pop music's great mysteries.

think

'Think' begins promisingly enough, propelled by an uptempo, fuzzy rock sound. Charlie Watts keeps a steady, driving beat as the rest of the Stones build a formidable wall of sound, with baritone guitar chords that succeed in filling the air like a full horn section. And yet it's a song that never fully takes off, even with Jagger's hectoring lecture at some girl to look back at her mistakes – "Tell me whose fault was that, babe?" he sings to her. The vocal melody only rarely strays far from a basic, flat reading.

Chris Farlowe had already released his own ignored version of 'Think' on Andrew Oldham's Immediate Records in January 1966. The Stones version was equally unsuccessful in reaching the pop masses.

what to do

'What To Do' was an odd place to conclude an album which otherwise represented significant growth for the Rolling Stones. This paean to boredom had little or nothing to do with where the Stones had been, and even less to do with where their sound was going. There were no blues here. No rock and roll. Just a simple mixture of acoustic and electric guitar that sounded closer to early Mersey Beat, with the bizarre addition of "bow-bow-bow!" backing vocals that could easily have been stolen from the Beach Boys.

This was the age of experimentation. If the content of *Aftermath* and the fast approaching *Between The Buttons* indicated a commitment to smoother pop ideas, it was really only a passing phase. Songs like 'Out Of Time' and 'Under My Thumb' displayed the Stones new mastery of the genre, but that's not where their ultimate commitment lay. Andrew Oldham certainly encouraged the Stones toward the most lucrative commercial sound available, but Keith Richards was a rock player to the core, and he was only then emerging as a dominant force in the band. None of the Stones could know that their most serious work was yet to come, in an era defined by their definition of rock and roll.

chapter five

1967 between the buttons

Some girls: The Rolling Stones cross the great sexual divide to uncertain ends.

Yesterday's Papers
My Obsession
Back Street Girl
Connection
She Smiled Sweetly
Cool, Calm And Collected

All Sold Out
Please Go Home
Who's Been Sleeping Here?
Complicated
Miss Amanda Jones
Something Happened To Me Yesterday

Don't even mention *Between The Buttons* to Mick Jagger. For him, it's an album best left forgotten, a failed experiment at multi-layered pop. That's a sour verdict for what is still among the most beloved albums of the band's mid-sixties pop phase. Frank Zappa always spoke highly of it. So have critics and members of rock bands as diverse as the Doors and Fleetwood Mac. But Mick will have none of it. *Between The Buttons* is forever spoiled for him by the four-track recording process, which saw layer after layer of fancy overdubs muddle the pristine pop sound he'd once imagined for it. Jagger was still complaining about it two decades later.

"Oh, I hate that fucking record," the singer moaned to engineer Dave Jerden during the making of *Dirty Work* in 1986. To Jagger, *Between The Buttons* was just one more good reason for the Rolling Stones to finally abandon the ways of pure pop in favour of their coming blend of rock and blues – even if that didn't actually occur until after the half-baked psychedelia of 1967's *Their Satanic Majesties Request*. The sounds of Chicago and the Mississippi Delta were beckoning Jagger and the Stones once again.

Of course, the band was enjoying the fruits of pop stardom just the same, hanging out with the young Guinness heir Tara Brown in Ireland, spending Christmas in Los Angeles, moving into slick new pads in the UK – Keith into a thatched Tudor mansion named Redlands, Mick into an apartment at the heart of fashionable London. The *Aftermath* album was another success, as were the singles of 'Paint It Black' and 'Have You Seen Your Mother, Baby, Standing In The Shadow?'. Even Chris Farlowe's version of 'Out Of Time', produced by the Glimmer Twins themselves, hit No. 1 in England. Stones tours of the UK and North America were met with the usual hysteria: rioting in Montreal, London fans knocking down Keith and nearly strangling Mick after rushing the stage at the Royal Albert Hall.

"We were in danger of becoming respectable," Richards happily said at the time. "But now the new wave has arrived, rushing the stage just like old times."

In the midst of their American tour, the Stones stopped in Hollywood for nine days of recording at RCA Studios, where they began the sessions for what would become *Between The Buttons*. But the bulk of the album would be recorded at Olympic Studios in London. When it was finished, *Between The Buttons* was further away from the band's core blues sources than any Stones album so far. At this time, the Stones were making waves of pure pop, and the results were frequently brilliant, in spite of Jagger's later disappointment.

The American version of the album deleted 'Back Street Girl' and 'Please Go Home' in favour of 'Ruby Tuesday' and 'Let's Spend The Night Together', which had already been released as singles in the UK. *Between The Buttons* was the final Stones album to have a different song list on opposite sides of the Atlantic, suggesting that the band was assuming more control over their music and career. It was the inevitable result of the success the Stones had enjoyed almost from the beginning. Unlike much of their earlier work, *Between The Buttons* was not recorded quickly between gigs in the US. Instead, the Stones camped out at Olympic Studios in London, ready to follow their muse where it took them.

In his 1990 autobiography, *Stone Alone*, Bill Wyman calls the album the "first studio session at which we concentrated on an album as a finished product."

"Working with the Rolling Stones never really changed," engineer Glyn Johns told journalist Craig Rosen in 1994. "Immediately they became successful enough to not have any financial restrictions on their recording budget. They did take an immense amount of time making a record. And they very rarely did any preparation before going in the studio. Most of the material throughout the period that I worked with them they wrote in the studio. They would play stuff for extremely long periods of time before they ever got a take that they were satisfied with. I found that extremely monotonous."

> **"Oh, I hate that fucking record"**
> Mick Jagger on Between The Buttons

Those habits would ultimately drive away Johns, who liked to work quickly and found that he could complete three or four albums with other bands in the same amount of time. Johns had been the first man to record the Stones, even before their discovery by Andrew Oldham, and he engineered most of their important albums throughout the sixties. He reunited briefly with the band during the making of 1976's *Black And Blue*, before moving on to work as a producer of bands ranging from the Eagles to the Clash. But his legacy with the Rolling Stones has haunted his reputation ever since. "It was fascinating working with them because of the abilities and personalities," Johns said. "A lot of the music they made I thought was amazing. I just didn't particularly appreciate the way they went about doing it... So in the end I quit. I wanted to produce, and I wanted to be recognized as a producer, which I never was going to be by the Rolling Stones. And I wanted to do something other than sit and wait for someone to show up, which is what I spent a large portion of my youth doing.

> **"I am really proud to have been involved with the records I made with them... I think we made some fucking great records"**
>
> Glyn Johns, engineer

"I am really proud to have been involved with the records I made with them. Although when anybody asks me about working with them my memories are not tremendously pleasant – there was a lot of boredom involved – the fact is that when they played and got it together it was fantastic. They were unbeatable and I'm really glad that I was around. I don't regret a minute I spent with them. I think we made some fucking great records."

For many listeners, one of the greatest of those records remains *Between The Buttons*. It was the Stones' richest pop moment, but beneath the surface things were beginning to fray at the margins. Drugs had entered the scene, and soon had a devastating impact on the musical contribution of Brian Jones.

For the album cover session with photographer Gered Mankowitz, the band was somehow gathered at dawn. The resulting photograph was made with Vaseline smeared across the camera lens, and captures the Stones at their most bleary eyed and dishevelled. Only Keith looks utterly composed – probably because he had not bothered to sleep the night before. The picture's blurred edges suggest a fragmenting, psychedelic vibe. And at the center of the image is Jones, a spaced-out grin across his lips, his eyes swollen and unfocused, sinking obliviously into his coat. It was a telling image. Jones was still a key creative player within the Stones, but the golden-haired multi-instrumentalist was already beginning to lose touch with the world.

yesterday's papers

esterday's Papers' is the first song Mick Jagger ever wrote on his own for a Rolling Stones album, but its ambivalent tone and suggestion that girlfriends are as disposable as yesterday's newspaper was hardly a new theme from these masters of misogyny. The song was likely inspired by Jagger's just-ended relationship with live-in girlfriend Chrissie Shrimpton. She had survived a recent car crash with her famous boyfriend, but now could only watch in horror as young Mick made his first public appearance with a singer named Marianne Faithfull at the launch party for the International Times underground newspaper. For Jagger, women were easily replaced.

"Who wants yesterday's girl?" asks Jagger at the song's opening, singing with a typically cruel detachment. His very public life has been one of "constant change", he explains, and now a change is long overdue in his sex life. The song is a two-minute farewell to Miss Shrimpton, a "horrible public humiliation" for poor Chrissie, according to Faithfull. They were unofficially engaged when Jagger broke up with his once-fashionable girlfriend of three years in December 1966.

"We were very much in love but we argued all the time," Shrimpton bravely explained at the time. "As time goes on you begin to feel different about life and each other. There wasn't a row. We broke by mutual agreement." Soon enough, Shrimpton attempted suicide, with Jagger refusing to pay her hospital bill. Instead, he had all her belongings removed from his home.

The lyrics of 'Yesterday's Papers' may have been about Mick's indifference to heartbreak and abandonment, but the music behind him was completely upbeat and hypnotic. It was a festive blend of marimbas, harpsichord, unidentified wind instruments, the low, low rumble of bass, brief shards of guitar and overlapping vocals, straddling the right and left stereo channels. The final mix offered a more natural psychedelic excursion than much of the coming *Their Satanic Majesties Request*.

The richness of instrumentation on 'Yesterday's Papers' and elsewhere across *Between The Buttons* owed much to Brian Jones, who had created a new role for himself within the band by *Aftermath*. His ability to wrestle interesting new sounds from whatever exotic instruments were within his reach put an indelible stamp on the Stones' pop era. His later firing from the band shortly before his death in 1969 inevitably stripped the Stones back down to a straight-ahead rock and roll band. As glorious as the post-Jones era was, there was a certain charm and excitement about the Stones' mid-sixties pop records, which remain as deeply influential on later acts as anything else in the Jagger/Richards catalogue.

For singer-guitarist Lindsey Buckingham, whose version of Fleetwood Mac found international success in the mid-seventies, often by exploring his band's own troubled relationships, the Brian Jones-era Rolling Stones was deeply influential. His favourite Stones albums are those with a sense of "the European and the element of colour and the ability to try things that Brian Jones brought in. I think there must be some intangible element that he was bringing to the group, you know, that kept it from being too Chuck Berry. There's some brilliant things on *Between The Buttons*. That was a good run they had there."

> "I think there must be some intangible element that he was bringing to the group, you know, that kept it from being too Chuck Berry"
>
> Lindsey Buckingham, Fleetwood Mac, on Brian Jones

my obsession

HIS is what Mick was complaining about: the muddled wall of sound, Ian Stewart's piano banging hopelessly in the distance, leaving only the vocals with any clarity. Blame producer-manager Andrew Loog Oldham. "Andrew used to think that anything was possible if you put enough echo on it," Richards said later.

It's just not the kind of thing Jagger had in mind when he sketched out these nonsensical lyrics, with his scattered ideas about girls who need TEACHING, and built mostly around words that rhyme with "obsession". But the fans ate it up, taking *Between The Buttons* into the top three on both sides of the Atlantic. That's not quite as successful as other Stones records of the period, but reasonably popular just the same. Jagger would rather just forget about these tracks. "I don't think I thought they were very good at the time either," he said.

between the buttons

back street girl

'Back Street Girl' was an early sign of the Rolling Stones' interest in the country/folk-flavoured pop that would re-emerge with great effect on *Beggar's Banquet*. The song enjoys a delicate mixture of acoustic picking, light percussion and swells of accordion. It's a sound that suggests warmth and affection. And yet Jagger's vocals are typically casual and cruel, singing to some poor "back street girl", and instructing her to service him sexually at his pleasure. Just don't bother his wife or call him at home.

Is 'Back Street Girl' wry social commentary on the downtrodden classes, or condescending male fantasy gone crazy? Whatever you may think, it's an affecting package, and the only song on *Between The Buttons* that Jagger remembers with any fondness. "That's the only decent song," he said in 1975. That favourable reaction was shared by many longtime Stones followers, even if, in the US, 'Back Street Girl' did not appear on record until the *Flowers* compilation.

In a pop era dominated by the Beatles, the songcraft of the Rolling Stones was too often overlooked, argues Mick Fleetwood, the drummer with Fleetwood Mac. His own band had emerged from the same London blues scene that launched the Stones. Both the Beatles and Stones remain his favourite bands of all time. "The Stones really put some vibrant stuff together," says Fleetwood, also a veteran of John Mayall's Bluesbreakers. "They wrote great songs, and they still do. The image of the Stones sometimes denigrated their worth as creative people."

On the road with Mick, Brian and Keith, the pace intensifies.

between the buttons

connection

Keith Richards is a rocker, a committed denizen of the road, devoted to bringing rock and roll to stages across the continents, but even he sometimes longs for home. 'Connection' addresses that yearning, and describes a life spent in airports, making and missing connections. It's a life of endless inoculations from worried doctors, and of irritating searches of his bags by customs officials seeking contraband. Illicit drugs would not enter the Stones story for a few more months, when the band was busted at Redlands, Keith's country home. For now, it was a futile search. "They're dying to add me to their collection," sings a slightly frantic Jagger.

'Connection' is a hard, pop nugget, composed more or less by Richards alone. The guitarist fires off a series of rough, Chuck Berry chords, mingling with an effective minimalist piano melody. Richards' voice harmonizes roughly with Jagger's, and Charlie Watts slaps a fierce, steady beat. Even then, simplicity was Keith's calling card, at a time when Eric Clapton and other new blues heroes were taking rock guitar to new extremes. The Stones were equally versed in the blues, but their interpretations were somehow different.

"They were always about songs, and they weren't about long fucking guitar solos," says Mick Farren, a member of the Deviants in the mid-sixties and a writer for the *International Times*. "They were really pushing the envelope, beginning with 'Satisfaction'. What the Stones were doing retained a massive amount of R&B power."

A commitment to simplicity would remain a key element of the Stones' music for decades. "I don't think rock and roll songwriters should worry about art," Keith Richards said in 1986. "I don't think it comes into it. A lot of it is just craft anyway, especially after doing it for a long time. As far as I'm concerned, art is just short for Arthur."

> " They were always about songs, and they weren't about long fucking guitar solos. What the Stones were doing retained a massive amount of R&B power "
>
> Mick Farren, The Deviants

she smiled sweetly

Young Mick Jagger is actually in awe of a woman on 'She Smiled Sweetly'. Ignore, if you can, all of those earlier messages of misogynistic hate and despair, Jagger's endless battle of the sexes, and drift into his arms. Mick is capable of love after all. Maybe not romantic love, but at least a weakness for warm, maternal guidance, and a source of wisdom to soothe his battered soul.

His voice erupts from ripples of solemn organ melodies, piano and the thick basslines of Bill Wyman. Master troubadour Bob Dylan is a perceptible influence on both the lyrics and Jagger's soothing delivery. It's all comfort and happiness, an unexpectedly humane sentiment from Britain's most notorious rock and roll hoodlums.

Unusual, but not unprecedented. Heartfelt balladry has been a recurring motif in the Rolling Stones legacy, from 'As Tears Go By' to 'Angie' in the early 1970s. "I always loved that Mick could write something as sensitive as 'As Tears Goes By'," says Fleetwood Mac's Lindsey Buckingham. "It always blew my mind that he had that streak in him, underneath all that other stuff."

between the buttons

cool, calm and collected

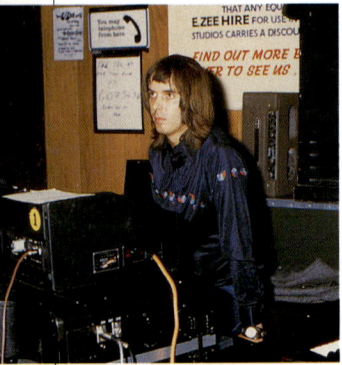

The innovative piano playing of Nicky Hopkins was first heard on *Between The Buttons*.

ccording to Andy Johns, "Nicky Hopkins was the best fucking rock and roll pianist who ever lived, apart from Jerry Lee Lewis." That's heavy praise, but Johns had ample opportunity to watch the man at work, first as visiting little brother to engineer Glyn Johns, and then while working himself as engineer on Stones albums stretching from *Sticky Fingers* to *It's Only Rock 'N' Roll*. Hopkins is a central figure on *Between The Buttons*, sending piano flourishes across tracks of various styles and moods.

Between The Buttons was the first collaboration between the Stones and Hopkins, then fresh from sessions with the Kinks. On 'Cool, Calm And Collected', Hopkins plays a vague approximation of ragtime as Mick Jagger adopts the tone of a Vaudevillian carnival barker, singing of a girl who is far too together, too competent, too independent, too wealthy, too respected, for his comfort. At the chorus, Brian Jones strums a sitar and Jagger's voice suddenly floats into the ether, as he adopts a mocking tone toward the supercool chick beyond his reach: "She knows all the right games to play."

The song is dark and comical, concluding with an accelerating thrash of drums, guitar, kazoo and harmonica. It's a lighthearted finish, much as the Stones would repeat later via 'On With The Show' at the close of 1967's *Their Satanic Majesties Request*.

all sold out

nger becomes the Stones. There's a convincing, raw quality to Mick Jagger's vocals on 'All Sold Out'. The song curdles in his throat, and is matched with some tense guitar work from Keith Richards, whose playing here is exceptionally reckless and dangerous. The guitars burst free from the sonic muddle of *Between The Buttons*. And Wyman and Watts thunder behind the Glimmer Twins, as Brian Jones blows on flute quietly within the blistering rock mix. Jagger is outraged at some unmentioned betrayal. The singer's been sold out by a girl, he sneers. Over love? Money? Fame? The intensity of the performance suggests the anger is real.

please go home

he shimmering beat behind Mick Jagger on 'Please Go Home' – which owes much to Bo Diddley – was just the starting point for the Rolling Stones on this strange psychedelic experiment. Charlie Watts smashes at the cymbals with extra fervour as Andrew Loog Oldham and the band overlay a dizzying array of echo effects and extra-sloppy guitars. Once again, the song appeared only on the UK version of *Between The Buttons*, and was not released in America until it appeared on the *Flowers* compilation released six months later. Bo Diddley would certainly have recognized his trademark rhythm, but very little else.

between the buttons

Not even the Beatles and Rolling Stones could escape the genre-shattering influence of Bob Dylan.

> **"He showed you that rock and roll didn't have to be quite so restricted by that verse-chorus-verse formula"**
>
> Keith Richards on Bob Dylan

who's been sleeping here?

Clapton wasn't God. Not while the likes of Jimi Hendrix still inhabited the earth. Guitar heroes were easy to come by in 1967. Less common was the kind of genre-shattering voice epitomized by Bob Dylan. Decades before he was entombed in legend, Saint Bob was merely the most dynamic songwriter of his generation, and a monumental influence on his contemporaries, from the Beatles and the Byrds to Hendrix and the Rolling Stones.

51

between the buttons

Dylan – born Robert Zimmerman – emerged from Duluth, Minnesota, as an edgy folk troubadour, drawing on the work of Woody Guthrie and the "Beat" writers, such as Kerouac, Ginsberg and Burroughs. After making a pilgrimage to Guthrie's deathbed, Dylan landed in Manhattan's Greenwich Village, where audiences discovered his explosive protest anthems and reflective folk, which often reached for a poetry utterly devoid of pretension. His songs were instead drenched in attitude, straight talk, mythic characters and ironic wordplay that was as devastating as it was amusing. By the time he "went electric" and embraced rock and roll in 1965, Dylan was the indisputable poet laureate of pop.

"Bob showed us all in the sixties a new approach, new ways of writing songs," Richards said in 1992. "He came from a folk tradition, which had much looser possibilities, and he showed you that rock and roll didn't have to be quite so restricted by that verse-chorus-verse formula."

Dylan was cocky, too. He once told Richards that he could have written '(Can't Get No) Satisfaction', but that the Stones could not have written his 'Desolation Row'. But Jagger later replied, "I'd like to hear Dylan SING 'Satisfaction'."

His influence can be heard loud and clear within the organic grooves of 'Who's Been Sleeping Here'. Jagger sings to a lover, demanding to know who's been sleeping in his bed, and eating off his plate, in his absence. The singer's imagery is plainly Dylanesque, and so is the music: the folky acoustic guitars and harmonica, the steady piano melody. Keith Richards briefly escapes the Dylan oeuvre with a flash of rock and roll riffing at the bridge.

The song is one of the highlights of *Between The Buttons*, and is free of the muddled overproduction that Jagger so dislikes. 'Who's Been Sleeping Here' also demonstrated that the Stones could draw honestly from contemporary sources without losing their own voice in the process.

complicated

'Complicated' begins like a surfing track, with Charlie Watts beating out a rolling rhythm before the song erupts into a charged Stones pop blend, with Brian Jones playing organ. The basic sound and rhythm is virtually identical to 'My Obsession'. Dark musical textures notwithstanding, the song's content is mostly light-hearted, with the complicated, educated, sophisticated, dedicated, soft and underrated female character most likely inspired by his new girlfriend Marianne Faithfull. "We talk together and discuss what is really best for us, 'cause she's so complicated." The complications were only beginning.

miss amanda jones

A raw electric guitar melody launches this hyped-up rock and roller. Keith Richards piles up the charged riff passages as Mick Jagger sings of Amanda Jones, a young girl from a good, wealthy family, who spends her nights at balls and discotheques, chasing good times at the risk of her own reputation. She's a party girl who maybe gets around a bit too much for her own good. "She's losing her nobility", Jagger warns. When she's not going down and down and down, young Amanda is "delightfully stoned", going up and up and up. By now in the Rolling Stones universe, young women like Amanda Jones were just another part of the scenery.

between the buttons

something happened
to me yesterday

Consider this the Stones' acid test. Their ultimate LSD freakout via *Their Satanic Majesties Request* was still 11 months away, but 'Something Happened To Me Yesterday' was an early expression of acid fascination. Jagger and Richards sing of "something" happening, without specifically calling it acid. It's enough just knowing just how trippy, drippy and groovy the whole experience was.

The Glimmer Twins duet happily together, having a good time while parodying popular TV personality PC George Dixon (of *Dixon Of Dock Green*). The poor British bobby doesn't seem to know whether the stuff is legal or not, or even if it's right or wrong. Adding to the comedy are soaring, vaudevillian sounds made by the horns of Brian Jones, weaving a quasi-Dixieland feel on his saxophone.

Only months later, the Rolling Stones would not be laughing quite so hard. Proper authorities had been watching these five London boys with increasing alarm. It was perhaps only a matter of time before the cops launched a crackdown on these obnoxious troublemakers, who were already making waves with drug-references in such songs as 'Mother's Little Helper' and '19th Nervous Breakdown'. Although this action seems all the more strange when none of these references actually PROMOTED drug use. If anything, those tracks were grim cautionary tales, but that hardly seemed to matter now. The Rolling Stones were deemed to be enemies of society, a threat to the state. The coming years would send Jagger, Richards and Jones through a gauntlet of courtrooms and jail cells – it was the price paid by youngsters who grow too successful outside the mainstream.

He may have smiled for the cameras but beneath the surface Brian Jones was beginning to fray at the edges.

chapter six

1967
their satanic majesties request

"Where's the joint?" Drug arrests only sent the Stones deeper into acid-fuelled experimentation.

Sing This All Together

Citadel

In Another Land (WYMAN)

2000 Man

Sing This All Together (See What Happens)

She's A Rainbow

The Lantern

Gomper

2000 Light Years From Home

On With The Show

"So how are our two jailbirds then?" Very funny, Charlie, but so true! Weird, scary times had now come to the Rolling Stones, sending poor Mick, Keith and even fragile Brian into the angry maelstrom of a British justice system fed up with these bad boys of rock. Perhaps it was inevitable. Just how long were the proper authorities supposed to watch this loathsome quintet parade around while Andrew Loog Oldham bragged about how dangerous they were? Why lock away your virgin daughters in fear when you could lock up the Stones?

These are hard lessons for the young rock star. Not everyone is amused at the idea of fabulously wealthy, young and promiscuous delinquents thumbing their noses at their elders. At least the Beatles were discrete about such matters. Certainly Lennon and McCartney lived lives just as appalling as Jagger and Richards. And yet they'd been congratulated by the Queen, no less. But the Stones' notorious bust for "urinating in public" back in 1965 should have been clue enough that Scotland Yard was watching. The band now represented everything that was wrong with a certain troublemaking generation. And they were being made to suffer for it.

So 1967 was the year of despair. Jagger and the boys can laugh about it now, but there was nothing at all funny about the moment on February 12 when police came knocking at Redlands, Keith's thatched palace in West Sussex. There was a party that day, and George Harrison had just left. Now cops were marching through the door in search of illicit substances. Their first discovery was Miss Marianne Faithfull, wearing nothing but a convenient fur rug. Jagger, Richards and art dealer Robert Fraser were detained and later charged with various drug crimes: Jagger for possessing four tablets of amphetamine – bought legally in Italy; Richards for allowing pot to be smoked in his home; and Fraser for possession of heroin. All were found guilty the following June.

Jagger was sentenced to three months in jail, while Richards got one year, and Fraser six months. Bad news, to be sure. Public outcry ensued, including an influential editorial in the London *Times* that questioned the severity of the sentences under the headline "Who Breaks A Butterfly On A Wheel?" But after just a few days in the lockup, the Glimmer Twins were released on bail pending an appeal of their cases – not being a rock star, Fraser still had to serve four months. Meanwhile, Brian Jones was arrested May 10 and charged with drug possession, with a trial date set for October 30. So Charlie's little wisecrack about jailbirds during the sessions for *Their Satanic Majesties Request* was no joke.

No wonder the embattled Rolling Stones were ready to escape into a lovely puddle of psychedelic mumbo-jumbo at Olympic Studios. It wasn't only escapism, but the fashion of the moment. The Beatles had just released *Sgt. Pepper's Lonely Hearts Club Band* to a stunned pop world. And Jagger didn't want to be left behind – he and Faithfull even travelled with the Beatles to North Wales to study Transcendental Meditation with the Maharishi Mahesh Yogi. The singer argued passionately with Jones and Richards that the band also needed to submerge into some drippy acid-fuelled pop. They went along with the plan, which resulted in the sonic muddle of *Their Satanic Majesties Request*, although the Stones never quite managed to escape the pressures of their lives outside the studio.

"It was made in between court sessions and lawyers with everyone sort of falling apart," Richards told *Rolling Stone* in 1971. "I ended up with chicken-pox. At the appeal, when I got up, I was covered in spots, man."

The record took almost a year to finish, as the band struggled to cope with the distractions of court dates and acid trips. Oldham was losing patience with the Stones' behaviour by then, and showed up only sporadically to "produce". What emerged were not just the usual lucrative pop tunes – although there were a few – but a collection of freakout jams. While a handful of tracks on *Their Satanic Majesties Request* are marked by a powerful grace, a good deal of the rest comes off like

> **" It was made in between court sessions and lawyers with everyone sort of falling apart "**
>
> Keith Richards on 'Their Satanic Majesties Request'

their satanic majesties request

'Revolution #9' out-takes, hopelessly adrift in the ether. It was an odd move for a band with its roots in the hard-edged blues of Muddy Waters. By following fashion so slavishly, the Stones recorded what is now easily their most dated album, closer in spirit to an old Seeds album than to the earth-shaking signature sound of 'Satisfaction'.

Richards admits now that the album was a shameless attempt at passing styles, a bow to the peer pressure of *Sgt. Pepper's Lonely Hearts Club Band* and too many hits of LSD. He told Kurt Loder in 1987 that he was never that interested in flower-power, though he did pay it a modicum of lip service at the time. "I am quite proud that I never did go and kiss the Maharishi's goddamn feet, you know."

The album title was not meant as a clue to the band's later interests in things satanic, but was only a play on words found in UK passports. During the making of *Their Satanic Majesties Request*, Jagger and Richards never actually slowed down long enough before the recording sessions to work out their tunes. This was their first album made away from the road and they were winging it.

"I used to defend it, but I suppose it's really indefensible," says George Chkiantz, who acted as the album's tape operator and assistant engineer. "I used to think we were the nightclub that was open after all the other nightclubs had closed. So heaps and heaps of fashionable London would appear at 3:30 or 4:00 in the morning. Which if you happen to be working at the place isn't actually what you want, thank you very much."

By the early summer, both Mick and Keith's drug charge sentences were overturned by an appeals court. Events overpowered Brian, however, and he was soon hospitalized from strain. In court during October, he admitted to possessing marijuana, but denied charges that he had cocaine and methedrine. He was found guilty, and sentenced to nine months in prison. He spent a single miserable night in a Wormwood Scrubs cell before being freed on bail, pending an appeal. The sentence was later set aside following a psychiatrist's report describing the fast-deteriorating Jones as an "extremely frightened young man" with suicidal tendencies.

> **"I am quite proud that I never did go and kiss the Maharishi's goddamn feet, you know"**
>
> Keith Richards on the psychedelic era

their satanic majesties request

The Stones had survived their most dangerous year, even if it was a far cry from Keith's deadly serious bust in Toronto in 1978, when the Mounties really did have the goods to put the guitarist away for decades. It was still enough to send poor Brian deeper into the paranoia that alienated him from the band.

Later during 1967, the Stones flew to New York City for the album's photo session. The final cover image is a silly rip-off of *Sgt. Pepper's Lonely Hearts Club Band*, with the Stones wrapped in rainbow silks, Mick wearing a sorcerer's dunce cap, and a model of Saturn hanging from the ceiling. The image originally

The Stones failed to surpass the psychedelic pop already mastered by the Beatles.

their satanic majesties request

Shiny happy people: The Stones greet the psychedelic 1960s.

appeared in a plastic 3-D panel glued to the album cover. Acid was clearly still the fuel of choice. "It was like being at school, you know, sticking on the coloured bits of paper and things," Jagger said in 1995 about making the cover. "It was really silly. But we enjoyed it. Also, we did it to piss Andrew off, because he was such a pain in the neck. Because he didn't understand it. The more we wanted to unload him, we decided to go on this path to alienate him."

That September 29, the Stones announced that Andrew Loog Oldham was no longer their manager or producer. He was immediately replaced as business manager by Allen Klein – a move that would have ramifications for the rest of the band's career. Producer Jimmy Miller would be recruited in time for *Beggars Banquet*, helping the Stones usher in the era of their most important work.

Not that everyone was so quick to dismiss *Their Satanic Majesties Request* – even Jagger says he still likes 'She's A Rainbow' and '2000 Light Years From Home'. It remains one of the Rolling Stones' most controversial records, for reasons not easy to explain. It stands virtually unconnected with any other Stones work, either before or after. And decades later, it remains both loved and despised.

"I thought it was a good album," says Marty Balin, singer with Jefferson Airplane. In the late-sixties, his band joined the Grateful Dead in presiding over the San Francisco psychedelic movement. Balin experienced the so-called "Summer Of Love" firsthand, drawing inspiration for an inventive blend of acid rock and tie-dyed folk.

"It was the psychedelic era, so that album was right on for me. It had that cool cover with the 3-D picture. They disowned it right away, but it's always been a favourite of many people. 'She's A Rainbow' was great, man. I still sing that to myself once in a while."

> " I thought it was a good album... they disowned it right away, but its always been a favourite of mine "
>
> Marty Balin, Jefferson Airplane

sing this all together

Take this as a warning. The first seconds from the Rolling Stones' psychedelic opus sound like nothing their followers could have expected in 1967. Atonal banging on the piano, blasts of high-strung brass, aimless picking on the acoustic guitar. Free jazz, at last. That is soon interrupted by the pure pop vocals of Mick Jagger, leading a chorus happily through a message of peace, love and brotherhood, but the precedent has been set. Beware of noodling.

Jagger sounds relatively innocent here, as if he really, truly believed the dawn of a new age was upon us – if only we could just get our hands on the right drugs. Not that his voice has gone to mush. Mick was inherently too cynical to ever embrace anything quite so blindly, no matter how much he wanted to believe in the hippy dream. An edge remains. He wouldn't be the first man facing prison to turn spiritual.

The track includes several layers of buzzing and clicking percussion parts, sounds which are best appreciated over a pair of headphones. Exotic and frantic, the vaguely Indian rattling is the product of Brian Jones, who also mastered the Mellotron, the harp, the saxophone, and whatever else happened to be lying around. He was the blues purist theoretically least inclined to psychedelia, except that the free-form music allowed him to experiment around the edges of songs, much as he had done on 'Paint It Black' and elsewhere. Jones was growing ever more estranged from the band he founded, but he still had a crucial role within the Stones.

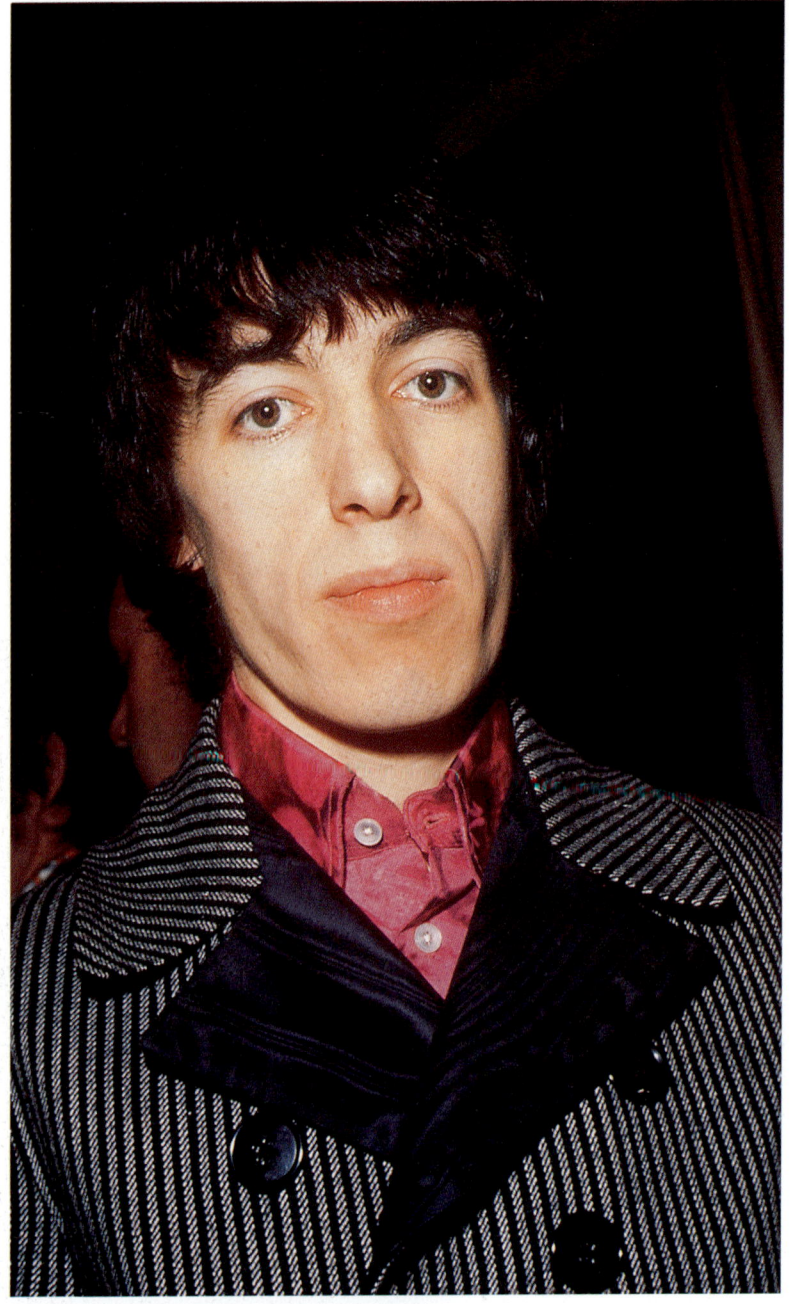

"The only time Brian looked like coming into his own"

Ian Stewart on 'Their Satanic Majesties Request'

The talent and ability were there, but he just screwed himself up."

While 'Sing This All Together' did not suffer from the same degree of self-indulgence as some of the other tracks, a new spaced-out vibe was obvious. The taunting, cynical tone of such earlier signature songs as the self-explanatory 'Under My Thumb' and 'Stupid Girl' was now gone.

Things were also less controlled. All that acid had clouded their judgement throughout the album, and the delicate process of weeding out the bad from the good failed them. "It's a fractured album," Richards told *Rolling Stone* in 1981. "There are some good bits, and it's weird, and there's some real crap on there as well."

"The only time Brian looked like coming into his own was when they did that awful *Their Satanic Majesties Request*," Ian Stewart told Bill Wyman for his 1990 *Stone Alone* autobiography.

"It was a terrible shame… He had the ability to actually sit down and fiddle with [any musical instrument], and got something out of it very easily.

citadel

Meaty electric guitar riffs are in short supply on *Their Satanic Majesties Request*. Where was Keef? Lost in the mix, and awash in a pool of acid and paisley. On 'Citadel', Richards asserts himself – and redeems the song – through a muscular burst of charged rhythm work. It's one of the album's few links to the Stones' rock and blues past.

The sound of 'Citadel' is otherwise charmingly dated, documenting the era's psychedelic vibe for hipster cultists and unrepentant Deadheads. Mick's unique edge is blunted and relaxed, as if trapped within the lethargic conventions of a limited genre. And as he serenades a mysterious "Candy and Cathy" with glancing social commentary – "Flags are flying dollar bills, from the heights of concrete hills" – he could just as easily be singing about incense and peppermints.

Critic Robert Palmer has suggested that 'Citadel' was one of a number of tracks on the album that inadvertently encouraged the unfortunate excesses of progressive rock. If so, bands such as Yes and the bombastic Emerson, Lake and Palmer overlooked one crucial point: not even the Stones took this seriously.

their satanic majesties request

in another land

The quietest Stone speaks. The Rolling Stones had already declared "it's the singer, not the song" to the world. Now Bill Wyman was about to test that philosophy with 'In Another Land', the bassist's only lead vocal and songwriting credit on a legitimate Rolling Stones album. Here was further indication of just how distracted Jagger and Richards had become by the outside world.

Wyman, Watts and pianist Nicky Hopkins arrived on schedule for a session at Olympic Studios on July 13, only to discover that the Glimmer Twins would not be attending. With costly studio time already blocked out, engineer Glyn Johns asked Wyman if he had a song to record. What Wyman had was something he had just written at his Thomas organ at home. The working title was, fittingly, 'Acid In The Grass'.

On the final version of 'In Another Land', Wyman sings of a romantic, dreamlike encounter of uncertain meaning. His flat delivery is drowned beneath a thick layer of tremolo and Hopkins' genteel harpsichord melodies. Consequently, Wyman doesn't try very hard to emote. The Small Faces were working next door, so singer Steve Marriott was invited to help out with the vocals.

"A lot of people were meandering around the studio," says Chkaintz. "A lot of groups – and the Faces were certainly one of them – were either doing a session in the other studio or had just finished or were thinking about starting."

At the next day's Stones session, Mick and Keith were played the tape of 'In Another Land'. The sweet waves of melody were clearly right for the album. They both agreed, and overdubbed some additional background vocals on to the recording. Mick's voice erupts during the chorus, adding a much-needed spark of energy to the pop ballad – "Then I awoke, was this some kind of joke?" The snoring that closes the track is Wyman's.

The Jagger/Richards songwriting monopoly was broken at last, even if it did not permanently alter a situation that Wyman often found creatively frustrating. He wasn't alone in that feeling. Although he'd started the band, Brian Jones, too, had been continually shut out. Jagger even went as far as to say of him: "I've never known a guy with less talent for songwriting." In later years, guitarist Mick Taylor – Jones' replacement – reportedly quit the Stones largely because he was not receiving the songwriting credit he felt was deserved.

Wyman eventually found his own outlet, embarking on the most prolific solo career of the original Stones. He recorded two solo albums in the 1970s – *Monkey Grip* and *Stone Alone* – enjoyed a major international hit single in 1981 with '(Si Si) Je Suis Un Rock Star', and, in 1985, released an album of early rock and roll credited to Willie and the Poor Boys – a band that included Wyman, Watts, Ringo Starr, Jimmy Page of Led Zeppelin and vocalist Paul Rodgers of Free and Bad Company. In spite of this, to most fans of the Stones the spacey 'In Another Land' remains Wyman's best-known recording.

"It came out because it seemed to work with the rest of the songs on the album," Wyman told *Guitar Player* magazine in 1978. "But you have to look on it as a complete coincidence. I mean, if everybody had turned up that night, that song never would have appeared on record. That's the way it is."

Bill Wyman (opposite) made his compositional debut when Jagger and Richards didn't make it to the studio.

> "It came out because it seemed to work with the rest of the songs on the album. But you have to look on it as a complete coincidence. I mean, if everybody had turned up that night, that song never would have appeared on record"
> Bill Wyman

their satanic majesties request

2000 man

ick Jagger is no prophet, but even at the age of 23 the singer was wise enough to understand that generational conflict was nothing new, and wouldn't end with the 1960s generation. In '2000 Man', Jagger looks to the future and predicts the same gaps – "My kids, they just don't understand me at all".

He could have been been referring to a destiny that both he and his own peers would have to face in coming decades. The song also questions what lasting legacy his era would leave. "Oh, daddy, is your brain still flashing like it did when you were young? Or did it come down crashing, seeing all the things you done?" These are serious considerations for a rock god who would by the 1990s be older than both the British Prime Minister and the President of the United States.

A crisp acoustic guitar pattern guides '2000 Man', blending into waves of organ, as the song repeatedly shifts gears and tempos. And why not? By the 1967 sessions, the Stones were a tight unit. They may have stopped touring in 1966, but with the likely exception of Brian Jones, drugs hadn't yet affected their chops.

Keith Richards can often now be heard talking with reverence of the mighty Charlie Watts, who he credits for much of the Stones' muscle. While the rhythm section of Watts and Wyman has come to enjoy a reputation of near-mythic proportions, their role was less clear back in the prickly, sensitive days of *Their Satanic Majesties Request*. Mick may have been reaching for a sixties utopia, but he and Richards were a bit high-strung from being in and out of courtrooms and jail cells.

Sitting cooly above the fray, Charlie Watts observes the madness of psychedelia and drug busts.

That was clear the day Watts made a rare suggestion in the studio. Andy Johns, who later worked with the Stones between 1969 and 1974, remembers visiting the sessions engineered by his brother Glyn, and seeing "Mick and Keith fall over laughing that Charlie had made a suggestion. Mick put the talkback button down, laughing, so everyone could hear him: 'Keith ha-ha-ha! Charlie just made a suggestion!' It was a little mean."

Over the years, Watts assumed a more important position. His opinion mattered, particularly on the choice of the bassists who would join the band after Wyman retired in 1993.

"They didn't really use to listen to what old Charlie had to say, and they would run him through the ringer on drum parts all the time," says Johns. "Some of those drum parts on the earlier records are really unusual."

Watts often seems to have viewed the Stones as if were just his job. As he once told the teenaged Johns, "You don't think I take this seriously, do you? It's just a fucking rock and roll band."

> "You don't think I take this seriously, do you? It's just a fucking rock and roll band"
> Charlie Watts

sing this all together (See what happens)

Here is where *Their Satanic Majesties Request* veers off into aimless noodling. Here the Stones try to push the musical envelope beyond where the Beatles and the Beach Boys last left it. But in the context of the Stones' oevre, of the band's strengths and lasting importance, this eight-minute free-for-all is practically an embarrassment. A bad trip.

Improvisation was never the Stones' mission. And yet on this reprise of the album's opening track, Keith and the others jam to no discernible conclusion. The "song" opens with giggling and chatter from the left speaker, and the comment, "Where's that joint?" Where indeed? What follows is a gurgling of brass, bells and whistles, during which Mick works hard at his chanting, moaning and heavy breathing. In a moment, Jagger's vocals suddenly find clarity through the song's central melody.

'Sing This All Together (See What Happens)' is not without some charm. It at least represents a period where they were not locked into the hard-rock mould that would carry them from the 1970s through the 1990s. But there's no plan, and the song is ultimately unsatisfying.

The overall failure of *Their Satanic Majesties Request* should not suggest that the Stones had lost touch with their central talents. George Chkaintz remembers being directed by engineer Glyn Johns to fetch a new reel of tape from the Olympic Studios store. He took a shortcut through Studio B. "That was a time when there were just oodles of people – hangers on, Beatles, various and so on," Chkaintz says now. "I hurried through this room, which was full of people, and Keith is playing a little white Hammond organ, which belonged to one of the advertising geezers who used the studio. And he was just tapping it rhythmically, not really playing any kind of tune; it was all to do with rhythm. I must have got about two-thirds of the way down the room, and I got frozen. It was fascinating, I just got caught by this thing."

When Glyn impatiently came looking for his tape operator, he too was hypnotized by Keith's organ recital. "The quality of his rhythm I've always found exceptional anyway," Chkaintz says. "But this wasn't from his instrument or anything. It was just mesmerizing. It's important to realize that you were dealing with people of that calibre, who just could do it in a way that very few others can."

their satanic majesties request

she's a rainbow

The world's greatest pop band? No one ever made that claim for the Rolling Stones. Pop was for nice people, not those shaggy anti-Beatles from London. But by the mid-sixties, pop had become the Stones' language of choice. Even if they had rockers ('Satisfaction') and R&B covers ('Time Is On My Side') at their disposal, the Stones mastered the frazzled pop melody long before the drug-addled menace of *Exile On Main Street* took hold. This was the era between the Rolling Stones' days as blues purists and their later years as the masters of hard rock and roll.

'She's A Rainbow' was the final pure pop moment for the Stones. It was the last time Mick Jagger would ever sound child-like, singing fairy tale lyrics utterly devoid of his usual sex-baiting cynicism. The irony here is that the album's most accessible pop track rises from the depths of a brief, but grating introduction of pre-industrial electronic moaning, scraping and found dialogue. Then out pops a blissful piano melody and a regal blast of horns fit enough for Buckingham Palace.

"Have you seen her dressed in blue?" sings Jagger with almost heartbreaking innocence. If the rest of the album had been of this calibre, even the Beatles would have been worried. No acid necessary. The soft, euphoric textures owe a good deal to the presence of strings, arranged by John Paul Jones, destined two years later to play bass with Led Zeppelin. Jones was a regular presence at Olympic. He found work in a variety of genres, much as his future bandmate, guitar deity Jimmy Page, paid his rent with session work for the Kinks, Marianne Faithfull and others.

"John Paul Jones did quite a lot of session work," says George Chkiantz, who also engineered for Led Zeppelin. "Olympic was a sound stage for quite a lot of films, not to mention all the jingle work we did as well. We met John Paul Jones in that capacity quite often."

John Paul Jones (opposite) was a busy session player before finding fame with Led Zeppelin.

the lantern

An experiment in stereophonic sound, 'The Lantern' offers the album's strangest, most barren, and jumbled mixture of elements. The creamy background vocals and Keith's rocking riffing erupt from nowhere, and then disappear again just as quickly. A horn section drones loudly, and Mick sings with some restraint, performing enigmatic lyrics in a dreamy mood. It's a story fit for Edgar Allen Poe – "My face, it turns a deathly pale, you're talking to me through your veil".

Nonetheless, the track contains a link to the rock and country sounds at the Stones' deepest roots, most notable within the sudden, ecstatic flashes of guitar. Even amidst the swirling chaos, 'The Lantern' rocks, but only in frustrating spurts.

In many ways, 'The Lantern' is like much of *Their Satanic Majesties Request*, offering many fine moments, mixed in with a collection of ill-conceived or unfinished ideas.

"It had interesting things on it, but I don't think any of the songs are very good." This was Jagger's final verdict delivered to *Rolling Stone* magazine in 1995. "It's a bit like *Between The Buttons*. It's a sound experience, really, rather than a song experience."

> **"It had interesting things on it, but I don't think any of the songs are very good... It's a sound experience, really, rather than a song experience"**
>
> Mick Jagger on 'Their Satanic Majesties Request'

gomper

Watch now as the Stones try very hard to become George Harrison. Their own *Sgt. Pepper's Lonely Hearts Club Band* would be incomplete without it. 'Gomper' is largely a throwaway, hardly a "song" at all, though it's buoyed with a dazzling array of exotic percussion by Brian Jones. The track begins and ends within an Indian-influenced rhythmic pattern, making sudden shifts into pop, rather like Harrison's 'Within You Without You'.

'Gomper' is one of the album's most deeply psychedelic excursions, but the ultimate result is disjointed and derivative. The Stones had already discovered the dynamic instrumentation of North Africa for themselves, but Jagger even sings a bit like Beatle George on 'Gomper', painting an idyllic picture of a woman communing with nature. Most satisfying, Jones' percussion work suggests that he might have re-emerged as a force within the Stones if only he'd been healthy and clear-headed enough.

2000 light years from home

Before the Rolling Stones resurrected this dark, swirling pop number for their 1989 *Steel Wheels* tour, it was just another forgotten track from an album few cared to remember. Hardcore Stones fans always understood its charms. However, the Stones' larger-than-life performance on a multi-million-dollar stage gave new life to a song that is now widely seen as one of the highlights of the psychedelic era.

The track unfolds into a wave of drifting, spacey instrumentation, creeping slowly into the twilight zone. A rumbling beat from Charlie Watts mingles with a guitar riff resembling one of Ennio Morricone's spaghetti western themes. And Jagger sings of interplanetary isolation, perhaps inspired by his few days in jail. Helping bring the tune to life is Brian Jones, making sense of those dreamy Mellotron sounds.

'2000 Light Years From Home' was a brief tangent for the Stones. It was a sound they would never again attempt.

"That was one of the great space songs," says Marty Balin of Jefferson Airplane. "We were into that kind of stuff, too. When I first heard that I loved it. The sounds on there were real unique. I think a good song can be done in any field by anybody. Anybody could do '2000 Light Years From Home'. It wouldn't sound like the Stones, but it would translate for anyone, because you could identify with what he was talking about, and with the funky keys."

Like the rest of *Their Satanic Majesties Request*, the science-fiction epic was recorded on to the Olympic four-track machine, no more complicated than any other Stones track. Repeat echo effects, and thuds and thumps from an orchestral bass drum that was laying around the studio were slowed down and later added to the basic track.

"When it came to the overdubs all hell was let loose. We just tried anything and everything," says Chkiantz. "It was all basically conventional recording. We tried to do funny things with vocals and make funny sounds with various bits and bobs, and most of them got left off in the end."

> "That was one of the great space songs. We were into that kind of stuff, too. The sounds on there were real unique"
>
> Marty Balin, Jefferson Airplane, on '2000 Light Years From Home'

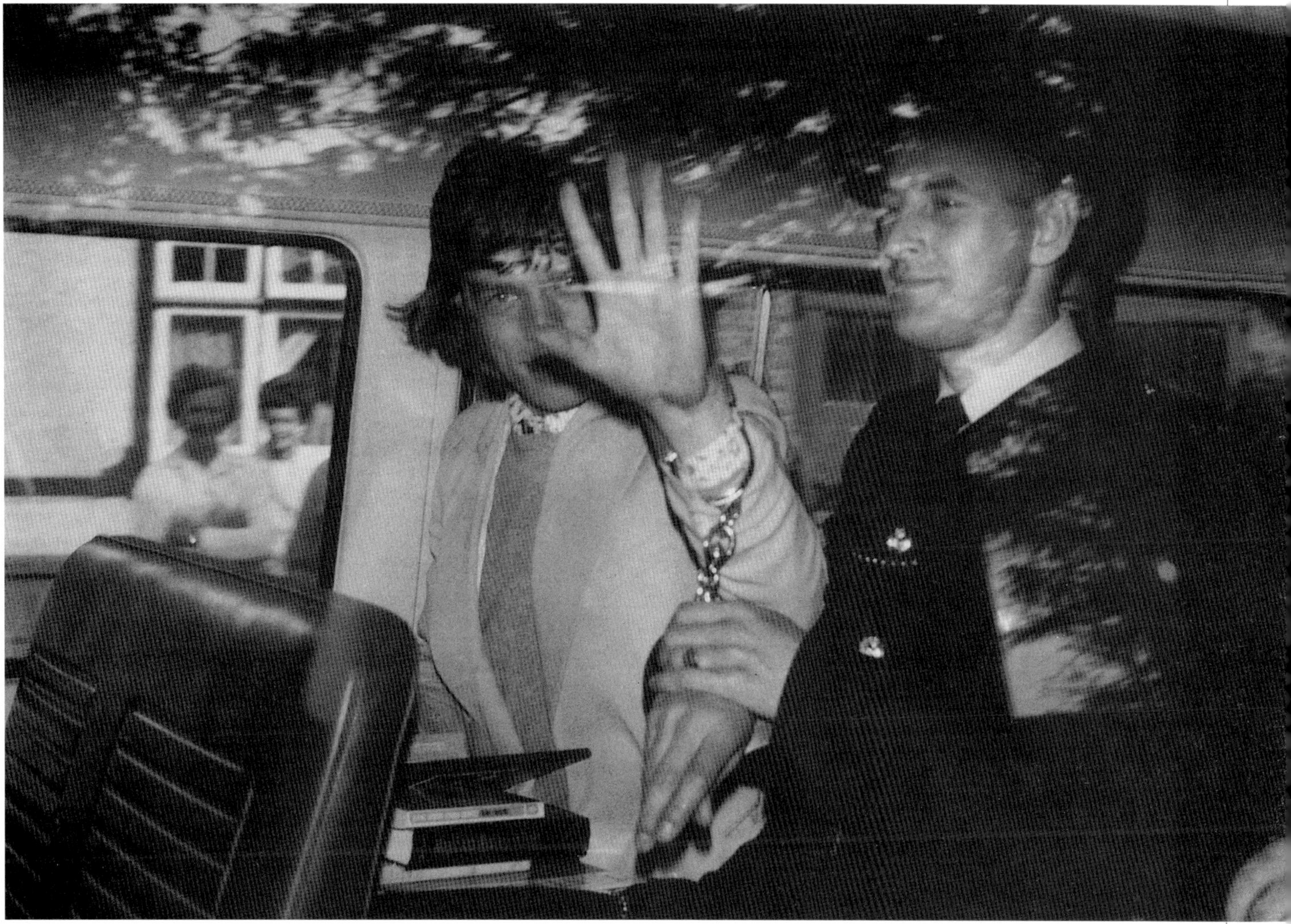

their satanic majesties request

on with the show

n With The Show' is the album's most playful track. It opens with the sidewalk pitch of a gentleman barker working to draw customers in to see his naked girlie show. Keith Richards snaps out a sharp little guitar lick, and Jagger announces that "Bettina starts her show at two o'clock."

What follows are Jagger's lyrics of light burlesque humour, made frenetic through layers of percussion and other bits and pieces added by Brian Jones, before an inevitable finale and some heated cocktail party chatter.

The song is rather light-hearted for a band that would be singing songs about Lucifer and fighting in the streets in just a matter of months. The coming transformation would spark the band's most important work. In 1967, however, escapism was surely inevitable, even if the promised prison sentences that awaited Mick, Keith and Brian never materialized. If not for those knawing distractions of the law, the Stones just might have pulled off a more consistent psychedelic exploration. Even so, *Their Satanic Majesties Request* climbed the charts to No. 3 in the UK, and No. 2 in the US. It remains the strangest chapter in the Stones' recording history.

"It was a very self-indulgent mess in many ways," Chkiantz says. "But it's very difficult for me to hear *Their Satanic Majesties Request* without getting the smells and colours of the room back. I quite like it, but that doesn't mean it's good."

Jailhouse rock: Mick Jagger is shuttled between court dates.

chapter seven

1968 beggars banquet

French avant-garde film maker Jean-Luc Godard (centre) documented the recording of 'Sympathy For The Devil'.

Sympathy For The Devil
No Expectations
Dear Doctor
Parachute Woman
Jig-Saw Puzzle

Street Fighting Man
Prodigal Son (WILKINS)
Stray Cat Blues
Factory Girl
Salt Of The Earth

he Rolling Stones found their moment of absolute clarity in 1968, after a long season of drug busts, bad press, and that swirl of forced experimentation called *Their Satanic Majesties Request*. Confusion was replaced by a new sense of purpose, where passing psychedelic fashion was cast aside in favour of the blues and rock roots that had first inspired them. Here was a band back in control of its destiny.

Beggars Banquet emerged from a brief period of relative calm. Not that there weren't the usual moments of high misadventure. The early morning album sessions at Olympic Studios were interrupted on June 11 when fire engines were called out to extinguish a blaze ignited by a faulty arc lamp hung from the ceiling. It had been put there by one of the film crew working on Jean-Luc Godard's *One Plus One,* a film that inadvertently documented the recording of 'Sympathy For The Devil'. By the time the fire crews left, much of the band's equipment was soaked, but the Stones were back at work the next morning. "It was bloody frightening," Charlie Watts commented at the time.

While the band's legal problems were not yet completely behind them, there was no longer the feeling of impending doom that had clouded the previous year. Mick Jagger was actually enjoying a relatively quiet life with Marianne Faithfull in a rented house in London's Chester Square, spending his days reading poetry and philosophy. "It was a wonderful time," Faithfull says now of that era. "The biggest thing in the air was love."

Faithfull was involved in the theatre, and had just finished work on the X-rated art film *Girl On A Motorcycle*. Both were mingling happily with a young crowd of stage directors, film-makers and gallery owner Robert Fraser's hipster art crowd. "I wasn't taking so many drugs that it was messing up my creative processes," Jagger told *Rolling Stone* in 1995. "It was a very good period, 1968 – there was a good feeling in the air. It was a very creative period for everyone."

The result was not just a haunting new rock sound *a la* 'Sympathy For The Devil', but a rustic country flavour already being explored on Bob Dylan's *John Wesley Harding* and the Byrds' *Sweetheart Of The Rodeo*. Richards' renewed interest in acoustic country and western put the Stones squarely within that movement, with compelling results. The band had rarely before approached the scratchy authenticity now on display in their rendition of the Reverend Robert Wilkins' 'Prodigal Son', sung by Jagger on *Beggars Banquet* in a nervous, twangy warble. The Stones were finally tapping into the soul of their beloved blues in a way their early cover versions had never quite managed. Likewise, Jagger sounded more nasty, amused and dangerous than ever in the torrid opening seconds of 'Stray Cat Blues'.

Beggars Banquet also marked the final meaningful contribution from the rapidly fading Brian Jones, who emerged from his wounded stupor long enough to provide elegant slide guitar work on 'No Expectations' and elsewhere. Jones' relationship with actress Anita Pallenberg had ended in Morocco, where she had taken up with Keith Richards. But his slide playing could still generate the same shivers of emotion Mick and Keith first encountered when Elmo Lewis – as Jones had once liked to be known – played his earliest licks at the Ealing and Marquee clubs. "Brian was absolutely brilliant when he was on form, remembers George Chkiantz, who worked as assistant engineer on *Beggars Banquet*. "The trouble is that when he wasn't on form, it was not to be borne easily."

Producer Jimmy Miller was brought into the Stones fold early in the sessions, beginning a collaboration that would last until 1973. During those years, Miller and the Stones would record some of the most powerful albums in the history of the genre – *Beggars Banquet, Let It Bleed, Sticky Fingers* and *Exile On Main Street.* Jagger recruited Miller after hearing his work with Traffic. The American-born producer arrived just as the Stones

> "It was a very good period, 1968 – there was a good feeling in the air. It was a very creative period for everyone"
> Mick Jagger

beggars banquet

Street fighting man: Beggar's Banquet was fuelled by a period of protest throughout Europe and America.

were finding a new hardened flair in their sound, as demonstrated in their very first project together, the single 'Jumpin' Jack Flash' – introduced to television viewers via an alarming film clip of the band vamping in war paint, with both Jones and Richards wearing bug-eyed shades.

"You get someone like Jimmy, who can turn the whole band on, make a nondescript number into something, which is what happened on *Beggars Banquet*," Richards told *Crawdaddy* magazine in 1975. "We were just coming out of *Satanic Majesties*... Mick was making movies, everything was on the point of dispersal. I had nicked Brian's old lady. It was a mess. And Jimmy pulled *Beggars Banquet* out of all that."

If the Stones' provocative new interest in all things Satanic was ultimately a put-on, it suited the dark times that were coming. Swinging London, flower power, the Beach Boys' 'Good Vibrations' were beginning to fade in a new season of political assassinations, calls for revolution and the deepening morass of the Vietnam War. 'All You Need Is Love' no longer seemed appropriate. Any rock act hoping to be taken seriously by the increasingly troubled youth culture marching in the streets was required to deal in some way with the new socio-political rumblings of the era. The Beatles responded with 'Helter Skelter' and 'Revolution'. The Stones, already feared by parents and the proper authorities as the bad boys of British rock, could do no less.

Jagger was well-suited to the role of provocateur, inspired by many of the same works of literature and old blues recordings that lit a fire beneath the Doors in Los Angeles. While Jagger's new persona was the demonic gentleman, Jim Morrison sang of explosive journeys into hedonism and rebellion, following a troubled psyche to apocalyptic confrontations with the ruling generation. According to Ray Manzarek, organist with the Doors, the desire to explore man's darker impulses – an approach they shared with the Stones – came from "knowing that the other side of life is death, and you better dance madly".

As ever, Manzarek says, the experience of black America provided an alarming resource. "The idea that you are going to die infuses your life with a depth and a meaning, which is why the blues were so powerful. As a black man in America – not so much in the fifties but in the earlier years – you could be hung at any moment. They would hang you, or they would harass you, they would cut you, they would shoot you down. So walking the streets of white America as a black man was always a matter of life and death."

Jagger was happy to be the bearer of bad news, but he was no activist or working-class hero. He would never hold a press conference with Yippie leader Jerry Rubin or any other political gadfly. Better to let Lennon play that game. After Jagger's drug conviction was overturned following an appeal, the singer was interviewed live on UK television as a reluctant spokesman for his generation. The habits that had brought him so much trouble, he declared, were simply "a matter of one's own private life", not a revolutionary act.

A more pressing issue was the launch of *Beggars Banquet,* unexpectedly stalled when both Decca in England and London Records in the US refused to release it with the intended cover art. As originally designed, the cover was a photograph of a bathroom wall and toilet covered in graffiti. For nearly four months, the Stones refused to discuss changing the design, before finally agreeing to release the album with a simple white cover – in spite of an unfortunate resemblance to the Beatles' *"White Album"*. The original *Beggars Banquet* cover would not see the light of day until the 1980s.

During the delay, Jagger began work on the film *Performance,* starring alongside Anita Pallenberg in a psychodrama directed by Donald Cammell and Nicolas Roeg. He returned in time to celebrate the album's release with a Stones food-fight during a press conference at London's Kensington Gore Hotel.

The band, however, was not prepared to tour in 1968. The very idea of rehashing the old hits was now a profoundly uninteresting idea to Jagger. "People say that audiences are listening now, but to what? Like the Rolling Stones on stage isn't the Boston Pops Symphony Orchestra. It's a load of noise," Jagger said in 1968. "On record it can be quite musical, but when you get to the stage it's no virtuoso performance. It's a rock and roll act, a very good one, and nothing more."

> "It's a rock and roll act, a very good one, and nothing more"
>
> Mick Jagger

sympathy for the devil

Enter Lucifer. Not as a way of life, nor even as a partner in crime, but as a telling metaphor for the dark side of the human soul. Here was the ultimate outlaw anthem, an expression of the danger and dread that Andrew Loog Oldham had long promoted as the band's mission. Maybe Robert Johnson sold his soul to the Devil in return for his supernatural chops, but Mick Jagger's exploration of the satanic was for his own ends, not for anyone else.

Jagger was inspired to write 'Sympathy For The Devil' after Faithfull gave him a copy of Mikhail Bulgakov's *The Master And Margarita*. The book features the Devil as its debonair central character, the host of a fabulous ball in Moscow, and a master of high society. Jagger's reaction was a challenge to mainstream values, depicting Satan in the song not as a beast, but as a sophisticated "man of wealth and taste", a role the singer embraced.

His phrasing is vaguely Dylanesque, but more agitated, even confrontational across the song's relentless samba beat. The lyrics travel through dark moments from history – the Crucifixion, the Russian revolution, World War II – before putting a new spin on recent events. It was a notable accomplishment, even within an epic six-minute pop song. Jagger's suggestion that "it was you and me" who killed the Kennedys is a provocative and memorable line, even if its implications are less than clear. More disturbing is an unsettling use of role-reversal, disrupting the accepted rules of society. "Every cop is a criminal," he warns, "and all the sinners saints".

The persona Jagger created with 'Sympathy For The Devil' was so effective that it would haunt the band for years, causing some fans to abandon them in fear. Suspicions on Jagger's true motives only intensified after the blood-soaked disaster of 1969's free concert at Altamont Speedway. But Faithfull

beggars banquet

called the song "pure papier-mache Satanism" in her 1994 autobiography. And Jagger says he never intended the song as an endorsement of black magic, nor as an inspiration to the laughable brand of satanic metal that emerged in the seventies and eighties. "The satanic imagery stuff was very overplayed," Jagger said in 1995. "We didn't want to really go down that road. And I felt that song was enough. You didn't want to make a career out of it."

> **"The satanic imagery stuff was very overplayed. We didn't want to really go down that road... I felt that song was enough. You didn't want to make a career out of it"**
>
> Mick Jagger on 'Sympathy For The Devil'

But for Keith, at least, this dance with the devil seemed less a metaphor than a new hobby. Both he and Anita dabbled in the black arts, and seemed to actively encourage others to do the same. "It's something everybody ought to explore. There are possibilities there," Richards told *Rolling Stone* magazine in 1971. "Why do people practice voodoo? All these things bunged under the name of superstition and old wives' tales. I'm no expert in it... I just try to bring it into the open a little. When we were just innocent kids out for a good time, they were saying 'They're evil, they're evil.' Oh, I'm evil, really? So that makes you start thinking about evil."

The metamorphosis of 'Sympathy For The Devil' from a simple folk ballad into its final state as a hypnotic rocker is well documented, thanks to the fortuitous presence of Jean-Luc Godard's *One Plus One* cameras at Olympic. "Godard happened to catch us on two very good nights," Jagger said in 1968. "He might have come every night for two weeks and just seen us looking at each other with blank faces."

In the film – which mingles the tedious in-studio shots of the Stones with absurd scenes of black poet revolutionaries loudly worshipping white women – the song slowly takes shape as Jagger, Richards and Jones slowly strum acoustic guitars. Richards is later seen playing bass, as Wyman performs percussion alongside Watts and Rocky Dijon. The finished track also includes rare straight-ahead lead guitar playing by Richards, who patches together a progression of stinging notes that is occasionally awkward, but always exciting.

"'Sympathy For The Devil' was a nightmare from start to end," George Chkiantz says with a laugh. "It went on for several days. There was all the film crew

mucking around in it. The song changed out of all recognition, from one end to the other. You could see a development and it was quite interesting, and it was very tiring."

The lengthy sessions were nothing unusual for the Stones, who would often enter the studio unrehearsed, with only the barest sketch of a song prepared. "There were loads of people that said this method was super expensive for no good purpose. But I don't think that's actually true. Jagger really felt that unless you had gone through it until nobody could stand it anymore you didn't purify the material. The record companies don't like that, when they're paying the bills. The curious thing is that I can scarcely remember anything of the earlier takes, which makes me feel they got the best track."

The Glimmer Twins, hard at work on the devil's music.

beggars banquet

no expectations

Witness the vagabond blues, as true for the Willy Lomans of the road as for the anonymous bands of young men making music in one town after another. 'No Expectations' is a tender acceptance of that life on the road, where love is a fleeting experience at best, and commitment an impossibility. The sound is elegant and raw, just the quiet strumming of acoustic guitars, while Brian Jones creates a moving passage of bottleneck guitar right out of the Mississippi Delta. "Our love is like our music," Jagger sings regretfully, as if forever en route to some airport, train station or highway. "It's here and then it's gone."

'No Expectations' was recorded at Olympic Studios with the band gathered in a circle, singing and playing into open microphones. The track also marked one of Jones' last flashes of brilliance on a Stones recording. By now, drugs, paranoia and fading health were pulling him away from the muse that had once inspired him to launch the Rollin' Stones. But 'No Expectations' showed that Jones was still capable of deeply moving instrumental flourishes. "That was the last time I remember Brian really being totally involved in something that was really worth doing," Jagger told *Rolling Stone* magazine in 1995. "He had just lost interest in everything."

Not everything. Jones would periodically emerge from his cloud to demonstrate a continued interest in creating music, and in exploring new ideas. While the Stones impatiently awaited the release of *Beggars Banquet* in 1968, Jones travelled to Morocco that July to record the Master Musicians of JouJouka, whose soulful trance rhythms had captured his excited imagination. Jones was introduced to this family of players in the hills south of Tangier by expatriate writer Brion Gysin. Engineer George Chkiantz was soon summoned from Olympic for the recording.

"My plane arrived at 9 o'clock in the morning," Chkiantz recalls now. "The Stones office asked me to phone him up – 'Brian says he'll meet you. If he does, give us a ring because nobody will believe that he's going to be anywhere at 9 o'clock in the morning.' But he was. He was there."

Most surprising was Jones' demeanour during this period. "He was the most extraordinarily together person there, in JouJouka, up in the hills. Not when he got back to Tangiers. Different story," says Chkiantz. "In JouJouka he was extraordinary."

Jones was travelling with his new girlfriend Suki Potier, and quickly slid back into his addictions once he returned from the hills. At one point he collapsed on the balcony of his Tangier hotel room. But Jones never lost his obsession with the JouJouka project. After three days of work, Chkiantz happily stumbled back into his room at the Es Saadi Hotel and collapsed, only to be summoned again by Jones. "I remember being woke up by Brian saying he couldn't get the tape recorder to work," Chkiantz says. "So half in my sleep I sort of stormed out, waggled some connection, pressed a play button and said 'There, see,' and went back to bed. To my great embarrassment I remember having no clothes on at all. I have no idea who was in the room. I remember apologizing to Suki afterwards."

The final result of Jones' last great enthusiasm wouldn't emerge until 1971, when *Brian Jones Presents The Pipes Of Pan* was finally released on Rolling Stones Records. It wasn't exactly music for the pop masses, but Jones' foray into the hills of Morocco would have ramifications as late as 1989. That's when Jagger and Richards returned to the village of JouJouka during work on *Steel Wheels* to weave some of those hypnotic rhythms into the Rolling Stones' sound via 'Continental Drift'.

> "That was the last time I remember Brian really being totally involved in something that was really worth doing. He had just lost interest in everything"
>
> Mick Jagger on 'No Expectations'

A friendship was shattered when Anita Pallenberg left Brian Jones for Keith Richards.

beggars banquet

dear doctor

Country music was nothing new to the Rolling Stones. Back in 1964, the band recorded a hyped-up rendition of Hank Snow's 'I'm Moving On'. But the *Beggars Banquet* sessions suggested a deepening interest in the universal torch and twang of the redneck waltz, which already shared a surface accent with the Stones' beloved deep blues. With 'Dear Doctor', these London rockers sounded about ready for the Southern honky tonk circuit, appropriating yet another American pop style.

"Keith has always been country," Jagger told *Rolling Stone* magazine in 1968. His earliest memory of Richards is that of a toddler dressed like Roy Rogers. "That's what his scene was. We still think of country songs as a bit of a joke, I'm afraid. We don't really know anything about country music really. We're just playing games. We aren't really into it enough to know."

On 'Dear Doctor', Jagger sings as a confused young man overcome with doubt on his wedding day. "Oh the gal I'm to marry is a bowlegged sow," Jagger moans. "I've been soaking up drink like a sponge." His voice is embraced by a warm blend of acoustic guitars and harmonica as Jagger's groom is relieved to discover he's been jilted by his bride.

This isn't country music, not yet. Look forward a few years to the terrible torture and twang of *Exile On Main Street*. What we have in *Beggars Banquet* is straight-ahead rock, played by the absolute masters of the form with an occasional folk spin or southern warble. And if this comical vignette is less than a respectful tribute to the world of Hank Williams and Merle Haggard, then 'Dear Doctor' at least showed the Stones could get the sound right. For that, they owe a debt to the influence to two other albums released in 1968: Bob Dylan's *John Wesley Harding* and the Byrds' *Sweetheart Of The Rodeo*. Both were country-flavoured milestones, and Jagger acknowledges their impact on *Beggars Banquet*.

Following his 1966 motorcycle accident, Dylan embarked on an introspective trek into country-flavoured rock and folk music. The Byrds, meanwhile, had recruited new keyboardist Gram Parsons, who immediately began lobbying bandleader Roger McGuinn to record a full country album. The Byrds had already dabbled in bluegrass and country by then, so McGuinn agreed. "It was just a coincidence," remembers McGuinn. "We really had no contact with Bob Dylan at that point. It was after his motorcycle wreck and he was up in Woodstock recuperating, and evidently writing country songs. We didn't know it until we asked for some material from Bob, as we did periodically to see what

The country-rock of the Byrds strongly influenced the sound of *Beggar's Banquet*.

he was up to. We got 'You Ain't Going Nowhere,' and it was obviously a country song. It's really one of those nebulous, almost mystical things. It was something that affected a lot of people independently in different parts of the globe at the same time. Maybe it was time to get laid back because things had been so intense with the psychedelic era."

On *Sweetheart Of The Rodeo,* there was none of the Stones' playful disrespect for the country genre or its audience. It had been a faithful attempt at the heartfelt sounds Parsons knew from his George Jones and Porter Wagner records. The Byrds even travelled to that Taj Mahal of country music – the Grand Ole Opry in Nashville, where this band of West Coast hippies was greeted by tepid applause. Soon, Parsons was urging McGuinn to hire a steel-guitar player and permanently transform the Byrds into a full-time country act. McGuinn wasn't interested, so Parsons and bassist Chris Hillman left to form the Flying Burrito Brothers.

Three decades later, *Sweetheart...* remains deeply influential, helping inspire a new generation of country rock bands, epitomized by Wilco and Son Volt. And the reputation of Parsons, who became a close friend to Keith Richards before his death in 1973, has since grown to legendary proportions. "He was a colourful character," McGuinn says. "We had a lot of fun together. We used play pool, ride motorcycles and drink beer together. I just know him as a picker. I don't see him as James Dean."

When McGuinn heard the new country flavours of *Beggars Banquet,* it somehow made sense. "I knew Gram was hanging out with Mick and Keith in London," McGuinn says, "so it didn't surprise me too much."

> "Maybe it was time to get laid back because things had been so intense with the psychedelic era"
> Roger McGuinn, the Byrds

parachute woman

Old blues metaphors are drafted into this seething expression of young lust from a heavy breathing Mick Jagger. He delivers his message with lascivious glee, rolling his tongue around lyrics of coarse sexual innuendo that would have a hard time getting past would-be censors if released today – "My heavy throbber's itchin' just to lay a solo rhythm down."

Jagger is joined by a roaring harp finale and one of Jones' harshest passages of slide guitar. Beneath it all is a low rumble the Stones created by recording a rhythm track on a simple mono cassette recorder, much to the astonishment of the recording engineers at Olympic. "They fell in love with the sound of this thing," says Chkiantz. "If you got the distortion just about right it had a curious kind of warble, which was a remarkably gutsy sound."

The band would gather around the cassette recorder, armed with instruments suited to the machine: Bill Wyman on a fretless acoustic bass guitar; Charlie Watts pounding a street drummer's kit; Jagger on percussion; Richards on acoustic guitar; Jones on various instruments, including sitar. Once completed, the cassette track would be added to the studio four-track machine, to be overdubbed by another electric track.

"That was really fascinating. It worked incredibly well," says Chkiantz. "The Stones, never known for efficient and quick work, were actually in serious threat of getting more than a track done in a night, rather than one track in seven days."

Elsewhere on the album, 'Street Fighting Man' owes Jones' sitar-playing to the same lo-fi process. "It twangs away," Richards said in 1971. " He's holding notes that wouldn't come through if you had a board, you wouldn't be able to fit it in. That was really an electronic track, up in the realms... It's nice to make it simpler sometimes."

beggars banquet

jigsaw puzzle

Bob Dylan – his influence on the music of the 1960s is inestimable.

ot even Mick Jagger could escape the influence of Bob Dylan, that high priest of meaning in 1960s pop music. Neither could the likes of Lennon and McCartney. But even the devil himself must eventually succumb to the word according to Saint Bob, which helps explain 'Jigsaw Puzzle', with its lyrics loaded with clever detail, and Jagger's unusually flat but determined delivery.

"He was like the big guy that you all looked up to," says Roger McGuinn of the Byrds, a band that recorded several of Dylan's songs. "Even McCartney says that. Everybody was looking up to Dylan the way people would read Kerouac. He was the person with the most to say, with the greatest amount of artistic integrity. He really did represent the whole generation. So we all listened to what Bob was doing, and it trickled down."

Jagger could at least rest in peace knowing that he would never suffer that unfortunate label – "The New Dylan". On 'Jigsaw Puzzle', Jagger almost sounds uncomfortable with all these words, as if he really could express more with less – like the great bluesmen who had been such an influence on the Stones. Jagger has never been overly fond of the song, although it would be a mistake to ignore its strengths, such as the rumbling slide guitar licks. Meanwhile, Jagger sings a wry description of a band much like his own whose "singer looks so angry at being thrown to the lions".

street fighting man

ick Jagger is no revolutionary. Make no mistake, for all the mainstream anger against long hair and funny clothes, the Glimmer Twins were never out to destroy you and "your petty morals", as young Keith once described them. The only jail time the Stones ever suffered was for illicit drugs. Hardly the stuff of revolution. Even David Crosby and James Brown were busted on weapons charges. But if things were quiet at home in London, there was serious trouble brewing in Paris and America, where questions about the Vietnam War, free speech and civil rights, brought young people on to the streets. Jagger understood the inherent passion behind such an impulse, enough to make one of the most unexpectedly meaningful statements of the era.

If Dylan was then the essential voice of protest in pop music, the Rolling Stones at least emerged

beggars banquet

Demonstrations by young people were commonplace in Europe and America during the 1960s.

ready to step into the fray, if only long enough to check out the scene. "Summer's here and the time is right for fighting in the streets," Jagger sings in a tone of urgency and near-confusion. "What else can a poor boy do 'cept sing in a rock and roll band?"

Here was a taunting note of ambivalence that suggested the Rolling Stones had given more thought to the day's events and their consequences than a thousand bands of beaded, bearded hippies screaming "Up against the wall, motherfuckers!" They may have craved a certain hedonistic anarchy within their own lives, but the Stones stopped short of calling for the same across society.

The music begins in a driving, militaristic rhythm, as duelling acoustic guitars, a pounding tom-tom beat and some vaguely psychedelic undertones coalesce into a lo-fi mantra. With Brian Jones on sitar, and Dave Mason blowing a shelani – a primitive Indian reed instrument – the sound swells into the kind of swirling pocket symphony the band had failed so miserably at on *Their Satanic Majesties Request*.

The Rolling Stones may have been on the outside looking in on this sudden flare-up of youthful political rebellion, but the trip from Muddy Waters to 'Street Fighting Man' was less suspect than the distance between the Beatles' 'I Want To Hold Your Hand' and 'Revolution'. For front-line rock and roll agitators like the Motor City 5, 'Street Fighting Man' and the later, apocalyptic visions of 'Gimme Shelter' were at least a signal of acknowledgment for the movement. "We never really felt like the Stones were in the street, so to speak," MC5 guitarist Wayne Kramer says now. "It was nice they were sharing those sentiments, and they were great songs, but we never felt they were exactly part of the struggle."

Few sixties rock acts attacked the US political establishment with the same vehemence as the MC5 and the radical White Panther Party. Their manifesto promised "Rock and roll, dope, and fucking in the streets!" Thus the MC5 were the only band to show up outside the 1968 Democratic Convention in Chicago for a protest concert that was to have included the Jefferson Airplane, the Grateful Dead and Country Joe and the Fish. "They all chickened out," says Kramer, who remembers how nicely the noise from police helicopters overhead added to their usual nerve-rattling finale of avant-rock feedback, 'Black to Comm'. "When we said we were going to send the youth of America screaming down the streets, tearing down anything that would stop them from being free we meant it," Kramer says now, "although it was all in a certain amount of marijuana haze and uproarious laughter."

The Stones made rock and roll palatable to the bohemian aesthetic of bands like the MC5, bringing the rougher, challenging moods of blues back into the mix. While the early Beatles represented the good and clean side of sixties pop, the Stones were everything that was rude and surly about rock and roll. And the likes of 'Street Fighting Man' proved the Stones were brave enough to ask questions neither side wanted to hear. The song was banned from the Chicago airwaves during the convention.

"I'm not sure if it really has any resonance for the present day," Jagger said to *Rolling Stone* in 1995. "I don't really like it that much. I thought it was a very good thing at the time. There was all this violence going on."

> "We never really felt like the Stones were in the street, so to speak... It was nice they were sharing those sentiments, and they were great songs, but we never felt they were exactly part of the struggle"
>
> Wayne Kramer, MC5

beggars banquet

stray cat blues

As an exhibition of raw sexual appetites, 'Stray Cat Blues' lived up to every nightmare inspired by Andrew Oldham's slogan "Would you let your daughter marry a Rolling Stone?" The song's opening moments are all grunts and coos between Mick Jagger and some anonymous young woman, as Keith Richards amplifies the heavy breathing with a wickedly lean guitar lick. "I can see you're 15 years old," Jagger growls suggestively. "Bet your mama don't know you scream like that."

The menacing seducer is a recurring character in the blues tradition, preaching an insatiable lust without fear or apology. By now, the Rolling Stones had developed their own special brand of hedonism, exploring the limits of sex and drugs for all to see. The Stones were hardly unique in their reputation for devouring young groupies, but no band had dared transform it into a public celebration. This was at least partly role-playing, with Jagger tweaking a horrified establishment by living the life of Turner from his role in the film *Performance*.

The low rumbling of 'Stray Cat Blues' owes much to the Velvet Underground's example, songs such as 'Sister Ray' and 'Heroin' – all grim examinations of humanity spread across a canvas of stark rhythm and distortion. Richards puts his own blues-based spin on it, and Jagger welcomes yet another victim.

The darker side of the 1960s: New York's Velvet Underground.

factory girl

Beggars Banquet begins with an outrageous ode to the dirty work of Lucifer, but the scratchy country-blues textures across the rest of the album finally lead the Stones to a pair of songs on the working classes. In 1968, the lives of band members already shared little with the sad little people of these last two tracks, even if there is some affection between the lines of 'Factory Girl'.

Jagger seems to be singing adoringly of a woman he's waiting to emerge from her factory job – hardly one of the women of wealth and taste the Stones were now mingling with.

It's left to the picking and strumming of Keith Richards to bring some warmth and uplift to the song. If Jagger's feelings for the working women he had never met remain forever ambiguous, the organic acoustic sounds behind him at least seem able to tap into their world.

It's very possible that Richards knew nothing of any ironic twist in Jagger's lyrics during the recording of basic tracks for the song. "Quite often the words would get written afterward," George Chkiantz says of the *Beggars Banquet* sessions.

While Richards often played a part in crafting lyric ideas for songs, most of the details were left to Jagger. But the guitarist maintained some veto power if he didn't like something. "Mick is the one who does all the talking," says Chkiantz. "Keith will lay down on the sofa and listen, though he's obviously active and concerned. But Mick is very much the one who sits at the producer's desk and does things. But I very distinctly got the feeling that if Keith decided he didn't like it, that was the end of it. No arguments."

> **" I very distinctly got the feeling that if Keith decided he didn't like it, that was the end of it. No arguments "**
> George Chkiantz, engineer

salt of the earth

The final song on *Beggars Banquet* begins with a disarmingly simple sound: just the strumming of acoustic guitar, and the cracked vocals of Keith Richards. He's singing a song straight from the pub, raising his glass: "Let's drink to the hard-working people... the salt of the earth."

The track ultimately swells into an epic gospel number, with a choir and excited piano melody. But, once again, Jagger's response to the masses is ambivalence – "They don't look real to me, in fact they look so strange". But it's that first verse sung by Keith that makes it real.

'Salt Of The Earth' marked the first significant vocal appearance by the guitarist. "He didn't really know how to do vocals," says Chkiantz of Richard's big moment in front of the microphone. "He'd watched Mick do a million of them, but when it came to himself he seemed rather charmingly diffident."

Beggars Banquet remains among the very best rock albums ever recorded. And yet the Rolling Stones never considered themselves to be the voice of a generation – Mick Jagger left such pronouncements to others. His passion was in the sexual danger of 'Stray Cat Blues' or in the eternal threat of 'Sympathy For The Devil'. With *Beggars Banquet*, a scattered multitude of basic elements of blues, rock, country and soul coalesced into the mature sound of the Stones. The days of pop and psychedelia were behind them. Everything the band would later become had its roots in *Beggars Banquet*. And with or without Brian Jones, they weren't ready to stop now.

chapter eight

1969 let it bleed

Guitar prodigy Mick Taylor (second from left) joined the Stones in time for a new era of live performance.

Gimme Shelter

Love In Vain (JOHNSON)

Country Honk

Live With Me

Let It Bleed

Midnight Rambler

You Got The Silver

Monkey Man

You Can't Always Get What You Want

"THIS RECORD SHOULD BE PLAYED LOUD". Pay attention to these words, stamped on to the cover of *Let It Bleed* in great, bold letters. Read them not only as operating instructions, but as a warning. The Rolling Stones meant to assault your senses in 1969 – in ways both overt and wickedly subtle – with sounds that reflected the turmoil then rolling through the streets of America and Europe, and across the rice paddies of south-east Asia. It was a storm of sex, death and fear, where shelter and redemption seemed a distant dream.

For anyone who hadn't already noticed, *Let It Bleed* was here to proclaim the collapse of everything that had once seemed so sweet and innocent about the 1960s, a decade of utter extremes. Swinging London and San Francisco's Summer of Love were fading quickly. The muddy, good vibes of Woodstock still lay ahead, but so too did Altamont, which only added to the era's growing unpredictability. By now, both Robert Kennedy and Martin Luther King had been murdered. Men visited the moon that July, just as President Richard Nixon began a reign of dirty tricks, paranoia and ruthless calculation, with vague wartime promises of "peace with honour". Charlie Manson descended from the foothills of Los Angeles to lead a murder spree of the rich he hoped would unleash a race war, just as The Beatles' 'Helter Skelter' had somehow promised him. Another kind of insanity was sweeping China, where radical Red Guards continued a violent purge of the intelligentsia and all things foreign in Chairman Mao's Cultural Revolution. Russian tanks in Czechoslovakia. Bombs in Northern Ireland. Ted Kennedy at Chappaquiddick. Casualties everywhere.

Laying amidst the dead and wounded was Brian Jones. He did not live to see the December release of *Let It Bleed*. But Jones had long since ceased to be a creative factor within the Stones, the band that had once been his obsession, his creation. His masterplan of bringing the blues to the masses, to spread the word about the immortal Muddy Waters and Elmore James, had worked beyond his wildest fantasies – even if it also meant enduring the occasional Chuck Berry rocker at the insistence of Keith Richards. Yet fame and fortune hadn't been good for Jones. "He was very talented," Mick Jagger told *Rolling Stone* in 1995, "but he was a very paranoid personality and not at all suited to be in show business."

That paranoia had come from repeated drug busts, his failing health, the loss of lovely Anita Pallenberg to Keith, and his obsession with being known as the leader of the Stones even after the band's creative energy shifted to the songwriting of Jagger and Richards. Meanwhile, his own talent slowly slipped away during a lifestyle of endless partying, lack of sleep and too much hanging out. Speed, morphine, cocaine, acid, booze. Even on *Beggars Banquet*, Jones' useful moments of inspiration had been few. But during the early *Let It Bleed* sessions, his appearances were sporadic and, ultimately, not welcome. At Olympic Studios a year earlier, Jones had asked Jagger, "What can I play?" The singer's reply: "Yeah, what can you play, Brian?".

When the Stones decided to tour in 1969, largely for financial reasons, it was obvious that Jones was not up to the task. He would have to be replaced. So Jagger, Richards and Watts went to Jones' new home at Hartfield, Sussex, outside London, to accept his resignation. On June 8, Jones officially announced his departure from the band: "I want to play my kind of music, which is no longer the Stones' music," Jones said. "The music Mick and Keith have been writing has progressed at a tangent as far as my own taste is concerned."

In reality, of course, he'd been kicked out of the Rolling Stones. Although this was – to say the least – an impossible act for Jones to follow, he was hardly suicidal. He had already started cleaning up his habits. And at his new country home, the former house of Winnie the Pooh author A.A. Milne, Jones made plans for a new band. He was soon talking with

> **"He was very talented, but he was a very paranoid personality and not at all suited to be in show business"**
> Mick Jagger on Brian Jones

increasing excitement about his future with friends such as Alexis Korner and other members of the Stones. Then, on July 3, after a night of partying and swimming in his pool, he was dead. An unfortunate mixture of alcohol and barbiturates, combined with a hopelessly frail nature, led to his drowning. Richards sensed foul play at the time, but Jagger remains unconvinced. And the cause hardly mattered. Elmo Lewis was gone.

His replacement in the Rolling Stones was Mick Taylor, who emerged from the London blues virtuoso tradition that had already produced the likes of Eric Clapton, influenced by the stinging lead playing of B.B. King and Freddie King.

It wasn't Jagger or Richards who discovered the 20-year-old guitarist. Veteran British bluesman John Mayall had already encountered Taylor years before at a Bluesbreakers gig when the young musician offered to fill in for an absent Clapton. "He was only about 16 or 17, but we had nothing to lose," Mayall remembers. "We had two sets to play that night in some town hall somewhere, and he just joined us for the second set. He was astonishing. He knew all of our versions of the material. I guess he'd been down to the club many times and heard it. Very gifted young fellow."

Mayall lost touch with the blues prodigy, until he needed a new guitarist for the Bluesbreakers – both Clapton and Peter Green had since moved on. Taylor answered an advert in *Melody Maker*, and was quickly hired. "He has his own style, and is exceptionally good on slide guitar," says Mayall, who recorded four albums with Taylor.

Two years after Taylor joined the Bluesbreakers, Mayall disbanded the group to free himself to explore acoustic blues. Jagger was by then looking to replace Jones and called on Mayall, a man with a reputation for unearthing supernatural young musical talent. He recommended Taylor and the young guitarist was soon spotted at the Rolling Stones sessions. "He just jumped from one to another", says Mayall, who has periodically reunited with Mick Taylor over the years.

The full impact of Taylor's presence would not be felt until 1971's *Sticky Fingers* album, but the guitarist appeared at a crucial time for the Stones. There was the coming international tour, playing for a more sophisticated audience: no more little girls screaming through puberty, but massive arena crowds who actually expected to hear what the boys were playing.

Expectations for the Stones were bumped even higher with the single 'Honky Tonk Women', released the day after Jones' funeral. The song had been transformed during sessions from Richards' original country bumpkin concept into a brash, mid-tempo rocker through Taylor's influence. As 'Jumpin' Jack Flash' had done a year earlier, 'Honky Tonk Women' found the Stones pushing their straight-ahead rock and roll to an exciting new level.

The first look fans got of Mick Taylor came just days later at the previously scheduled free concert in London's Hyde Park on July 5. Accompanying the band on stage was a life-size cut-out of Jones, to whom the concert was now dedicated. Jagger read from Shelley's *Adonais* in Brian's memory, and released hundreds of white butterflies into the crowd. "We played pretty bad. Until the end, 'cause we hadn't played for years," Richards told *Rolling Stone* in 1971. "And nobody minded 'cause they just wanted to hear us play again. It was nice they were glad to see us 'cause we were glad to see them. Coming after Brian's death, it was like a thing we had to do."

Thus began a new era of live performance for the Rolling Stones. "It was the biggest fucking deal of the year", remembers Mick Farren, leader of the Deviants and a writer for *International Times*, London's first underground newspaper. He attended the concert with feminist writer Germaine Greer. "It was a whole fucking garden party backstage, and to penetrate that you had to go through lines of police, and then lines of Hells Angels. The British Hell's Angels were jovial, fairly friendly fellows."

> **" He was astonishing... Very gifted young fellow... He has his own style, and is exceptrionally good on slide guitar "**
>
> British blues veteran John Mayall on Mick Taylor

let it bleed

The death of Brian Jones in 1969 only added to a perception of the Stones as a band dancing too close to the edge.

Most recollections of the event neglect to include the scene brewing that same evening across the park at the Albert Hall, where the Who and Chuck Berry were performing. For some fans at Hyde Park, it was all part of the same full day of music. "There was a sort of rerun of the Mods and Rockers culture clash at the Albert Hall," Farren says. "All these Teddy Boys came out to see Chuck Berry and started throwing things at the Who. It was quite a spectacular evening."

The Rolling Stones were then in the midst of finishing *Let It Bleed*, a work destined to stand as one of the key albums of the 1960s. If *Beggars Banquet* was an explosive comeback after a season of muddled psychedelia, then *Let It Bleed* emerged as a more profound statement, a survey of the wreckage of an era.

The album cover bordered on the ridiculous, depicting a pop art five-layered cake – complete with

85

let it bleed

gimme shelter

bicycle tyre and movie film canister. It couldn't possibly represent the grim contents within. Lyrics were inspired by the months Mick was now spending in the US, along with constant reminders of the Vietnam War and campus uprisings.

Produced once again by Jimmy Miller, the Rolling Stones returned to their beloved blues, diving right into the source with Robert Johnson's 'Love In Vain'. Adjusting the arrangement to their own comfort, the Stones added extra chords and a deeper country flavour. On the album, and in published sheet music Jagger and Richards brazenly took full songwriting credit for the immortal blues tune.

Let It Bleed is also notable for Keith Richards' playing, which reached near-heroic proportions on the album. In the absence of Brian Jones, Richards' did most of the guitar work himself, layering both rhythm and lead work into passages of stirring nuance and gut-bucket drive.

The basic tracks for most of *Let It Bleed* were recorded at Olympic Studios in London, with final overdubs and mixing being completed in Los Angeles. The final album was an instant success, widening the boundaries of rock and roll possibility a little bit more. But back at Olympic, there was always some lingering frustration among the studio crew that some of the great moments they remembered would be wiped away by the time the album masters returned from the US. "If you work on a Stones album it takes about two years to come to terms with realizing it's going to be like that," says engineer George Chkiantz with a laugh. "At first it's like 'What on earth has he done to it now! How could he!'"

And yet, details aside, the final outcome could not be denied. If any work proved that what the Stones were doing was more than just rock and roll, it was *Let It Bleed*.

> **"** If you work on a Stones album it takes about two years to come to terms with realizing it's going to be like that **"**
>
> George Chkiantz, engineer on 'Let It Bleed'

Welcome to the apocalypse according to Mick Jagger. And why not? The Rolling Stones were suitable messengers on the troubles shaking the populace. And fiction was hardly necessary at this point. No need to dance with Lucifer when napalm is already boiling earth and flesh in the name of freedom.

The West was still enjoying a post-war economic boom, but a crisis of conscience was emerging amidst a youth culture unhappy with the war in Vietnam and mainstream attitudes toward race, sex and free speech. Revolution was brewing, or so it seemed. And as rape, murder and war crept closer, Jagger's message was both a warning and a cry for escape. If war is "just a shot away", then so too is love but "a kiss away".

As Richards builds an ominous, shimmering backdrop of guitars, a haunted Jagger describes "the fire sweepin' our very street today". It's a story of the end of the world, as told through a song that critic Greil Marcus once declared as "the greatest rock and roll recording ever made".

The grim tremolo effect underneath Jagger's dreadful tale owes much to the Stones' endless search for interesting new sounds. "They discovered these Triumph amplifiers, tall stacks with an amp-top built in," says engineer George Chkiantz. "They were pretty terrible really. But Keith got into the fact that if you got these things just hot enough and on the way to breaking down, you suddenly got this sound out of them. They didn't use them a lot after that."

Singing alongside Jagger on 'Gimme Shelter' is Merry Clayton, emerging from Richards' distorted canvas with an angelic delivery of pure, haunted gospel. The veteran R&B backing vocalist had already appeared on records by Darlene Love and Ray Charles when she was summoned by the Stones. Her career would later lead her to some mildly successful solo albums and occasional acting parts, including a recurring role on TV's *Cagney And Lacey* in the eighties. Clayton's presence on the track added a crucial layer of warmth and power.

Producer Jimmy Miller used to tell a story of the Stones' first encounter with Miss Clayton, who was no wallflower at the Los Angeles vocal sessions. When she arrived at Elektra Studios, Clayton sauntered up to Jagger, looked him up and down, and said, "Man, I thought you was a man, but you nothing but a skinny little boy!".

Further discomfort came after Clayton had finished singing the first chorus of the song: Perfect! Amazing! Mick and Keith raved. It was then, Miller recalled to friends, that this woman with the lovely voice wanted to discuss royalties before moving on to that second verse.

Merry Clayton added a crucial layer of warmth and power to 'Gimme Shelter'.

let it bleed

country honk

To some ears, this country and western remake of the Stones' immortal 'Honky Tonk Women' was an act of sacrilege. But this is exactly how Keith intended it all along. If 'Country Honk' does not ring with the same kind of authenticity as the band's later forays into the white man's blues, the track at least reveals genuine affection for the genre.

It's been said that Gram Parsons used to spin George Jones discs for friends, and then mumble through his tears, "That's the king of broken hearts." No doubt, the Glimmer Twins were treated to a similar spectacle during their frequent trips to the US. It was Parsons who first brought Jagger and Richards into contact with real honky tonks. He shared his Merle Haggard and Jimmie Rodgers records, and sat at a piano patiently explaining the shades of difference between the sounds of Nashville and Bakersfield.

Richards' renewed interest in all things country emerges in a rich musical tapestry on 'Country Honk', which opens with sounds culled from the roadside: passing cars, car horns, tyres on gravel. He's soon strumming an acoustic guitar, joined by the tender fiddle-playing of Byron Berline. The song also marks the first appearance on a Stones album by Mick Taylor, who plays slide guitar. Vocals are more restrained than on 'Honky Tonk Women', and Jagger is joined by Richards and Nanette Newman for a rousing chorus around a jug of moonshine.

"That's how the song was originally written, as a real Hank Williams/Jimmie Rodgers/1930s country song," Richards told *Crawdaddy* magazine in 1975. "And it got turned around to this other thing by Mick Taylor, who got into a completely different feel, throwing it off the wall another way."

'Honky Tonk Women' was conceived in the tradition of country stars such as Hank Williams (opposite).

live with me

Here was a clue to the future. Listen closely and you'll hear the sound of the 1970s – of *Sticky Fingers* and *Exile On Main Street*. Here was everything that would epitomize the Rolling Stones, circa 1971: Jagger's nasty rap, the rollicking sax of Bobby Keys, Keith's relentless rhythm. 'Live With Me' was another prototype of a sound in the making.

The song glides along an aggressive bass-line played by Richards himself. But the key element is a the dual-guitar assault of Richards and Taylor – making the second of his two appearances on *Let It Bleed* – riffing toward some hypercharged rock and roll nirvana. Charlie Watts pounds a sinister rhythm, as keyboardists Nicky Hopkins and Leon Russell trade upbeat bar-room melodies.

Jagger meanwhile taunts a lover into woeful cohabitation: "I got nasty habits... Don't you think there's a place for you between the sheets?" Jagger sings of weird scenes and the promise of nightmarish domesticity, his flair for decadent humour – the ultimate manifestation of which would be 1978's *Some Girls* – growing ever sharper.

Saxman Keys makes his first appearance on a Stones track with 'Live With Me'. Here the band was at last incorporating horns as more than an afterthought, closer in spirit to soulman James Brown than ever before. Keys' ballsy honking would remain a central ingredient to the Stones sound both on record and on tour up through the 1980s.

Earlier in his career, to the never-ending amazement of Keith Richards, Keys had played with Buddy Holly. Keys finally recorded with the Stones in Los Angeles, but he was already a well-known commodity back in England. He and trumpet-player Jim Price were a couple of Texan boys who first

let it bleed

let it bleed

arrived in the UK in 1969 as part of the illustrious 11-piece Delaney and Bonnie band. The duo quickly became in-demand session players in London, adding their horn chops to records by John Lennon, George Harrison, Ringo Starr, King Crimson, Mott The Hoople and Bad Company. Although they wouldn't be credited together on a Stones album until *Sticky Fingers* in 1971. Keys and Price sold themselves as a team: Jim Price wrote the charts, and Bobby Keys took the solos. "People would call us up, and we'd go over in the middle of the night," Price remembers. "They'd be stuck on something, and we would go and add a little colour that kind of solved the problem."

Between 1969 and 1974, Keys and Price recorded and toured regularly with the Stones, keeping pace in the fast lane. "Despite all this cowboy goddamn-them bravado bonhomie affect, underneath all that Bobby's got a mind as sharp as a fucking saber," says engineer Andy Johns, who worked with the Stones during those same years, and later produced solo albums for both Price and Keys. "If you try and play chess with Bobby he always beats you in three or four moves. Every fucking time. Jim would come up with the parts, but his mind would drift, and often you'd see Bobby nudge him with his elbow to remind him to play something he'd written. So it was the cat's pyjama twins, man."

let it bleed

on't be fooled by the hint of deep blues suggested in Keith's opening passage of bottleneck guitar. Even surrounded by an ocean of decadence, violence and drugs, there's virtually nothing within the grooves of 'Let It Bleed' to suggest any regret. Jagger may be drowning in blood and decay, but it's merely some warmth and comfort – "a little coke and sympathy" – that he seeks, yelping across a stormy country tune from the Stones, including Ian Stewart on piano. Boogie-woogie in the service of blissful disintegration.

"They tended to lay the tracks down with Keith on acoustic," says engineer Chkiantz. "It's amazing how much of this type of rock stuff is actually founded on acoustic instruments. The acoustic or 12-string or harpsichord is very often welding the track together, even if you're not really that much aware of it."

Keith Richards surely understood the importance of that acoustic foundation, and worked hard at perfecting it. Chkiantz remembers one session when Richards took that commitment to the extreme, playing the same acoustic guitar chords endlessly in the vocal booth while Mick Jagger and Jimmy Miller argued about the most minute differences in the drum sound. When Chkiantz walked down from the control booth to adjust the microphones, Keith asked him what was going on. Chkiantz told him that his singer and producer were arguing about the drum sound. "Look, my hands are beginning to bleed," said Richards, who had been sitting quietly without complaint until that moment. "I've been playing the acoustic now for several hours. I won't be able to play it for much longer, and I really want to get this track down tonight. So you tell them to get their finger out of it."

The message was transmitted to Mick and the producer, who left the drums as they were. As Chkiantz passed through the vocal booth, he spotted Keith's guitar. "It was just covered with blood," says Chkiantz. "He must have been in considerable pain." Let it bleed, indeed.

> "It's amazing how much of this type of rock stuff is actually founded on acoustic instruments. The acoustic or 12-string or harpsichord..."
>
> George Chkiantz, engineer

Saxman Bobby Keys (opposite) began his long collaboration with the Stones on 'Live With Me'.

let it bleed

let it bleed

midnight rambler

Dread is a recurring theme on *Let It Bleed*. It hovers over the album, exploding with terrifying assurance on 'Midnight Rambler'. During the 1969 tour, the Stones turned the song into a violent chant, drawing on fears attached to such twisted personalities as the Boston Strangler – aka serial murderer Albert DeSalvo. Jagger stood on stage, singing gravely of this nebulous force of darkness stalking your streets, your home, before whipping the floor in a frenzy. "Did you see me make my midnight call?"

Mick and Keith wrote the song while on holiday in Pasitano, nestled into the hills of Italy, a strangely pleasant setting for such a malevolent tale. They sat together in small cafes, Mick playing harmonica and Keith a guitar, cobbling together the chord changes, the tempo, the explosive horror story. "Why we should write such a dark song in this beautiful, sunny place, I really don't know," Jagger said in 1995.

There are scenes of greater violence elsewhere on *Let It Bleed*. For most of 'Midnight Rambler' the violence is implied, and therefore more weighted with impending doom. "Usually when you write, you just kick Mick off on something and let him fly on it," Richards said in 1971, "just let it roll out and listen to it and start to pick up on certain words that are coming through – it's built up on that."

Richards preferred the live version heard on *Get Yer Ya-Yas Out!*, which drew shattering force from the added guitar of Mick Taylor. The psychotic vibe of the tune emerged in the songwriting sessions. "It's just something that's there," Keith said. "Some kind of chemistry. Mick and I can really get it on together. It's one way to channel it out. I'd rather play it than shoot it out."

> **" Why we should write such a dark song in this beautiful, sunny place, I really don't know "**
>
> Mick Jagger

'Midnight Rambler' was partly inspired by serial killer Albert DeSalvo (opposite).

let it bleed

you got the silver

Brian Jones did not live to see his final contributions to a Stones album.

monkey man

'ou Got The Silver' is the first song to be carried entirely by a Keith Richards vocal. It's a tender love ballad, no doubt inspired by Keith's new love affair with Anita Pallenberg. As ever, his raw vocals lack the richness and power typical of a Jagger performance, but there's something poignant and real about his delivery.

The track also marks one of the final appearances of Brian Jones, who plays autoharp here. He had by now burnt up his creative energies in an orgy of drug use, boozing and fear. So the person who arrived at Olympic Studios occasionally in rock star finery was but a glamorous, empty husk of what was once Brian Jones. As far as the rest of the Stones were concerned, he needn't have bothered coming at all.

"There were sessions where it was getting very, very ropey with Brian," says Chkiantz. So bad, in fact, that even when Brian gathered enough energy and interest to show up for a session, he often wasn't even plugged in by the band. "After that, things went slowly and then faster downhill. By *Let It Bleed* they were trying to keep him out of the sessions," Chkiantz adds. "And when he came it was just dreadful. The trouble is that you never knew if he was going to come up with a good one or not. It's true that at times nobody bothered to plug him in. But I don't think it was a consistent policy. It must have been pretty desperate for all of them."

icky Hopkins had many great moments playing piano for the Rolling Stones, inventing enough riveting passages to wonder aloud why he wasn't a full member of the band instead of a hired hand. That was perhaps a reasonable question, but one impossible to answer as long as Ian Stewart resided in the Stones universe. Even if they had been crass enough to fire poor Stu for image reasons, the band was forever grateful that he'd stuck around just the same. If Hopkins was destined to never enjoy his fair share of the rewards attached to the music he helped create, his playing was still a key element in some of the era's most important recordings.

Not that 'Monkey Man' stands as a particularly profound statement from the Stones, particularly in context with the rest of *Let It Bleed*. It's a showy, tuneful track, with a jumble of lyrics, making no particular statement, even if Jagger tosses in a "Satanic" reference. 'Monkey Man' is built on a very clever, up-tempo arrangement, mixing the elegant pop progressions of Hopkins with Keith's charged guitar riffs.

Hopkins had played with the Stones since the recording of *Between The Buttons* in 1967. "With his right hand he'd come up with these astounding melodic things, and his touch was perfect," remembers Andy Johns. "He never really screwed up. It was like a weapon you could use, really, on tracks. If you asked him to come in and dub something, it was like 'Oh, we'll use the Nicky Hopkins effect on this.' It was fantastic."

Not only that, but Hopkins fitted in. "For anyone to work with them, you had to have a certain strength of character, otherwise they'd roll right the fuck over you," says Johns. "You had to be very strong."

you can't always get what you want

The close of *Let It Bleed* remains one of the Stones' most famous epics, a sermon to the throngs of agitated youth awaiting guidance. To the streets? To the country? To Carnaby Street? Minister Jagger has your answer, or so he'd have you believe. And who wouldn't? The singer's voice is bolstered here by a massive singalong chorus, raising the stakes of 'You Can't Always Get What You Want' to Biblical proportions.

Yet it wasn't always this way. On *The Rolling Stones' Rock And Roll Circus* (finally unearthed in 1995 after decades in the vaults), the song is performed without the London Bach Choir. It's just the band stripped to its core, revealing a song with a quieter, darker message that touches on the desperation of the drug life and the unsettled times.

On *Let It Bleed*, Jagger begins the track singing against a backdrop of acoustic guitar, with a forlorn note blown on French horn by Al Kooper. Producer Jimmy Miller sits in on drums. By the time Jagger describes his meeting with the hipster junkie "Mr Jimmy", the singer is shouting above the beautiful racket of a gospel chorus and shards of electric guitar.

These are difficult subjects he's dealing with here, but for many listeners, the message of the song went no further than the title, a metaphor to the era's continuing disappointments, the falling short of one's youthful ideals – the song was used to melodramatic effect in *The Big Chill*. Appearing on the B-side to the massive 'Honky Tonk Women' single, 'You Can't Always Get What You Want' was widely heard.

"People can identify with it: no one gets what they always want," Jagger said in 1995. "It's got a very good melody. It's got very good orchestral touches that Jack Nitzsche helped with."

Profound or not, the song put a close to an era. The Rolling Stones were heading into a new decade, where the Gothic flourish of a classical choir would never again seem necessary. They would instead crawl ever deeper into their own version of the blues, committed to an ever-hardening brand of riff-rock. With the Beatles about to implode, the Rolling Stones were well on their way to earning that ridiculous title: "The World's Greatest Rock And Roll Band".

> **"People can identify with it: no one gets what they always want. It's got a very good melody. It's got very good orchestral touches..."**
>
> Mick Jagger

chapter nine

1971 sticky fingers

Pop art icon Andy Warhol designed the album cover for *Sticky Fingers*, which included a working zip.

- Brown Sugar
- Sway
- Wild Horses
- Can't You Hear Me Knocking
- You Gotta Move (McDOWELL)
- Bitch
- I Got The Blues
- Sister Morphine
- Dead Flowers
- Moonlight Mile

Behold Rolling Stones Records. Behold the mighty tongue, those bright red lips, and a sound both confident and fine, bringing rock and roll into a strange new era. The 1970s were finally upon us, and the snappy lips-and-tongue cartoon logo signalled that Jagger and his cohorts were now somehow "in charge". A ghastly development, no doubt, for the cops and tastemakers out to bring down these loud-mouthed London minstrels. Now they weren't even within reach – by 1971 the Stones had declared themselves tax exiles from Mother England, and were living in heathen splendor in the south of France, or wherever, and not much concerned about any bad news they might have left behind.

No longer would there be those irritating battles over taste and decorum. The first sign of a new enlightened age came in the form of *Sticky Fingers*, released by Rolling Stones Records, a "boutique" label distributed via a licensing agreement through Atlantic Records. Running the company was Marshall Chess, the 29-year-old son of Leonard Chess, the sainted founder of Chess Records. And for the label's first release, pop artist Andy Warhol created an audacious cover that depicted a suggestive pair of jeans, complete with bulging crotch and a working zip. Sticky fingers, indeed.

The Rolling Stones had been reborn yet again in the months leading up to the release of *Sticky Fingers*. Young Mick Taylor's guitar was now fully incorporated into the band, and to great musical effect – evidence enough of this could be heard on the single 'Honky Tonk Women'. Jagger was even threatening to become a movie star, with three films – *One Plus One*, *Ned Kelly* and *Performance* – all released in 1970. And the Stones were finally free agents, no longer indentured labourers for Decca Records in the UK, London Records in the US, or former hero and manager Allen Klein.

Equally important was the band's return as a touring unit. The sudden exit of the sadly dazed and confused Brian Jones now made it possible for the band to perform across Europe and the United States during 1969 and 1970. Powered by new sound technology, the Rolling Stones were now capable of filling sports venues with ear-rattling rock and roll. The screaming teenage girls were long gone, instead they had been replaced by enormous crowds ready to tap into the Stones' dark, bluesy groove. Outside the halls were the usual clashes between fans and police.

Then, of course, there was Woodstock, that massive rock festival happening in upstate New York that seemed to represent the hopeful side of sixties pop culture. JImi Hendrix, the Who, Janis Joplin, Creedence Clearwater Revival, Crosby Stills Nash and Young, Santana, Melanie (!) and countless others had mixed with the rain, mud and acid for three days of mostly good vibes. All that was missing was a representative of one of the decade's great pop triumvirate: the Beatles, Dylan or the Stones.

At the end of 1969, the Rolling Stones sought to recreate Woodstock in their own image with a free concert in San Francisco's Golden Gate Park. After a experiencing a variety of problems with red tape, "Woodstock West" was moved to the Altamont Speedway in nearby Livermore, California. At the suggestion of the Grateful Dead, security was provided by the Hell's Angels motorcycle gang. It was here, in the days after the December release of *Let It Bleed,* that the Stones presided over an ignoble event that pop pundits would later declare the symbolic death knell for the era of peace and love – not that the Stones had ever fully identified with the hippie subculture, anyway.

Trouble began as the Hell's Angels rolled their motorcycles through the crowd toward the stage, solving security problems with pool cues and knives. Even Jefferson Airplane vocalist Marty Balin was beaten in mid-song for openly criticizing the Angels. And before the night was over, 18-year-old Meredith Hunter was stabbed to death while the Stones performed 'Under My Thumb'. Jagger was left to plead from the stage: "Who's fighting?

> "Who's fighting? What for? This could be the most beautiful evening"
>
> Mick Jagger, on stage at Altamont

sticky fingers

What for? This could be the most beautiful evening..."

Instead, it turned into the ultimate nightmare, witnessed by 300,000 fans, and captured by the documentary cameras of David and Albert Maysles and Charlotte Zwerin, whose footage would later be seen in the film *Gimme Shelter*. By the time the Rolling Stones made their escape via helicopter from Altamont, at least 850 concertgoers had been treated for LSD overdoses. Three others died as a result of various accidental causes. Already, the darkness was threatening to overtake them.

By the time the Rolling Stones arrived in Muscle Shoals, Alabama, for the first sessions of what would become *Sticky Fingers,* the disaster of Altamont was still a week away. Right now, they were a tightly wound rock and roll machine, riding the euphoric high of their first American tour since the demise of Brian Jones. As a result, the band experienced three impossibly productive days within the concrete tomb of Muscle Shoals Sound. It left them with the backing tracks for 'Brown Sugar', 'Wild Horses' and 'You Gotta Move', each song a career-defining anthem.

Mick Jagger makes his acting debut in the film 'Performance'.

sticky fingers

The Stones decamped at the nearby Sheffield Holiday Inn with little fanfare from the locals. Few in town seemed to recognize the celebrities in their midst, even with Keith Richards aswirl in scarves and snakeskin boots. Muscle Shoals session keyboardist Jim Dickinson remembers sitting at breakfast with the band when a waitress innocently asked: "Are you in a group?" "Yes", Bill Wyman replied, "We're Martha and the Vandellas."

The only limitation on the Stones was time – three days squeezed between the end of the official tour and the fabulous free love-in scheduled for San Francisco. So there was little of the meandering freedom the Stones enjoyed back in London.

The band entered the bare-bones studio (nestled within an old coffin factory) at the usual ungodly hour to begin working on 'You Gotta Move', a mournful examination of the soul by the North Mississippi blues immortal Fred McDowell. It was a song Jagger and Richards were already performing on the road as a duet. But what should have been a simple return to their roots was immediately bogged down in untested ideas, new arrangements, and Mick even attempting to improvise his own lyrics.

"I watched them for an hour, maybe a little more, and it just wasn't working," Dickinson says now. "I thought 'Well, here I am at a Stones recording session and I'm going to watch them blow it. This really sucks.' It really just wasn't working."

Dickinson left the studio briefly with writer Stanley Booth (who would later document his travels with the band in his book *Dancing With the Devil: The True Adventures of the Rolling Stones*) to make a phone call and smoke a joint. When they returned, the studio was filled with the grim, languorous thumping of Charlie Watts, the electric piano of Wyman, and the forlorn scratching acoustic guitar. It was 'You Gotta Move', working at last, with the dual moaning of Mick and Keith offering a shivering authenticity.

Three days in the Deep South could hardly transform the Rolling Stones into the real bluesmen they once admired as teenagers. And yet that first early morning session at Muscle Shoals demonstrated the ability of these five British players to tap into the raw essence of the real American folk blues like few others. "It's like they had turned into the Rolling Stones while we were gone," Dickinson says. "From that moment on everything they did worked."

> "Everything they did was at the peak of their competence... When Charlie Watts got up from the drums it was a master take, and that was it. Nobody discussed it"
>
> Jim Dickinson, Muscle Shoals session keyboard player

sticky fingers

brown sugar

Mick Jagger began writing 'Brown Sugar' while filming 'Ned Kelly' (above) in the Australian Outback.

The Rolling Stones hadn't come to Muscle Shoals on a whim. Not now, only days before the band's first American tour in four years was set to end with the free concert at Altamont. They had travelled to the Deep South in search of cultural ambience, to tap into the kind of musical source material they discovered back at Chicago's Chess Studios, mingling with the likes of Muddy Waters. And yet this time the Stones would not be satisfied with a mere rehash of the ancient blues. Their recording of Fred McDowell's 'You Gotta Move' notwithstanding, the band's three days at Muscle Shoals were devoted to perfecting a sound that was undeniably their own.

The rich, edgy guitar that launches *Sticky Fingers* is the ultimate realization of what has been the band's signature sound ever since. The eclectic pop that had characterized such early work as 'Ruby Tuesday' now seemed forever behind them, replaced by a new darker wave. 'Brown Sugar' set an arch tone for *Sticky Fingers,* and rode a harsh groove borrowed from fifties rocker Freddy Cannon (best known for 'Tallahassee Lassie' and 'Palisades Park'). The song emerges from a blend of electric and acoustic guitar, some rude sax squealing from Bobby Keys – added later in London – and the nervous percussion of Jagger. 'Brown Sugar' moved like a supercharged locomotive, slicing through the Alabama air as rich as syrup. In short, it was straight ahead, state-of-the-art rock and roll.

Mick Jagger first sketched out the song during the filming of *Ned Kelly,* sitting alone in the Australian outback with an electric guitar to exercise an injured hand. By the time he reached Muscle Shoals, Jagger was slurring and mumbling words as confounding as 'Louie Louie', but leaving enough clues to suggest the man was singing happily about heroin, slavery and eating pussy. "God knows what I'm on about on that song," Jagger told *Rolling Stone* magazine in 1995. "It's such a mishmash. All the nasty subjects in one go."

The early morning sessions at Muscle Shoals benefited greatly from the band's tour, which had left them in fine playing form. "The way they did those songs, Jagger stayed on the floor with a hand-held microphone, walking around between musicians until he had all the lyrics nailed," remembers Jim Dickinson, who witnessed the entire three-day session. "And then he went in the control room with the engineer as the band played the rhythm track, at which point Keith took over the floor."

At one point, Dickinson remembers, a small problem emerged within the rhythm section. Charlie Watts' tom-tom was clashing harmonically with the bass, so it was suggested that he retune the drum. "No," Watts said casually, "I don't ever tune my drums." For a moment no one seemed concerned by this declaration, until Ian Stewart said, "Wait a minute, you can't just say blatantly 'I don't tune my drums.' That's a terrible thing to say." Watts remained unconvinced: "Why should I tune something I'm going to go out there and beat on? I'll just go out there and hit it and it will change."

The Stones would later re-record 'Brown Sugar' during a birthday party for both Richards and Keys, and were joined by Eric Clapton and Al Kooper at Olympic Studios. But not even that kind of firepower could capture the special ambiance of the band's three days at Muscle Shoals.

"Everything they did was at the peak of their competence," says Dickinson. "They reached the point where they did as well as they could do it, and that was their take. It was never discussed: 'Should we do this again? Is this a good take? Is this too slow? Is this too fast?' When Charlie Watts got up from the drums it was a master take, and that was it. Nobody talked about it."

sway

agger counts off a weary, lumbering beat at the beginning of 'Sway', before easing into the role of a man caught desperately adrift, his mind fragmenting from too many nights spent living "that evil life". A slow progression of twangy guitar chords suggest a dazed state of mind, as Jagger awakes to discover a new day that "destroyed your notion of circular time". He's still in search of some redemption when young Mick Taylor embarks a swelling blues lead that brings sudden and explosive clarity alongside the frantic piano runs of Nicky Hopkins and a subtle layer of strings.

For listeners still mourning the loss of Brian Jones, 'Sway' offered a graphic demonstration of the new musical possibilities his replacement brought to the Rolling Stones. In some ways, the result was truer to the band's initial blues fantasies than the endless pop experiments on sitar, dulcimer, and other exotic instruments, that Jones had pursued during the Swinging London years.

"After Mick Taylor came along, and they got a little bluesier – just straight-up blues rock and roll – it was fan-bloody-tastic," says Andy Johns, who witnessed many of the *Sticky Fingers* sessions as a sound engineer. "I used to like to watch the tracks come together, because they would literally write in the studio. So you would be able to see the whole procession of ideas that led to the finished song."

'Sway' also marked the beginning of another experiment for the Stones. It was the first track to be recorded at Stargroves, Jagger's Berkshire mansion. At the time of these first sessions in 1970, the typical mobile recording unit was a van packed with equipment that was then unloaded into a room, where the machines were held together unsteadily with string and gaffer tape. By then, however, the band had built the Rolling Stones' Mobile – a truck with the first self-contained portable recording unit, complete with control room. "I was petrified," remembers Johns, who was working on his first full album with the esteemed band his elder brother, Glyn, had engineered since the beginning of their career. "We're at Mick's house, I've never used this sort of gear before, and it's their new baby. So their expectations are pretty high. So I better dial it in or I'm up shit creek."

The band played together in a huge room at Stargroves, where Johns set up Taylor's amplifier in the fireplace – with microphones placed up the chimney – and Charlie Watts' drum kit in a big bay window. The results for the tracks recorded there were spectacular. "It was fucking cool," says Johns of those *Sticky Fingers* sessions, "it really was."

> "After Mick Taylor came along, and they got a little bluesier…it was fan-bloody-tastic"
>
> Andy Johns, sound engineer

sticky fingers

wild horses

'Wild Horses' began life as a lullaby. Keith Richards' first son, Marlon, had just been born, but the guitarist knew he would soon be leaving him behind for the crucial 1969 American tour. "It was a very delicate moment," Richards told *Rolling Stone* in 1971. "The kid's only two months old and you're goin' away."

The critical element that transformed a simple love ballad into a wistful, epic exploration of devotion came when Mick Jagger rewrote most of Richards' original lyrics, keeping only the guitarist's signature line – "Wild horses couldn't drag me away". The inspiration would seem to have emerged from Jagger's own romantic life, still shaken from Marianne Faithfull's recent overdose-induced coma and their rapidly disintegrating relationship.

"Jagger was like a high-school kid about it," says Jim Dickinson, who watched as Jagger sketched out the final lyrics at Muscle Shoals. "He was crushed."

'Wild Horses' was the final song the Stones would attempt in Alabama. But as the band prepared to begin recording, Ian Stewart calmly packed up to leave. Dickinson was then recruited. It wasn't until years later that Dickinson discovered the reason behind Stewart's disinterest in 'Wild Horses' – Stu had always hated minor chords. And the song begins with a minor chord. Even when playing live with the band on tour after tour, the committed boogie-woogie man would regularly engage in an act of perverse defiance, lifting his hands from the keys whenever a minor chord came up. "He was an extreme dude," says Dickinson. "He kept them honest. There was no bullshit when Ian was around."

For Dickinson, such as revelation was small compared to the spectacle of watching his beloved Rolling Stones up close in the studio. As he struggled to fit some appropriately tinkly Floyd Kramer country licks into the song, Dickinson realized the band was playing defiantly, if not obliviously, out of tune – a fact that demonstrated that in the world's greatest rock and roll band precision counted for little. As late as the mid-eighties, witnesses to their sessions would come away astonished at the rank amateurism of the Stones in the studio, where they were capable of showing little more expertise than the newest band of nobodies working on their worthless demo tapes.

Family Man: Keith Richards with Anita Pallenberg and daughter Dandelion.

But that recklessness was essential to the Stones process. And since Dickinson was unlikely to tell Richards how to tune up his guitar, he turned to an old beat-up tack piano in the back of the studio – where the band's roadie was storing the dope – and found an octave-and-a-half range he could play with one hand that was in tune with the Stones. It wasn't easy, but the immortal results of the final 'Wild Horses' track was ultimately a revelation to Dickinson, whose later career as a producer for the likes of the Replacements and the Texas Tornadoes has partly hinged on a certain looseness borrowed from the Rolling Stones, circa 1969.

"I've virtually based a career around what I learned in those three days," Dickinson says with a laugh. "It was so organic and natural, you just had to stop to think, 'Who's right and who's wrong here?' And they literally didn't have a clue as to what they were doing. They were making a record the way people off the street would come in and make a record."

As the sun finally came up at the end of the band's third day in the studio, Jagger packed up the final masters of their three new tracks and made sure he was leaving nothing behind. "When the session was over, and they had the rough mixes, Jagger sat there and shredded the tape, except for the masters," says Dickinson. "He erased every mix and every outtake that they weren't taking with them. And he shredded the eight-track except for the masters, and ran the tape off on the floor. There ain't no bootlegs on that session."

> "They were making a record the way people off the street would come in and make a record"
> Jim Dickinson

can't you hear me knocking

The quick, grinding bursts of guitar that open 'Can't You Hear Me Knocking' are as minimalist as any punk riff that would emerge later that same decade. Never mind the Sex Pistols. This was a sound both brutal and wickedly real: the staccato riffing, the screech of fingers sliding across steel strings, the distant yelp from Jagger – in fine ragged voice – taking the role of the Grim Reaper himself.

These are moments clearly dominated by the harsh rhythm playing of Keith Richards. From that tough-as-nails groove, the song soon drifts into the ether, shifting into an unexpectedly expansive second half that still has rock purists fuming. In the middle of this epic track – at over seven minutes, the album's longest – saxman Bobby Keys rolls into rich R&B runs and rude, jazzy honking as the Latin conga rhythms of percussionist Rocky Dijon guides the Stones into some rocking jazzbo that drifts perilously close to Santana territory. To some listeners, this was nothing more than pretentious junk. But 'Can't You Hear Me Knocking' was solidly within the rock and roll pantheon, not an exercise in aimless noodling. And *Sticky Fingers* was better for it.

If nothing else, the track further demonstrated the dramatic horizons suddenly open to the band via the slippery young fingers of Mick Taylor. The new guitarist introduced himself here as the kind of rock and blues virtuoso Brian Jones had once dreamed of becoming, before bad drugs and paranoia sent him speeding toward irrelevance, and a once-charmed life into sad oblivion. Taylor's presence did not change the Stones fundamentally. The overall sound of *Sticky Fingers* era was established at least as far back as 'Jumpin' Jack Flash' in 1968. But Taylor did enable the band to expand on a purely musical

sticky fingers

level, and that was something both Jagger and Richards seemed to ready to explore.

"He had a big contribution," Jagger said of Taylor's playing to *Rolling Stone* magazine in 1995. "He made it very musical. He was a very fluent, melodic player, which we never had, and we don't have now. Neither Keith nor Ronnie plays that kind of style. It was very good for me working with him. I could sit down with Mick Taylor and he would play very fluid lines against my vocals. He was exciting, and he was very pretty, and it gave me something to follow, to bang off."

For Andy Johns, who mixed the Olympic Studios session engineered by his brother Glyn, witnessing the emergence of Taylor was a singular event in his career.

> "He was a very fluent, melodic player, which we never had, and we don't have now… He was exciting, and he was very pretty, and it gave me something to follow, to bang off"
>
> Mick Jagger on Mick Taylor

Over the years, Johns would work in the studio with such guitar luminaries as Jeff Beck, Jimmy Page, Eric Clapton, Jimi Hendrix and on up to Eddie Van Halen. Even today, Taylor remains his favourite. "I could sit and listen to Mick Taylor all night," says Johns. "He would never make a mistake and every take would be different. And he'd make you cry. It really was good. He was a little bit hard to get in touch with as a person. He was a very private man, didn't put out much. But I loved listening to him play night after night after night. It was not boring. Whereas working with Eric or Jeff or Pagey or even Hendrix you could get really bored. They're not on all the time, you know."

"I really think Mick Taylor had a big influence on the direction the band took. Who knows? After Brian left, and they started working with Jimmy Miller, and they did 'Jumpin' Jack Flash' and 'Street Fighting Man', obviously it got very much more rock and roll. Then Mick Taylor comes along and it really sort of put the icing on the cake. They went in that fantastic direction because they could start jamming again. They hadn't been jamming for a long time."

bitch

ere was another explosive, archetypal Stones riff, another flash of rhythmic brilliance from the guitar of Keith Richards amidst the comforts of Stargroves. Yet the sessions for 'Bitch' actually began without Richards. By the time the guitarist arrived at the studio carrying a bowl of cornflakes, the Stones had struggled with the track for a full day without success. "It sounded bloody awful," remembers Andy Johns.

Richards calmly ate his breakfast as he watched the band at work, until he could stand no more of the terrible screeching: "Give me that fucking guitar!"

He quickly found a simple chord pattern that somehow transformed the song into a tight, agitated package. It was an absolutely relentless riff, a fiendish attack on the senses. On the final track, Richards' rhythm guitar is joined by the horns of Bobby Keys and Jim Price, with some minimal lead guitar work at the edges. "Instantly it went from not very good, feels weird, to BAM! and there it is," says Johns of the moment Richards stepped into the studio. "Instantly changed gears, which impressed the shit out of me."

The sound was well suited for the lustful message from Jagger, grunting excitedly "When you call my name, I salivate like Pavlov's dog!" Further pushing the era's delicate boundaries of mainstream taste and decorum was the song's title – nearly two decades before gangsta rap and MTV welcomed the word into the common pop vocabulary – which was merely a more graphic expression of a theme that had held Jagger's interest at least since the self-explanatory 'Stupid Girl' and 'Under My Thumb'.

sticky fingers

I got the blues

Jagger doesn't even try to adopt some cartoon drawl here, and 'I Got The Blues' thus comes off less as another blues tribute than a deeper reflection of the singer himself. Too often in his work, Jagger has been strangely compelled to comically ape the vocal quirks and mannerisms of the original blues and country masters, as if he were still chasing those adolescent dreams of becoming a true bluesman. But as he sings this wrenching manifesto on heartache – presumably inspired by the end of his affair with Marianne Faithfull – Jagger glides sadly across the soulful gospel organ of Billy Preston and a soaring horn section arranged by Jim Price to an expressive style of lowdown blues that is undeniably his own – "I'll tear my hair out, just for you".

sister morphine

The roots of 'Sister Morphine' stretch back to 1968, and a garden in Rome, where Jagger first began strumming this mournful tune. "It was a tune that Mick had that he didn't seem to have any words for," Marianne Faithfull says now. He played those acoustic guitar chords for months without lyrics before Faithfull offered her own, telling the bleak tale of a dying man crying out desperately for morphine. It was a story far from the delicate balladry of 'As Tears Go By', but it was also a chance for Faithfull to expand her repertoire to deeper, even dangerous material.

"I was envious of Mick and Keith," she wrote in her 1994 autobiography, *Faithfull*. "They had moved far beyond the boundaries I was still locked in… I had seen what the Stones were doing, what pop music could become. 'Sister Morphine' was an attempt to do that myself. To make art out of a pop song!" Other influences were in the air, including the Velvet Underground's 'Waiting For The Man', another junkie's tale.

Faithfull modelled her own song's structure after John Milton's *Lycidas,* and drew inspiration for the line "the clean white sheets stained red" from an incident aboard a boat en route to Brazil where a pregnant Anita Pallenburg suddenly began bleeding. At a hospital, she was given a shot of morphine, much to the envy of her friends.

But at the time she collaborated with Jagger on the song, Faithfull had yet to fall into any serious drug problem of her own. For all the press about the "Naked Girl At Stones Party!" headlines, Faithfull was, like Jagger, still just a dabbler. For more than two decades, both have insisted the song is fictional, and not about Faithfull's subsequent experiences. "It was a story, literally a story, long before I ever took heroin or any other opiate," Faithfull says. "It was just a story that I had in my mind of a man who's in a car crash, and he's really in pain, dying in hospital, and he is the one asking for more morphine. It was really just an image. I wasn't really taking anything."

It was Jagger who arranged Faithfull's recording of 'Sister Morphine' during the mixing of *Let It Bleed*. On this recording, Ry Cooder plays accelerating bottleneck guitar like a man on edge, flailing across the rock-solid rhythm of Charlie Watts and Bill Wyman. The vocals were recorded in London.

Guitarist Ry Cooder, once considered a replacement for Brian Jones, performs on the haunting 'Sister Morphine'.

sticky fingers

Though left officially uncredited for more than two decades, Marianne Faithfull was the co-author of 'Sister Morphine'.

During the Los Angeles session, pianist Jack Nitzsche scolded Faithfull after he spotted the singer drinking booze and snorting cocaine. "How can you call yourself a singer and do coke?" Nitzsche demanded "Don't you know what that stuff is doing to your vocal chords and mucus membranes? Forget about Keith and Anita. Everyone in the band can get wrecked except the drummer and the singer."

Faithfull's first attempt to break free from her image as pop-chanteuse/rockstar's girlfriend was cruelly ended when Decca pulled her 'Sister Morphine' single from the shelves after just two weeks. By the time the Rolling Stones finally released the song on *Sticky Fingers,* laying Jagger's haunted vocals over the same backing track, Faithfull had begun her own struggle with hard drugs, including heroin. And the song would become what she calls her "Frankenstein", a dark creation that doggedly overshadowed her own life.

By the end of the 1970s, Faithfull had beaten back those addictions enough to re-emerge as the wonderfully hard-bitten singer of *Broken English*, an album of stark intelligence and brutal experience. In 1997, her newest incarnation was as the wizened, refined interpreter of the Weimar catalogue of Kurt Weill and Bertold Brecht. 'Sister Morphine' has been left to her past, and she hasn't sung it in years.

"People can think what they want and take what they want, but I'm not going to promote morphine," Faithfull says with a laugh. "I'm not in the advice- and lecture-giving business, you know. These are big decisions that people have to make on their own. But I don't take morphine and I don't like it, and I don't see why anyone else needs to. That's probably a very old-fashioned view. But I don't stand in the way of people. They have to decide their own way of death."

Faithfull was left uncredited on *Sticky Fingers* for co-writing 'Sister Morphine'. The Jagger-Richards team received sole credit for more than two decades. Jagger now acknowledges that Faithfull wrote at least some of the lines, though he disputes the idea that she wrote all of the lyrics. "She's always complaining she doesn't get enough money from it," he said in 1995. "Now she says she should have got it all."

On the newest re-issue of Sticky Fingers on Virgin Records, Faithfull was finally acknowledged as co-author of the song. "Isn't that wonderful?" Faithfull says. "Sweet of them!"

dead flowers

If 'I Got The Blues' proved that Jagger didn't need phony accents to tap into the organic roots of American music, 'Dead Flowers' returned the singer to a style that was more play-acting than interpretation. Jagger later took that unfortunate inclination to the utter extreme with 1978's 'Far Away Eyes', which treats country music as a complete joke. This track is at least redeemed by a loose country groove, bouncing along a joyous boogie-woogie piano roll by Ian Stewart.

"I'll be in my basement with a needle and a spoon," Jagger sings happily, "and another girl to take my pain away". It's as if the singer has adopted the inherent optimism of country and western music to disguise some lingering sadness and other troubles.

"I love country music but I find it very hard to take seriously," Jagger told Rolling Stone magazine in 1995. "I also think a lot of country music is sung with the tongue in cheek, so I do it tongue in cheek. The harmonic thing is very different from the blues. It doesn't bend notes in the same way, so I suppose it's very English, really. Even though it's been very Americanized, it feels very close to me, to my roots, so to speak."

> **" I love country music but I find it very hard to take seriously. I also think a lot of country music is sung with the tongue in cheek, so I do it tongue in cheek "**
>
> Mick Jagger

moonlight mile

Sticky Fingers closes on an epic, wistful note. While Mick Taylor strums a rich musical canvas, Jagger sings wearily of being endlessly on the road "with a head full of snow," yearning to return to the bed of a loved one.

After a night of working on the track at Stargroves, with Taylor banging away at his guitar, and Jim Price plucking at the piano strings with a pedal down, 'Moonlight Mile' emerged in its final form at day-break. "We got it four or five in the morning, just as the sun was coming up," says Andy Johns. "It was dawn filtering through the windows, so it had that almost half-asleep feeling. It was gorgeous. I still listen to that song now and again."

Years later, Jagger would fondly recall 'Moonlight Mile', Taylor's restrained guitar and the lush string arrangement. Richards had missed the session, but was equally upbeat about the result. "I wasn't there when they did it," he told Rolling Stone in 1971. "It was great to hear that because I was very out of it by the end of the album and it was like listening, really listening. It was really nice. We were all surprised at the way that album fell together."

chapter ten

1972 exile on main street

Hide your love: Mick Jagger and his new wife Bianca step out for an early public appearance.

Rocks Off

Rip This Joint

Hip Shake (MOORE)

Casino Boogie

Tumbling Dice

Sweet Virginia

Torn And Frayed

Sweet Black Angel

Loving Cup

Happy

Turd On The Run

Ventilator Blues

Just Wanna See His Face

Let It Loose

All Down The Line

Stop Breaking Down

Shine A Light

Soul Survivor

"I gave you diamonds/You give me disease". There's no escape from the real world of decay and desperation the Rolling Stones found themselves in by the early 1970s. These were lyrics scrawled right on to the cover art of *Exile On Main Street,* a musical document so fierce and chaotic that the Stones' early songs of sex and rebellion seemed almost wholesome by comparison.

Witness how far these London bad boys had come since the days of overgrown bowl haircuts. The Stones now seemed well beyond the reach of any recognizable authority, exiled to Keith Richards' villa in the south of France to wallow happily in a world of their own making, where middle-class values had gone terribly, terribly wrong.

This was no longer just rock and roll, but a rough, decadent sound with all hipster pretense stripped away. *Exile On Main Street* rolls through a mushroom cloud of urgent foreboding as grim as 'Gimme Shelter'. That its sense of danger hasn't dimmed over time owes much to a fanatical return to the rawest blues sound imaginable, finally transformed into a sound and fury that is undeniably theirs. As a package, *Exile...* is a mess of scattered images and sorrows, sending listeners on a travelogue of dysfunction and defiance.

Reactions to *Exile...* in 1972 were heated and mixed. On first listen, the album's 18 tracks sounded like a catastrophe of sloppiness. Jagger was virtually unintelligible. That still didn't prevent it from topping both the British and American charts that year. But it wasn't until the seventies rolled onward that a critical consensus emerged, declaring the album a crucial pop document. And yet the singer himself still needs convincing. "It's a bit overrated, to be honest," Jagger told *Rolling Stone* magazine in 1995. "It doesn't contain as many outstanding songs as the previous two records. I think the playing's quite good. It's got a raw quality, but I don't think all around it's as good."

That thumbnail analysis misses the album's larger effect. *Exile On Main Street* is not a collection of singles, but a bristling wall of sound. Jagger's judgment is undoubtedly clouded by the weird times that inspired the album's murky tales. His arrival at the sessions in the south of France followed his wedding to Bianca Rose Perez Moreno de Macias in St Tropez – a ceremony attended by Eric Clapton, Ringo Starr, Stephen Stills and Paul McCartney, among others. At this time, tax problems, lawsuits and ex-managers still hounded the band. Keith had just survived a car crash, but was sinking deeper into various drug habits at Nellcote, his rented palace in Villefranche-sur-Mer.

Although several tracks on *Exile...* were salvaged from earlier sessions at Olympic Studios and Stargroves, the essential core emerged during nearly six months of work in the south of France. Keith's villa overlooked a quiet fishing village on the coast of the Mediterranean. His rent was $10,000 a month. The plan was originally for the Stones to find another house for recording, but Ian Stewart was unable to find a suitable location. Sessions began in Keith's basement in the summer of 1971.

The Nellcote sessions were relaxed but difficult. The electricity often failed, and it was so humid during the summer months that instruments repeatedly fell out of tune. Among the Stones cast and crew was Gram Parsons, who was AWOL from his duties leading the Flying Burrito Brothers to some promised country-rock nirvana. Although not credited, Parsons may well have sung backing vocals on 'Tumbling Dice'. He was certainly responsible for influencing Richards' increasing fascination with country music.

Final vocals were overdubbed later in Los Angeles, where the band's visitors included Neil Young, Joni Mitchell and Marc Bolan. What they witnessed was a band digging deeper into its roots, ignoring a growing trend toward the pretensions of classical music, where epic overkill from the likes of Emerson, Lake and Palmer rang laughably hollow.

> "It's a bit overrated, to be honest. It doesn't contain as many outstanding songs... It's got a raw quality, but I don't think all around it's as good"
>
> Mick Jagger on Exile On Main Street

> **"People say 'Why the south of France?' It's just the closest place where we can relax a bit and then record"**
>
> Keith Richards

The Stones would drift into their own bloated excesses soon enough, but *Exile On Main Street* captured them at a moment of charmed recklessness. It was there in the band's lecherous take on Slim Harpo's 'Hip Shake'. The Stones cut the track as raw Texas boogie, with duelling guitars, the clipped rattling of Charlie Watts, and Jagger moaning like a man caught in a trance. He falls deeper into Harpo's ancient spell during a harmonica wheeze that carries the low rumble of the sorriest of life's blues.

If *Exile...* is less memorable for its individual pop songs, the album's overall effect is profound, shaping a lasting monument to the most primal blends of rock and blues. "People say, 'Why the south of France?' It's just the closest place where we can relax a bit and then record," Richards told *Rolling Stone* magazine in early 1971, as the band prepared to begin work in his basement. "That's why we're all living in the same place...to transfer all that equipment. I hope it's worthwhile."

rocks off

o now begin the begin. *Exile On Main Street* starts off, fittingly enough, with a sharp progression of mid-tempo riffing, and a gravelly yowl from Mr Jagger. In these first few seconds, the tone for the album's 18 songs is indelibly set, and it's disarmingly relaxed.

There is a barely hidden fire that soon explodes with joyous abandon, cutting across a roaring riverbed of piano and horn. Jagger's voice is just another part of the mix, rarely demanding any more attention than the epic muddle of rock and blues going on around him. The dual-guitar assault, the tidy, vicious beat, Bill Wyman's thick, breezy basslines, all roll as one. It was if the "World's Greatest Rock And Roll Band" was just another juke joint jam session.

Thus the six months of recording on *Exile On Main Street* often depended on sudden bursts of inspiration. 'Rocks Off' was an early success at Villefranche-sur-Mer. Sessions for the basic track had gone extremely well, and by sunrise the next day even Keith had passed out. That was usually a signal to engineer Andy Johns to head off to bed himself. But once he arrived at the villa he shared with trumpet-player Jim Price a half-hour drive away, the telephone was ringing. It was Keith. "Where the fuck are you?" "Well, you were asleep," Johns replied. "I thought I'd go home seeing as it was five in the morning." Normally, Richards would have been inclined to wait for the next night's session. What was the hurry? But Keith was ready, supremely prepared for the delicate task at hand, and he wasn't about to let this moment pass. "Oh, man, I've got to do this guitar part," he said. "Come back!"

Johns returned. "So I get back, he plugs in his Telecaster, and he does the second rhythm guitar part, and the whole thing just came to light, and really started grooving," Johns remembers. Richards had the thing nailed in two takes.

The relentless riffing on 'Rocks Off' propels another tale of profound sexual frustration and impotence. Much that could be explicit is brilliantly slurred by Jagger, suggesting the steamy contents of a Henry Miller novel.

During the mixing of 'Rocks Off' months later, a strange echoing warble effect was added to Jagger's vocals, adding a dreamy layer to the bridge of this otherwise straight-ahead rock tune. "We got lucky on the sound of that," says Johns. "It's very cohesive."

The finished track also served to introduce horn-player Jim Price and saxman Bobby Keys as crucial figures throughout the album. The brassy sound from these Texan sidemen was big, brash, impudent and rude, much like the Rolling Stones themselves. Price acted as arranger for the horn section, and was delegated an unusual degree of autonomy. When the Stones were finished with the basic tracks, and left for a holiday in Montreaux, Price, Keys, keyboardist Nicky Hopkins, producer Jimmy Miller and Johns were left to handle the overdubs. "It was obvious which songs lent themselves to having horns," Price says now. "What was played was left up to us. They kind of liked what we did."

rip this joint

This quick roadhouse rave-up is a blistering salute to the Stones' deepest rock and blues roots. Jagger's vocals are a frantic blur within a supercharged Chuck Berry groove, though even the old master himself never rocked this hard and fast. Look forward half a decade or more to the Clash and X for a suitable comparison.

The slashing Richards–Taylor guitar assault runs on pure adrenaline here, joined by the standup bass of Bill Plummer and a rollicking solo by Bobby Keys. 'Rip This Joint' was just one result from the all-night jam sessions the Stones led at the beginning of work on *Exile On Main Street*. "When we were in France we just jammed every night for two months," says Price. "We just played from about nine at night until about four in the morning. We'd just play, play and play. Then the songs would fall together. Mick started singing 'Mmmumngn-mmumbng' – nothing, just syllables, just mush. He would keep singing until words started to come out of it."

Price remembers that most tunes would begin with Richards working something out on guitar, in search of an appropriately snarling groove. "Sometimes Keith and Mick would write upstairs," says Price. "They would play and sing until something would take form."

> **"We just played from about nine at night until about four in the morning. We'd just play, play and play. Then the songs would fall together"**
> Jim Price, horn player

casino boogie

The slow shuffle of 'Casino Boogie' offers typically mush-mouthed vocals from Mick, making way for another energetic Bobby Keys solo. Richards plays bass. Some inspiration for both this track and 'Tumbling Dice' most likely emerged from the convenient proximity of casinos to these sessions in the south of France. Richards often spent his days at the craps and roulette tables near the villa shared by Johns and Price just outside Monte Carlo. It was a fine way to ease into the day, before crawling into the studio that night at Keith's house.

"Those albums weren't very difficult to make," Price says of his work on *Exile On Main Street* and *Sticky Fingers*. "It just took a long time, because it was very relaxed and kind of went on and on forever. But there wasn't any fighting or anything."

The raw, muddled sound on much of *Exile On Main Street*, Price says, "really comes from the instruments, because Keith would play with a certain kind of distortion on his rhythm guitar. That's just what it sounds like."

exile on main street

tumbling dice

Mick Jagger is the unlikely preacherman here, testifying to some great life lesson as the band eases into a throbbing groove. He's embraced by the warm gospel harmonies of Claudie King and Vanetta Fields as he flubs his words to great and frustrating effect, neither saying what he means nor meaning quite what he says, just as Fats Domino always said it should be.

Jagger also plays guitar here, while Mick Taylor handles bass. But the groove is all Richards. 'Tumbling Dice' glides along the album's richest musical arrangement, aligned with a steely Charlie Watts backbeat that brings some discipline to Jagger's sermon of defeat. Even a printed lyric sheet, free from Jagger's haunted soulman growl, leaves its message far from clear, but its loser's ambivalence is undeniable. "I don't think it's our best stuff," Jagger told *Rolling Stone* magazine in 1995. "I don't think it has good lyrics. But people seem to really like it, so good for them."

For many listeners, 'Tumbling Dice' ranks among the Stones' most memorable tracks. But what sounds so natural and subtly hypnotic on record actually provided one of the most difficult recording and songwriting challenges during the making of the album. Originally entitled 'Good Time Women', with a different set of lyrics, the song stumbled through endless sessions of trial and error as Richards struggled to finesse its central riff.

"With 'Tumbling Dice' we worked on that for a couple of weeks at least, just the basic track," remembers Andy Johns. "I know we had a hundred reels of tape on the basic track. That was a good song, but it was really like pulling teeth. It just went on and on."

The making of 'Tumbling Dice' was an extreme case, but it symbolized the atmosphere of lingering detachment that prevailed for much of the Stones' six months at Nellcote. Drugs, lawsuits, sex, the decadence of isolation in the south of France, all the usual suspects were to blame. "We cared, but we didn't care as much as we had," Jagger said in 1995. "Not really concentrating on the creative process, and we had such money problems... We were really in a very bad way. So we had to move. And it destabilized us a bit. We flew off all edges." The lasting power of *Exile On Main Street* emerged during those moments when inertia was suddenly overtaken by inspiration – when the Rolling Stones finally coalesced into a band that mattered.

"They were the worst bloody band on the planet, the worst bunch of musicians in the world, they could be for days at a time," Johns says with a laugh. "Really fucking horrible. And you sit there wondering how on earth are we going to get anything out this. They would play very badly, and that's how they played most of the time, very poorly, and out of tune. Most of it had to do with attitude. They did take a long time in those days, so Bill and Charlie were kind of waiting for the real spark to happen before everyone really bothered."

Watts and Wyman usually arrived at Nellcote by 8 pm. Richards typically made it downstairs to the studio by midnight, but was soon gone again – "Oh, hang on, I've got to put Marlon to bed." And he'd be absent for another hour or two.

"Trying to get all those guys in the room at the same time and actually really bother to nail something back then was very difficult," says Johns. "They were the worst band on the planet, BUT, when it happened, they were transformed almost instantly from this dreadful band into the Rolling Stones, and blow you away. It was almost magical."

> " They were the worst band on the planet, BUT, when it happened, they were transformed almost instantly from this dreadful band into the Rolling Stones... It was almost magical "
>
> Andy Johns, engineer

Mick Taylor's epic lead playing helped return the Stones to the deepest blues within their reach.

sweet virginia

The fabulous church of the Rolling Stones never rang with more crisp religious fervor than on this slow acoustic hootenanny. Waves of longing harmonica preside over 'Sweet Virginia', a track with all the spiritual force of a folk revival meeting on a backwoods porch.

"We can't play country music like authentic Chicago bluesmen," Jagger told *NME* in 1978. "We do our best, but we can't copy – that's not the idea. And so it comes out the way it does…different."

The track is a leftover from the Olympic Studios sessions for *Sticky Fingers*. Thus, the better separation between instruments, a marginal improvement over the muddle of Keith's basement. And yet the raw country blues of 'Sweet Virginia' fits easily within the thick sonic gumbo of the album. Ian Stewart scatters some piano runs deep in the mix, while the acoustic guitars do their delicate dance toward hipster transcendence.

Jagger isn't singing of salvation of the normal variety. His oeuvre remains that of the casual rock and roll outlaw, blending sex, drugs and rebellion to uncertain ends. He sings here of "tryin' to stop the waves behind your eyeballs", while cataloguing a fistful of reds, greens and blues from his local street pharmacist. "And I hid the speed inside my shoe." Lord have mercy.

torn and frayed

Hard truths emerged from Keith Richards' basement. The Stones eased into the long, wearying *Exile On Main Street* sessions never quite knowing if what they were creating was a wonderful, profound mess, or simply a tragic waste of tape and talent. "I don't think it was particularly pleasant," Jagger told *Rolling Stone* magazine's Jann Wenner in 1995. "I didn't have a very good time."

The great irony of *Exile On Main Street* is that while the Stones were en route to one of their greatest creative triumphs, maestro Richards was falling deeper into drug dependency. And booze and drugs certainly flowed freely at their Mediterranean hideaway. These were habits Richards wouldn't be able shake until his monumental 1977 drug bust in Toronto, when it became terribly clear that his addictions not only threatened his own health and freedom, but the future of his beloved Stones. And yet the guitarist performed brilliantly throughout the album, leading the band to a vast timeless sound, a defiantly organic mixture of blues, folk, country and rock, all marked by a troubled fraying at the edges. The recordings had a tendency to drift off course within the regular unstructured scenes at Keith's villa.

Jagger remembered the sessions later as "Just winging it. Staying up all night… It was this communal thing where you don't know whether you're recording or living or having dinner; you don't know when you're going to play, when you're gonna sing – very difficult. Too many hangers on. I went with the flow and the album got made. These things have a certain energy, and there's a certain flow to it, and it got impossible. Everyone was so out of it."

The implications of that life were brought into sharp focus on 'Torn And Frayed'. Jagger rides a breezy country groove here and sings of a rock and roll desperado, trapped on the uncertain edges of a world of the Stones' own making. It's a rock fable that's all too real. Did Richards recognize himself in the character of Joe the guitar player? Jagger sketches Joe as a figure of profound restlessness, lost in a haze of stardom and decadence.

Gram Parsons was a constant presence during the making of *Exile On Main Street*.

The presence of Gram Parsons at Nellcote is likely to have provided a jolt of Bakersfield-Nashville country and western inspiration on 'Torn And Frayed'. Al Perkins adds some springy steel guitar, as Jagger sings in a countrified drawl of ballrooms, smelly bordellos and parasite-filled dressing rooms. The lyrics could as easily have been about Parsons as his pal Richards. Both shared a rootless and reckless existence, and both found themselves within a lingering crowd of dubious hangers on. Parsons became a casualty of that world in September 1973, when he died in the California desert idyll of Joshua Tree from a probable drug overdose.

"There were a lot of funny people always drifting in and out," says Andy Johns recalling the sessions for *Exile On Main Street*. "When I showed up, there were a lot of people still there from when Mick got married, which was months earlier, just leeching off of Keith, and various dope dealers who would arrive and disappear. Keith used to have a lot of fucking wankers hanging around, let's be honest. The fucking dregs, but they were all getting him high. And Mick had his posh friends hanging around, but they really wouldn't come to the sessions that much. Some very disastrous people."

> "Keith used to have a lot of fucking wankers hanging around, let's be honest. The fucking dregs, but they were all getting him high... Some very disastrous people."
>
> Andy Johns, engineer.

sweet black angel

'Sweet Black Angel' was another leftover from *Sticky Fingers,* this time from the sessions at Stargroves, Jagger's manor in Berkshire. The working title – 'Bent Green Needles' – had been Keith's idea of a joke. It was recorded in a similar casual style as the Nellcote sessions, with two acoustic guitars, Jimmy Miller on percussion, and everything bleeding into one another's microphones.

"That was done all of them in a room in a circle at the same time, because there was this one room away from the main hall that had no furniture in it, with a wooden floor, quite high ceilings and plaster walls," says Andy Johns. "We wanted to get the sound of the room." The result was a crisp hillbilly shuffle, upbeat and funky, with marimbas to add a vaguely Caribbean feel. Across that rich acoustic fabric, Jagger penned an example of extreme black caricature to rival *Uncle Tom's Cabin*. Finding the appropriate sharecropper's twang, he sang of "Ten little nigga, sittin' on de wall…free de sweet black slave!" Jagger's foray into bonehead quasi-Ebonics was meant as great irony, an unusual gesture of political support for the black American radical Angela Davis. The singer had previously shown little patience for specific political movements even as the Stones documented a darkening mood in the late-sixties via 'Street Fighting Man' and the apocalyptic 'Gimme Shelter'. And yet Jagger found something compelling about the dramatic image of Davis, whose hair was grown into a tall "afro" – a symbol of cultural pride in the era of the Black Power movement. "She's a sweet black angel," Jagger sang, "not a gun-totin' teacher, not a red-lovin' school mom."

Davis was openly communist and aligned herself with the Black Panthers when outraged California Governor Ronald Reagan targeted her for removal as a teacher at UCLA. She went into hiding in 1970 and landed on the FBI's "10 Most Wanted" list after being accused of aiding an attempted courtroom escape in Marin County that ended with four people dead. By the time of the album's release in June 1972, Davis had been captured at a Howard Johnson's motel in Manhattan and was awaiting trial. She was ultimately acquitted by a jury after a high-profile court battle that struggled with issues of class and race.

Along the way, Davis called for the overthrow of the US government and declared in her 1974 autobiography, "Jails and prisons are designed to break human beings, to convert the population into specimens in a zoo – obedient to our keepers, but dangerous to each other." That's tough talk for a jet-setting rock star to be embracing, though Jagger

> **" Rock and roll isn't protest, and never was… It promotes interfamilial tension… Now it can't even do that, because fathers don't ever get outraged with the music "**
> Mick Jagger

The final recording of 'Torn And Frayed' also marked a rare appearance on organ by trumpet-player Jim Price. It was typical of the often accidental nature of the Stones' creative process. During sessions for the song, listening to the band, Price was inspired to tap at a nearby Hammond organ. He didn't realize that he could be heard in the control room, and that Johns and Miller would decide to record it.

"There were a lot of rooms and all the different instruments were set up in separate rooms," says Price. "I went into that room, picked up the headphones and started listening, and just started playing the organ. It was just for fun. They did a bunch of takes on it, and I never knew that they had used it until I saw it on the record." Log another triumph for reckless abandon.

was likely more attracted to Davis as compelling feminine symbol – more smitten than engaged. It's doubtful, too, that Davis would have appreciated Jagger's other tribute to African-American women – 1978's 'Some Girls', which suggested that "black girls just want to fuck all night…"

Davis became the vice-presidential candidate of the US Communist party in 1980, and spent the Reagan–Thatcher era drifting into middle age. She travelled the world in support of civil disobedience, racial parity, the feminist and peace movements and the fight against apartheid in South Africa. Jagger, meanwhile, was occasionally spotted at the British House of Lords watching longingly from the gallery.

"Rock and roll isn't protest, and never was," Jagger told Rolling Stone in 1980. "It's NOT political… It promotes interfamilial tension. It USED to. Now it can't even do that, because fathers don't ever get outraged with the music… So rock and roll's GONE. It's all gone."

American radical Angela Davis was the inspiration for 'Sweet Black Angel'.

exile on main street

loving cup

Amidst all the tracks of grim foreboding on *Exile On Main Street*, the Rolling Stones find a hopeful vibe on this passionate estimation of the gospel sound. 'Loving Cup' was first heard in rough form at the Hyde Park concert in 1969.

By the time of this recording, Mick Jagger had clearly decided the song could do without any attempts at the exotic lingo of the Deep South. Instead, his delivery is natural and direct, and thus a more authentic reflection of the ancient musical influences that inspired him.

The track plays out against the bouncy piano uplift of Nicky Hopkins, as Jagger portrays the usual down-on-his-luck hustler, looking for some spiritual redemption in small favours. "Yes, I'm fumblin', and I know my car don't start," he sings. "Just one drink from your loving cup?"

Tough riffing and a sharp backbeat soon emerge in the mix, but retreat in time for a deep wheeze from the horns of Keys and Price, who probably played this brand of American soul for real back home.

happy

Keith Richards had clearly been a key creative force in virtually everything written and recorded by the Rolling Stones. He was no god-like lead guitar hero in the mould of Eric Clapton or Jimmy Page. But this was the man who had DREAMT the central riff and key phrase to '(Can't Get No) Satisfaction', no less. And during a relentless decade of work, Richards had refined the underappreciated fine art of rhythm guitar to spectacular new ends. Yet it is the casual, euphoric mess of 'Happy' that is so often seen as the Richards signature tune – the guitarist's special moment behind the mike on most of the band's subsequent tours. For fans, 'Happy' captured the reckless joy at Keith's core.

There is the usual rhythm pattern charged with attitude and drive. Richards' vocals are more ragged and thin on 'Happy' than on some of his other performances, but the spirit captured here is hard to resist, further uplifted with well-positioned harmonies from Jagger. "That was a lot of fun," says Andy Johns of the session. "It made us happy."

The initial session in France for 'Happy' was casual even by *Exile On Main Street's* standards: Richards sang, and played guitar and bass; on drums was Jimmy Miller, while Bobby Keys added some percussion. The horns were overdubbed later, says Johns, "and it really came to life."

The recording of 'Happy' was so effective that there was soon talk of a Keith Richards solo album. Not that Keith was interested in the idea. Further evidence of the possibilities of such a project emerged at the most casual of moments. Johns remembers some of those moments coming during the elaborate lunches the band and crew often shared at Richards' villa, where a French chef was hired to keep the rock and roll commune sated on the delicacies of his stuffed tomatoes, sautéed asparagus and other fine foods. "This guy would make this luncheon deal on a big table out on the terrace, gorgeous to look at, let alone eat," says Johns. "This guy was a genius, a real artist. You'd sit on this big terrace and look out on the Mediterranean, and all these big yachts.

Songwriters Jagger (opposite) and Richards (above) chronicled the world of decay and desperation they found themselves in by the early 1970s.

exile on main street

Then Keith would come down and go 'I wanna cheeseburger.' After these great lunches Keith would sit down on these steps that went down to the garden, and just bang around on his guitar and sing. He was just wonderful on his own."

Johns was among those who repeatedly told Richards he should make a record of his own. But Keith's response was always the same: "Well, if I did that I would just want to use the guys in the band, so it would be a Stones album. So what's the point?"

Over the next few years, Richards gradually began to entertain the idea. At one point, Richards and Johns even had a meeting to discuss a solo project, which would include some heavyweight sidemen that Johns had already approached. "We had talked about it on the phone several times," says Johns. "We were going to do this, it was going to happen." But their big meeting was inconclusive. "He had been up for three or four days, and was passed out. He only woke up for five minutes... And then he went back to sleep."

They met again in New York in 1976. "Yes, you're right, we're going to do this!" said Keith. Then nothing, until 1978, when Richards released a single of Chuck Berry's 'Run Run Rudolph' and Jimmy Cliff's 'The Harder They Fall' as a lark. This was right in the midst of the Stones' rebirth as a band via the acclaimed *Some Girls* album, so he was in no mood to strike out on his own. Not yet. Richards' debut as a solo artist wouldn't come until 1988, but by then the Stones' future seemed very much in doubt. Mick had forced the issue by releasing two solo albums of his own during a growing estrangement with Richards. Although his *Talk Is Cheap* was critically acclaimed (unlike the Jagger LPs), Keith was not a happy man in 1988. "I kept putting off making a solo album for a long time, because making it would mean that I had to admit to myself that I failed to keep my band together," Richards told the *Chicago Tribune* that year. "How am I going to play, without Charlie Watts to give me the beat?" It was a scenario unthinkable back in those days of decadence in the South of France.

> "I kept putting off making a solo album for a long time, because making it would mean that I had to admit to myself that I failed to keep my band together"
>
> Keith Richards speaking to the Chicago Tribune

turd on the run

The blood-hot hoodoo of 'Turd On the Run' features some of Jagger's most driving, hypnotic harp-playing. He sets in motion a twangy North Mississippi trance rhythm here in the tradition of the late blues immortal Fred McDowell – the composer of 'You Gotta Move', covered on *Sticky Fingers* – whose fine example taught a young Mick Jagger the crucial rules of sex and sorrow.

As Richards and Taylor send tears and fireballs from their guitars, Jagger plays and moans ominously, spitting out his lyrics on tortured love like a hyperactive hillbilly. Love, sex, diamonds, disease. The man's on his knees and crying – "I've lost a lot of love over you!" He's Mr Bad News on 'Turd On the Run,' rushing through these straight-ahead madman blues with raw, primal force. It's an utterly authentic recasting of the folk blues in the Stones' own image, played like some euphoric, mesmerizing revelation on the neglected roots of pop music.

During his wheezing moments blowing harmonica passages alongside Richards' acoustic chicken scratching, Jagger was at his most musically pure. "He's not thinking when he's playing harp," Keith told Lisa Robinson in 1989. "It comes from inside him. He always played like that, from the early days on."

ventilator blues

It wasn't just lingering vibes from the old blues immortals that cast a dark spell over the *Exile...* sessions. And Robert Johnson wasn't the only man ever said to have sold his soul to the devil. If the Stones were in search of inspiration regarding the dark side of the human soul, they need not have looked any further than Keith's fabulous villa, which served as a local Gestapo headquarters during the Nazi occupation of Vichy France during World War II. Visitors noticed the floor vents to the basement were in the shape of Swastikas. "I imagine that downstairs in the basement, where things were always peculiar – we had fires – is where they would interrogate prisoners," Johns told journalist Craig Rosen in 1994. "So God knows what sort of behaviour was going on down there." On this track Taylor earns his first and only co-writing credit on a Stones album. Jagger sings 'Don't fight it!" forcefully. According to Johns, the song was inspired by the real-life conditions there. Just one small window served the room where most of the band was set up, with a tiny electric fan spinning above Watts. Ventilation was at a minimum. "It would get very steamy down there," Johns says of that summer in the Mediterranean, "so we would have the ventilator blues."

Jumping Jack Flash: Mick Jagger captured in full flight.

just wanna see his face

This thumping, muddy track was another of the album's accidental ingredients. It began simply as a lo-fi recording of Jagger sitting in a chair singing while Keith played keyboards, and its deep echoes sound as if they were captured in some cavernous old cathedral. 'Just Wanna See His Face' was initially taped for reference, but the recording captured a haunting, soul-searching vibe that was worth preserving. Miller's percussion comes on like distant thunder. Both Taylor and Bill Plummer play low, rumbling bass-lines. And Jagger is practically scat singing here, moaning and grunting and mumbling about Jesus. The ghostly backing vocals were added later.

exile on main street

let it loose

There's no mistaking that voice on the other end of the line. Singer Tammi Lynn had heard it many, many times – the vaguely irritated New Orleans growl, rasping like Louie Armstrong with a migraine. "Hey, Tammi," her caller croaked into the phone. "Hey,

Tammi Lynn (above) was one of many backing vocalists the Stones used on *Exile On Main Street*.

man! Check this out…fuckin' session cat called me, said be at the session, gonna be a session and shit, I don't know who it is, let's meet down there."

This was, of course, Mr Mac Rebennack calling, otherwise known as Dr John Creaux, the Night Tripper, master of the voodoo blues, who had often called on young Tammi to sing on his own records.

Both shared a musical background rooted in the sounds of New Orleans, the same festering gumbo that spawned the Meters, Allen Toussaint and Professor Longhair. Although Dr John's only Top Ten American hit single – 'Right Place Wrong Time' – would not come until the following year, the singer-keyboardist had already been an established solo act since 1968. And when he travelled to England in 1971 to record his album *The Sun, Moon & Herbs*, he was joined by the likes of guests Mick Jagger and Eric Clapton.

Now Dr John was summoning Tammi Lynn down to Sunset Sound studios in Hollywood for another session. "He didn't tell me it was the Stones," Lynn says now. Not that it would have fazed her. She began her career as a jazz singer, bouncing from be-bop to Creole funk, and over subsequent years would appear on records by Wilson Pickett and Bob Dylan, among many others. When Lynn arrived at the session, she found not only the Rolling Stones in charge, but discovered she was to be part of a vocal group that also included veteran New Orleans R&B singer Shirley Goodman. During the 1950s, Goodman launched her career with Shirley & Lee, and enjoyed the hits 'Feel So Good' and 'Let The Good Times Roll'. (In the mid-seventies, Shirley & Company tapped into the disco craze with the breathy New Orleans funk of 'Shame, Shame, Shame'.)

Together, Lynn, Goodman and Dr John were among a half-dozen singers harmonizing until dawn. Lynn remembers working on four songs that night, though the singers are credited on *Exile On Main Street* only for the regretful gospel track 'Let It Loose'. Bathed under a soothing blast of horns, the gospel harmonies join the desperately pleading vocals of Jagger.

The basic track had been recorded at Olympic Studios in London months earlier, with the backing vocals added later at Sunset. "There was one particular line in something that was really raunchy," says Lynn of her night with the Stones. "It was a really, really raunchy line. I thought, We're out there, this is kind of good. This is like breaking all the rules." There was much common ground in the room that night between these singers, each of them exiles from London or New Orleans, which became obvious from Jagger's instructions to his makeshift choir. "What he wanted was this funk feeling, this real honest church feel. He had an appreciation for black music, and he said it openly," says Lynn, "so that was out of the way. We knew he had this affinity for the blues and where it came from. Wilson Pickett came clearly out of a church, out of a black experience. Mick came out of a respect for black experience, or black music. The greatness comes out of the spirit."

Years later, Dr John would grumble bitterly about the lack of credit the Stones had given to the richly talented players and singers he'd brought to the Los Angeles sessions. On 'Sweet Black Angel', the marimbas are mysteriously credited to "Amyl Nitrate", which Dr John insists should have gone to percussionist Richard Washington.

Lynn remembers the all-night session more fondly, describing it a quarter-century later as "very loose, very creative, very artistic." She adds, "When you're making music you don't know you're making history. You go in to have fun, you hang out all night and you party."

Her lasting impression of Richards is that of a quietly open player, absolutely honest and even humble, the furthest thing from a superstar. She'd had no contact with the Rolling Stones since then, other than bumping into Jagger years later at a Hollywood restaurant. But when the *Voodoo Lounge* tour passed through Los Angeles in 1994, Lynn left her front row seat at the Coliseum, and strolled up to the side gate. "I'd like to speak to Mick," she told the security guard, realizing she probably sounded like any other groupie crowded near the stage. Mentioning that she had appeared on *Exile On Main Street,* word got backstage to Richards, who had her sent to his dressing room. She noted that little had changed. "Keith just seems real human. He's a musician and he knows he's had a life that has had good and bad in it, and it's made him a better person for it."

After the concert, Richards sat amidst an ocean of food with friends and family. "It was very relaxed, laughing and talking about yesterday. He felt good."

> "Keith just seems real human… He's a musician and he knows he's had a life that has had the good and bad in it, and it's made him a better human for it"
>
> Tammi Lynn, backing singer

all down the line

ll that tape. All those months in France. Certainly the Rolling Stones had achieved SOMETHING. But just what? This was the question Jagger and Richards had begun to ask themselves when they arrived in Los Angeles to finish vocals and other bits and pieces for *Exile On Main Street*. No doubt, their new pals at Atlantic Records were asking much the same thing. The Glimmer Twins had long grown accustomed to working at their own pace, burning up time and tape like cigarettes as the band pounded away at some riff or bridge in search of that transcendent moment. In France, the only schedule that mattered was their own. And yet that internal pressure to put out a new single, to get back on the air, to maintain their presence in the ever-churning flow of pop culture hadn't faded from the early days.

So 'All Down the Line' was chosen, not because it was the track best suited for pop radio, but because it was the song closest to completion. Certainly, the song offered a driving rock sound, built on the charged chords of Richards, along with brief flashes of lead from Taylor. The elegant, blissful horns of Keys and Price mingle with a chorus of urgent backing vocals as Jagger inquires, "Won't you be my little baby for a while?" Soulful and rocking.

That musical balance was still a distant goal when Andy Johns was summoned to mix down the track in Los Angeles. The individual elements were ready when Johns and the band began work on the final mix, but it just wasn't coming together. After hours of ear-numbing work, Johns felt he was losing perspective. He muttered, "Too bad I can't hear this on the radio." Jagger replied, "Oh, we can do that." The singer handed Stu a copy of the tape, with directions to deliver it immediately to a local radio station. In late 1971, any Los Angeles rock broadcaster would have been ecstatic at the opportunity to preview a new Stones single for its audience, even in the middle of the night. So at about 2 am, Jagger, Richards, Watts and Johns climbed into a limousine for an early morning moonlight drive. "Next thing I know, I'm going up and down Sunset Boulevard, and one of the stations is playing it over the air so we can listen in the car," Johns says. "I still couldn't tell. It was a bit too surreal."

stop breaking down

If *Exile On Main Street* did not present Mick Taylor with the kind of showcase for epic lead playing that certain tracks on *Sticky Fingers* had, the double album's deep rock and blues canvas at least inspired some memorable flashes from the youngest Stone. 'Stop Breaking Down' was a leftover track from Olympic Studios that had captured Taylor's dynamic slide-guitar work.

"I learned a lot from Mick Taylor because he is such a beautiful musician," Richards told *Guitar Player* magazine in 1977. "I mean, when he was with us, it was a time when there was probably more distinction, let's say, between rhythm guitar and lead guitar than at any other time in the Stones. The thing with musicians as fluid as Mick Taylor is that it's hard to keep their interest. They get bored, especially in such a necessarily restricted and limited music as rock and roll. That is the whole fascination with rock and roll and blues... how far you can take those limitations and still come up with something new."

Besides Taylor, another key element on 'Stop Breaking Down' was a keyboard performance by Ian Stewart. It was one of only three appearances on the album for the man who had been ejected from the Rollin' Stones for essentially looking too square. And he didn't seem much different now, looking like a rugby coach in his golf shirts amidst the storm cloud of sex, drugs and rock and roll that was Stones. Stu was a pillar of strength under such circumstances, and always welcome on band recordings. A song like 'Stop Breaking Down' was well-suited to his passionate boogie-woogie rolls. Stu was around for most of the sessions, but as a player he often just didn't seem interested. Most of the keyboard work was left to Nicky Hopkins. One time during the sessions in France, Johns suggested to Jagger that Stewart was perfect for a particular track. Why not have him play? "Oh, well, if you can." Jagger replied. When Johns approached Stewart, the road manager huffed: "No, I'm not playing for those fucking bastards anymore. They never fucking pay me! All the hits I've played on..." In the end, of course, Stu played.

"They had a very weird relationship," says Johns. "Stu dressed very straight, was very down to earth, loved the band, but when everything was going wrong Stu would stand firm in the centre of the eye of the hurricane. If they couldn't tell what they were doing, they'd ask Stu 'How's it going?' And he'd go: 'A load of fucking rubbish! Sounds like a bunch of fairies playing!' They'd laugh and pretend not to take any notice, but they would listen to Stu, because he'd been there forever."

> **" I learned a lot from Mick Taylor because he is such a beautiful musician "**
>
> Keith Richards

exile on main street

shine a light

Mick Jagger was once asked in the pages of *Creem* magazine if he would rather have been born a black man. "Yes, perhaps so," the singer replied, if only half-seriously. Blues, reggae, R&B, rock and roll – all of them had come out of the African experience, and all would forever fascinate Jagger and the Stones. Yet by 1971, the band was no longer simply copying the examples of Muddy Waters and James Brown and Chuck Berry. On *Exile On Main Street*, the Rolling Stones were playing music that still owed much to those forefathers, but it was also a sound they had made indelibly their own. There is an ease and understanding demonstrated on this album. Tracks like 'Shine A Light' and 'Let It Loose' reveal gospel elements that are noticeably earthier and deeper. A profound spirituality is at work within the harmony vocals that was missing on the lush chorale sounds of such earlier recordings as 'Salt Of The Earth' and 'You Can't Always Get What You Want.' With 'Shine A Light', the Stones leaned heavily on the organ sounds of Billy Preston, who was a prominent collaborator during the band's albums and tours of the early 1970s. "He had that gospel feel, you know, which Nicky didn't have," says Johns, who worked with Preston years earlier for the keyboardist's first solo sessions for the Beatles' Apple label. "He became pals with them. Billy was part of the scene back then because he'd been on Apple. Billy was always hanging out, and they liked the idea of that gospel thing."

The man with the mighty organ: Billy Preston graced albums by the Stones and the Beatles.

soul survivor

The final moments of *Exile On Main Street* hinge on a sharp, edgy guitar riff that rolls on endlessly like a tape loop. Jagger may shout religiously above the fray, but it is the relentless chord pattern that keeps the tune in motion. That 'Soul Survivor' retains so much energy within such a limited – if dynamic – pattern says much about the rhythmic power in the hands of Keith Richards.

"If you want to understand Keith Richards' guitar playing, you watch him play snooker," says engineer George Chkaintz, who worked often with the Stones. "He has some difficulty in keeping any of the balls on the table. It's just extraordinary to see the way the point of decision happens with him. And he recognizes that as a weakness in his game of snooker. But it is absolutely explosive."

It's evident also in the guitarist's snakey, almost self-absorbed moves on stage, where Richards' instrument appears like just another physical part of himself – another appendage, much like John Coltrane's tenor sax. Richards is the sort of extremist who will strum a guitar until his fingers are bleeding all over the damn floor. It is that utter commitment that inevitably led to the twisted greatness of *Exile On Main Street*.

There would be more important peaks in the band's career, scattered across such albums as *Some Girls* and *Tattoo You,* and on selected tracks all the way up through the 1990s, despite the growing distractions of middle age and competing interests. But *Exile On Main Street* was the high water mark for the Rolling Stones. And what came after would never mean quite so much.

chapter eleven

1973 goats head soup

In with the in-crowd: Mick Jagger and his celebrity pals keep the bubbles flowing.

Dancing With Mr D

100 Years Ago

Coming Down Again

Doo Doo Doo Doo Doo (Heartbreaker)

Angie

Silver Train

Hide Your Love

Winter

Can You Hear The Music

Star Star

itness as a new era begins for the fabulous Rolling Stones, a band whose legend was secure, and a band with nothing left to prove. Or so they believed. Jagger and Richards had entered the 1970s as one of the most powerful forces in rock, riding a crest of popular and critical acclaim for their every move, their every guitar riff and inflammatory lyric. Now what? Decay. The brilliant recklessness that had made *Exile On Main Street* such a profound and chilling return to the rawest blues and country imaginable had all of a sudden descended into rock-star befuddlement.

Goats Head Soup was not without its charms. A handful of tracks do shine through the haze, but the Stones had clearly fallen prey to distraction. By now, Jagger had lost whatever connection he might have had with the middle-class Bohemianism that had guided his best early work, succumbing instead to the alarming "Jet-set" world of Lady Bianca. And what should have been a continuation of the band's most creative period was seriously hobbled by the further encroachment of heroin into the life of Richards. It was not simply decadence that knocked the Stones off-balance, but a sudden lack of will. In 1973, the attitude of the Glimmer Twins seemed to be saying "we've done it." Jagger later described the general mood of the band as "...general malaise. I think we got a bit carried away with our own popularity and so on. It was a bit of a holiday period."

Consequently, a mild atrocity like the new album's 'Dancing With Mr D' only demonstrated a failure of the imagination, leaning heavily on old ideas about evil and danger that had inevitably lost their edge the third or fourth time around. However, the mystery is why this deterioration came so soon after the band's creative peak, even if they were hardly the only major artists from the 1960s to stumble awkwardly into the new decade. But although John Lennon's *Mind Games* and Paul McCartney's *Red Rose Speedway* were both arguably their weakest albums, this was hardly true of their entire generation. Pete Townshend remained an ambitious voice, confirmed by the Who's recording of *Quadrophenia*. And the epic Led Zeppelin had emerged from the ashes of the Yardbirds to create a sound and vision of ominous power that even the Stones could not deny. The title of "World's Greatest Rock And Roll Band" was already beginning to ring hollow.

"This album will be less freaky, more melodic than the last one," Jagger promised *Rolling Stone* magazine in January 1973, during the making of *Goats Head Soup*. "We've recorded a lot of fast numbers already, maybe too many."

Fast or slow hardly mattered. When the Stones arrived in Jamaica for the *Goats Head Soup* sessions, heroin was the increasing obsession of Keith and other members of the Stones' entourage. The Stones had sought the isolation of Jamaica to escape the distractions of home, to allow them to work without interruption. Drug habits were harder to shake. "Consequently, those sessions weren't quite as much fun," Johns remembers now. "And there are a couple of examples on there where just the basic tracks we kept weren't really up to standard. People were accepting things perhaps that weren't up to standard because they were a little higher than normal. But there still are some fantastic things on there. There really are some jolly good moments."

The band and and crew shared a hotel in Kingston, an old mansion called the Terra Nova, which was the family home of Island Records founder Chris Blackwell. They all ate breakfast together, but it wasn't quite a repeat of the communal feeling of the *Exile On Main Street* sessions in the South of France. Bobby Keys, for one, had been left behind – he would overdub his sax parts later. Sessions were recorded at Dynamic Sound Studios, a facility run by bandleader and producer Byron Lee, and where reggae singer Jimmy Cliff recorded his big-selling *Wonderful World, Beautiful People* album. But *Goats Head Soup* never tapped into the rich musical legacy surrounding the Stones in Jamaica. In 1973, Bob Marley and the Wailers would release the politically charged reggae

> " I think we got a bit carried away with our own popularity... it was a bit of a holiday period "
>
> Keith Richards on 'Goats Head Soup'

albums *Catch A Fire* and *Burnin'*, featuring a deep rhythm that wouldn't infect the Stones' sound until 'Luxury' the following year. After that, reggae would remain a permanent part of their repertoire.

Johns was sent ahead to Jamaica before the sessions to prepare the studio for the Stones' arrival. He discovered a good working area, but also a control room that was less than state-of-the-art. Speakers were strangely positioned, there were no sound screens to separate individual musicians, no grand piano or Hammond B3 organ, and some of the equipment was inadequate for the band's needs. Nonetheless, the studio's management agreed to provide the improvements, and Johns returned home. "Of course, I show up with the band two months later and none of this shit's been done," Johns says. "They work on a completely different time scale down there. After we were down there for two or three months, some of these things started to appear. So on the last day we had everything, when it was too late."

More disturbing was a vibe of violence that seemed to hover over the studio. "My assistant was telling of these nightmares about these guys hacking each other to death in the studio with these fucking machetes when they have arguments," says Johns. "The bass player would go over to his bass case and he'd have a machete, the other guy would have a fucking gun, and they'd go at it."

The Stones entourage suffered their own taste of that violence one night about six weeks into the recording, when a man with a knife broke into Bill Wyman's hotel room. The intruder demanded money and ordered Wyman underneath the bed. He then raped Wyman's longtime girlfriend, Astrid Lündstrom. Minutes later, Johns heard a knock on his door. It was Astrid. "Oh Andy, you'll never guess," she told Johns. "I've just been raped!"

> **"Throughout most of the seventies, I was living in another world from him...it kind of got up my nose a bit, that jet-set shit"**
>
> Keith Richards on Mick Jagger

Alarming news, and yet she seemed so clear-headed, says Johns, who was standing shoeless and in his shorts in the doorway. The engineer immediately grabbed some heavy object to use as a weapon and ran outside and down the road, cutting his feet on broken glass. But the rapist had escaped across the lawn in another direction. "Bill, obviously, was totally freaked because he'd had to lie under the bed while all of this went on," says Johns. "If he had done anything the guy would have cut his fucking head off. He really didn't have any fucking choice. It was a tough thing. It was another Rolling Stones thing. Shit like that was always going on. There was always something bizarre happening. There were some very unfair comments like 'Why didn't Bill do something? What a fucking weed!' Which I thought was totally uncool and uncalled for."

That kind of tension was often felt elsewhere within the band, as even Jagger and Richards drifted apart. Keith was lost to his drugs, Jagger to high society. In celebration of his glittery lifestyle, the singer would soon have a diamond planted into his front tooth. Marvellous!

"Throughout most of the seventies, I was living in another world from him," Richards told Kurt Loder in 1987. "I didn't blame him – he'd earned the right to do whatever he wanted. It was just that I couldn't relate to that...it kind of got up my nose a bit, that jet-set shit and, like, the flaunting of it. But he's a lonely guy, too. He's got his own problems, you know?"

Bill and Astrid moved into another hotel, and the sessions continued. The ultimate result was little more than a few energetic singles, and an album that inadvertently documented the uncertain focus of a once-great unit. Time was also an issue. While the Stones spent a year working on *Exile On Main Street*, the band this time was churning out the material much faster. Among the songs recorded just in their first month in Jamaica were 'Angie', 'Star Star' and 'Coming Down Again'. Also recorded during this same period was 'Waiting On A Friend', which wouldn't emerge until 1981's *Tattoo You*.

"I didn't think there was any one song on there that really stood out," says Bobby Keys, whose saxophone solos were not enough to lift the album's spirits. "I thought *Goats Head Soup* was kind of bland, shall I say, after *Exile On Main Street*."

Goats Head Soup would also mark the final appearance of Jimmy Miller as producer. When it came time for the Stones to record *It's Only Rock And Roll* the following year, his services were no longer required. It was the end of an important era for the band, which had recorded its greatest works, from *Beggars Banquet* to *Exile On Main Street*, with the producer. "When they first started working with him, he was a lot of help," Johns says of Miller. "Then after a year or two, they kind of used Jimmy for what they wanted, and learned Jimmy's tricks, and started shutting him out a bit. So by the time of *Exile On Main Street* they weren't listening to Jimmy very much, and it did him in. They weren't really being rude, but they would ignore him a lot more than he would have liked."

It would be a near-tragic fall for Miller, the Brooklyn-born percussionist and producer who had co-authored the Spencer Davis Group's 'I'm A Man' and produced classic albums by Traffic and Blind Faith. He would produce only a handful of records over the next two decades, before his death from liver disease in 1994. After the Stones, Miller worked with the likes of Motorhead and Johnny Thunders. Hardcore characters to be sure. But the Stones had left him shaken, and forever changed. "Jimmy," Keith later told *Crawdaddy* magazine, "went in a lion and came out a lamb. We wore him out completely. Same with Andrew Loog Oldham. Burned out like a light bulb. Andrew wanted to be Phil Spector, meanwhile I'm screwing his wife, nobody gives a shit and it's just…just ridiculous." Miller was neither the first nor the last casualty of the Rolling Stones.

> "I thought *Goats Head Soup* was kind of bland, shall I say, after *Exile On Main Street*"
>
> Bobby Keys, sax player

dancing with mr d

ere comes Mick Jagger, a man of unquestionable wealth and taste, who by 1973 had indeed been around for many a long, long year. Stolen many a man's soul and faith? Maybe. But if anyone still believed that Mr J was in fact a sympathetic soldier for Satan, then the cartoonish 'Dancing With Mr D' must have been very enlightening indeed.

It's not a bad rock track by any standard other than their own, but the song inevitably suffers from comparison to 1968's chilling 'Sympathy For The Devil', which examined the darker corners of the human soul across a riveting samba beat. In those days, Jagger boasted of dark events from history, such as war, assassination and crucifixion. The effectiveness of the song could be measured by the numbers of listeners who truly feared that Jagger was promoting black magic and violence. By contrast, 'Dancing With Mr D' is a tale best told on Halloween.

Mick sings of traipsing around a graveyard, and being confronted by Mr D himself, a big-shot with a necktie made of human skulls – images more appropriate to the likes of horror novelists H.P. Lovecraft or Clive Barker. Nothing to fear here.

On 'Sympathy For The Devil', Jagger taunted his listeners with "Pleased to meet you, hope you guessed my name". This time, Jagger breathlessly sings, "Now I know his name, he's called Mister D, and one of these days he's gonna set you free." Silly, although no more ridiculous than the theatrics of Alice Cooper from the same era or the laughable death metal bands that emerged in the 1980s. At least '…Mr D' rocked convincingly.

For the Jamaican 'Dancing With Mr D' sessions, the Stones once again travelled down that dark road to the ominous funk of a sharp Keith Richards riff, a sound that later bands such as the Black Crowes would imitate endlessly. By now, though, this was

goats head soup

merely coasting for the vampire guitarist. The riff's arch tone hints at evil, but never fully delivers.

Thus, the opening shot on *Goats Head Soup* at once represented everything that was right and wrong with the Rolling Stones in the middle of the 1970s. The band's continued ability to conjure up at least a handful of driving rock tunes was enough to make it a third straight number one album on both sides of the Atlantic. But critics only heard failure, finding professionalism where there had once been profound inspiration. It's a verdict that the Stones themselves would later come to agree with.

100 years ago

Billy Preston's clavinet gave a new dimension to the Stones' sound.

These were strange days for the Stones. With their rock and roll heroes of the fifties now virtually irrelevant and a new generation of pop voices fast emerging, the Stones stood in the early 1970s as lonely journeymen of rock. Was their best behind them?

Jagger seemed to ponder this question on '100 Years Ago', a dissatisfying funk rocker that still included lyrics of real soul-searching. Even if the Stones' music on *Goats Head Soup* was falling out of focus, Jagger proved he could still pen lyrics that cut directly to personal experience when he sang "Don't you think it's sometimes wise not to grow up?"

His vocals are slurred, laid across the fluid jazz-rock of Mick Taylor, mingling with the ultrahip clavinet melodies of Billy Preston. The music is launched promisingly with driving mid-tempo funk, but it never fully erupts, even during a Taylor solo windout that's buried too deep in the mix to connect. The Stones would have better luck with funk in subsequent years, probing that seething rhythm more convincingly with the albums *Black And Blue* and *Some Girls*.

coming down again

This is Keith Richards at his most tough AND vulnerable. It's a sensuous declaration of self, and of an imperfect lifestyle of love he shows no interest in abandoning. And that's just the way it is, darlin'!

'Coming Down Again' opens with a lilting piano melody played by Nicky Hopkins, but quickly descends to a slow junkie's pace, rolling along Keith's lethargic wah-wah playing. Likewise, Keith's lead vocals emerge in an exhausted tone, far from the ragged euphoria of 'Happy'. He's joined by Mick on quiet harmonies. If Richards often let Mick do the talking on the raunchier cuts, here the guitarist shows he can be as nasty as he wants to be with sexual innuendo: "Slipped my tongue in someone else's pie".

The track would be hopelessly weighted down by its numbing pace if not for a pair of muted, overlapping sax solos by Bobby Keys at the bridge. Although Keys had been present for the recording of basic tracks for *Exile On Main Street* in Keith's basement in the South of France, his parts on *Goats Head Soup* would be added long after the Stones had left Jamaica. Keys explains: "Keith and Mick get together before they go into the studio and write. Their writing can consist of just coming up with little pieces, ideas, riffs here and there. They'll go in the studio and put something down. When they cut an album they cut quite a few tracks, and then go back and review it and see what fits together. And then they decide what needs strings or voices or horns or whatever. My part of the recording usually comes at the very tail end of it."

goats head soup

doo doo doo doo doo
(heartbreaker)

'Doo Doo Doo Doo Doo (Heartbreaker)' is not exactly social commentary – at least not in the traditional sense. But Mick Jagger skilfully exploits some inflammatory subject matter to create the most potent rock track on *Goats Head Soup*. The song opens with a scene of urban violence, as New York City Police kill an unarmed youth in a case of mistaken identity. Jagger sings angrily "Heartbreaker with your forty-four, I wanna tear your world apart!" He goes on to describe a 10-year-old girl sticking hypodermic needles into her arm, only later to be found dead in an alley. It's all grist for Mick's pumped-up rock and roll shouting – his own view on the deeper implications of these matters is left inconclusive.

The power of the song owes much to the duelling guitar attack of Richards and Taylor, along with the driving piano of Billy Preston. But the element that finally uplifts the track is a fitting blast of horns arranged by trumpeter Jim Price and overdubbed later. It would mark Price's final appearance on a Stones recording project. He would soon embark on a career producing the likes of Joe Cocker, Herbie Hancock and Wayne Shorter.

The song become a hit single in America, but the prospects of 'Doo Doo Doo Doo Doo (Heartbreaker)' were far from certain back in Jamaica. "The track was really out of tune," Andy Johns told journalist Craig Rosen in 1994. "Everyone was so out of it that instead of recutting the track, Keith spent four months trying to get the bass in tune, and there was no way to make it work, because the electric piano and the guitar were out of tune with each other. Things were getting a little fuzzy there."

David and Angie Bowie. Did she inspire Jagger?

angie

'Angie' stands as one of the most tender ballads in the Stones catalogue. In 1973, that was almost like a throwback to another era. The delicate acoustic guitar, Jagger's wounded, yearning tone, the romantic subject, all had more in common with earlier Jagger/Richards compositions like 'As Tears Go By' than with the charged rock sound the band had perfected by the early 1970s. A song that was heartfelt AND pretty is not what most listeners now expected from a band best known for cynicism and danger.

There were early rumours that 'Angie' was dedicated to Angela Bowie, and her marriage to Jagger's new friend David Bowie. But a close reading

of the song suggests something much closer to Jagger's personal experience. In a promotional video made for the song, Jagger is seen in white silky threads, singing "Baby, dry your eyes… ain't it good to be alive…they can't say we never tried".

It's a sentiment that could easily have been inspired by Jagger's relationship with Marianne Faithfull. Once considered among London's most daring artistic couples, their relationship had finally collapsed in 1969 after an endless storm of troubles, which included a miscarriage, repeated drug busts and an attempted suicide.

Whatever the source material, the song struck a chord with listeners. The single of 'Angie' hit No. 2 in the UK, and topped the charts in the US.

silver train

The Stones recorded 'Silver Train' at Island Studios in London, seemingly inspired to reconnect with some chugging blues rock. And who better to send the boys along than that erstwhile Stone, Ian Stewart? His spirited boogie-woogie keyboard work is joined here by the slippery bottleneck of Taylor and the frantic harp-playing of Jagger, who blows a stirring train whistle between lyrics describing another jolly encounter with a prostitute.

Hearing an early take of the song, Texan blues-rocker Johnny Winter was sufficiently smitten to record his own version. Appearing on his *Still Alive And Well* album of March 1973, Winter's take of 'Silver Train' hit the streets months before *Goats Head Soup* was released.

hide your love

Basic tracks for much of *Goats Head Soup* were recorded back in Jamaica, but the crucial overdubs of horns and vocals were largely completed in England. One day at Olympic Studios, Jagger was sitting at a piano, killing time between tracking sessions.

"He was banging away at the piano and it sounded really cool," remembers Andy Johns. "Fuck, I'm going to tape this, because we could turn this into something later, you know? I said 'Come on man, let's do a whole pass on that, because you can use this. This is a really good vibe.'"

Jagger continued playing his lumbering piano melody, a sound with roots in gospel, and not unlike some of the most casual bits and pieces of *Exile On Main Street*. Johns played the tape for Mick and Jimmy Miller a week later, and both agreed it was worth exploring. Mick Taylor added a bluesy guitar lead, Miller a bass drum. Hand claps were also brought into the mix, as Jagger again adopted the tone of a country preacher, testifying to his woman, shouting and rhyming lyrics that often sound improvised: "Oh, babe, I'm sinking, I wanna cry, well I've been drinking, but now I'm dry."

A close listen reveals a small voice in the distance that sounds suspiciously like Jagger. Though his proper vocals were later overdubbed, his singing during the recording of the basic track had bled into the piano microphone. At last, a touch of *Exile On Main Street*'s recklessness.

> **"He was banging away at the piano and it sounded really cool"**
> Andy Johns on Mick Jagger

winter

inter' was the first track cut in Jamaica for *Goats Head Soup*, and one of two tracks on the album recorded without Keith Richards. This left the track wide open for the kind of fluid melodies Mick Taylor had first explored on 'Sway' and 'Moonlight Mile' from *Sticky Fingers*. Though a less inspired composition than those 1971 recordings, 'Winter' reaches for the same epic heights.

Mick Jagger sings here like a man cast adrift, yearning wistfully for a failed romance: "It sure has been a cold, cold winter, and the light of love is all burned out".

It's a rare moment of vulnerability from the singer, and it's played out against an epic soundscape of strings and guitar. Taylor's rich leadwork flows in and out of a lush bed of strings arranged by Nicky Harrison. As with 'Angie', the song stood in 1973 as a monument to the Stones' ability to craft a tender ballad, even as the band's overall sound and purpose seemed to unravel. Andy Johns today calls the song "one of the best things they ever did".

Apart from the song's musical value, 'Winter' also demonstated a human side of Johns' rock and roll paymasters, in spite of their well-deserved reputation for bitchiness. Shortly, before travelling with the Stones to Jamaica, Johns was producing an album with Jack Bruce, with whom Johns shared an apartment on New York's Park Avenue. After a night of debauchery, Johns awoke to find one of his arms numb, and the feeling wasn't coming back. Johns told Jagger about his arm, and offered to bail out of the *Goats Head Soup* sessions. "That's bullshit," Jagger told him. "You're coming. Look, it's all in your head anyway. I bet you get better real soon." A few days into the sessions, and just as they were finishing 'Winter', the feeling in his arm returned.

Several weeks later, the band and crew were working toward their Christmas break, which was still two weeks away. "Stu comes in, and he goes, 'I've got some really bad news: Your father is dying and he's asking to see you.' Mick put his arms around me and he says, 'We'll just stop now, you go home and see you're dad.'"

For Johns, whose father ultimately died of colon cancer, these were surprising signals of humanity from these notorious princes of darkness. "Which was unlike them. Their loyalty thing didn't stretch very far," Johns says with a laugh of the band he first met as the 14-year-old brother of engineer Glyn Johns. "They used to use people up very like a consumer society with their minions."

Mick Jagger tries hard to look cool in 1973.

goats head soup

can you hear the music

'Can You Hear The Music' sums up the problems that the Stones faced in the middle of the 1970s: self-indulgence, aimlessness and pointlessness. It would have fitted well within the psychedelic mishmash of 1967's *Their Satanic Majesties Request*, if that album hadn't been so energetic and memorable by comparison.

'Can You Hear The Music' opens with the delicate clamour of a ringing bell, percussion and the lilting flute of Jim Horn. They're soon swallowed up by spacey wah-wah guitar and Jagger moaning in a strangely nagging tone about his love for music. It emerges rather like an unfinished work-in-progress, with an odd clash of aesthetics. While *Their Satanic Majesties Requests* rightly built its psychedelic tripping on a solid pure-pop base, Jagger perversely chooses to sing here in a mush-mouthed bluesman's voice. It's an aggressively ethereal package best enjoyed with an unclear head.

Jagger can be heard singing "When you hear the music floating in the air, can you feel the magic?" That's an idealistic sentiment, coming as it did at a time when the music itself seemed to be losing the purpose and conviction the Rolling Stones once epitomized.

star star

Even groupies need an anthem. And who better qualified to document their comings and goings, their acrobatic skills and unique hygienic habits, than Mick Jagger? This was, after all, the same man listed as "number one on my far-fetched fuck list" by proto-groupie Pamela Des Barres. By 1973, groupies had long been part of the scenery. "Groupies? Oh yeah, man," Bobby Keys remembers. "In the early seventies? Like flies."

Des Barres was known throughout the sixties and seventies as Miss Pamela, a member of Frank Zappa's all-female GTOs (Girls Together Outrageous) "band" of fellow groupie chicks. Her eventual conquests included Jimmy Page, Keith Moon and Waylon Jennings, according to her 1987 book *I'm With The Band*. Her diary entry for November 25, 1969, reads: "I am extremely happy. I slept with Mr Jagger last night, and we got along SO well; honesty, freedom and joy. Genuine. I helped him pack his seven suitcases, and he gave me some lovely clothes... The sexual experience was quite a joy."

So 'Star Star' was not just another song about girls. Originally entitled 'Starfucker', the tune told the story of the young girls whose men of choice are rock stars and movie stars. To the sounds of some rowdy Chuck Berry riffing, Jagger sings of a groupie "giving head to Steve McQueen", betting that she'll "get John Wayne before he dies".

Not everyone was happy about the song. Atlantic Records chief Ahmet Ertegun was aghast, and insisted that the song title at least be changed to the innocuous 'Star Star'. Sheet music at the time changed the word "Starfucker", used extensively in the chorus, to the laughably censored "Starbucker".

"At the time it was seen as incredibly outrageous," says Andy Johns. "To actually say 'FUCK' on a record. Nobody did that much, especially a record Mick knew was going to be a big record."

> "Groupies? Oh yeah, man...in the early seventies? Like flies"
>
> Bobby Keys, sax player

goats head soup

When *Goats Head Soup* was finally released in August 1973, 'Star Star' immediately won the attention of enraged feminists. In the context of so much of the Stones catalogue, 'Star Star' was seen as just another misogynistic attack. Miss Pamela may have called herself a "freewheeling feminist", but hers was not a brand of feminism that all women could rally around.

Jagger was unrepentant: "That's real, and if girls can do that, I can certainly write about it because it's what I see," Jagger told *Rolling Stone* in 1978. "I'm not saying all women are star-fuckers, but I see an awful lot of them, and so I write song called that. I mean, people show themselves up by their own behaviour, and just to describe it doesn't mean you're anti-feminist."

Jagger had worked up a demo of the song in Jamaica the night before recording, with Johns playing bass. The greatest challenge came months later, when an Atlantic representative paid a visit to Johns. Apparently, John Wayne had refused to give permission to include his name on the record. "Andy," the Atlantic man told him, "we've got to cover up this thing where it says John Wayne, otherwise we can't release the record." Johns then put a light repeat echo effect over the Wayne reference, and convinced the label rep that the average person would not be able to make it out. He lied. "Of course, when it came out you could still hear John Wayne," says Johns. "I was always happy about that." The CD reissue of *Goats Head Soup*, saw the band return to the original clearer version.

"That's the only song with any slice of cynicism," Mick explained to *Rolling Stone* in 1973. "All the others are into beauty. It's very hard to write about those primitive emotions without being cynical about it – that's when you sound old. I mean, if you can't go into a coffee shop and sort of fall in love with every glass of coffee, and listen to the jukebox – that's difficult to portray in a song."

The controversy did not end with the album release. When the Rolling Stones went on tour in 1975, Jagger's performance of the song was accompanied by a giant inflatable phallus, much to the horror of proper authorities everywhere. "Police chiefs were waiting for it all over America," Keith Richards said later. "It was like a dare."

The band's willingness to document their lifestyle only went so far, which acclaimed photographer and film-maker Robert Frank discovered with his brutal documentary of the band's 1972 tour. Entitled *Cocksucker Blues* (after an unreleasable song of the same name recorded by the Stones), the film captured a world of sex and drugs in graphic fashion. *Cocksucker Blues* also captured moments of musical euphoria, including a duet of Mick Jagger and Stevie Wonder performing 'Satisfaction'. More notorious were scenes aboard their private tour jet, which showed the road crew stripping several groupies naked. After seeing the finished product, the Stones refused to allow the release of the film.

Cocksucker Blues has been seen infrequently ever since, mainly at unannounced screenings at small independent theatres and on college campuses. "What goes on on the tour was worse than what you see," Frank said at a 1976 screening. The tour, he continued, "was a hard trip to survive, but I was never disgusted. I didn't follow the whole tour – you get involved in a trip like this and you get so strung out it's impossible to work...and it shows. I'm told that Keith Richards liked the film, but his attitude is, he doesn't really care. He liked it better than Jagger."

Among such attempts to document the everyday debauchery of life with the Stones, it's those moments with the groupies on the airplane that remain the most memorable. "That wasn't typical. That was staged," insists Bobby Keys, a regular presence on most Stones tours during the 1970s. "Those chicks were brought on my a couple of the guys who handled the luggage. Robert Frank was wanting some material for his movie. That shit didn't really happen. It doesn't portray a totally wrong impression, but we didn't carry chicks around all the time, grab 'em up, take 'em on a plane and take their clothes off."

Jagger finds himself under perpetual assault from groupies. And that's just the way he likes it.

chapter twelve

1974 it's only rock 'n' roll

If You Can't Rock Me

Ain't Too Proud To Beg
(WHITFIELD/HOLLAND)

It's Only Rock 'N' Roll
(But I Like It)

Till The Next Goodbye

Time Waits For No One

Luxury

Dance Little Sister

If You Really Want To Be My Friend

Short And Curlies

Fingerprint File

In 1974, 31 was a grand old age for a rock star. But did Mick really think he'd still be doing the same thing 20 years later?

Why argue with success? In 1974, the magnificent Rolling Stones were the most beloved, feared, studied, praised and hated rock and roll band in the universe. *Goats Head Soup* was their third consecutive transatlantic No. 1 album, with more destined to come. They were the kings of rock, the potentates of pop, sitting pretty on a throne so secure that not even the Who or Led Zeppelin could claim it.

But the Stones knew better. Or at least Mick did. The singer probably hadn't been fully satisfied by a Stones record since *Let It Bleed*. Soon enough he would realize (and speak about it openly) that *Goats Head Soup* was the band's weakest album since 1967's *Their Satanic Majesties Request*. At least they were still trying in those crazy psychedelic days, making a record that is still worth a listen as a failed crackpot experiment gone half-wrong. Now they were beginning their second decade as a band, too often just going through the motions and hoping their ideas would be enough when execution failed them.

It's Only Rock 'N' Roll offered some improvement, a slight glimmer in the morass that the Stones had allowed themselves to become. Engineer Andy Johns remembers the sessions for the album as being even more submerged in drugs than *Goats Head Soup*, but there was a more consistent energy at work here. The hooks are sharper and the playing is more animated. Junior partner Mick Taylor's typically elegant playing on 'Time Waits For No One' is filled with troubled assurance and subtle regret. Not that the entire album reaches those heights.

It's Only Rock 'N' Roll is a great title for a concept album the Stones were uniquely qualified to make but never did. Instead, it's just the Stones following their usual formulas once again. Jagger does touch on the possibilities on the title track, briefly exploring the sick love-hate relationship the band had developed with its audience – "If I could stick a knife in my heart, suicide right on stage, would it satisfy ya?" – but the possibilities are largely left unfulfilled. Leave the concept albums to Pete Townshend.

A full recovery would not come to the Stones until *Black And Blue* the following year. And who would notice anyway? Many fans had undoubtedly preferred *Goats Head Soup* to the rough-hewn mess of *Exile On Main Street*, which had little of the slick good-time boogie of 'Doo Doo Doo Doo Doo (Heartbreaker)'. This meant that Keef could continue chopping out the same brand of riff-rock he mastered with 'Jumpin' Jack Flash' and 'Brown Sugar', even if the time to move on had long since passed.

Keith's worsening drug habits prevented much else, but the ramifications were growing ever more profound. His pal Gram Parsons had just overdosed in the California desert. Overindulgence, too, was partially to blame for the recent banishment of producer Jimmy Miller. And now Keith and Anita were banned from entering France for two years and each fined 5,000 francs, the result of a bust at Richards' villa in the South of France.

Trouble also brewed elsewhere in the band. Creative frustration had finally led Bill Wyman to release *Monkey Grip*, his first solo album, the previous May. More serious, however, was Mick Taylor's growing estrangement from the band, just as he had begun to assert himself. His guitar playing had deeply impacted the direction of the Stones over the previous five years, but he had only been awarded one co-writing credit – 'Ventilator Blues' from *Exile On Main Street*. And the guitarist had grown increasingly particular about how he played. During album sessions at Musicland Studios in Munich, West Germany, Taylor often arrived early to record a bass overdub or try some other idea he had for a track. Keith usually erased them later.

"I don't know that Mick Taylor ever really fit in," remembers George Chkiantz, who engineered the overdubs for the album back in England. "In a sense, he was almost more of an outsider than Nicky Hopkins." In Munich, Johns remembers the Stones playing at a session when Richards suddenly turned to Taylor and said, "Fuck you! You play too loud. You're really good live, but you're no good in the studio. So you can play later."

> "I don't know that Mick Taylor ever really fit in"
> — George Chkiantz, engineer

it's only rock 'n' roll

Johns and Taylor were about the same age, in their mid-twenties, and had by then spent a lot of time together, most recently hanging out during the 1973 European tour and at the Jamaica sessions for *Goats Head Soup*. In Munich, Johns says, "He was whining and moaning: 'I never get to do what I want, and I don't think I'm going to be able to do this much longer'. And I'm going, 'What are you crazy?! You're going to quit the Stones? You're out of your fucking mind!'"

Before *It's Only Rock 'N' Roll* was finished, Johns' own heroin problem had grown so severe that he wasn't invited back to the sessions after the holiday break. He eventually went to work for Jack Bruce, formerly singer and bassist with Cream, who was then organizing a new band. Johns called Taylor. "Come on man, you've been talking about this for ages, quitting the band," he told Taylor, who was preparing to leave again for Munich to begin work on another album. "Come and play with Jack! It's the real thing! Jack's a genius and so are you!"

So Taylor quit the Rolling Stones. He released a statement to the press: "The last five-and-a-half years with the Stones have been very exciting, and proved to be a most inspiring period. And as far as my attitude to the other four members is concerned, it is one of respect for them, both as musicians and as people. I have nothing but admiration for the group, but I feel now is the time to move on and do something new."

For Taylor, the quiet, blond, young blues virtuoso, his exit from the Stones was inevitable. It was also a brutal career choice. "He would have left anyway," says Johns. "But the timing of it was obviously that my phone call instigated it. It was the worst thing I ever did. It wasn't a smart move...though they were jolly surprised when he quit. *What is he insane? No one's ever left us before!*"

> **"The last five-and-a-half years with the Stones have been very exciting, and proved to be a most inspiring period"**
>
> Mick Taylor's press release on leaving the Stones

The Stones' public reaction was more diplomatic. Jagger told *Rolling Stone*, "I'm sorry to see him go, but I think people should be free to do what they want to do. I mean, it's not the army, it's a sort of rock and roll band." But in 1995, he added, "I think he found it difficult to get on with Keith."

Mick Taylor's solo career never fully took off after that. The supergroup with Jack Bruce turned into "this miserable heroin festival, and nothing really much came of it," says Johns. Just a tour and little else. Taylor has since recorded a handful of eclectic albums, both under his own name and as a sideman to others. He made an appearance on Keith Richards' first solo album – 1988's *Talk Is Cheap* – and he was invited to join the Stones for their 1989 induction into the Rock and Roll Hall of Fame. The decline of his own fame with contemporary audiences can't erase a well-earned legacy as a key player on some monumental rock albums.

Young Mick was gone, but a clue to the future Stones was already planted within the title track of *It's Only Rock 'N' Roll*, which had been recorded at the home studio of Ronnie Wood of the Faces. But the album was still very much rooted in the early seventies. The band's cover of the Temptations' 'Ain't Too Proud To Beg' rolled with energy and bad attitude, adding to what amounted to a decent party record from the 1974 monsters of rock.

Of course, coming from a band with such a rich history, an album like *It's Only Rock 'N' Roll* could only be seen as something of a disappointment. It was surely more than a mediocrity, yet it contained fewer surprises than we had come to expect by the beginning of the 1970s.

it's only rock 'n' roll

if you can't rock me

Enter the Glimmer Twins, producers extraordinaire. Maestro Andrew Loog Oldham was by now a fading memory, and poor Jimmy Miller a forced evacuee. Which left *It's Only Rock 'N' Roll* in the hands of Jagger and Richards themselves, officially in charge of producing a Stones album for the first time since the band had been left to their own devices on *Their Satanic Majesties Request*. Although a dubious legacy, the duo had learned much in the years since, having grown seasoned and sophisticated with time, as befitting their *nom de plume*.

These were men of wealth and taste. Certainly the Glimmer Twins knew what they were doing, launching the album with 'If You Can't Rock Me', a song of great sonic urgency in its opening moments. Jagger shouts frantically of being on stage, lusting for the crowd of women gathered in the front rows. It's just a few hours of warmth and love he needs tonight, not marriage or a lasting romance. To these ladies of "leather and lace" he makes his standard offer – if it's not you who indulges "somebody else will".

The song is carried by the seething force of Jagger's vocals and the pounding of Charlie Watts, and is a vast improvement over much of *Goats Head Soup*. Except that the winding, grinding groove never quite falls into focus. Richards and Taylor scrape their guitars in search of a memorable riff, but barely end up with even a middling melody. Is this how Jimmy Miller would have started things off?

it's only rock 'n' roll (but i like it)

No band born in the 1960s pushed the boundaries of taste and decorum further than the Rolling Stones, a band forever tarnished by Oldham's bad press. Sex, drugs, revolution, Satanism, violence and decay – all subjects explored *in extremis* by "The World's Greatest Rock And Roll Band". But even Mick Jagger had to wonder if maybe things had been carried too far, serving an insatiable audience hungry for endless shock and titillation.

The Stones had seen their early shows erupt into dangerous rioting, been mobbed in the streets, had young girls fling their bodies at their moving limos, had to literally run for their lives. Meanwhile, their worst experiences – the drug busts, car wrecks, the death of Brian Jones, Altamont – were somehow interpreted in the most romantic light possible, marking just another chapter in the Stones' great outlaw legend.

At first glance, 'It's Only Rock 'N' Roll (But I Like It)' appears as just another light-hearted anthem celebrating the music. And yet Jagger sounds both in command and truly spooked as he contemplates the entertainment value of self-mutilation and public suicide. Perhaps real tears and insanity would also be amusing. "Would it be enough for your teenage lust? Would it help to ease the pain?" These are heavy questions, even if Jagger is playing them mostly for laughs, and partly as a jibe, perhaps, at the new generation of exhibitionist glam-rockers and proto-punks – but imagine these same lyrics in the hands of Iggy Pop.

The Faces, featuring Ron Wood (centre), their very own "Keef".

Jagger had always talked disdainfully of rock, as if he regretted dropping out of university and the respectable life he might have led.

The very title of the song and album was taken as an insult by some listeners for whom rock and roll provided transcendence, not just cheap thrills. But between the wisecracks are haunting observations of the demanding relationship between audience and rock star, where the threshold of expected behaviour is raised ever higher.

Although Jagger and Richards were the song's credited composers, 'It's Only Rock 'N' Roll (But I Like It)' was first sketched out by Mick and Ronnie Wood, the ever-playful guitarist with the Faces. The Stones had known Wood since he was a baby guitarist hanging around the Crawdaddy and Marquee clubs. He was now partnered with singer Rod Stewart, and together they had left their own trail of rock and roll debauchery with the Jeff Beck Group and then the Faces.

Engineer George Chkiantz was quickly summoned one night to Wood's home studio in Richmond, where he found Jagger and Wood both strumming acoustic guitars. The basic track was recorded with Willie Weeks on bass, and a brutal crash of drums and cymbals by Kenny Jones of the Faces. The final recording was finished in Munich, where Richards added sharp bursts of Chuck Berry-style riffing. Ian Stewart's piano can be heard in the distance. Although it was Wood's first appearance with the Stones it's likely that his parts were erased by Keith. That explains Wood's credit as "inspiration" for the song, but nothing else. The final result is a song of relentless rock and roll crunch, but the central instrument here is Jagger's voice, shouting his explosive cautionary tale.

till the next goodbye

right acoustic guitars bathe a soft vocal melody from Mick Jagger, who manages to create a folksy groove touched with romance and regret. 'Till The Next Goodbye' is a troubled Manhattan love story, with vague suggestions of a rendezvous at some local coffee shop or movie theatre. The tale of endless tears and goodbyes is told through a smooth blend of guitar and Nicky Hopkins' piano. It's far from the rugged country-folk of *Beggars Banquet*, but the song sparks to emotional life at the chorus with Jagger's words of warmth and longing. The Stones may have fallen out of sync with the casual greatness they enjoyed only two years before with *Exile On Main Street*, but 'Till The Next Goodbye' demonstrated that the band was still capable of a quiet grace.

time waits for no one

ick Taylor changed the Rolling Stones. But not forever, and not in the way that Brian Jones and his teenage blues fanaticism continued to haunt the band well into the 1980s. Taylor's influence depended entirely on his presence, and the graceful, intricate lead work that for five crucial years took the Stones into new musical territory. For all the grumbling from rock and blues purists about the guitarist's occasional self-indulgences, 'Time Waits For No One' demonstrated his profound strengths as a guitarist. This was a sound as much about subtlety as rock muscle. And once Taylor was gone, the Stones would rarely pass this way again.

During these final days with the Stones, Taylor's playing did often feel detached from the rest of the band, and undoubtedly reflected the guitarist's deteriorating relationship with the others. But a connection was made with 'Time Waits For No One', as Taylor's graceful, almost rushed leads reflected the drama and breathless emotion of Jagger's lyrics. If the playing had more to do with Carlos Santana than Chuck Berry, it still meshed seemlessly with Nicky Hopkins' cascading piano melodies and the steady tick-tock beat of Charlie Watts.

Jagger's message may seem an obvious one, but the note of regret in his voice sounds real. Nothing is safe from the passage of time, he warns, not man-made monuments, not a woman's face, not the Stones. "Hours are like diamonds," Jagger sings. "Don't let them waste." In 1974, Jagger turned 30, a milestone once unthinkable for the modern rock star, though he was hardly alone – not with the ex-Beatles still around, and grandpa Chuck Berry scoring his first No. 1 hit in 1972 with the ridiculous 'My Ding-A-Ling'. Yet it's unlikely that it was simply age that inspired these philosophical musings on wasted time. No one better illustrated his theme than Keith Richards, now spending what might have been his most productive years trapped in stupor and decay, bringing the Stones' chance at continued greatness down with him.

In time, Jagger acknowledged that the era of *Goats Head Soup* and *It's Only Rock 'N' Roll* were lost years for the band. Their inherent gifts meant that memorable music still emerged from the Stones even while they were coasting, but it was here that the band relinquished their position as rock and roll trailblazers. The Stones still came up with the odd thrill, and no act could draw a bigger crowd on the concert circuit. They continued to inspire a new generation of rockers in their own image, whether it was the glam-blues boogie of Aerosmith or the bitchy personality crisis of the New York Dolls. And the Stones would enjoy remarkable comebacks, such as 1978's *Some Girls* and 1981's *Tattoo You*. But the 1970s would ultimately belong to others, much as they had once shared credit for the 1960s with the Beatles. Even before the advent of punk, listeners and critics were already turning to a new wave of artists: David Bowie, Neil Young, Al Green, Bruce Springsteen, Bob Marley, all of them introducing new sounds and ideas to pop. Not even the late-eighties retro of the Black Crowes and other Stones wannabees could bring it back to the way it once was.

Basic tracks for 'Time Waits For No One' dated back to the *Sticky Fingers* sessions at Jagger's Stargroves mansion, but final overdubs for the entire album were done at London's Island Studios. Engineer George Chkiantz remembers that Watts commuted to the sessions by train, wearing pink-striped trousers while sharing the ride with crowds of businessmen in bowler hats and grey handlebar moustaches.

A song like 'Time Waits For No One' demanded a rich, layered texture to reflect the quasi-spiritual message. So one day Jagger announced he was bringing in a percussionist named Ray Cooper. Which came as surprising news to Chkiantz, who considered Jagger an exceptional percussionist himself, given to wild dance steps with the maracas behind the microphone. Who could possibly shake, rattle and roll more spectacularly than Mr Jumpin' Jack Flash? And Cooper's history playing with Elton John wasn't the sort of thing to endear him to the rock and roll set.

"No, no, you wait till you see this guy," Jagger told Chkiantz, clearly excited about the prospects. "You will not BELIEVE it. This is a treat for you as much as for anybody else." Cooper soon arrived at Island for two efficient days of work, with his congas and tambourines, his various sticks, blocks, bones, bells, gongs, triangles and things. He was a tall man, with hair cut extremely short, practically shaved to the scalp. Cooper played it all, but it was his work on tambourine that was most astonishing. The man coaxed an amazing range of sounds from the thing, putting the simple instrument through an ordeal of

> **"What do you do with a tambourine? This guy was getting a symphony out of the thing"**
>
> George Chkiantz on percussionist Ray Cooper

it's only rock 'n' roll

Mr Tambourine man: Ray Cooper performs with Elton John.

shaking, pounding, tapping, caressing, thumping, knocking, coddling, cuddling, snuggling, nuzzling, whacking and jabbing.

"Let's face it, what do you do with a tambourine?" says Chkiantz. "Shake, shake, thwack! And this guy was getting a symphony out of the thing. He was just unbelievable, running his hands around the rim. His precision was just incredible. He'd actually tell you a story on this stupid bloody instrument. If you haven't seen it you've really missed out."

The percussionist's work appears all over *It's Only Rock 'N' Roll*, but it's within the lush mix of 'Time Waits For No One' that Cooper's presence is most felt. The final track is a lavish meditation on fate.

It isn't the album's most memorable tune – Keith's rockers were often best at sticking to your ribs – but there is something poignant in Jagger's message of regret, and his clear desire to push the Stones ever higher.

luxury

he rhythms of reggae had failed to penetrate the Stones' universe when the band recorded *Goats Head Soup* in Jamaica, but 'Luxury' suggests the band might have been paying attention after all. Not that this track has much in common with the Wailers, other than a certain hypnotic rhythm. Richards twists the genre to his own ends here, adding guitars that crunch more like the music of Chuck Berry than Bob Marley. The Stones would, of course, soon explore a more traditional reggae sound with 'Cherry Oh Baby' on *Black And Blue*.

On 'Luxury', Jagger adopts another of his notorious dialects. As his vocals slowly drift deeper into the mix, he sings as a man working hard to keep his woman and daughter out of poverty. Why must he spend his Sundays at the oil refinery while his millionaire bosses grow even richer?

it's only rock 'n' roll

dance little sister

Pray for Keith? Not at all! The man was merely indisposed. Try to ignore the image of walking, talking death, the head full of rotting teeth, the veins flooded with unfathomable toxins. He was, after all, a family man. Richards would never be caught strangling on his own vomit, drowning in a swimming pool, falling out a hotel window or choking on a ham sandwich. His heart would not explode in this decade, nor would he pass out on some inconvenient railroad tracks. This was no drug casualty, not really. Keith knew his limits. And if he seemed somehow diminished in the mid-seventies, Richards never once abandoned his role as key collaborator and Glimmer Twin.

Others have tried to be Keith, his bad example leaving a trail of rock-star bodies caught in its sway. In the end, even Johnny Thunders was proved an amateur. The implications of Keith's demon life seemed to be of little concern to the guitarist himself, depicted on the cover of It's Only Rock 'N' Roll as a dishevelled wreck, slouching in ill-fitting clothes. He was no longer the musician he had been on Let It Bleed, when Richards played most of the guitars and created a new, harrowing sound to close out the 1960s. That kind of clarity and musical ambition was inevitably clouded by continued drug use. But his ability to craft a flaming guitar riff never wavered, as the brutal opening to 'Dance Little Sister' demonstrated once more.

Leave the ethereal wispyness of 'Time Waits For No One' and other epics to Mick and Mick. There is no doubt which is the lead instrument on 'Dance Little Sister', no matter how busily Taylor twists his guitar to some excitable passages at the margins. Keith's rhythm guitar sends the Stones on a savage course, bolstered by a fierce pounding from Charlie and Stu's rolling bar room piano deep in the mix. Jagger vamps and seethes at the image of women in high heels and tight skirts and painted lips out on the town, urging them to dance and shake for him all night long.

'Dance Little Sister' has all the elements needed for the best kind of devil's music, and yet the song never fully erupts, never clicks into a perfect groove. Whether it was Keith's fading energy, uncertain band cohesion or some other cause, the Stones were no longer thriving musically as they once had.

In Munich, the Stones attempted to recreate the community vibe that had worked so well for 1972's Exile On Main Street. Band and crew shared the same hotel, just as they had done in Jamaica. "Everyone used to take their old ladies with them everywhere in those days," says engineer Andy Johns. "I'm not saying it was like a hippie thing back then. But when you were doing a project like that,

It's a hard life for Keith Richards in "The World's Greatest Rock And Roll Band".

it's not like it is now; there was a lot more sense of family and community and we're all in this together kind of a thing."

Johns remembers Ronnie Wood hanging out a bit, and jamming with Keith on Dobie Gray's 1973 hit 'Drift Away', a song Richards listened to every day for a month. The Stones abandoned that for the Temptations' 'Ain't Too Proud To Beg', an early high point for the album, recast with an echoing Richards riff. But not even these few moments of inspiration, and an attention-grabbing graffiti publicity campaign for the album, disguised the sound of a band in decay.

if you really want to be my friend

or a godless quintet of British rock stars, the Rolling Stones were surprisingly fluent in American gospel. 'If You Really Want To Be My Friend' is no match for the stirring likes of 'Let It Loose' from *Exile On Main Street*, but the Stones find a soulful groove here which is both relaxed and moving. With the air of a confessional, Jagger sings of love and trust across more than six minutes of spirited gospel. Mick Taylor erupts with a lead that is equal parts strength and melancholy. Vocal group Blue Magic add soothing harmonies, and Nicky Hopkins draws typically elegant harmonies from his piano. "Looking back at these albums, Nicky's contribution is enormous in my view," says George Chkiantz, who had watched Hopkins work with the Stones since 1967. "So many Stones tracks that we know and love are almost inconceivable without Nicky on them."

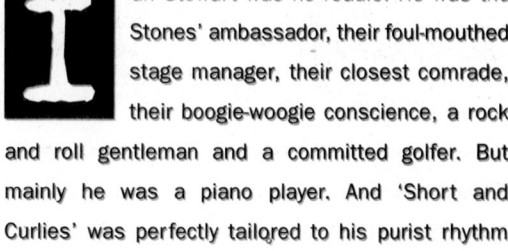

I an Stewart was no roadie. He was the Stones' ambassador, their foul-mouthed stage manager, their closest comrade, their boogie-woogie conscience, a rock and roll gentleman and a committed golfer. But mainly he was a piano player. And 'Short and Curlies' was perfectly tailored to his purist rhythm and blues sensibility.

"He loved the band, hated what they were doing a load of the time and moaned about it," remembers Chkiantz. "But he was devoted to the band, and stuck with them through thick and thin." He had never expressed any lasting bitterness at being ejected from the early Rollin' Stones. And maybe it was for the best, since Stu's boogie-woogie sensibility might have clashed with some of the wilder musical turns explored by the Stones over the years. By standing outside the band, Stu could play only what he liked, and leave the rest to Nicky Hopkins. "He wasn't overly convinced by Nicky Hopkins' playing," Chkiantz says with a laugh. "He said, 'Do you really like that sort of thing?' Stu was one of the nicest guys. Wonderful character. I'm sure that if Stu wanted to play on something he had a way of making it known."

On 'Short and Curlies', Stu's piano is right out front, not buried in the mix, and it rolls with a boys-will-be-boys impishness. It's joined by the dual guitars of Richards and Taylor as Jagger sings of a man comically under the thumb of a woman. She's spent his money, crashed his car, and yet he can't (or won't) get away. "She's got you by the balls!" Naughty, haughty, sexist boogie-woogie heaven.

it's only rock 'n' roll

fingerprint file

'ingerprint File' was a clue to the coming funk of *Black And Blue*. The thumping bassline and wah-wah guitar owe something to the sounds of Hollywood blaxploitation films – such as *Shaft* and *Superfly* – not to mention Stevie Wonder, Sly Stone and the coming disco explosion. It's a fitting beat for Mick Jagger's private-eye paranoia, sounding the alarm for an age of diminished privacy.

"Some little jerk in the FBI is keeping papers on me six-feet high," Jagger sings, and he's not kidding. Revelations on the US government's extensive surveillance of John Lennon confirms whatever worries Jagger is expressing here – of the mountain of FBI paperwork on Lennon, sections remained classified even into the 1990s. His own history of drug arrests, supposed devil worship, and his association with any number of long-haired commie troublemakers undoubtedly made Jagger a threat to the "American way". So satellites, phone-taps, ultraviolet photography, G-Men and old-fashioned snitches have all got him feeling down and desperate.

The track would mark Mick Taylor's final appearance on a Stones album – at least until the vault-raiding *Tattoo You* – ending an important period for the band. The Rolling Stones soon found some renewed energy, resulting in the comeback albums *Black And Blue* and *Some Girls*. Guitarist Ronnie Wood, who was Taylor's replacement the following year, played in a style more like Keith Richards. Together, they traded riffs and rhythms and headed toward the 1980s with a more driving hard rock sound.

Some listeners would forever miss Taylor's fluid elegance. During the next decade, interviewers rarely failed to ask the Glimmer Twins to evaluate the different Stones eras: Jones versus Taylor versus Wood. They couldn't very well answer that their best years were behind them, but acknowledged the special achievements during Taylor's tenure, from 'Honky Tonk Women' to *Exile On Main Street*. These were monumental recordings for the Stones, and anything they created in the future would surely be judged against them.

He may have been a great musician but Mick Taylor was always an outsider.

chapter thirteen

1976 black and blue

The presence of Ron Wood on second guitar gave the Rolling Stones a much-needed boost of vitality.

Hot Stuff

Hand Of Fate

Cherry Oh Baby
(DONALDSON)

Memory Motel

Hey Negrita

Melody

Fool To Cry

Crazy Mama

black and blue

The day after Mick Taylor quit the Rolling Stones, Keith Richards sent a telegram. "Really enjoyed playing with you for the last five years," it read. "Thanks for all the turn-ons. Best wishes and love." Taylor cried when he read it. Such a touching note of goodwill, so generous and merciful. Or so it seemed. Some observers have interpreted its brevity to reflect a sarcastic send-off to the boy guitarist. It was, after all, just a telegram, not an essay. In any case, neither Jagger nor Richards were shaken enough by Taylor's departure to abandon plans for their next album. Sessions for what would become *Black And Blue* began according to schedule in Munich.

That meant the Stones were once again a quartet, just as they had been during the making of *Let It Bleed*. No one performed more heroically than Keith on that album, filling the gaps left by a quickly fading Brian Jones with music that was inventive, foreboding and alive. His guitar work on 'Gimme Shelter' and 'Midnight Rambler' carried the Stones to a new level of creative intensity in 1969. *Let It Bleed* had been 43 minutes of scorched vinyl, music thick with danger and enlightenment. No way Keith was up to that now, not in this season of smack. It was enough that he could still play at all, and still create those crucial four-chord riffs. So at the end of 1974, the Stones NEEDED a second guitarist, someone to fill in the band's new empty spaces.

It would prove a hotly contested gig, and recording sessions for *Black And Blue* were all of a sudden transformed into auditions for Taylor's replacement. The Stones spent the next eight months jamming and recording endlessly with a long line of guitarists. The top candidates were British guitar hero Jeff Beck, Americans Harvey Mandel and Muscle Shoals session man Wayne Perkins, and, finally, Ron Wood of the Faces. Not a lot in common among that group. Beck, for one, had just released his acclaimed *Blow By Blow* album, an all-instrumental jazz-funk windout with little obvious connection to the rock and blues frenzy of his Yardbirds days, or even to the contemporary Stones. At the other end of the spectrum stood happy Ronnie Wood, rock and roller to the core, whose collaborations with Rod Stewart were a mixture of ragged joy (Faces albums) and focussed brilliance (Stewart's solo discs). The final version of *Black And Blue* would include playing by each of them, except for Beck, who is said to have insulted the legendary Stones rhythm section. His parts were erased.

The cross-section of styles and temperaments made *Black And Blue* the band's most eclectic batch of tracks since the late 1960s, opening with Harvey Mandel's astonishing hyperfunk on 'Hot Stuff'. The fluid lead lines of Wayne Perkins on 'Hand Of Fate' came closest to the sound of Taylor, while Woody's rugged riffing on 'Hey Negrita' was most like Keith's. If replacing Brian Jones had seemed such an easy, an almost casual choice – a recommendation from John Mayall was almost enough – replacing Taylor was more agonizing. Just as Taylor's elegant blues leads had helped the Stones master a new sophisticated rock blend at the beginning of the decade, the choice of Keith's new sideman would obviously have long-term ramifications.

"Basically, the Rolling Stones are a two-guitar band, that's how they started off," Richards told *Crawdaddy*. "And the whole secret, if there is any secret behind the sound of the Rolling Stones, is the way we work two guitars together. As far as records go it's no big hassle for me not to have another guitar player 'cause I'm used to doing all the parts. It's just I LIKE working with another player, that's the turn-on for me."

Perkins came achingly close to winning the gig, until Wood returned late to the *Black And Blue* sessions. He could finally be heard playing on three album tracks, compared to Wood's two, but Ronnie had long ago made a special connection with the band – and especially Richards. Both Mick and Keith appeared on his *I've Got My Own Album To Do* solo disc in 1974, and the seeds of 'It's Only Rock 'N' Roll' were recorded at Wood's home the same year. Band folklore has it that Wood was actually offered

> **"The whole secret, if there is any secret behind the sound of the Rolling Stones, is the way we work two guitars together"**
> Keith Richards

the job back in 1969, before the Stones settled on Taylor. True or not, Wood was an easy fit in 1975, and a needed burst of positive energy in a band fraying at the edges from drug use and internal resentments.

"I loved Mick Taylor for his beauty," Bill Wyman said later. "He was technically really great. But he was shy, maybe like Charlie and me. Mick wasn't so funky, but he led us into other things. Ron is a bit like Keith, he takes us back. He's not such a fantastic musician, but he's more fun, got more personality."

> "He [Mick Taylor] was technically really great. Ron is a bit like Keith, he takes us back. He's not such a fantastic musician, but he's more fun, got more personality"
>
> Bill Wyman

But Woody wasn't about to abandon his mates in the Faces, even if Stewart's solo career had long since eclipsed his work in the band. A new Faces album and tour was already in the planning stages. So officially, at least, the guitarist signed up only as a temporary Rolling Stone, helping the band finish *Black And Blue*, posing for the dramatic album cover photograph by Hiro, and touring the US that summer. Then Ronnie would be back with the Faces again, he promised.

Of course, the Faces were already in the final stage of a sad breakup. Never as lauded as the Stones, they had only scored a handful of UK hits in their career, and only the rocking 'Stay With Me' had made an impression in the US. Furthermore, bass player and occasional vocalist Ronnie Lane had already quit. Both Stewart and Wood saw the end coming, and finally used each other's extracurricular activities as justification for their inevitable departures. The Faces were gone.

"Woody and Rod were like Mick and Keith," says singer-guitarist Bobby Womack, a longtime friend to both Wood and the Stones. "They were tight. And when Rod left, Woody had no other choice but to say, 'Well, the Stones always wanted me, I'm going to go with them'." On February 28, 1976, Ron Wood was announced as the newest Rolling Stone.

The earliest sessions for *Black And Blue* marked a reunion between the band and engineer Glyn Johns, who had been the first to record the young Rollin' Stones in the early days. Later, Johns recorded such era-defining albums as *Beggars Banquet* and *Let It Bleed*, before drifting off into other projects and leaving the Stones to his younger brother, Andy.

His return to the Stones fold was the result of a preliminary agreement that Johns would receive a co-producer's credit on *Black And Blue*, unless he failed to finish the album for any reason. In December 1975, Johns and the band arrived in Munich. "We got on tremendously well and we cut an immense amount of material in a very short period of time, under extremely pleasant circumstances," Johns told Craig Rosen in 1994. "It was great for me to be back with them because I hadn't seen them for a while, and we were all extremely close friends for several years. That was really nice."

For Glyn Johns, the absence of Mick Taylor at the sessions was a welcome surprise. Although he acknowledged the guitarist's important role during a crucial stage of the Stones' career, he had grown increasingly finicky, contributing almost as much as Keith in the amount of time spent (and wasted) in the studio. "Frankly," Johns said, "I didn't get on with him very well."

So much else had changed within the Stones universe since Johns had last worked with them, recording tracks that later appeared on *Sticky Fingers* and *Exile On Main Street*. In Munich, Keith was still suffering from the death of his second son, Tara – named after Tara Browne, the young royal and scene-maker eulogized in the Beatles' 'A Day In The Life' – who had been born prematurely 10 days earlier. And Mick was battling a paternity suit with Marsha Hunt – a suit later settled out of court. Keith also had a brand new set of teeth, replacing his rotted junkie fangs with a row of pearly whites more appropriate to a jet-setting rock star. Meanwhile, Bill Wyman had just released his first solo album, *Monkey Grip*, and already had plans to release another, *Stone Alone*.

There was also the irritation of *Metamorphosis*, an album of barrel-scraping outtakes and misfires from the 1960s released by former manager Allen Klein. It was a collection best left on the shelves, and not even Andrew Loog Oldham's liner notes of loving beat poetry could disguise the weakness of what was inside. Balancing that atrocity was *Made In The Shade*, which gathered some of the band's best tracks of the new decade.

The most astonishing change within the Rolling Stones, at least for Johns, was the band's new willingness to work quickly. In Munich, the band managed to cut 11 tracks in 11 days, a dizzying pace against the agonizingly slow sessions that Johns remembered from London. But it wasn't to last. After the Christmas break, the Stones gathered in Rotterdam to continue work on *Black And Blue* in a rehearsal facility designed for symphony orchestras. The Rolling Stones Mobile unit was parked outside. This was Mick's idea to save money, but to Johns it made no sense at all.

"The whole environment in this place in Holland was not really right and extremely inconvenient," said Johns, who was growing irritated that recording time was being used for guitarist auditions. "I was parked in the street. They were on the third floor of this building. Every time I wanted to go and adjust a mike, I had to walk up four flights of stairs and down ten corridors. In the end, there was a misunderstanding between Keith and I which caused an argument from me. I lost my rag, and suppose it was years and years of nonsense that had built up... I said my piece and told the Rolling Stones they could go fuck themselves. That was the end of that."

At the time, Johns figured that the album was just about finished anyway. But the band still managed to spend several more months in the studio. For Johns, who has not worked with the Stones since, it was one big disappointment: "I've never listened to the record," he said later. "I'm sure they fucked it up."

The new Mick Taylor? US guitar virtuoso Harvey Mandel.

hot stuff

Black And Blue opens with a jarring blast of high-tension funk, a sound that was unexpected and extreme coming from the "World's Greatest Rock And Roll Band" in 1976. Here, at last, was a sign of life from the embattled Rolling Stones, a band that had long since drifted into predictable, straight-ahead riff-rock. Inertia was now replaced by Mick's alarming first declaration of dance fever. Rock extremists were horrified. Were the Stones being swept up within a disco scene fast emerging from the underground via international hits like Donna Summer's 'Love To Love You Baby'? Was rock dead?

Not while Keith Richards walked the earth. 'Hot Stuff' wasn't the enemy, but rather the Stones' twist on a classic funk groove, closer in spirit to James Brown and Sly Stone than to any of the slick disco tracks beginning to haunt the radio. The song was built on the high-pitched riffing of Keith, with melodramatic accents from the rumbling piano chords of Billy Preston. Guitarist Harvey Mandel sends flames across this heavy groove as Mick chants passionately about lives lived to a big beat, and improvising wildly to all those going broke in New York City that "I know you're tough!"

> "A large percentage of American women wouldn't be half as liberated if it wasn't for the Rolling Stones"
>
> Keith Richards

The track was recorded in March 1975 at Musicland Studios in Munich, where the Stones were augmenmted by percussionist Ollie E. Brown. "That sucker felt good that night," Brown says now. "It really came together that night."

If not all listeners were overjoyed at the prospect of the Rolling Stones "going disco", a song like 'Hot Stuff' was in fact a logical extension to the band's longtime commitment to the sounds of Black America. This was merely the Stones' mid-seventies take on what they had already witnessed during their first visits to the Harlem Apollo. 'Hot Stuff' was no more of a departure than the sudden mid-nineties interest in electronica and jungle beats by the likes of David Bowie and U2.

Even more controversial than these first moments of *Black And Blue* was the album's advertizing campaign, which depicted a blonde woman tied up and covered in bruises. Feminists and many others were appalled at the image, which was soon scattered across billboards and magazine pages. "I thought it was quite funny," Richards told *Creem* magazine in 1979. "Trouble is, not too many people have a sense of humour, especially institutions... Goddamn it, a large percentage of American women wouldn't be half as liberated if it wasn't for the Rolling Stones in the first place, and people like us. They'd still be believing in dating, rings and wondering whether it was right to be kissed on the first date or not."

hand of fate

o mistaking the sound behind 'Hand Of Fate' – the grinding electric guitars, the tough, driving rhythm. The opening riff passage was clearly Keith's, but there was a new clarity and energy here. On *Goats Head Soup* and *It's Only Rock 'N' Roll* the riffs had fallen from the ringed fingers of Richards a little too easily, rarely rising beyond the prototype he'd created years earlier with 'Jumpin' Jack Flash'. On *Black And Blue*, Keith momentarily emerged from his cloud.

As with the entire album, the sound of 'Hand Of Fate' was crisp without seeming sterile, thanks to the work of engineers Glyn Johns, Keith Harwood and Phil McDonald. Each element, every drum beat and vocal line, was strong and unblemished through a staggering variety of rock blends, from funk to rock riffing to the reggae breeze of 'Cherry Oh Baby' to the wistful balladry of 'Memory Motel'.

After the superfunk of 'Hot Stuff', the Stones returned immediately to the land of the superhuman riff. Despite its vaguely spiritual tone, Jagger sings 'Hand Of Fate' as a man on the run after committing murder over the love of a woman.

Following a precedent set by the departed Mick Taylor, guitarist Wayne Perkins fires a jazzy rock lead across the band's charged rhythm. But 'Hand Of Fate' ultimately belongs to Keith.

"It doesn't matter about the B.B. Kings, Eric Claptons and Mick Taylors 'cause they do what they do. But I know they can't do what I do," Richards said later. "They can play as many notes under the sun but they just can't hold that rhythm down, baby... Everything I do is strongly based on rhythm 'cause that's what I'm best at. I've tried being a great guitar player, and – like Chuck Berry – I have failed."

memory motel

Richards leaves the guitar playing to Wayne Perkins and Harvey Mandel on 'Memory Motel', a story of endless, lonely nights on the road and of the good women met along the way. Jagger and Richards duet on the song in an often wounded tone, singing longingly for nights and memories long past.

Some memories are more intense than others. "I saw this girl pin Mick against a wall and try to take her clothes off on him," remembers percussionist Ollie E. Brown. "She just started undressing herself. Fans would scream, scratch, just like you see on TV. He just laughed."

Jagger and Richards sing across a lavish blend of keyboards: Mick on acoustic piano, Keith on electric piano, Preston on string synthesizer. Perkins strums an acoustic and Mandel plays electric, as Keith groans sagely, "She's got a mind of her own, and she uses it well."

As ever, sessions in Munich usually began in the evening and ended at sunrise. It would seem that Richards' rock muse only awoke after midnight. His night hours are spent with a guitar, not in bed. And songs often emerge from late-night jam sessions, as Ollie E. Brown discovered while touring with the Stones in the mid-seventies. "Keith would have an amplifier sent up to his room after a concert," Brown says. "Him and Woody might be sitting in the bedroom, noodling around; the next you know Mick walks in there and he might start singing to it. Then they might tape it for reference. The next thing you know you have a song."

hey negrita

That's Ron Wood's face on the back cover of *Black And Blue*, drifting in from stage left to a waiting world as the newest member of the Rolling Stones. His face is uncommonly proud and serious, clean-shaven and upright, even if the guitarist only plays on two album tracks here. They're enough. The first was Eric Johnson's quiet reggae song 'Cherry Oh Baby', but Wood's presence is most felt on 'Hey Negrita', which finds an appropriate voodoo groove within the scratchy, staccato guitars of Ron and Keith. Mick sings another lurid tale, this time shouting passionately of watching the street walkers before offering up one last dollar.

The song's Bayou rhythm was largely Wood's creation, erupting with twangy country-rock lines at the song's bridge. It was nothing that he couldn't have done with the Faces, but now it was in a different context, and the stakes were suddenly higher. Everything with the Stones was at a greater scale than anything Wood had known as a member of the Faces or, earlier, the Jeff Beck Group.

Wood sometimes asked his friend Bobby Womack for advice. "I remember him asking me, 'What do you think I should ask them? How much do you think I should ask them for?' I said 'Man, I have no idea. Ask them for a million dollars,'" says Womack. "But they put him on a salary. He proved himself not only as being loyal, but with being a Stone they could count on."

Being a Stone has come at a price. In later years, Wood has managed to win songwriting credits from the Glimmer Twins. But the Rolling Stones would always focus first on the needs and desires of Jagger

Ron Wood quickly blended in with the Rolling Stones.

black and blue

and Richards. The modern Stones were THEIR creation, THEIR personal venue, just as the Faces had been for Wood. With the Faces, at least, Wood had been the central musical force, crafting passages of passionate acoustic slide guitar and chunks of Stones-style rock to his own liking. Now he was part of the Stones machine, inevitably subverting his own musical voice. By the beginning of the 1980s even his solo recording career was essentially over.

But Wood came at another crucial time for the Stones. If *Black And Blue* represented a band finding renewed creative energy, then Wood was determined to keep the good vibes rolling. By 1978's *Some Girls*, young Ronnie was a key player within the band, a crucial presence that kept them together. And his raw, grinding guitar chunks locked in snugly with Keith's, just as if he'd been there all along.

"I certainly expect to contribute," Wood told *Rolling Stone* in 1977. "I've written a bit with Mick, a lot with Keith wherever we've been – New York, Paris, Munich – we've just collected all the ideas, like the stuff we were trying out in the studio. I've gotta make sure I do contribute. After all, I'd hate to become the dormant member of the Rolling Stones."

Stepping Out: Billy Preston forged a successful solo career during the 1970s.

melody

'Melody' was the only track recorded at the Rotterdam sessions to make it on to *Black And Blue*, and it's unlike anything else on the album. With an excited rush of horns arranged by Arif Mardin, it's an unlikely foray into jazz, with Charlie Watts on brushes. (Finally!) Mick stomps his feet, rolls his tongue, and sings a sloppy duet with Billy Preston. The song is warm and nasty, as Jagger struts through a sad, sad tale of a woman who spent all his money before falling into the arms of another man. "I'm looking for her high and low/like a mustard for a ham..."

The song slides across some spirited bar-room piano and soulful organ from Preston, who brings a measure of R&B into the mix. He joins Jagger for a lengthy session of joyful moaning, shuffling, groaning and scat singing at the track's end. During the 1970s, Preston enjoyed several hits of his own – 'Nothing From Nothing' and 'Will It Go Round In Circles', among others – enjoying the momentum of his work with the Beatles and the Stones. But none of it outclassed this stylish blend of jazz and blues.

fool to cry

For some listeners, the weepy ballad 'Fool To Cry' was even more disturbing than the strange dance-floor epic that had heralded the start of the album. This was music you expected from the Carpenters or Barry Manilow, NOT the Rolling Stones.

Jagger sings with rare vulnerability of being a father, a lover, a friend overcome with emotion and self-pity. It was not exactly rock and roll, but it was deeply effective, giving the Stones a top 10 hit in both Britain and America. "It's a fabulous song, and Jagger sings it brilliantly," Glyn Johns said later.

Johns had completed what he thought was the final mix of 'Fool To Cry' on December 4, 1974, only to see the band continue working and re-working the song when they returned to the studio after the Christmas break. The final version offers a slow blend of keyboards and guitars. Proof enough that even the most notorious of rock stars can master syrup if necessary.

> **"It's a fabulous song, and Jagger sings it brilliantly"**
>
> Engineer Glyn Johns on 'Fool To Cry'

crazy mama

Black And Blue closes with another straight-ahead Stones rocker, this time with Mick Jagger playing rhythm guitar, and Keith Richards firing off bits of country-funk lead. The talents of would-be sidemen Mandel, Perkins and Wood are not needed here, suggesting that Richards would have easily been up to the task alone if he'd wanted.

Recorded on March 29, 1975, 'Crazy Mama' is buoyed by layers of excited, dynamic guitar work. For Richards, who played guitar on Alexis Korner's *Get Off Of My Cloud* album of the same year, it may have been a simple exercise. But it was enough to reassure the fans that within the Rolling Stones, the slow decline had been at least temporarily halted. The blood was still boiling.

chapter fourteen

1978 some girls

Satisfaction: *Some Girls* was hailed as a new beginning for the Rolling Stones.

Miss You
When The Whip Comes Down
Just My Imagination
(WHITFIELD/STRONG)
Some Girls
Lies
Far Away Eyes
Respectable
Before They Make Me Run
Beast of Burden
Shattered

some girls

bserve Mick Jagger's new motto for 1978: IF YOU CAN'T TAKE A JOKE, IT'S TOO FUCKING BAD. And it worked. *Some Girls* was the Rolling Stones' most audacious, incendiary, bitchy, fearless and most wickedly funny album ever, with Jagger cutting loose through a series of stream-of-consciousness raps that tapped into a mutant New York groove. The Stones had been funny before, but the likes of 1967's 'Cool, Calm And Collected' had been the innocent merry making of youngsters. *Some Girls* was different – the sound of grown men laughing harshly among themselves, with all the swagger and grim sarcasm that image implies.

This was urban country music, a grimy blend of punk, funk and speedy Chuck Berry riffs, all of it dripping with attitude. It wasn't totally unexpected. *Black And Blue* had been an encouraging sign in 1976, an energetic signal that the Stones were at least interested again in making music, even if that album leaned heavily on old formulas and borrowed funk. *Some Girls* was also indelibly linked to the Stones' past, but with a sound that was new and vital. Jagger and Richards sang of outlaws and romance, and mercilessly ridiculed both redneck country and western music ('Far Away Eyes') and women of every stripe and temperament. "Black girls just want to get fucked all night," Jagger sings on the title track. "I just don't have that much jam." Not everyone was amused.

To the pop masses, *Some Girls* was perhaps just another in a continuing series of international No. 1 albums, another pop source for the home stereo. But for critics and other rock and roll shut-ins, *Some Girls* was a revelation, a long-awaited return to form by the kings of rock. Here the Stones were not only recapturing a certain energy from the past, but they were making it sound fresh again. Jagger even showed a vulnerable side on the band's tender version of the Temptations' 'Just My Imagination'.

"I thought *Some Girls* was the most immediate album we had done in a long while, and you can't argue with seven million sales," Richards said in 1979. "It took off just at the right period in the band's evolution."

Some Girls might also have been the end for the Stones. In 1977, the band arrived in Toronto, Canada, to record a series of shows at the El Mocambo for the *Love You Live* album. But at the airport, Mounties discovered 10 grams of hash and a blackened spoon (heroin paraphernalia) in one of Anita Pallenberg's 28 pieces of luggage. She was immediately arrested. Three days later, Mounties descended upon Keith Richards' hotel room and found an ounce of heroin, enough to charge the guitarist with drug trafficking. If convicted, Richards faced a possible life sentence.

With Keith out on bail, the El Mocambo shows went on as planned, but the Stones were caught in another scandal with revelations that Margaret Trudeau, Canada's First Lady, had reportedly been spotted at the band's hotel in a bathrobe. The local headlines ("Stones Scandal With The First Lady" and "The First Lady Who Got Turned On By The Stones") caused an uproar, and the Canadian dollar even slipped in value. "If she goes to rock concerts she has to expect to be noticed and written about," Mr Trudeau bravely told the *Toronto Sun*. "I have no complaints about that, but I believe that my wife's private life is her affair and mine."

In court, Anita was fined $400 for her trouble, and Keith was scheduled for a hearing several months away. Both were allowed to leave Canada for a drug treatment centre in New York. By October, the Stones were in Paris, gathered at EMI's Pathé Marconi studios to begin work on *Some Girls*.

"It was quite electrifying," said Chris Kimsey, who engineered and mixed the album. "No one was quite sure what was going to happen to Keith's drug busts from Canada, whether he was going to go down or not. So it was a very anxious time. A lot of studio hours. There wasn't much time spent out of the studio. The atmosphere of the studio was a lot like a live show because a lot of people would come

> " I thought *Some Girls* was the most immediate album we had done in a long while, and you can't argue with seven million sales "
>
> Keith Richards

some girls

down. It wasn't like a closed session. There might have been anything like 10 to 30 people milling around the studio."

That crowd doesn't seem to have been a distraction. *Some Girls* was recorded on a relatively low-tech 16-track machine in what was considered to be Pathé Marconi's demo room, a massive space more like a soundstage. A bar was set up, adding to the informal atmosphere. More than 40 songs were recorded there, with the occasional help of such guest sidemen as pianist Ian McLagan (formerly of the Faces), saxman Mel Collins and Sugar Blue on the blues harp. Most songs were virtually written on the spot. "Mick or Keith would come in with a riff or an idea," Kimsey told journalist Craig Rosen in 1994. "No one else in the band had heard it until that moment. Paris is a very good environment for them. It was a great place for them to work."

The album took only seven months to complete, from the Paris recording sessions to mixing in New York. And despite his continuing legal troubles, Keith was there for all of it. "Keith never records his parts separately," said Kimsey. "He always plays live to the band. That's the magic of the Rolling Stones. They either play together or not at all."

Also emerging as a key player was Ronnie Wood. The guitarist couldn't take much credit for the renewed energy heard on *Black And Blue*, but *Some Girls* owed a bit of its wry, prickly flavour to Wood. Despite the presence of 'Miss You', the so-called "disco" track, the Stones were emphatically a rock and roll band. And Woody was now a creative force, even if he would never again enjoy the same creative freedom he had known in the Faces.

Even Woody's growing role would be small consolation if Keith went down on the Canadian drug charges, though. Mick vaguely promised to carry on if his Glimmer Twin landed in prison. But he knew the Stones would be over without Keith. Just as the band completed their best album in years, the very future of the Rolling Stones was more uncertain than ever.

"Gossip is always bigger than the music," Mick told *Creem* in 1978. "It's really difficult to get out of the gossip columns once you've gotten in. I try to be as emphatic as possible about the music, but most of the reporters just want to talk about who you're fucking or what happened to Keith. I don't think they really want to know about the music, especially the English dailies. They don't want to know about NO music crap so, you might as well forget it."

> "It's really difficult to get out of the gossip columns once you've gotten in"
> — Mick Jagger

miss you

In 'Miss You', Mick Jagger crafts one of his most memorable tales of romance. This isn't about sex. Nor is it about a bitter battle of the sexes. His lover has gone away, and he's begging for her return. The song is rare show of vulnerability and sadness from the singer, who perhaps found some inspiration in his fast disintegrating marriage to Lady Bianca.

'Miss You' is rich in the imagery of loneliness and regret: the empty bed, the haunted dreams, the solitary walks through Central Park, a friend who offers to bring over "some Puerto Rican girls just dyin' to meet you!" *Some Girls* opens without a hint of sarcasm. Just love and unhappiness.

Those sentiments were matched by a sound that alarmed many longtime Stones followers. Charlie Watts slapped a steady, danceable beat as Richards and Wood strummed glancing funk riffs and sideman Sugar Blue added winsome harmonica melodies. It was undeniably Stones-like, and yet strangely close to dance music. Jagger had come up with the basic groove with the help of Billy Preston (who doesn't actually appear on the album) during the 1976 European tour. And Bill Wyman first worked out the

some girls

song's oozing four-on-the-floor bass pattern during rehearsals at the El Mocambo. The result was an overture to the growing disco movement, but not a surrender. 'Miss You' slipped into the seventies dancefloor zeitgeist as easily as '(Can't Get No) Satisfaction' once shared playlists with the sounds of Motown. An extended version of the song – timed at 8:36 minutes – pressed on 12-inch vinyl was even produced especially for club DJs.

"I think if you were to mention DISCO to Keith and say 'Let's do a disco song', you might have a problem on your hands," says longtime Stones saxman Bobby Keys. "I can't imagine anything like that going down consciously."

The Rolling Stones had not exactly abandoned rock and roll. The same day the band recorded 'Miss You', the Stones also came up with 'Start Me Up', destined to appear on 1981's *Tattoo You* and become one of their most popular rock anthems. But that was for another era. Right now the Stones were in the heart of the seventies. "'Miss You' really caught the moment, because that was the deal at the time," Jagger told *Rolling Stone* in 1995. "And that's what made that record take off. It was a really great record."

Bianca Jagger: the jet-setting couple would soon no longer be an item.

> **"** 'Miss You' really caught the moment, because that was the deal at the time... that's what made that record take off. It was a really great record **"**
>
> Mick Jagger

157

some girls

when the whip comes down

In just a few moments, the Stones were able to step comfortably into contemporary dance culture via 'Miss You'. Now the band set out to reclaim rock and roll from a new generation of loudmouthed punks. The Rolling Stones were a prime target for derision from the likes of Johnny Rotten of the Sex Pistols. And the Clash declared boldly: "No Stones or Who in '77!"

When he wasn't being defensive, Mick Jagger actually sounded as if he was quite amused by the punk movement. He argued that for new rock bands to rebel against the legacy of the Stones was silly. To rebel against the Stones was like Jagger and Richards rebelling against Eddie Cochran and Elvis. It can't be done. The connections between rock and roll generations run too deep. Besides, Jagger added, "Keith is the original punk rocker. You can't out-punk Keith – it's pointless."

But could the Stones recapture the feeling of edgy rebellion they remembered from the sixties? That wasn't Jagger's goal. To him nostalgia was a hopeless dead-end. So 'When The Whip Comes Down' was clearly influenced by the pace and energy of punk. The duelling riffs and leads, Charlie and Bill's driving, rattling rhythm and Mick's anxious growl all combined into a spirited, volatile groove.

Lyrically, the track had very little to do with contemporary punk. No politics or class warfare. It was instead classic Stones decadence. Jagger sings a coming-of-age story of a young gay hustler who arrives on the streets of New York to ply his sordid trade, engaging in hapless scenes of sado-masochism. It was the kind of message even the he-men of punk might find horrific.

> **"Keith is the original punk rocker. You can't out-punk Keith – it's pointless"**
> Mick Jagger

The riveting sound underneath was something anyone could understand, the result of breaking the Stones down to its bare essentials. "The more musicians you use the longer it takes," Richards told *NME* in 1978. "The bigger the band the slower the process. Without any conscious effort, this time around we stripped things right down to the bare bones."

According to the likes of John Lydon, punk was supposed to finish off the Stones and their generation.

some girls

Mick Jagger loves women. LOVES them. And he has theories, observations and tips for lovers. Really, he's just trying to help. 'Some Girls' is the Jagger manifesto on the women he's known, all the white girls, black girls, English girls, French girls, Chinese girls, American girls, married girls, inconveniently pregnant girls. Every kind of female he's seen up close during his life as a master of the rock and roll universe. Hope it helps.

Jagger's not about to apologize, certainly not to the usual angry feminists always at him about this or that sexist song. 'Some Girls' was special, a perverse twist on the Beach Boys' 'California Girls'. And why not? He'd done the research, enough to testify to the gentleness of Chinese women, the greed of American chicks, and enough to tell us emphatically that "black girls just want to get fucked all night". Maybe Mick was only joking anyway, singing these outrageous sexist, racist words across

some girls

a soaring, eccentric urban blues. Sugar Blue's harmonica wails only added to the jeering tone. Much of it had been improvised anyway. The original track was 24 minutes of Jagger's ramblings before being reduced to four-and-a half minutes of the most outrageous, comical passages.

Jesse Jackson was not amused. He called the song a "racist insult" that "degrades blacks and women." On October 6, 1978, he met with Ahmet Ertegun, the embattled president of Atlantic Records, a man still likely to have been shaken from the Stones 'Starfucker/Star Star' controversy just a few years earlier. This time he was forced to face Jackson, a one-time aide to Martin Luther King Jr, a future candidate for president of the United States, and in 1978, the man who was calling for a boycott of the *Some Girls* album.

Jesse Jackson, like many black Americans, didn't see the funny side of 'Some Girls'.

On the eve of their July 8 concert in Chicago, writer Cynthia Dagnal noted in the Chicago *Sun-Times* that Jagger's "comments on the sexual appetites of black women are insults. They fit a pattern." Not a pattern, but a *tradition*, one epitomized by 'Brown Sugar' and its scenes of slave ships, whips and midnight rounds by the slave-owner. None of it should be taken seriously, pleaded Ertegun: "Mick has great respect for blacks. He owes his whole being, his whole musical career, to black people."

Which is true. The label chief also suggested that future pressings of *Some Girls* would have the offending line edited out. That never happened, and no copies of the album were ever recalled from stores. Earl McGrath, president of Rolling Stones Records, issued the statement: "It never occurred to us that our parody of certain stereotypical attitudes would be taken seriously by anyone who heard the entire lyric of the song in question. No insult was intended, and if any was taken, we sincerely apologize."

Jagger's reaction was more blunt. He told *Rolling Stone* magazine, "If you can't take a joke, it's too fucking bad." Keith also tried to explain. "We write our songs from personal experiences," he told *Creem*. "OK, so over the last 15 years we've happened to meet extra-horny black chicks – well I'm sorry, but I don't think I'm wrong and neither does Mick."

lies

ever mind the fashion. The Rolling Stones weren't about to openly embrace the punk movement. Yet new tracks like 'Lies' at least argued that the Stones were quite able to keep pace with the younger, rude rockers. Here, a dizzying rhythm sends the band careening forward as Jagger angrily denounces the LIES he confronts daily, from history books to the sweet nothings in his ear. He finally reverts back to a common Stones theme, attacking the nearest female, shouting: "You dirty Jezebel!"

'Lies' is a song of minimal lyrics, blind anger and disgust, and is likely to have emerged from one of the *Some Girls* jam sessions. As was now a tradition, the Rolling Stones did not rehearse before entering Pathé Marconi studios in Paris. Mick might come in with one of his slower songs on cassette, or Keith would walk in with a riff idea. "It's done very casually, and it's really jamming," Wyman said in 1978. "We don't work it all out or anything like that. Actually, it's quite easy that way, but it can also be very boring. If you've got your bit together, but the whole thing isn't together, you can play it for eight hours. And by the time you go to bed that night, all you can hear going through your head is that riff. It drives you mad."

far away eyes

T his isn't what Gram Parsons had in mind. This is isn't why the wayward Flying Burrito Brother took Mick and Keith by the hand through all his favourite honky tonks. This isn't why he jammed endlessly with Richards in the South of France when he should have been back home working on his own albums. He loved country music, and only wanted to help the Stones to UNDERSTAND. Keith knew this, of course. But Mick never approached the genre with the same kind of reverence, never granted it the respect he reserved for the blues. One listen to 'Far Away Eyes' confirms that.

Not that the musical backing to 'Far Away Eyes' is anything less than a loving tribute to the classic country – part Bakersfield, part old-time Nashville. It moves at a relaxed, loping pace, with both Mick and Keith on piano, and Woody on crucial pedal steel. The Stones here sound about ready for the American honky tonk circuit. Until the vocal begins, that is.

Jagger sounds like he received his entire country education by watching reruns of *The Beverly Hillbillies*. He adopts another of his unfortunate caricatures, this time of the shit-kicking, Bible-thumping, oafish, gullible, Gomer Pyle rednecks he imagines listens to country music. The stereotypes continue with his story of preachers, truckers and loose women.

"Mick feels the need to get into other caricatures," Keith said later. "He's slightly vaudeville in his approach. 'Far Away Eyes' is like that. He did it great every time except for the final take. It's good when he does it straight 'cause it's funny enough without doing a pantomime. When he sings it as a caricature it sounds like it would be great for a show. You expect Mick to walk out in his cowboy duds on an 18-wheeler set. Or sing it into his CB as part of his skit."

If the song comes off as a big joke on first listen, what emerges later is a bit more affection, although not respect. Even Jagger is partly redeemed by a chorus of warmth and romance. It's the music that makes 'Far Away Eyes' worthwhile.

Andy Johns, who engineered the band's albums of the early 1970s, marvels at Bill Wyman's bass lines. "You listen to 'Girl With The Far Away Eyes' at 45 rpm and you really see what Bill's doing, and it's genius," says Johns. "It really is. I was always trying to copy the way he played, and it's impossible. And I'm not a bad bass player. But the way he walks through changes is so unique. To try and cop it is pretty tough."

Engineer Chris Kimsey noted that 'Far Away Eyes' was a track that demonstrated the versatility of Ron Wood, who had explored country-flavoured sounds during his time with Rod Stewart and the Faces. "Ronnie was quite diverse in his playing," Kimsey said later. "He can play peddle steel. That was great on 'Faraway Eyes'. And he could play a number of different types of guitar, which was good fun, very helpful. A lot of slide guitar, too. It was working very well together."

Wood's work on *Some Girls* laid an important foundation for his ultimate acceptance as a full member of the Stones. "Now he's got power and he's accepted," says Bobby Womack, a longtime friend to both Wood and the Stones. "And he's never changed, regardless of what people would say. He went through hell and high water. I felt sorry for him a lot of times. This guy's got the spirit. *How long are they going to test him?* When Keith embraced him, he was in. He reminds you of a kid who just got in the music business. His attitude is the same way. He's like the guy that keeps everything running smooth."

Wood also gave Jagger some timely guitar lessons, making it possible for the singer to play some of the punk-flavoured sounds he felt boiling inside for 'Respectable', 'Lies' and 'When The Whip Comes Down'.

> **" He did it great every time except for the final take. It's good when he does it straight 'cause it's funny enough without doing a pantomime "**
>
> Keith Richards on Mick Jagger singing 'Far Away Eyes'

some girls

respectable

The Glimmer Twins didn't always agree on the ever-increasing tempos Keith wanted to play. The guitarist was perhaps just protecting the Stones from allowing Jagger to turn *Some Girls* into a disco album. In any case, on 'Respectable' the guitarist fortunately prevailed, turning the song into the band's most intense, rip-roaring rocker since 'Rip This Joint' from *Exile On Main Street*. "This is kind of the edgy punk ethos," Jagger told Jann Wenner in 1995. "The whole thing was to play it all fast, fast, fast. I had a lot of problems with Keith about it, but that was the deal at the time."

Jagger's lyrics poke fun at the band's own newfound respectability as rock journeymen, imagining joining the President at the White House for a casual heroin session – a sly nod to Mick's "high society" image and the days when Bianca frolicked on the White House lawn with President Ford's son.

The recording is tight but ragged – all driving guitars, hyped-up Chuck Berry riffs and rockabilly flair. "None of us are superb musicians in a technical or performing sense," Wyman told *Guitar Player* in 1978. "It's just that we have that mixture within the band, and Ron Wood has really dropped into that. Mick Taylor didn't really. He's very technical and a very clever musician – much more clever musically than the rest of us. Woody's a very good musician, of course, but much more Stonesy, if you like, more like Keith's playing than pretty."

before they make me run

The sky was falling in on Keith Richards by 1978. The bust in Toronto was no hallucination. The charges against him – possession of heroin with the intention to sell – meant he faced losing not only his freedom, but the Stones. He was prepared for the worst. "Being famous is OK," Richards noted, "but in the courtroom it only works against you."

'Before They Make Me Run' was recorded in Paris while Keith was on bail and awaiting a court hearing. The song began under the working title 'Rotten Roll', but soon took shape as a timely outlaw anthem. The sound was sloppy and crude – all rock and roll, defiance and dissipation – with Keith's voice a casual groaning on the desperado life.

> **" I've never had a problem with drugs, only with policemen "**
> Keith Richards

Richards sings of a life spent in front of the crowd, and of pills and powders and booze, and the friends lost along the way. "Unfortunately, many of my closest friends have died suddenly," Richards told *Creem* in 1979. "It's like they've always been very compulsive people and Gram was no exception. Maybe it's the attraction of opposites?"

He offers no apologies. "I've never had a problem with drugs, only with policemen," Richards told *NME* in 1978. "The actual busts have always been utter farces…to wake up with 15 Mounties standing around your bed after they've spent an hour trying to wake you up."

Things continued to look grim for Richards through most of 1978. *Some Girls* was a popular and critical success, and fans crowded stops on the American tour. But underneath was the understanding that Richards still faced his drug trial in Toronto, and that this could be the last anyone ever saw or heard from the Rolling Stones.

some girls

The Mounties get their man: Keith's arrest sends panic waves through the Stones camp.

In Canada, officials were suffering their own anxious moments. The Keith Richards bust was a giant public relations nightmare, a no-win situation. And no doubt some remembered stories of Keith's earlier bust in Fordyce, Arkansas, during the 1975 tour, when angry Stones fans surrounded the jail until the guitarist was allowed to leave quickly on a jet plane. In the end, a Toronto judge avoided rioting in the streets of Canada after Richards pleaded guilty to the lesser charge of heroin possession. He was sentenced to one year of probation and required to continue his drug rehabilitation and perform a benefit concert for Toronto's Canadian National Institute for the Blind. "No incarceration or fine would be appropriate because of Mr Richards' continued treatment for drug addiction, and his long-term benefit to the community, the large community," declared Judge Lloyd Grayburn.

In the end, the entire experience allowed Richards to break with his pattern of addiction, though he insisted later that heroin hadn't fully diminished him. "When I was a junkie I used to be able to play tennis with Mick, go to the toilet for a quick fix, and still beat him," Richards said later. In 1989, he told Stanley Booth: "I always felt I had a safe margin. That's a matter of knowing yourself, maybe just on a physical level. I come from very tough stock, and things that would kill other people don't kill me. To me the only criteria in life are knowing yourself and your capabilities, and the idea that anybody should take on what I do or did as a form of recreation or emulation is horrific."

some girls

beast of burden

Some Girls was the Rolling Stones in balance, an album of sudden clarity after several years adrift. Why the title? "Because we couldn't remember their fucking names!" Keith joked. But for all the jokes and outrageousness elsewhere on the album, there were just as many moments of vulnerability like 'Beast Of Burden'. Within Jagger's passionate growl is the sound of a man pleading his love for a woman who will not have him.

Songs of misogyny and decadence earned the headlines for Some Girls, but they were redeemed by the sort of genuine feeling found in 'Beast Of Burden'. Jagger's lyrics may have been inspired by the turmoil in his own romantic life. By now he was living with model Jerry Hall, and poor Bianca – who has called her 1971 wedding to Mick "the worst day of my life" – filed for divorce. The marriage, Jagger later noted, had basically been over since 1973.

Listeners were drawn to Jagger's testimonial and the arrangement of rich guitars. Released as a single, 'Beast Of Burden' was a top-10 hit in America.

> **"Because we couldn't remember their fucking names!"**
>
> Keith Richard explains his choice of album title

Mick Jagger and Jerry Hall quickly became one of the world's most prominent celebrity couples.

shattered

The Glimmer Twins were New Yorkers now. They were Big City boys, rockers who understood the ways of the Great Metropolis, the noise and mad scenery. *Some Girls* reflects that hardened view, tapping into both punk and disco – otherwise disparate sources that blended into a fine, brassy mixture of state-of-the-art rock and roll. The charming irony of such older Stones tracks as 'Complicated' had de-evolved into the leering, dangerous sarcasm of the late seventies. Welcome to Manhattan, Jagger sings, "don't mind the maggots!"

'Shattered' is the Stones at their most nervous and bitchy, spinning a singular blend of white funk and testy punk rock into a new sound of their own. Jagger raps through a rushed list of grim New York scenes as the band agitates through the song's mutant fusion. The hurried rhythm, the handclaps, Woody's lead guitar erupting near the end, the strangely flat background vocals that sound borrowed from Devo's version of '(Can't Get No) Satisfaction' – 'Shattered' was the oddest piece of music to hit the American pop singles chart.

As elsewhere on the album, Jagger's vocals are the driving force, setting a hyper pace, while reflecting the fragmenting mind of a New Yorker overwhelmed by the city's frightening decay. It is simply too much to bear.

The song emerged during typically early morning sessions at Pathé Marconi Studios. "A lot of that album was so much fun," remembered engineer Chris Kimsey. "It was like being at a club every night, like a nightclub atmosphere. What they would do – it was either Mick or Keith's song – was to jam it for a couple of hours and then fine tune it and get it down."

Some Girls is a lasting document of those sessions, and the music made by the Stones during 1978 remains just as exotic and exciting two decades later. Critics were largely pleased, judging the disc second-rate only in comparison to the monumental albums that preceded it. *Some Girls* was either a dramatic comeback for the "World's Greatest Rock And Roll Band", or the last meaningful work from a group destined to fray during the 1980s.

> "A lot of that album was so much fun. It was like being at a club every night. What they would do was to jam it for a couple of hours and then fine tune it and get it down"
>
> Chris Kimsey, engineer

chapter fifteen

1980 emotional rescue

Dance (Pt. 1)
(JAGGER/RICHARDS/WOOD)
Summer Romance
Send It To Me
Let Me Go
Indian Girl
Where The Boys Go
Down In The Hole
Emotional Rescue
She's So Cold
All About You

Disco may suck but Mick's not ready to stop dancing.

emotional rescue

"Keith! Whatcha... Whatcha doin'?!" Mick sounds genuinely concerned, shouting out these words at the beginning of *Emotional Rescue*, and marking the Rolling Stones' entry into the awesome 1980s. He's babbling and whistling and raving like any other curbside crank on the streets of New York City. And just what was Mr Richards doing? Finding clarity. He was FREE, not only of the long prison sentence he'd just escaped in Canada, but free of the smack, and the cloud of addiction that hounded him throughout the seventies. Keith Richards was back in his role as Glimmer Twin extraordinaire, maestro of the biggest rock and roll act in the universe, and just in time for...disco?

The Stones had already dabbled in the stuff to great pop success on 'Miss You', with its cocky blend of throbbing four-on-the-floor dance rhythm and the rock and blues at the band's core. Not all of their fans were pleased. Not everyone liked the idea of the Stones mingling with the white polyester suit crowd, in a world of strobe lights and mirror balls. Bad enough that Jagger was regularly spotted at the fashionable Manhattan discotheque Studio 54, dancing and drinking with Bianca and Andy and Liz and Liza. Now the entire band looked ready to join him in the disco inferno.

They weren't alone. For one terrifying moment, it seemed like the sounds of Donna Summer, the Bee Gees, the Trammps, KC and the Sunshine Band, the Village People and a thousand other pumping-thumping disco acts were about to eclipse rock permanently with their cartoon synths and big beats, singing of love and sex and sex and sex.

Summer helped launch the movement back in 1975 with 16-minutes of orgasmic panting, gasping, moaning and groaning called 'Love To Love You Baby'. These were strange times, crowded with punk and funk and soft rock and the multi-million-selling likes of Fleetwood Mac and the Eagles. Somehow disco looked like the quickest way to commercial ecstasy, leading even the most unlikely rock acts to the dance floor. So now Rod Stewart ('Do Ya Think I'm Sexy?') and the Grateful Dead ('Shakedown Street') were dabbling in the genre, no doubt looking to their own survival in an era without rock and roll. It was time to do the hustle.

Which meant that disco was the enemy to the die-hard rock crowd, who scrawled "Disco Sucks!" on public walls and bridges in response to the disco culture dominating the airwaves. It was this hatred that culminated during the late 1970s in events like the anti-disco rally in Chicago's Comisky Park. It was not unlike the kind of hatred generated in the nineties by the wave of acts bringing drum and bass, jungle and other brands of high-adrenaline electronic music to the masses. (In 1997, the Stones would again look to appropriating modern textures by hiring the Dust Brothers to co-produce several tracks.)

Sacrilege or not, the Stones had a certain flair for seventies dance music. To them, disco was just another strain of American R&B. And the very idea that the premier rock and roll band would dabble heavily in the sound at the height of a DISCO SUCKS! campaign was just perverse enough to suit Jagger.

Not all fans were appalled. Some longtime followers understood straight away, recognizing the lineage that stretched from Robert Johnson to James Brown to Chic to the Sugarhill Gang. The Stones' excursions into disco and other styles made perfect sense, even to committed rockers like Lindsey Buckingham, singer and guitarist with Fleetwood Mac. "It all still had the spine of being the Stones, even when they were changing their context a little bit," says Buckingham, whose band was enjoying its greatest success with a moody blend of rock and folk at the height of the disco era. "It never got into an area where it was a caricature. It was still their own. They were always good at copping what was intelligent to cop, and just enough of it."

Still, *Emotional Rescue* is not a dance album. Only two tracks – 'Dance (Pt. 1)' and the title song – are built on the controversial big beat. And the

> **"It never got into an area where it was a caricature. They were always good at copping what was intelligent to cop"**
>
> Lindsey Buckingham, Fleetwood Mac, on disco and the Stones

emotional rescue

Stones soon abandoned the genre altogether. They were already in danger of falling behind the curve. Disco still dominated the US pop airwaves in 1980, but the club scene was suffering an undeniable fade. So dance music was just another flavour on an album that explored a variety of styles, from the blues of 'Down In The Hole' to the reggae of 'Send It To Me'.

As the band entered Compass Point Studio in the Bahamas in January '79, the Stones were still on a high from the commercial and critical comeback of *Some Girls* and Keith's escape from hard time. Now it was time to make another album. "The material on *Emotional Rescue* was a little bit more diverse than had gone on before," said Chris Kimsey, associate producer and engineer for *Emotional Rescue*. "If anything, it was a little more soul-orientated and laid back than the *Some Girls* album. A lot more relaxed. The writing for that album was a little bit more experimental. There hadn't been a long writing period. All of this built-up frustration had come out in *Some Girls*, but the *Emotional Rescue* felt a little bit left over."

Album sessions were soon moved to Pathé Marconi in Paris, where recording was typically done in the early morning hours. Keith broke a new personal record by going without sleep for nine consecutive days. Hard drugs were now gone from his life, but Keith was still a rock and roll vampire to the core.

"They're pretty unique in the way they do that," remembers saxophonist Bobby Keys. "That was the hour when everyone's adrenaline started working at the same time. I guess it's taken for granted that rock and roll and the Rolling Stones being a dark and forbidden subject should only take place in the cover of night. Daytime was for sleeping back then."

For Keys, daytime hours were largely spent unconcious on a couch in Richards' Paris apartment on Rue Victor Hugo. Together, Keys and Richards travelled to the nightly sessions for *Emotional Rescue* in Keith's orange-pink Bentley, a car once owned by the Queen Mother. "It seemed like Keith and Mick were a little bit more polarized at that time," says Keys, a veteran of Stones sessions since *Let It Bleed*. "There wasn't quite the same vibe when everyone was gathered together as there had been in the *Exile On Main Street* days."

When the sessions for *Emotional Rescue* ended, the Stones had amassed enough material for two albums. Some of that would emerge on 1981's *Tattoo You*. Left off of both albums was 'Claudine', an uptempo country tune inspired by the story of Claudine Longet, the former wife of crooner Andy Williams who was convicted of murdering her lover. As a cautionary tale of the fast and rich, it was irresistible, but possible litigation has kept 'Claudine' languishing underground on lo-fi bootlegs ever since. Even in 1980, the Stones were capable of looking for trouble, and finding it.

> " I guess it's taken for granted that rock and roll and the Rolling Stones being a dark and forbidden subject should only take place in the cover of night "
>
> Bobby Keys, saxophone player

dance (pt. 1)

here's no mistaking the intentions behind 'Dance (Pt. 1)'. Mick Jagger is serious about his funk, urging his minions to the dance floor. At more than four-minutes, the track was already well-prepared for international discotheque turntables. Not that the Stones were the only rock act stepping out to the big beat. In 1978, Blondie forged a dynamic blend of dance pop via 'Heart Of Glass' while somehow managing to keep their New Wave integrity intact.

'Dance' wasn't exactly the bold creative move that the funked-up 'Hot Stuff' had been for the Stones back in 1976. Four years later, the anti-disco backlash was spreading on both sides of the Atlantic.

"English people hate it 'cause they say it's all disco. That's what they think it is, you see," Jagger told *Rolling Stone* in 1980. "It's just black music."

Yet this wasn't quite like an Otis Redding soul jam. The Stones played 'Dance' with typical looseness and warmth, but there remained a certain emotional distance within its grooves, the glancing funk riffs, the heavy beat and crash of cymbals. The balance of emotional heat and dancefloor finesse that emerged so brilliantly on 'Miss You' was gone, no matter how often or how fervently the horn section erupted. 'Dance' existed in an emotional vacuum, and was about nothing more than the ecstacy of life under the strobe lights, with a few of Jagger's meaningless observations on the rich and poor. Back in the early days, the Stones had somehow expressed more when Jagger was singing of king bees and back street girls.

How could Keith have gone along with such a scheme? He felt the funk in his bones, too. After all, that's his playing (alongside Woody) on 'Dance' and 'Emotional Rescue'. He had a knack for the glancing funk chord pattern, a not-so-distant cousin to the fiery riff-rock Richards had played since the sixties. Just don't call this stuff DISCO to his face. Bad enough that Jagger cluttered up 'Dance' with his hyper partymaster ramble. "I saw 'Dance' as more of an instrumental, like Junior Walker's 'Shotgun'," Richards said later. "And Mick immediately came up with reams of paper and lyrics. I thought it should be a minimal lyric, and Mick comes up with *Don Giovanni*."

In 1981, the Rolling Stones released 'If I Was A Dancer (Dance Pt. 2)' on the compilation *Sucking In The Seventies*. The track was virtually identical to 'Dance (pt. 1)', but had lengthier, altered lyrics, with Jagger proclaiming: "If I was a politician, I'd make sure I was a fancy dancer."

Four-to-the-floor: there was no escaping the disco phenomenon of the late 1970s.

summer romance

he dance floor boogie of 'Dance' had its place in the vast Stones oevre, but it wasn't about to usurp the quintet's core sound. Rock and roll remained their true calling. And for that, *Emotional Rescue* listeners could turn to the anxious roots-rocker 'Summer Romance'. The band slides into a joyous dual-guitar groove here, as Jagger sings with a shrug about the end of a romance with some schoolgirl. Summer's over, so it's back to class for her, back to the pub for him.

Jagger's vocals are vaguely teasing, and the band rolls urgently forward, but 'Summer Romance' is ultimately an unremarkable track. Most astonishing is that it exists at all. Only a year before the release of *Emotional Rescue*, Mr Richards was a world-famous junkie who appeared headed for the big

emotional rescue

house, and was likely to take the Stones down with him. Now the Stones had a future again. Their playing had lost little of its verve, even if the the Glimmer Twins' songwriting potency had faded in the two years since *Some Girls*.

> " For at least five years, undoubtedly, I was the weak link in the chain "
>
> Keith Richards on his years as a junkie

"For at least five years, undoubtedly, I was the weak link in the chain," Richards told *Spin* in 1985. "From my point of view, no way. But I was, in retrospect, in no condition to judge. That's the horrible, terrible fascination of dope. That when you're on it everything's cool. And the more you take the more cool it is, and the more necessary it is to be cool. When all is said and done, I'm either damn lucky or, as I like to kid myself, real smart that I didn't manage to top myself in that period."

In September 1978, Wyman and Watts attended the funeral of the Who's drummer Keith Moon, who overdosed after a life of extremes in sex, drugs and rock and roll. Richards had survived the junkie years, but his days of adventure weren't yet behind him. Months before the *Emotional Rescue* sessions, the guitarist narrowly escaped death in Los Angeles when his rented house nestled in the hills of Laurel Canyon burst into flames, destroying everything except for his passport, some threads, a gun and 500 rounds of ammunition. Some outlaw habits are harder to shake.

send it to me

Rock stardom is not exactly the same as being rocksteady. God knows the Rolling Stones have tried. The band's love of reggae runs deep, but their own luck at recreating the sound has been confoundingly erratic. While the band finds a true, shuffling rhythm within 'Send It To Me', the song inevitably falls far short of the profoundly spiritual power of reggae's most important masters. Bob Marley was no prude, but it's hard to imagine him joining Mick for a duet on this crass call for mail order lovers. Jagger just wants to be your friend, so send your huddled masses of females from as far away as Australia, Romania, Albania, Hungary, the Ukraine, wherever…one at a time. "I guarantee her personal security," he promises. The examples of Marley and Peter Tosh – himself signed to Rolling Stones Records during the late 1970s – seemed far, far away.

let me go

Breakup is Mick Jagger's specialty. It's fun, entertaining and just so amusing. Jagger perfected the cruel science back in the mid-sixties with such brutal breakup tunes as 'Gotta Get Away' and 'Out Of Time'. As pop music, the songs were brilliant – as messages to various girlfriends, they were devastating. 'Let Me Go' is in much the same vein, although seemingly less cruel, and more comical, even as Jagger shouts "Can't you see the party's over?"

The song is a double-barrelled rocker, with both guitars firing at will, snapping at the low strings with the festering "clickity-clack-clack" guitar sound first heard on *Some Girls*.

'Let Me Go' doesn't rank high in context of the entire Stones song catalogue, but the band plays here with refreshing energy, finding inspiration again in one of the group's core themes.

indian girl

Innocence lost is not a recurring theme in the Rolling Stones catalogue. And politics leaves them cold. However, the Glimmer Twins are occasionally distracted from their usual tales of love and sex by larger questions of life and virtue, even if it doesn't always suit them. The Stones glide into a romantic exploration of a civil war's impact on the idyllic life Jagger imagines for the indiginous peoples of Central and South America. Jagger's interest, of course, is with the Indian GIRLS. But the imagery here is undeniably grim – soldiers steal food and rape women, a girl's parents are drafted into Cuban President Fidel Castro's battle for the proletariat on the bloodied streets of Angola. Bad news all around.

The Stones soften the blow with music that is soft and tropical, accented by pedal steel and mariachi horns, arranged by Jack Nitzsche, veteran sideman to the Stones, Phil Spector and numerous others. Jimmy Buffett would feel right at home.

Whatever serious message Jagger intended is lost amid the music's lazy, island paradise vibe. And Jagger mumbles his vocals, which suggests the man wasn't all that serious anyway.

where the boys go

'Where The Boys Go' is another archetypal Stones riff-rocker that has the band blurring past in a mild panic. Jagger sings here in a Cockney drawl of all the drinking, primping, pumping, dancing and stomping undertaken by members of the boys club while on their way to their next "piece of arse". The track is a leftover from the *Some Girls* sessions.

Ron Wood insists that the rollicking guitar solo at the song's bridge is just him doing his best Keith Richards imitation. Keith still thinks he did it. Which indicates how deeply Wood had by now integrated himself within the band, blending in with the founding fathers in a way that Mick Taylor never quite did with all his blues guitar heroics.

The rhythm guitar brotherhood of Richards and Wood was further cemented during the band's hiatus between *Some Girls* and *Emotional Rescue*. Wood was about to release his *Gimme Some Neck* solo album, and planned to gather a band for a tour. Richards simply needed something to do. Thus, the creation of the New Barbarians, a new travelling boys club led by the guitarists that included saxman Bobby Keys, bass guitar virtuoso Stanley Clarke, drummer Joseph Modeliste and Ian McLagan, former keyboardist with the Faces.

The New Barbarians were launched as the opening act for two Stones charity concerts for blind children at Toronto's Oskawa Hall. The shows had been a condition of Keith's suspended sentence for heroin possession – a lenient sentence heavily criticized by Canada's right-wing press. But the New Barbarians went on to perform 20 more concerts, ripping joyfully through Wood's solo material and such Richards signature tunes as 'Happy'.

In 1978, Richards had released a Christmas single of Chuck Berry's 'Run Rudolph Run' as a lark, but it was with the New Barbarians that fans saw their first glimpse of the guitarist's potential as a solo artist.

Ron Wood, Bobby Keys and Keith Richards rehearse the New Barbarians.

down in the hole

The blues still matter to the Rolling Stones. The profound pain and madness and wisdom of the great bluesmen, of Muddy Waters and John Lee Hooker and Elmore James, still burn at the core of this London quintet. That connection has only grown deeper with the passing years, even if it rarely manifests itself in straight-head blues recordings from the band. Which made 1980's 'Down In The Hole' a surprising, and welcome flexing of those blues muscles.

Jagger passes judgement on a vague figure of corruption and exploitation. His performance is direct and passionate, just as the band's playing is dark and brooding.

'Down In The Hole' is late evidence that the Rolling Stones could have remained a fine blues band if fashion and rock and roll hadn't intervened. The song's appearance on *Emotional Rescue* was a heartfelt reminder of the band's roots. But the track's warmth inevitably left listeners utterly unprepared for what was coming up next.

emotional rescue

Disco was already fading in 1980, ending up as just another seventies fad passing into history, along with Pet Rocks, eight-track tapes and Farrah Fawcett-Majors. Dance music would never really disappear, much to the relief of playboy Mick. This particular brand of dancefloor fodder would soon drift into nostalgia, but not before Jagger twisted it to his own ends.

Many listeners were unprepared for Jagger's vocal performance on 'Emotional Rescue'. He sings here in a weird falsetto, edgy and strained, and a thousand light years from the soft and pretty Bee Gees. When his voice returns occasionally to its normal growl, it's comes with a sense of relief, and is a fine payoff for what is otherwise a standard romantic ballad.

Barry Gibb of the Bee Gees discovered the falsetto late in life, just in time to create one of the most distinctive vocal quirks of the late-seventies. His frantic, badgering whine made songs like 'You Should Be Dancing' nagging touchstones for an era. Jagger's rendition was simply nagging, gliding across tinny synth effects, Watts' relentless disco beat, strangely thin horn sounds and bits of guitar in the distance.

The song and vocal earned ridicule from some critics, and inspired confusion even among the Stones' own collaborators. Saxman Bobby Keys appears on the track, but left before the vocals were finished. "It was pretty disco-sounding, but pretty good," Keys says now of the instrumental track. "When Jagger put that Minnie Mouse vocal on it I just couldn't believe it. I thought it was a joke. I really couldn't believe it."

Jagger wrote the song on electric piano, and was joined by Watts and Ron Wood in the studio, where it was quickly cut live. The final vocals, with Jagger muttering about coming to some poor woman's rescue, riding a "fine Arab charger", were ad-libbed. "You would NEVER really write a song like that in real life," Jagger assured *Rolling Stone* in 1980.

In the end, of course, it was less the content than the character of Jagger's vocals that made 'Emotional Rescue' a strange, memorable curve in the Stones catalogue. That awkward high, high voice sent the song into the top-10 on both sides of the Atlantic. "I always found it a bit twee, myself," Chris Kimsey said of the falsetto. "It was a novel idea. A lot of that album was going that way. It was very experimental, that album."

emotional rescue

she's so cold

No explanation needed. The title says it all. The man is seething, panting, practically drooling on the floor, and pleading to some impossibly gorgeous babe: "I'm a bleedin' VOLCANO!" Yes, Jagger's in heat again, ablaze in blind lust, and absolutely amazed, utterly aghast that this little woman could possibly resist his aggressive charm.

All of which makes 'She's So Cold' a kind of 'Satisfaction' for bored adults. The message is simple, as it should be at times like these. Likewise, the band plays at full throttle, both excited and tense. Watts and Wyman build an anxious rhythm, as Richards and Wood pluck at the low tones, creating a sound not unlike that of *Some Girls*. By now the Stones could fall into that groove with ease, though the impudent, dangerous wit of that album's sexist manifesto was harder to come by.

all about you

'All About You' is Keith Richards at his sloppiest. And most direct. The song is a lethargic love-hate ballad long understood to be his bittersweet farewell to Anita Pallenberg. Richards' determination (and legal neccesity) to kick his heroin habit partly required a separation from the mother of his two children. But the final break came during 1979, when a 17-year-old boy shot himself in the head at the couple's house in South Salem, Westchester County, during a lonely game of Russian Roulette. Pallenberg was questioned for 12 hours by police about the boy found dead in her bed. She was released without any charges filed, but Keith had been through enough. "If you call this a life," Richards sings, "why must I spend mine with you?"

'All About You' sounds unfinished, as if the band members were still figuring out their parts. Guitars twang to no discernable direction or purpose, and Keith's vocal performance stumbles and cracks. But the result is genuine, organic barstool blues. Within the mix are slow, downcast sax melodies by Bobby Keys, who, according to Richards, "played his ass off on this album." It was about as far from some of the album's thumping dance music as possible.

Anita Pallenberg: an incident with a 17-year-old boy was the last straw for Keith.

Keys insists that the bitter lyrics may perhaps have been less about Keith breaking up with Anita than they were an irritable description of current state of affairs between the Glimmer Twins. "It had a little bit of sentimental input there about his feelings for Mick at the time," says Keys with a laugh. "Just listen to the lyrics."

More love and hate within the ranks. Though little-noticed at the time, 'All About You' was maybe a small warning about the Rolling Stones' combative decade which was just then getting started.

chapter sixteen

1981 tattoo you

Up against the wall? *Tattoo You* restored faith after the disappointment of *Emotional Rescue*.

Start Me Up

Hang Fire

Slave

Little T&A

Black Limousine
(JAGGER/RICHARDS/WOOD)

Neighbors

Worried About You

Tops

Heaven

No Use In Crying
(JAGGER/RICHARDS/WOOD)

Waiting On A Friend

The Rolling Stones mean well. Really they do. But the blissed-out seventies were a strange decade for everyone. Even the once-divine John Lennon and Paul McCartney saw some extreme highs and lows as solo artists. For the Stones things had certainly started well enough with *Sticky Fingers* and *Exile On Main Street*, and true believers found hope once more in the edgy spunk rock of *Some Girls* in 1978. But even Jagger and Richards had doubts about the so-called "me" decade, a time that found the Stones awash in drugs and decadence, and hobbled by a lengthy creative drought. Their own verdict on the last ten years came in the form of an album title given to their newest greatest hits collection: *Sucking In The Seventies*.

So how do we explain *Tattoo You*? It arrived in the summer of 1981 to rescue the band's reputation just as fans and critics were again beginning to lose faith. And yet nothing new was recorded for the album. Instead, the Stones dug into the same vat of material that had harmed their reputation for much of the previous decade, and somehow emerged with a better collection of songs than anyone could have expected. *Tattoo You* was a gathering of outtakes and rejects, forgotten leftovers from sessions for *Goats Head Soup*, *Black And Blue*, *Some Girls* and *Emotional Rescue*. What they showed was not a band in creative decline. If anything, the new album demonstrated that the raw materials for greatness were there all along. The Stones had simply lost the touch to pull it all together. Until now.

"*Tattoo You* really came about because Mick and Keith were going through a period of not getting on," producer Chris Kimsey said later. "There was a need to have an album out, and I told everyone I could make an album from what I knew was still there. They used to put so much stuff down, and a couple of years later they'd forget all about it."

It was from that material that *Tattoo You* was made. Could we have been so wrong? Had *Goats Head Soup* and *Emotional Rescue* in fact been great rock and roll discs? Not exactly, except perhaps in the context of much of what had come since. The punk revolution hadn't yet overthrown the rock establishment as planned, especially in America. Conservatism reigned as usual. So here were the Stones chugging through one of Keith's most obvious riffs on 'Start Me Up', the kind of thing he used to dismiss in the days of 'Gimme Shelter' and 'Brown Sugar'. The song erupted as a welcome blast from the past and a reminder of the core ethics of rock and roll in the face of such current horrors as Journey and REO Speedwagon.

The Rolling Stones weren't about to chart any new creative territory in 1981, particularly if they were simply raiding the vaults. They had played their part in the sixties and early seventies. Let the Clash or Talking Heads come up with some crazy new sounds for the kids. Nothing could eclipse the Stones' role as a primal source – like Bill Monroe singing 'Blue Moon Of Kentucky' or Louie Armstrong blowing a solo with the Hot Fives. The Stones were history, not nostalgia. Kimsey had provided the needed early enthusiasm for *Tattoo You*. As the co-producer of both *Some Girls* and *Emotional Rescue*, he knew just how much was left waiting in the vaults. He'd always made a point of recording everything the Stones did during the sessions, even if it was just an old Jimmy Reed blues jam. And he kept a comprehensive log of how many songs were recorded and where they were hidden. There were 150 reels of tape from the *Some Girls* sessions alone.

"If it was happening I made sure it got on tape," Kimsey said. "So I wasn't surprised at all to go back and find that from *Goats Head Soup* and *Black And Blue* some really good material had just been forgotten about really. The organization was really bad of their tapes as well. It took me a very long time to find the masters. They were sort of scattered all over the place and nobody had bothered to log anything. Nobody knew what was going on."

Kimsey finally unearthed two tracks from the dusty *Goats Head Soup* tapes, another from the Rotterdam sessions for *Black And Blue*, and rounded off the album with outtakes from *Some Girls* and

> **"If it was happening I made sure it got on tape"**
>
> Chris Kimsey, engineer

tattoo you

Emotional Rescue. Jagger and Richards then began work on writing and recording the lyrics.

"They're all from different periods," Jagger told *Rolling Stone* in 1995. "Then I had to write lyrics and melodies. A lot of them didn't have anything, which is why they weren't used at the time – because they weren't complete. They were just bits, or they were from early takes. And then I put them together in an incredibly cheap fashion. I recorded in this place in Paris in the middle of the winter. And then I recorded some of it in a broom cupboard, literally, where we did the vocals. The rest of the band were hardly involved."

The Glimmer Twins had by now got past their little feud. But finishing up *Tattoo You* still took a good nine months, mainly because in December 1980 Mick left for Peru to begin filming *Fitzcarraldo* with director Werner Herzog. Filming was halted months later when star Jason Robards fell ill and the set was attacked by Amazonian Indians. By the time filming resumed later in the year Mick was on the road with the Stones, and no longer available for his close-up.

In the months prior to the album's summer release, the rest of the band also kept busy. Bill Wyman composed the soundtrack to the film *Green Ice*, a thriller starring Ryan O'Neal, and enjoyed a UK hit single with '(Si, Si) Je Suis Un Rock Star'. Rocket 88, the band led by Charlie Watts and Ian Stewart, released an album from a concert recorded at the Rotation Club in Hanover, Germany in 1979. Ron Wood's *1234* album was prepared for release. And in June, Keith stepped backstage at the Ritz in New York to say hello to his guitar hero Chuck Berry, who immediately punched Keith in the eye when he didn't recognize him. Berry later apologized to Ron Wood, thinking he was Keith.

The Stones soon announced their 1981 world tour, which would bring them through stadiums and arenas to a new generation of listeners. It was also the first rock tour to be "sponsored", after Jovan perfume paid $4-million for the privilege of attaching its name to the Stones roadshow. That raised some eyebrows before opening the floodgates for future tours by major acts to be sponsored by any number of beer and sneaker companies.

Even that sacrilege was largely overlooked with the release of *Tattoo You*, which earned the band its best reviews in years and topped the album charts in both England and America, where it dominated the top spot for nine consecutive weeks. Small, elegant touches like hiring bop saxman Sonny Rollins to solo on 'Slave' and other tracks hadn't gone unnoticed. And the presence of Mick Taylor's guitar on two of the tracks culled from the *Goats Head Soup* sessions returned the band to a certain musical grandeur and subtlety. In the end, even if the songs did emerge from different periods, the sound and vibe were held together thanks to the work of engineer Bob Clearmountain behind the mixing desk.

When the album was released, Richards suggested that the vaults still held other treasures that could be unearthed for future albums. "That's an advantage you don't think about, really, with a band that goes on for a long time," Keith told *Rolling Stone* in 1981. "One way or another, you end up with a backlog of really good stuff that, for one reason or another, you didn't get the chance to finish or put out because it was the wrong tempo or too long – purely technical reasons, you know? Sometimes we write songs in installments – just get the melody and the music and we'll cut the tracks and write the words later. That way the actual tracks have matured just like wine – you just leave it in the cellar for a bit, and it comes out a little better a few years later."

> **"Sometimes we write songs in installments – just get the melody and music and we'll cut the tracks and write the words later"**
> — Keith Richards

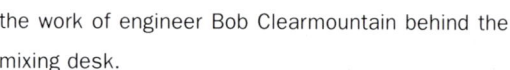

During the 1980s the Stones forged a reputation for their spectacular live shows.

start me up

Give the people what they want. In the case of the Rolling Stones, that doesn't mean quasi-disco numbers designed to compete with Donna Summer and the Bee Gees. If the rock and roll masses want to dance, they'll do it to the likes of the chunky riffing that slowly opens 'Start Me Up', a steady rocker that distilled the Stones down to their barest essentials.

'Start Me Up' became an instant standard in the Stones repertoire, with a sound that was both exciting and absolutely familiar: Richards chopping out a menacing chord, Watts and Wyman building a potent rhythm, and Jagger ranting lustfully – on 'Start Me Up' he uses an automobile engine as a metaphor for his sexual itch.

There was nothing new here, of course, nothing that hadn't already been done to greater effect through 'Jumpin' Jack Flash' and 'Brown Sugar' years earlier. But just how many pop revolutions were the Stones supposed to lead? These opening moments on *Tattoo You* argued that there was some value in simply refining their sound.

The song dates back to the *Some Girls* sessions, and was recorded the same day as the classic 'Miss You' at Pathé Marconi Studios in Paris. It began as a rock track, but after just two takes the Stones reworked 'Start Me Up' as a reggae number for nearly two-dozen miserable takes that the entire

tattoo you

band hated. The second take was the only complete rock version of 'Start Me Up' to be recorded, and was left off of Some Girls because Mick and Keith thought it sounded like something they heard on the radio. It was soon forgotten.

"I knew that was there, and I knew it was so good," Kimsey told journalist Craig Rosen in 1994. "It's really what inspired me to say 'I'm sure I can put an album together with what's already there'. That was my ground base, that song."

hang fire

Nearly a decade after becoming tax exiles from Mother England, the Rolling Stones could still cough up a knowing sneer for the folks back home. 'Hang Fire' sees Mick ranting on the state of Britain: "Where I come from, nobody ever works, nothing ever gets done".

'Hang Fire' was another Some Girls outtake, an uptempo rocker, but the lyrics were not added until the 1981 Tattoo You sessions. By now, the UK had entered the era of Prime Minister Margaret Thatcher, whose relentless critiques of the post-war welfare state made her a popular target for attacks from leftists. Rife with unemployment, inflation and despair, England had seen better days. But the debate seemed a thousand light years away from the daily reality of the Rolling Stones.

"They're going through their little traumas over there. It serves them right for kickin' us out," Keith told Rolling Stone in 1981. "It's coming to terms with a whole lot of problems that have been brewing for years, and the only thing it needed for these problems to come to a head was for the money to get tight. Politics is an ugly word these days, and the only people who make politics an ugly word are politicians, because they're ugly people."

The track's working title was 'Lazy Bitch'. Not surprisingly, 'Hang Fire' was released as a single only in the United States.

> "Politics is an ugly word these days, and the only people who make politics an ugly word are politicians, because they are ugly people"
>
> Keith Richards

Prime Minister Margaret Thatcher oversaw a period in which the divide between rich and poor grew ever wider.

slave

'Slave' began life as a lengthy jam at the Rotterdam sessions for Black And Blue, and blends a charged rock sound with a smooth funk rhythm. Guitars rumble to an arch beat, and Jagger repeats his agonizing mantra: "Don't want to be your slave!" He's joined during the chorus by guest Pete Townshend. Jagger pauses only to coldly rap out orders to his girlfriend of the hour to pick up a few things at the liquor store. Love hurts.

On the final version of the song, the Glimmer Twins went outside their normal rock and roll circles to recruit bop saxman Sonny Rollins. Once called the greatest tenor player of all time by Miles Davis, Rollins' recording career began in the late forties, playing alongside such jazz masters as Art Blakey, Bud Powell and Davis. Over the decades Rollins explored a variety of sounds, from bop to free-form to funk-based fusion. He remains a pace-setter even into the 1990s. On 'Slave', Rollins rolls into a fluid, passionate improvised solo. The sax master manages to set fire to the track without resorting to anything experimental that might mar one of the most commercial albums of the Stones' career.

tattoo you

little t&a

Sexism with love. Keith Richards sounds seriously moved as he groans of finding salvation from his "tits and ass with soul baby". And why not? Richards was a changed man. He'd just survived the threat of a lifetime in Canada, where he faced an existence behind bars for a drug habit that had overrun his life for too long. In 'Little T&A', Keith sings of abandoning those ways for the inspiration of a fine woman – his girlfriend of the hour. "That song's about every good time I've had with somebody I'd met for a night or two and never seen again," Richards explained.

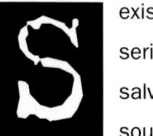

Patti Hansen (right): she helped to put Keith Richards on the straight and narrow.

Boys will be boys, as Ronnie Wood has said. But the song's sense of indebtedness may well have been inspired by model Patti Hansen, whom the guitarist met a year earlier at the Roxy Roller Disco in New York City – although what Keith was doing at a roller disco we can only begin to speculate. The couple would marry in 1983. Here he expresses his affection to a stirring blend of frantic guitars, Charlie Watts' thrashing drums and Bill Wyman's anxiously rumbling bass. Mick's testy background vocals can be heard in the distance. The song was first recorded during sessions for *Emotional Rescue* in the Bahamas with the working title 'Bulldog'. The final version of 'Little T&A' was released on the B-side of the quieter 'Waiting On A Friend', another song of companionship.

black limousine

In some ways, 'Black Limousine' is a kinder look at women than a typical Stones track. It's a harsh but loving remembrance of days sharing limousines, booze, dancing and dreams with the women of their lives. Recorded during the *Some Girls* sessions, the song is a mid-tempo boogie, a blend of guitars, Mick's wheezy harp and Ian Stewart's joyous piano.

The music of 'Black Limousine' is bright and excited, obscuring the haunted message within. By contrast, the lyrics look with a mixture of sadness and horror at the battle-scarred bodies that are left behind following years of fast living and abuse – Andy Warhol had once noted with surprise just how beat-up the Stones looked in the daylight.

On 'Black Limousine', Jagger could easily be referring to Anita Pallenberg, Marianne Faithfull or anybody else who might have been left in the Stones' wake as he sings: "Well now look at your face now, baby…and look at me".

neighbors

Welcome to Mr Richards' neighbourhood. Which also happens to be your neighbourhood, overlooking the big city from a fabulous Manhattan high rise apartment building. You're living in style, with a uniformed doorman downstairs, and Central Park is your front yard. Better still, Keith Richards lives next door! Hipster paradise! Except that the man has got his fucking stereo cranked up at all hours of the night and day, and God knows what sort of "friends" he has skulking in from the streets. But you can't expect Keith to check into the decadent Chelsea Hotel or shack up somewhere in East Village Bohemia. Not in the eighties. Keith needs a place suitable for his supermodel girlfriend. After all, Keith is RICH, just like his neighbours. The double-decibel

tattoo you

tattoo you

Sonny Rollins, one of the principal figures of modern jazz.

rock and roll is just part of the package, the price to be paid for mingling so close to rock star royalty. Hope you understand.

So 'Neighbors' is the story of Keith Richards, told via slicing guitars, a bluesy sax solo and Charlie's steady, thumping beat. The guitarist claims its the first song Mick Jagger ever wrote for him. No doubt Mick was inspired by Keith's eviction from his apartment earlier in 1981, after neighbours complained that his music was just too damn loud. And it wasn't the first time.

"I have a knack of finding a whole building of very cool people, you know, but there'll be one uncool couple – they're always a couple. And my apartment will always be either just above them or next door to them or just below," Keith told journalist Kurt Loder in 1981. "And they're the kind of people who'll knock you up at six in the morning, while you've just sort of got a little bit of music going... By now I'm aware I can't blast the sounds. So I'm trying to be cool about it. And these people come up to our door saying 'We can't even hear Bugs Bunny on our TV, you're music's so loud! Turn the kettledrums down!' So, I mean, I'm PLAGUED by that kind of thing." His youthful existence deep in the isolated countryside at Redlands, his thatched palace in West Sussex, seemed very far away.

On 'Neighbors', Jagger shouts about a nightmare of screaming babies, blaring TVs and would-be saxophone players practicing scales into the night. Flailing behind him are the Stones, making the kind of reckless noise designed to send your own neighbours up the wall. Jazzman Sonny Rollins makes another appearance in which he blows an appropriately howling solo.

In the video directed by Michael Lindsay-Hogg, Jagger sings from a tenement window, watching as his neighbours engage in various acts of sex, violence and boredom. The image is far from the reality of Keith's apartment life, but the guitarist related deeply to the song's underlying message: "It's one I wish I'd written, that."

worried about you

Mick ain't worried about you. He wants to know why you're treating HIM this way. He admits "you ain't the only one", and that he's out at night having fun, but now he's starting to wonder if you really love him. Credit the man for at least trying to figure things out.

'Worried About You' was recorded during the *Black And Blue* sessions and opens with a subdued blend of electric piano, light funk riffing on guitar and a light tapping of the cymbals from Charlie. From Jagger comes the falsetto that had earned him so much grief on 'Emotional Rescue'. But this is a sensitive reading, and the falsetto is used with some restraint, before his voice erupts into a full howl.

The Glimmer Twins cleverly omitted musician credits on *Tattoo You* – a ploy that not only disguised the age of some of the songs, but also who is playing the music. Mick Taylor complained bitterly when he wasn't rightfully credited for the tracks culled from *Goats Head Soup*. It's likely that the smooth funk lead, skirting across the bridge of 'Worried About You', is played by guitarist Wayne Perkins, one of several guitarists auditioned for the band during the *Black And Blue* sessions. If 'Worried About You' is a slow, almost lethargic ballad, in the context of the wide range of sounds on *Tattoo You*, the song emerges as an appropriate and welcome flavour.

tops

After quitting the Rolling Stones in December 1974, Mick Taylor virtually disappeared. Following his aborted supergroup with Jack Bruce, Taylor's career skirted below the pop radar, far from the high profile he enjoyed as a Stone. Until his long-awaited solo album in 1979, the guitarist spent his days working as a guest sideman to a variety of players, including old friend and mentor John Mayall. Meanwhile, the Rolling Stones juggernaut continued ever onward. Imagine his surprise in 1981 when some of his leftover performances from *Goats Head Soup* appeared on the Stones' new hit album. And the surprise was not only his. The Rolling Stones had undergone another transformation with the addition of Ron Wood, but now, on tracks like 'Tops'

tattoo you

and 'Waiting On A Friend', Taylor's fluid blues lines were once again in place.

On 'Tops', Mick Jagger rides a slow R&B groove, urging a young woman to leave her small town behind. Join him in the big city, Jagger sings, where he can make her a star. She's a natural, he insists, a rare talent just waiting for a turn up the ladder of success. As muscular piano rhythms pound behind him, Jagger warns, "Never, never let success get to your pretty head!"

For Taylor, pop success was a passing fancy. He'd apparently had his fill during his five years with the Rolling Stones. The years since have been spent largely on the road. His lack of credit on *Tattoo You* only further symbolized his disappearance from the rock and roll spotlight.

Mick Taylor was surprised to find his contributions gracing a 1981 Stones album.

heaven

More seething sexuality from Mick Jagger, this time to the sound of an ethereal guitar blend, light in touch, and with a vibe that would escape the Stones in later years as age sent them marching deeper into hard rocking grooves. 'Heaven' is a rare track cut especially for *Tattoo You*, but the shimmering instrumentation could just as easily have been culled from the band's later years with Mick Taylor.

Those were experimental times, but the Stones of 1981 felt little pressure to follow the new trend toward computers and automation. "The guitar, apart from its musical worth and versatility, also has a mystique about it – the way it looks at plays – that is very central to rock and roll," Keith told *Goldmine* magazine in 1983. "It's pretty much always going to be the central core of most rock and roll. We first used synthesizers in the early seventies to augment our sound, but I could never see us adding synthesizers to our lineup permanently."

> **"The guitar, apart from its musical worth and versatility, also has a mystique about it...that is very central to rock and roll"**
>
> Keith Richards

no use in crying

Ron Wood had been a creative force from his first moments as a Stone, beginning with 'Hey Negrita' on *Black And Blue*. However, along with 'Black Limousine', 'No Use In Crying' was a breakthrough, earning the guitarist his first co-songwriting credits on a Rolling Stones album. This was no small thing. The absence of songwriting recognition had partly led to Mick Taylor's sudden departure years before.

"It was a big thing for Ronnie to try to get it on there," said producer Chris Kimsey. "He had to do it carefully, rather than just saying 'Well I'm writing this song'. He was doing it cautiously, because there's a pact between Mick and Keith – everything is Jagger/Richards. That's changed over the years slowly, but the majority is always Jagger/Richards."

That's remained true even into the nineties, but the credit of Jagger/Richards/Wood slowly became a common presence on Stones albums as the years rolled forward. 'No Use In Crying' is a tortured love ballad, a Stones torch lament, with elements of country blues. But it's Jagger who's conducting the torture. As Richards and Wood pick lightly at their electric guitars, Jagger sings passionately about his fading love – "If you see your ship come a sailing, it's not me, it's not me".

tattoo you

waiting on a friend

'Waiting On A Friend' is another leftover from the *Goats Head Soup* sessions with Taylor, and it makes a quietly satisfying finish to *Tattoo You*. There's a touching warmth to be found here, a delicate mingling of guitars, percussion, piano and a wistful hooting from Jagger. He sings of finding enough maturity and self-control to just let the girls pass by today. It's not sex he's after now, but the simple goodwill of friendship. "I need someone I can cry to," he sings.

In the video to 'Waiting On A Friend', director Michael Lindsay-Hogg – who had worked with the Stones more than a decade earlier on *Rock and Roll Circus* – captured that relaxed, brotherly mood. Jagger is seen sitting on a New York stoop, casually waiting for Richards, who is shown strolling through the neighbourhood and toward the singer. Together they step into a local pub and find the rest of the Stones.

> " As long as I can play well and improve in my own life then, damn it, I'll be playing "
>
> Keith Richards

The song strikes an authentic mood, and may have been inspired by Mick and Keith's own long relationship. By now they lived largely separate lives, Keith solidly in the rock and roll trenches, Jagger amid the comfortable upper crust. There were no more road trips to Morocco, no more jamming endlessly at all hours of the night and day. Wives, girlfriends, children and age all inevitably took their toll on that lifestyle. But their bond was deep, going back to their days as anonymous toddlers in London, and then again after meeting as teenagers on a train, debating the finer points of Chuck Berry and Muddy Waters.

That friendship would be severely tested in the coming decade. Jagger would soon commit the ultimate sacrilege by launching a solo career, chasing after the new dancefloor sounds of the eighties and a new generation of fans. And now that he was finally free from the drugs that had limited

tattoo you

him for so long, Richards was eager to take the Stones into respectable middle-age. "As long as I can play well and improve in my own life," Keith said in 1983, "then, damn it, I'll be playing."

But the success of *Tattoo You* at least gave a demonstration that the necessary powers were still within their reach, if the Glimmer Twins could just focus their energy to make it happen.

The Glimmer Twins: they have their ups and downs just like any other couple.

chapter seventeen

1983 undercover

The original members may have passed their fortieth birthdays, but the Stones show no signs of slowing down.

Undercover Of The Night

She Was Hot

Tie You Up (The Pain Of Love)

Wanna Hold You

Feel On Baby

Too Much Blood

Pretty Beat Up
(JAGGER/RICHARDS/WOOD)

Too Tough

All The Way Down

It Must Be Hell

Credit the Rolling Stones for at least having some ambition left in middle age. Not that *Undercover* was much appreciated at the time by critics, who assailed the band for weak material, production overkill, strange guitar monkeyshines and a highly suspect new fascination with Latin American politics. Even Mick Jagger later declared that *Undercover* was "not a very special record".

True enough at the time, but the years have been kinder to the album. Within these grooves is the sound of a veteran rock act earnestly reaching for continued relevance in an uncertain new era, dabbling in new themes and textures. Most important, the Stones were still a tight, seething combo in 1983, playing fast and loose with reckless ease. Contemporaries like the Who could hardly claim so much at this late date. And even the album's most marginal tracks offer more heat than anything on the much-hyped *Steel Wheels* or *Voodoo Lounge*.

The Stones were aiming here for the darkness of *Exile On Main Street*, but landed somewhere closer to the raunch of *Some Girls*. Only this time the Stones were mixing politics with their poontang. *Undercover* returned the band and co-producer Chris Kimsey to EMI's Pathé Marconi Studios in Paris, and the oversize recording room they had called home since *Some Girls* – the studio has since been bulldozed to make room for a parking garage. They began by going over material left over from earlier albums, but soon resumed the jam sessions that had spawned so many worthy songs over the years.

"They record the same way as a bunch of kids starting out," says Jim Barber, who worked as Keith's guitar tech on *Undercover*, and was recruited to play guitar on 'Too Much Blood'. "They set up in the studio facing each other, and they can smell the drummer. They're not in another room on radio systems. No computers involved. It was very much one-to-one. Quite a bit of arguments about what key to do things in."

The Glimmer Twins were now ankle deep into the 1980s, but the sparkle hadn't yet faded from the "World's Greatest Rock And Roll Band", and nothing yet suggested serious decline. The Stones had just returned from the worldwide *Tattoo You* tour, the largest yet of their notorious arena rock cavalcades. They had also left the usual trail of casualties in their wake: teenage shoot-outs outside a concert in Texas, enraged gate crashers in Connecticut – it was just like the old days, when cops and politicians could blame the downward spiral of civilization on these superstar cretins of rock. French fans lit two fires at the Hippodrome d'Auteuil in protest at exorbitant ticket prices, but the fans still came, to hear these famed rockers, to see the monkeyman dance and sing in his day-glow jumpsuits.

Now, after a dozen eventful years with Atlantic Records, the Stones signed a new contract with CBS reported to be worth $25 million. It was the most lucrative record deal in history, coming a full decade before the likes of Michael Jackson, Madonna and Aerosmith were offered equally massive deals. CBS was immediately rewarded with *Undercover*, a top-10 album in both England and the US. It fell a little short of the Stones' usual position at the very top of the album charts, but business was still good.

The band also demonstrated a flair for the era's marketing medium of choice – the music video. They were already pioneers via their creepy promotional film for 1968's 'Jumpin' Jack Flash' and *The Rock And Roll Circus*. In director Julian Temple – the man behind *The Great Rock And Roll Swindle* – the Stones found a young collaborator to help them achieve MTV glory. That meant scenes of raw sexual comedy – the bursting zips of 'She Was Hot' – and random violence – Keith chasing after Mick with a gun on 'Undercover Of The Night', and with a chainsaw on 'Too Much Blood'. The BBC may not have approved, but MTV obliged, with only minimal editing of the most extreme moments.

So the Stones were aging with some dignity, enduring in a time not of their own making, even if

> **"They record the same way as a bunch of kids starting out. They set up in the studio facing each other…they're not in another room on radio systems"**
>
> Jim Barber, guitarist

undercover

Jagger's own daughter Jade much preferred the fashionable new pop sounds of Eurythmics and Boy George. The Rolling Stones could still move listeners in unexpected ways Jagger reported that one fan mailed a severed hand in the mail in response to the song 'Too Much Blood', with the note: "Hope this goes with your song and the album's successful".

That depended largely on what occurred back at Pathé Marconi. For the Stones, the process of making records was still much as it had always been, with the Glimmer Twins in search of that timeless blend of beat, riff and attitude. In Paris, Jim Barber remembers watching as Keith methodically pieced together tracks: first the key, then the tempo, and maybe a slight change of rhythm, and so on, with Mick watching his partner carefully. "He is very, very precise," Barber says of Richards. "And it's his band, not Mick's. Without Keith in the studio the whole thing is a mess. Once Keith walks in the door, suddenly it gels."

> " It's his band [Keith Richards'], not Mick's. Without Keith in the studio the whole thing is a mess. Once Keith walks in the door, suddenly it gels "
>
> Jim Barber, guitarist

Undercover illustrated Mick Jagger's unlikely interest in Latin-American politics.

undercover of the night

As they had done with *Emotional Rescue*, the Rolling Stones in 1983 responded to a hit album with a follow-up that was more experimental, in both form and content. That much was obvious from the first moments of 'Undercover Of The Night', which begins suddenly with the clatter of percussion and a heavy beat, sounding not unlike gunfire. Across that staccato funk rhythm, a spare guitar riff erupts sporadically, as if to underline the brutal action in Jagger's lyrics. The aggressive echo effects, ricocheting between beats, only add to the track's claustrophobic sense of doom.

This wasn't the Stones as we had come to know them, not the band of sublime dissipation and seedy glamour. This was the sound of violence and speed, a soundtrack for your local cut-throat dictatorship. Mick was thinking hard about politics in 1983. The Stones had rarely dabbled in the stuff, and even when they did, the message was one of ambivalence and scorn. But recent events in Latin America, with civil wars in El Salvador and Nicaragua, had caught Jagger's attention. A new battlefield for the Cold War was festering south of the US border, where a storm of class warfare and political oppression raged ever onward with the financial blessing of the American government.

Fuelling Jagger's enmity on 'Undercover Of The Night' was knowledge of the American government's support of right-wing dictators in the region, all in the name of anti-Soviet solidarity. Death squads in El Salvador, political assassination in Nicaragua. "People whisper, people double-talk," Jagger sneers.

Millions of American tax dollars went to support the "contra" rebels – "freedom fighters", according to President Ronald Reagan – challenging the Marxist government of Nicaragua. Even more flowed into the right-wing government of El Salvador, a country where less than two percent of the population owned

> " You have to be very careful. You dig pits that you fall into. You may have to eat your words more than once in your life "
>
> Mick Jagger

more than 60 percent of the land. More than 75,000 lives were claimed by the civil war, including the 1980 assassination of populist Archbishop Oscar Arnulfo Romero. A decade after the release of *Undercover*, a United Nations commission found that responsibility for the murder and disappearance of thousands of Salvadoran civilians belonged to senior figures of the rightist paramilitary National Guard.

On 'Undercover Of The Night', Jagger sings of death squads and dictatorships, of the disappearance of young men into the jails of South America and of young women with painted faces and dressed in lace for the pleasure of "dirty little GI Joes". Those dark forces are on display in a video directed by Julian Temple. Jagger portrays a man kidnapped in San Salvador, while Richards is an armed assassin wearing a Death's head mask.

The irony for Jagger was that for all the overt and covert support toward dubious international forces, the American government had laughably little control over its favourite dictators in Africa, Latin America, Asia and the Middle East. Real democracy was rarely the result of all those dollars. "That dictator [Anastasio Somoza] we supported in Nicaragua was definitely... I mean anyone could tell that guy had to go," Jagger told *Rolling Stone* in 1983. "So if the Americans had wanted to be in control of that – which they were paying these people to be – they should have said 'OK, your time is up, we're going to put somebody else in.' A centrist government, a left-wing coalition, whatever. Same thing with the Shah of Iran. We were supposed to be in control of events in those countries – and we just never really, in actual fact, were."

Power to the people was not Jagger's usual message. Indeed, the Stones had come under repeated attack by such hyper-political acts as the Clash precisely because of their distance from the little people. Now Jagger could cackle knowingly about pop revolutionaries "playing Philadelphia's JFK Stadium in Clash T-shirts," Jagger told Kurt Loder. "Yeah, you have to be very careful. You dig pits that you fall into. You may have to eat your words more than once in your life."

she was hot

> **"There's still disappointment when a single doesn't chart or is panned by critics"**
> Jim Barber, guitarist

Behold Mick Jagger in his vamping, leering, lip-smacking prime. There's no redeeming social value whatsoever. Just sex for its own sake, a tale of lustful fantasy. Yes, it may be dumb and crass, but there's life in these grooves, and a casualness that would be increasingly difficult for the Stones to find in the coming years. The band winds through an excited rocker as Jagger sings of repeated encounters with a woman as insatiable as the singer himself – Jagger had, in fact, once declared: "If I was a woman, I'd want a different man every night!"

The song's potential for blue comedy was explored in a video that starred red-headed dancer Anita Norris as the subject of Jagger's heated testimonial. Her very presence is enough to make guitar necks melt, enough to cause the crotch of a film executive to erupt, enough to leave Jagger's quivering body in cinders on his bed.

Sex, sex, sex. Maybe the man has run out of ideas. After all, is 'She Was Hot' really much different from the equally lustful dispatch of 'She's So Cold' from *Emotional Rescue*? The titles are self-explanatory, and indicate a certain limitation to Jagger's repertoire. But it's no fatal flaw as long as the band can still find that seductive boogie-woogie vibe. The humour and drive owe as much to the playing of Richards, Wyman, Watts, Wood and Ian Stewart. So many other survivors of the sixties were bands in name only, more a business partnership

undercover

than a continued creative endeavour. If relationships within the Rolling Stones sometimes grew prickly, there was so far not enough hatred to tear apart the music they had built together. The Stones entered the new decade as players on the contemporary scene, not peddlers of nostalgia.

"There's still disappointment when a single doesn't chart or is panned by critics," says Barber. "That's obviously important to them. It's not just a money thing that keeps them going. It's the love of playing. They do have that primitive element to it, which works still. The minute that goes, they'll stop doing it."

In spite of his age, Mick Jagger's live performances remain as athletic as ever.

undercover

tie you up (the pain of love)

'Tie You Up (The Pain Of Love)' is another track of wild sexual innuendo. Jagger's mush-mouthed vocals are mixed deep into the mix this time, leaving the exact details of his message unclear, even if the general nature of his song is obvious. Sex! Masochism! Tough, tough love! Please! His deepening growl is balanced against the feverish falsetto hooting of his background vocals. Richards and Wood provide some appropriately raunchy guitar passages, slicing across the soulful organ of Chuck Leavell and the big beat of Charlie Watts.

wanna hold you

Some critics were sceptical of the Rolling Stones' sudden interest in politics as expressed on 'Undercover Of The Night'. Naturally, context is everything. And virtually everything else on the album was obsessed with love and sex – hardly unusual for the Stones, or for the primal blues sources that inspired them so many years before. But where did the band's passions really lay? The answer can be heard in its most basic form on 'Wanna Hold You'. Keith Richards sings with overheated anxiety to a woman with promises of fidelity, offering free love for her time. The music behind him races along at a frantic pace, all winding guitars and boiling rhythm. The guarantees of loyalty are romantic, but hardly surprising coming from Richards, who maintained a long relationship with Anita Pallenberg before marrying Patti Hansen in 1983 on his 40th birthday. 'Wanna Hold You' is another ragged vocal performance by Richards, but the simple, upbeat promise rings true. "Yeah, I'm in love," Keith said of Hansen in 1981. "It's the greatest feeling in the world, right?"

feel on baby

No sixties rock and roll band embraced reggae more profoundly than the Rolling Stones. Reggae ultimately became another flavour of their sound, beginning with their recordings of 'Luxury' and 'Cherry Oh Baby' in the mid-seventies. They even signed original Wailer Peter Tosh to the Rolling Stones label. Thanks to bassist Robbie Shakespeare and drummer Sly Dunbar, 'Feel On Baby' sees the Stones achieve their most authentic reggae vibe yet. The Jamaican rhythm section had emerged as a key creative force by 1983, carrying reggae's influence forward when the sainted Bob Marley fell to cancer in 1980. As performer-producers, Sly and Robbie made rich, throbbing tracks for the likes of Black Uhuru, Grace Slick and Bob Dylan. For 'Feel On Baby', they joined the Stones in shaping this five-minute groove. Keith groans harmony alongside Mick's wistful vocal. And a crew of Senegal percussionists join the band to add exotic polyrhythms at the margins.

Reggae stars Sly and Robbie give the Stones a touch of authenticity.

undercover

too much blood

The scene at EMI Studios in Paris wasn't without its grim humour. Take the daily entrance of Mr Keith Richards, whose arrival at the *Undercover* sessions was greeted with great trepidation and awe among the tennis stars and modelling agents Bill Wyman was always bringing around the studio. After all, here was the Prince of Darkness himself – black hair askew, with that skull ring on his finger – a living, breathing casualty of the rock and roll passing lane, who had somehow survived to this point. And why not?

Richards wasn't without his own sense of fun on such matters. The guitarist often played up the legend, stumbling into the studio in a cape and carrying a cane, limping toward his guests with a mean glint in his bright red eyes. "They'd all be staring at him," laughs Jim Barber, who worked as Richards' guitar technician during those sessions. "He'd look like Orson Wells. He'd laugh at them, because they expected something outrageous."

Theatrics aside, the true horror of what Richards would later describe as "a very gory album" wouldn't emerge until one drunken early-morning session Jagger conducted for *Undercover* without the guitarist. The making of 'Too Much Blood' began with the Watts-Wyman rhythm section cutting a steady, rumbling beat. Jagger then turned to Barber – as he would several times during the album sessions – and said, "Can you put a bit of modern guitar on this? Can you do sort of an Andy Summers on it?" Barber picked up one of Richards' guitars – a fine Les Paul Jr – and chopped out a frenetic riff, a progression of funked-up jangling. Jagger also played some guitar at the session, but it wasn't used in the final mix.

The track finally edited down from that night's full 18-minute recording would later be mingled with additional guitar from Ron Wood, a layered blast of horns from saxman David Sanborn and the drums of Sly Dunbar. But all that came after those initial early morning hours in the studio, when Jagger began entertaining real thoughts of murder.

Not just murder, but cannibalism. By the time Jagger began tracking his vocals, the singer was quite drunk, and now reminiscing about a romantic evening gone terribly wrong. "A friend of mine was this Japanese with a girlfriend he met in Paris," Jagger rapped in his best Cockney drawl. "He took her to his apartment, cut off her head, put the rest of her body in the refrigerator, ate her piece by piece."

undercover

Jim Barber (right) provided the guitars on 'Too Much Blood'.

Jagger was, in fact, speaking of a Mr Issei Sagawa, a Japanese literature student at the Sorbonne in Paris, who in 1981 murdered his girlfriend, ate her flesh both raw and deep-fried, before surrendering to disgusted police. Sagawa had been spotted late one night burying the bones by a taxi driver passing through Bois de Boulogne, a park adjacent to this very same studio, and where the band and crew would pass almost daily to dine at their favourite restaurant-bar in one of Paris' seedier neighbourhoods. Now the singer was telling his tale, looking directly at both Barber and the studio tape-operator, when he said, "You don't believe me? You drive through there every day."

"I was standing there gob-smacked because the story was so horrific," remembers Barber, who is duly credited on the album for his playing on 'Too Much Blood'. That's when Jagger drifted into a series of increasingly dirty jokes, which, fortunately, were delicately edited out.

undercover

David Sanborn blows up a storm on 'Pretty Beat Up'.

pretty beat up

Disco had finally faded from the pop airwaves by the time of *Undercover*, but Mick Jagger wasn't about to lose the funk. 'Pretty Beat Up' is another track that is more driving groove than formal song, riding a driving funk riff and Jagger's scorching mantra. Saxophonist David Sanborn blows a typically elegant R&B solo across a bed of slicing guitars. Now that disco had faded back into the dance culture underground, 'Pretty Beat Up' could hardly be called a sell-out to passing fad. Here was proof that Jagger truly loved the beat, and that the Rolling Stones had a special knack for blending rock and roll with dance music. The heavy funk of 'Hot Stuff' in 1976 hadn't been a fluke. They made their own rules. Dance, dance, dance.

too tough

Keith Richards is not the usual kind of guitar hero. Not like B.B. King or Eric Clapton or Stevie Ray Vaughan. The blues runs through his soul, but Keef is no virtuoso, and he's never even been bothered to try. Mr Richards is the human riff, the master of rhythm guitar, the central ingredient of the immortal Rolling Stones sound. Think Pete Townshend without the windmill strumming. For Keith, rock and roll isn't about guitar solos, just songs.

"He understands the lost art of rhythm guitar playing," says Wayne Kramer, guitarist with the MC5. "From the point of Jimi Hendrix and Eric Clapton on, everybody wanted to be a lead guitar player, everybody wanted to play guitar solos. There was a time when being the rhythm guitar player in a band had a great sense of integrity to it. In our band Fred Smith was an absolute genius at it, and Fred really studied Keith and Brian Jones, and studied what are the elements of rhythm guitar and what makes it work. It's a tremendous discipline to stay locked into a rhythm pattern and play that pattern consistently and be locked in with the bass player and drummer. It's really a lost art. And Keith is one of the few guys out there."

Even during one of Richards' rare solo flourishes – 'Sympathy For The Devil', for example – there's no wild flurry of notes, no endless progression of lead lines to dazzle the kids. His playing is forever anchored by the rhythm, and he's careful not to fill in all the empty spaces with useless notes. Let the music breathe.

"In many ways he's a very inept guitarist, if you try and compare him to someone like Jeff Beck or Joe Satriani or Steve Vai or any of the modern guitarists," says Barber, now a successful session player. "He's not in that field. But he's got the best sense of rhythm guitar I've ever heard anyone play. He's got the best sense of timing, and in terms of what notes to put where."

'Too Tough' is neither the band's most memorable nor most forgettable piece of music. It's just another tune built on a classic Keith Richards riff pattern, with little to distinguish it from dozens of other tracks dating back to the late sixties. The song began life in 1975 under the working title 'Cellophane Trousers', and has Jagger irritably warning a lover not to pick a fight. Ron Wood eventually sends a frenetic blast of notes across Keith's chunky guitar rhythm. 'Too Tough' never really delivers anything beyond the basic, underlying pattern, but for a moment or two, that driving riff is everything it needs.

The simplicity of Keith Richards' craft can surprise guitar students brought up on the epic Stones catalogue. Keith is far closer to being the self-taught country bluesman than the studied modern rock guitarist. And yet his role in sculpting the sound of the Rolling Stones has made him one of the essential players in the history of rock and roll. "Our band does not follow the drummer," Bill Wyman noted in *Guitar Player* magazine in 1978. "Our band follows the rhythm guitarist."

> "Our band does not follow the drummer, our band follows the rhythm guitarist"
> Bill Wyman

all the way down

Mick Jagger is by no means a poet, but the man does have the ability to spin a reasonable tale with a minimum of words. He's a storyteller, much like the old bluesmen documented their highs and lows through chilling emotional extremes. So it was with some fascination that in 1983 the pop world read that Jagger had signed a contract worth a reported one million pounds to write his autobiography. Imagine the stories – the scenes of sex and drugs, his observations on the blues, Mother England and Lucifer.

A ghost writer was hired for the project, but Jagger ultimately returned the cash after an early manuscript was met with ambivalence and boredom. Either Jagger couldn't remember anything worth remembering, or he was still reluctant to discuss candidly the events of his life.

Rock and roll is Mick Jagger's true medium, though. 'All The Way Down' is a middling rocker, memorable less as a song than for an energetic performance from Jagger. But within his high-speed rap is evidence of storytelling skills, and a flair for small, telling details. 'All The Way Down' is a fictional reminiscence, a disdainful look at love and youth. "How the years rush on by, birthdays, kids and suicides." he sings. Now, if he could just remember...

undercover

undercover

it must be hell

Undercover ends much as it began, with Mick Jagger mulling over the failures of society and politics. He looks upon the streets and what does he see? Hunger, illiteracy and unemployment, that's what. Not only that, but...SOME KIDS OVER-EAT! Preacher Mick once again imagines the life of the lower classes, and finds only pessimism. And yet there's joy in the spectacular riffing of Keith Richards, who resurrects the ferocious chord pattern of 'Soul Survivor' from *Exile On Main Street*.

Pay attention to these closing moments. The Rolling Stones would not pass this way again. *Undercover* was the final chapter of an important era for the band, the period that had begun so gloriously with the 1978 "comeback" of *Some Girls*. There is little here to match the joyful nastiness of that album, but *Undercover* had at least maintained a certain hot-blooded sound, a certain raw texture. When the Rolling Stones reconvened in Paris and New York to record the fractious *Dirty Work*, that pulse would be gone, never to return.

There were other creative opportunities that remained open to the "Greatest Rock And Roll Band In The World", but the eighties would prove to be an uncertain time. Mick Jagger was already starting to imagine a life apart from the Stones, and was anxious to launch a solo career. Bill Wyman – at the age of 47, a good five years older than most of his colleagues – talked openly about retirement. Keith tried to ignore it.

The Rolling Stones needed to find a niche for themselves in an era crowded with pop, metal, hip-hop and a new wave of rockers – such as the Police and U2 – who threatened to assume their superheavyweight title. The Stones had survived this long with their reputation intact, but 20 years of making music was no guarantee that the embattled quintet would fit easily into yet another decade.

Mick Jagger is given a grilling by musician and TV presenter Jools Holland.

chapter eighteen

1986 dirty work

New blood: Steve Lillywhite (left), seen here with retro-rocker Marshall Crenshaw, is brought in to man the controls.

One Hit (To The Body)
Fight
Harlem Shuffle (RELF/NELSON)
Hold Back
Too Rude (ROBERTS)
Winning Ugly
Back To Zero
Dirty Work
Had It With You
Sleep Tonight

dirty work

Vampires don't only come out at night. And the midnight hour can't last forever, even in a world of perpetual darkness. Observe one Mr Keith Richards, prowling the streets of Paris and New York at sunrise after a night's work, facing the daylight in welder's goggles. He's dressed in black, and wears a skull ring on his right hand, but the edge in his voice is no decoration.

The hoodoo was rolling thick during the 1985 sessions for *Dirty Work*, and Keith was not a happy man. How could he be? He'd spent at least half the 1970s as a walking cadaver, lost between occasional moments of inspiration to a daily heroin fix, and regularly topping the annual "rock star most likely to expire" chart. But he'd survived that – as well as his horrific drug bust in Toronto – to reassert himself as a master rocker. Now the Stones were deep into the new wave 1980s, and Keef, for one, was ready to face the harsh fact that his youth was a thing of the past. His dream for the future, he said again and again, was to take his beloved rock and roll into middle age – into OLD AGE, even – just as Muddy and Wolf and John Lee had done for the blues. And to Richards' mind, no one was better positioned to do that than the holy Rolling Stones, the only band from his generation still standing more or less intact. But the angry funk Richards felt rising in his bones came with the realization that sweet Mick had begun looking at new career opportunities as a SOLO artist. Beware the angry vampire.

The Rolling Stones should have entered Pathé Marconi Studios in Paris on a high note, boosted by a new deal with CBS Records reportedly worth $25 million. But Mick was often absent during those early *Dirty Work* sessions, busy promoting his debut album, *She's The Boss*. The jet-setting vocalist insisted to interviewers that even if his solo career became a wonderful success, it did not mean he would abandon the Stones altogether. Not everyone believed him. Nor did Richards feel at all gracious about his partner's new hobby, which had inexplicably been encouraged by CBS chief Walter Yetnikoff, making the common A&R amateur's mistake that a band's core talent resided solely with the frontman. Richards also suffered a symbolic affront when Jagger took sole writing credit for many of the songs on *She's The Boss*, breaking the Jagger/Richards writing team of the past 20 years.

Mick was looking for a way out, and a way back into the hearts and minds of the young girls crowding the dance floors. Somehow the Stones were old hat. Mick was looking for something new, something fresh that poor old Keith just wouldn't understand.

Jagger suffered from a Peter Pan complex, grumbled Richards, who saw no reason to venture outside of the Stones. He'd avoided going solo himself, and never tried to be a movie star. Now, at nearly three years since *Undercover*, the distance between albums was growing longer. *She's The Boss* seemed like a threat – an insult to the history the band had together.

"I didn't think it was necessary for him to do THAT kind of album," Richards told *Musician* magazine in 1985. "Making a solo's fine by me. But apart from the timing of it being a little screwed up, I thought it'd be something he couldn't do with the Stones, rather than an obviously COMMERCIAL rock and roll album. If it was Irish folk songs with a lady harpist I would have respected it. If he had some burning desire to do an album like *Mick Jagger Sings Frank Sinatra* or *Mantovani* I would have understood."

The Who had called it quits only three years earlier, signing off with a highly profitably farewell tour sponsored by the usual liquor industry concerns. And why not? This was, after all, a game first played by the Stones themselves. Whether it was Jovan or Budweiser writing the cheques hardly mattered. Except that Keith was in no mood to shut down the firm, even if it meant a big payday. And besides, what would become of Pete Townshend in the years to come other than repeated trips down memory lane: a lighthearted stage

> **"I didn't think it was necessary for him to do THAT kind of album... I thought it'd be something he couldn't do with the Stones, rather than an obviously COMMERCIAL rock and roll album"**
>
> Keith Richard on Mick Jagger's solo career

dirty work

Mick Jagger and Keith Richards: not quite the best of friends.

musical version of *Tommy* designed for Broadway, another Who reunion to perform *Quadrophenia*, and the occasional release of a solo album to an increasingly ambivalent audience. Richards was too smart for that kind of sad farewell. That's not how Muddy went out.

Not that Jagger had shown complete disinterest in the newest Stones project. Both he and Richards agreed to bring in an outside producer for the first time in 11 years. The draftee was Steve Lillywhite, producer of U2's first three albums and popular releases by Simple Minds, XTC and Big Country. Hired as engineer was Dave Jerden, who had worked on *She's The Boss*, and who would later produce bands such as Jane's Addiction and the Offspring – energetic and multi-layered rock for a new generation. Thus on *Dirty Work* the Stones were presented in a modern context with BIG drums and a crisp sound. The charged blur explored between *Some Girls* and *Undercover* was now gone, never to return.

The making of *Dirty Work* was a typically nocturnal event, spread across nearly a year of sessions in Paris and New York City. In both cities, studio windows were covered by heavy curtains to blot out any creeping sunshine. At one time, the album was to be titled *19 Stitches*, and not just for the assistant engineer who had to be sewn up after falling through a glass table. "Besides just the angst of making the record, there was this weird voodoo going on too, people getting hurt," says Jerden. He remembers one night in New York when two punks were caught stealing a ghetto blaster out of Keith's car and then stabbed by a pair of Stones henchmen. "The people that hang around the Stones aren't lightweights, not by any means," Jerden says. "When you work with the Rolling Stones it's a lot like working with a motorcycle gang."

Likewise, song titles that emerged from the sessions were filled with violence and hate: 'One Hit (To The Body)', 'Fight', 'Had It With You', 'Winning

Ugly' and 'Dirty Work'. And yet there remained several moments of warmth and affection, as when Keith shared lead vocals with Jimmy Cliff on the reggae cover 'Too Rude' (which was another aborted title for the album). Bob and Earl's 'Harlem Shuffle' was a song Richards had long hoped to see the Stones record, slipping the original version on to mix tapes he sent Mick's way over the years. Then, as Richards was leading the band through the song during the *Dirty Work* sessions, Jagger walked in. "Let's do this," he said. The band had the song down in two takes. They were later joined by an overdubbed chorus of background singers that included Bobby Womack, Don Covay, Tom Waits, Patti Scialfa (who later married Bruce Springsteen) and Kirsty MacColl (Lillywhite's wife).

Richards by now was clearly the guiding force behind *Dirty Work*, although Keith himself saw nothing significant in this. "It's a Stones album," Keith told *Musician* magazine then. "If I've had a little more to do with it and a little more control over this one, it's the same to me as the middle seventies when Mick would cover my ass when I was out of it. Because of the timing of Mick's solo album, he wasn't there as much as the rest of us in the beginning when the mood was getting set. In that sense, yes, I took over the job. The same way he would if it happened to me. We cover each others' ass. We've done it very well for each other over the years."

At other times, of course, the tension was undeniable. "The record took a year to make, and it was hard," says Jerden. It wasn't an easy record to make. Mick and Keith were at loggerheads at times."

"I thought they were going to break up," says Bobby Womack, who had known the Stones personally since they topped the UK charts with his 'It's All Over Now'. As a backing singer at the New York *Dirty Work* sessions, Womack watched as the Stones seemed to fall apart. "They were having a lot of problems, a couple of the guys were stretched out, probably Charlie more than anybody at that time. They were working separately."

That turmoil occasionally bled over into unexpected directions. "When we were mixing in New York, Steve Lillywhite changed the speed in one song, sped it up a little bit, and it was hardly anything," says Jerden. "Keith walked in and he just went ballistic. He goes 'Nobody, fucking nobody, fucks with the Rolling Stones! That tempo was cut at that speed and it stays at that speed!'"

During the New York sessions, the studio was often crowded with guests dropping by, including Bob Dylan, Jimmy Page and others who were passing through town en route to the massive *Live Aid* concert in Philadelphia on July 13, 1985. The concert – designed to raise funds for Ethiopian famine victims – was a day-long event held simultaneously at Wembley Stadium in the UK and at JFK Stadium in the US. Paul McCartney, U2, Eric Clapton, Neil Young, a reunited Led Zeppelin, the Who, Madonna, Chuck Berry, Queen, David Bowie and George Michael all performed in the concert televised internationally. But not the Rolling Stones. Despite a five-year absence from the stage, the band decided not to appear.

Then, shortly before the concert, Jagger announced that he would appear solo, with backing from the Hall and Oates band. A video of a Jagger and Bowie performing 'Dancing In The Streets' was shown to great fanfare, but it was Jagger's high-energy live duet with Tina Turner that stood among the day's most memorable performances. By contrast, Richards and Wood were the unannounced accompaniment to Bob Dylan, who led the trio in to an acoustic muddle when he changed the song list immediately before going on. An embarrassing moment, perhaps, but it mattered little to Keith, knowing that there were plans for the Stones to hit the road themselves after *Dirty Work*. "Hey, this is our first album for CBS," Jagger told *Rolling Stone* in 1985. "We GOTTA tour."

When *Dirty Work* was released in March 1986, reactions were largely enthusiastic. 'Harlem Shuffle' was a top-10 hit on both sides of the Atlantic and many critics were encouraged by the hard rock muscle displayed on what was already being referred

> **"I thought they were going to break up. They were having a lot of problems"**
> — Bobby Womack

dirty work

to as "Keith's album". For a moment, the Stones once again seemed to be a healthy, happy unit. But the sharp neon colours on the cover photograph by Annie Leibovitz scarcely disguised a band drifting apart – in the picture, the band were scattered like victims of a bomb blast.

"The touring... I can't imagine it," Watts told journalist Nick Kent at the time. "I always have this image of me when playing in the Stones, and there are all these 16-year-old girls in the front screaming. My daughter's that age. I find it embarrassing."

Suddenly, the unthinkable happened: Keith Richards received a telegram from Mick Jagger announcing that he would not be touring with the Stones in 1986. With Jagger's solo career not slowing down, rumours soon emerged that the singer would be going out on the road with his solo band instead. When asked about this by *Musician* magazine, Richards was obviously disgusted. "If he was to say he don't want to go out with the Stones and goes out with Schmuck and Ball's band instead? I'll slit his fucking throat!"

By now studio tension had erupted into their most public feud, with accusations and name-calling in the press, and soon duelling solo projects. "This particular period is basically, I think, a reaction to 25 years of being forced to work together whether we liked it or not... I love working with those boys, and I don't see us not pullin' it back together," Keith told Kurt Loder in 1987. "Just give us a break and we'll come back for part two, you know?"

But back in 1985, Keith Richards was less than pleased with the state of the damned Rolling Stones. All of a sudden it really did seem possible that this could, indeed, be the last time.

> **" I always have this image of me when playing in the Stones, and there are all these 16-year-old girls in the front screaming. My daughter's that age. I find it embarrassing "**
>
> Charlie Watts on the thought of touring at the age of 45

one hit (to the body)

'One Hit (To The Body)' opens with one of the most dramatic guitar sequences in the Stones canon: a tense mingling of acoustic guitar and charged electric riffing. If the rest of the track fails to live up to that powerful introduction, these moments at least present a band ready to get down to some serious business.

The acoustic guitar was Wood's idea on 'One Hit (To The Body)', one of four tracks to include a Wood co-writing credit. "Woody went out and played acoustic on the basic track and everything just kind of fell around that," says Jerden. "He was trying to come up with an electric guitar part, and it wasn't grooving enough, so he went out and started banging on the acoustic. Woody's really great at coming up with ideas like that."

But Wood's role in the Stones was deeper than simply being a good sideman to Keith and Mick. In these days of tension and trouble, it was often Ronnie's lighthearted nature and communications skills that held the band's core duo together. "The peacemaker that kept that group together, as far as I'm concerned, was Ronnie," says Womack, who stayed at Wood's place in New York during the latter *Dirty Work* sessions. "He just had that extra spirit and life that it takes to be in a band. Plus he was younger, he had the energy, and he was willing to take the beating and be the fall guy for whatever that went down." Wood began referring to himself as the band's "Diplomatic Liaison Officer".

Womack, too, was sometimes recruited as a peace envoy. Jagger often picked Womack up on the way into the New York sessions. "He would always

Mick Jagger shares the limelight with Tina Turner.

dirty work

asked me, 'What did he say? What was he doing?' because they wasn't talking. And I think Bill might have had intentions not to do another tour at the time. He came in and did his part. Charlie put his parts there somewhere else. You can't cut an album like that. Not and be a unit."

The title of the track suggests another of the album's fight songs, but the story is more of violence to the soul from an intense love affair. Though hopelessly distracted by his new solo career, Jagger was still able to toss off some typically lurid passages for his own amusement.

Meanwhile, there was no shortage of heavy firepower in Mick's occasional absence. The rivetting solo on 'One Hit (To The Body)' was provided by Jimmy Page, who stopped by the New York sessions while en route to his Led Zeppelin reunion at the *Live Aid* concert. Page's solo career since the collapse of Zeppelin in 1980 had been somewhat low-key, both by design and circumstance. On *Dirty Work*, the guitar hero was reverting back to his earlier days as a professional session player, anonymously carving up immortal lead guitar lines for British hit makers.

"He was great to work with. He was very professional, like a session player," says Jerden. "A lot of guys will come in on a session like that and they kind of fuck around. But he came in like a session guy: he had his sounds all set up, and he just took direction and played."

Page's interaction with Keith was very friendly and respectful. "Everybody defers to Keith," says Jerden. "The control room could be full of people, and if somebody cracks a joke everybody looks at Keith to see what his reaction is going to be. He's got a very, very strong persona."

Led Zeppelin's legendary guitar star, Jimmy Page.

dirty work

fight

'Fight' is a furious, classic Stones rocker. It demonstrated that despite their differences – or maybe because of them – the band could coalesce into a tight, raging unit. The supercharged riffing between Richards and Wood create a roaring battlefield for Jagger's lyrics of endless, graphic violence: "Gonna pulp you into a mass of bruises!"

Most disturbing about Jagger's tale is the utter randomness of the song's wrath and brutality. For the central character it's just another Saturday night out on the town. And on *Dirty Work*, it was just another violent title, another agitated bit of noise that mirrored the growing tension between the Glimmer Twins. In this case, at least, their feelings coincided enough to bring a terrifying energy to the recording. "Keith wasn't happy about Mick making a solo record at the time," says Jerden. "He thought he should have been putting all his efforts into making the Stones record, preparing for it. There was definitely that going on."

Keith seemed to take out these aggressions through his guitar, which never left his presence. He and Ron Wood spent marathon sessions together working on their instruments. "They stood toe to toe with each other, just playing guitar. I never saw two guys play as much guitar as those guys. Keith literally always has a guitar on, even when he's just sitting around playing dominoes. I never knew anybody to this day that was so much into music. I mean so much into wanting to learn about music, wanting to play. He's just totally fucking into it."

That commitment was noticed by other visitors to the studio. "He's such a strong personality," Tom Waits said to *Musician* magazine in 1988. Waits had first watched Richards during the making of his *Rain Dogs* album, which features the guitarist on several tracks. "A completely intuitive musician. He moves like an animal. Gosh, he is just pure theatre – standing in the middle of a room and putting on his guitar and turning on his amp. All his stuff is irregular."

Likewise, Bono, the singer with U2, who recorded an impromptu early version of his 'Silver And Gold' with Richards and Wood, said: "You can see that all Keith's infamy and fortune don't matter much to him. When he puts on the guitar, the lines disappear from his face."

> "You can see that all Keith's infamy and fortune don't matter much to him. When he puts on the guitar, the lines disappear from his face"
>
> Bono, U2

hold back

Mick Jagger and the Rolling Stones have always demonstrated at least a passing interest in the sounds of the moment. In the late 1960s and early 1970s, it was a fashion of their own making. In subsequent years, Jagger has lobbied to have the Stones dabble in the sound of punk and the dance floor. If it was extremely successful on *Some Girls*, it had been far less effective on *Emotional Rescue*.

So in 1985, it was perhaps inevitable that at least a handful of tracks on *Dirty Work* would include loud thumping drumbeats, while the guitars were buried deep in the mix. It's a sound that was contemporary in the "big" 1980s, but now just seems odd. Ironically, given the deliberate lack of emphasis on guitars, 'Hold Back' is a classic Jagger/Richards collaboration with Mick providing most of the lyrics and Keith the music. "The message is don't hold back," Jagger said in 1986. "Trust your instincts."

dirty work

winning ugly

'Winning Ugly' was just one of two completed songs Jagger brought to the *Dirty Work* sessions – the other was 'Back To Zero'. "That was cut pretty fast," says engineer Dave Jerden.

Jagger worked in a different way to Keith on *Dirty Work*. The singer chose to work up his ideas on demo tapes before bringing them to the band. Richards tended to work on songs with the whole group.

For all the bad vibes brewing on *Dirty Work*, with Mick distracted by promotional schemes for *She's The Boss*, there were long periods where the Stones worked together as a classic unit. "There was a lot of jamming going on, and Mick would be there for the jamming. They were even doing some Beatles songs," Jerden says with a laugh. "They did 'Please Please Me' and a couple others. They would just jam on anything, old blues songs – 'Spoonful', stuff like that."

Jagger and Richards were face to face in those jam sessions – which were taped for posterity by Jerden – making music in a way some younger visitors to the sessions didn't understand. Keith told *NME* in 1986: "You get Duran Duran come down for a day, walk into our fucking sessions and say, 'What are you doing in that room together?' It's called playing music, man. That's the only way we record, you snotty little turd."

> **"You get Duran Duran come down for a day, walk into our fucking sessions and say, 'What are you doing in that room together?' It's called playing music, man. That's the only way we record, you snotty little turd"**
>
> Keith Richards

back to zero

Mick Jagger was worried about the future. In 1985, the Cold War reached some of its darkest days, as President Reagan continued to talk tough with the new Soviet leader, Mikhail Gorbachev. There were those in the Reagan administration who had actually suggested in the past that a nuclear war was winnable and survivable. All of which made nuclear obliteration seem like an unfortunate possibility, and not even rock stars would be able to escape it.

Although the title and song's underlying fear could be viewed as a metaphor for Jagger's new solo career, the singer's concerns about the bomb seem real enough, showing unprecedented concern for his great-grandchildren to the sounds of funky guitar and spacy jams from keyboardist Chuck Leavell and Bill Wyman on synthesizer.

For nearly two decades, songwriting for Stones albums had been the near-exclusive domain of the Jagger/Richards team. Bill Wyman's credit for 'In Another Land' from *Their Satanic Majesties Request* had been a fluke. Mick Taylor's inability to get co-writing credits was a factor in his leaving the band. But by the end of the 1970s, that policy had begun to loosen up, to the benefit of Ronnie Wood and later sidemen such as Steve Jordan.

So by the 1985 sessions for *Dirty Work*, the Stones were gracious enough to grant Leavell a co-writing credit on 'Back To Zero', which he had obviously earned. "Chuck was great," says Jerden. "He's a real country gentleman. He was a real stabilizing factor, because there was a lot of craziness going on, Mick was working on his record. He was real calm, cool and collected. He was always there. He played on everything."

The mid-eighties saw Jagger balancing the needs of the Rolling Stones with his fledgling solo career.

dirty work

dirty work

Keith Richards and Ron Wood engage in a little homework.

The album's title track speeds along at a frantic pace that would have given even the *Some Girls*-era Stones a nosebleed. Its peak comes with an excited clash of guitars between Richards and Wood, a dazzling duel that ranks among the album's high points.

Jagger sings with disgust at the exploitation of lesser mortals who perform dirty work and dirty deeds for their bosses, no doubt inspired by the gangster types and captains of industry Mick saw on the finer beaches of Europe. The song roars along at a dynamic pace before finally fading out in an ecstatic swirl of noise.

For the Stones, their dirty work did not follow any set schedule, but once started it could drag on for several gruelling hours or days. In Paris, Keith and Woody shared a house, while the others stayed at nearby hotels. Sessions often depended on the consciousness of Keith. "We were always on call," remembers Jerden. "Ian Stewart would call up and say 'Well, it's time. Keith has just gotten up'. So we knew we had two hours. We'd get up and go eat. But usually by the time we got to the studio it was pretty late. Midnight would be a normal call. Sometimes it was later. Then we would work until whenever. Sometimes it was a couple of days before we left."

had it with you

astiness personified, 'Had It With You' is built on a tossed off Chuck Berry riff, cranked to psychobilly extremes. It's not quite the roots rocking of *Exile On Main Street*, but a song of foul bitterness that hit listeners like armour-piercing bullets.

Jagger sings here of an outrageous incestuous brother-sister relationship, but it could easily be interpreted as a metaphor for a lifetime partnership with Keith Richards and two decades of built-up resentment. He taunts: "Serving out injunctions, shouting out instructions!" In later interviews, Jagger suggested that Keith was making a power play for control of the Stones.

"That song was done really quickly," says Jerden. "I think that whole thing you hear was all done in an hour." 'Had It With You' provided the proof that the Rolling Stones hadn't completely lost touch with their core rock roots. And nor had Jagger lost interest in provocation, singing of alarming subjects in the worst possible language. Richards said the band once considered putting a label on the sleeve of *Dirty Work*. It was to read: "FORGIVE THEM, FOR THEY KNOW NOT WHAT THEY RECORD".

sleep tonight

leep Tonight' is a ballad that emerged one day while Richards was dabbling on the piano. Ron Wood plays drums while Richards closes the album by singing a tender, masculine lullaby in his cracked whiskey rasp.

"That's Keith when he really exposes himself. He would sit in the control room and play that on acoustic guitar," says Jerden. "That's really what Keith is. Keith has got the tough image and rock and roll image, but he's really a sweet guy."

Though not primarily a vocalist, Keith's restrained, weary emotion was actually easier to capture on tape than the often explosive pipes of Jagger. If the guitarist's vocal style is often expressed just under his breath, Jagger's tendency is to attack his microphone, as if he were still trying to overcome the din of screaming girls at early Stones shows. "He's got a mike technique opposite to what I'm used to in the studio," says Jerden. "Usually when someone is going to sing loud they back off the mike a little bit so they don't distort the mike. Well, apparently because he couldn't hear himself on stage with bad systems in the sixties, when he wanted to get louder he moves up on the mike. Mick's got a real strong voice and he can just blow the shit out of microphones and compressors. Keith's got a real controlled voice."

The performance of Richards on 'Sleep Tonight' and 'Too Rude' would act as a virtual blueprint for the solo records he would make while waiting for the Stones to become active again. "I do feel better singing these days," Richards told the Los Angeles *Herald Examiner* in 1986. "Before, I was always just singing one song now and then, and in circumstances like that, you don't really get a chance to open the pipes up. On this album, with Mick not being around, I was in front of the microphone all the time, because you get a much better response out of the Stones if somebody's bellowing away on vocals. It doesn't

> "I do feel better singing these days... On this album, with Mick not being around, I was in front of the microphone all the time"
>
> Keith Richards

dirty work

even matter if you don't have sensible lyrics. The timing and phrasing of a vocal helps the band establish its rhythm and character.

"By the time it got around to recording my own vocals, my voice had thickened up quite a bit. I remember telling Bobby Womack that I hadn't done so much singing since I was a soprano in the Westminster Abbey. Come to think of it, that was probably the most prestigious gig of my career."

The sombre affection on 'Sleep Tonight' was a fitting end to *Dirty Work*, acting like a premonition of the impending departure of Ian Stewart, who died of a heart attack on December 12, shortly after the album was completed. He was 47. Stewart had been a constant presence in the studio during the making of *Dirty Work*, just as he had always been. Shortly after his work was done the album, Jerden talked with the boogie-woogie man one last time. "I was in New York working on something else, and I got a call at my hotel. It was Ian Stewart in Scotland," says Jerden. "He called up in the middle of the night, and he says 'Well, congratulations. You've just made a Rolling Stones record'. That's like the highlight of my life. Being accepted by Ian Stewart, because he was not easy to please."

The "Sixth Stone" had been a pillar of steadiness during the crazed years of the sixties and seventies, cutting through the rock star glamour to bring the boys back down to earth with his quips: "Come on my little shower of shit, you're on!"

"Stu didn't have some of the same habits that the others had," says saxophonist Bobby Keys. "Stu was the kind of guy who got up at 8 o'clock in the morning if something had to be done at 8 o'clock in the morning."

> **"Stu didn't have some of the same habits that the others had. Stu was the kind of guy who got up at 8 o'clock in the morning if something had to be done at 8 o'clock in the morning"**
>
> Bobby Keys, saxophone player, on Ian Stewart

His death came as a shock to the Stones, whose infighting had already left the band's future uncertain. *Dirty Work* was completely finished and mixed, and had been turned in by Jerden and Lillywhite by the time of Stu's death. But as a tribute to Stewart, the Stones added a 30-second fadeout of boogie-woogie piano. It was a bit of the old organic vibe that would rarely reemerge in the new age of the Stones in the finest studios.

dirty work

The Stones also managed to come back together to play a tribute blues show at London's 100 Club in February 1986 for invited guests. A few nights later, they appeared by satellite to receive a Grammy Award for lifetime achievement, an honour that could as easily been directed at Stewart. "Stu wouldn't have been comfortable as a pop star, so he became our roadie and when you're making records your roadie becomes one of the most important people," Keith later told journalist Lisa Robinson. "For whatever it's worth, it should have gone on longer, but Stu had a great life and it was perfectly compatible with the kind of personality he was. He was there on the records and if he felt like it he'd walk on stage and play – the piano was there for him. Sometimes he'd have *Golfing Monthly* on the music stand on the piano, but he was always the perfect counter for all the bullshit we had to go through."

A Stone by any other name: Ian Stewart (right) had been a constant presence from the beginning.

chapter nineteen

1989 steel wheels

The *Steel Wheels* tour confirmed that the Rolling Stones were still the biggest draw in live music.

Sad Sad Sad

Mixed Emotions

Terrifying

Hold On To Your Hat

Hearts For Sale

Blinded By Love

Rock And A Hard Place

Can't Be Seen

Almost Hear You Sigh
(JAGGER/RICHARDS/JORDAN)

Continental Drift

Break The Spell

Slipping Away

So the Rolling Stones were finally over. Washed up, crushed beneath the weight of their own long history. Ripped apart by competing interests. Gone. Mick Jagger was simply bored with the whole business. For him, it was a time to dance, to find new purpose, new music, a new audience. Times had indeed changed yet again, and the Stones simply did not fit in. At least not for the fabulous frontman hoping to find a new generation of admirers. "Man, I've got a band that's better," Jagger moaned to Bobby Womack during the making of *Dirty Work*. "They play TODAY'S sound."

That's dangerous talk, the kind of sentiment guaranteed to send fireballs of rage and terror into the heart of Keith Richards. A damned insult! The Rolling Stones had set a standard, had made much of what was now called rock and roll possible. They were not about to be replaced by a crowd of faceless session players, at least not without some painful consequences for Mick. The Glimmer Twins were at war. But if the Stones were destined to not survive the eighties, how much did it really matter? They weren't exactly going out on a high note with *Dirty Work*. The album certainly had its moments, built on the furious noise of Keith and Ronnie's guitars, but the atmosphere had been polluted by Mick's uncertain commitment.

Now Jagger's refusal to tour behind *Dirty Work* sent Richards into a rage, and began a feud that erupted with increasing bitterness in the tabloid press. In early 1987, Jagger complained in London's *Daily Mirror* that Richards was trying to run the Stones "single-handedly". He added, "I love Keith... but I don't think we can really work together anymore." The next day in the *Sun* newspaper, Richards was asked about the Stones' future and the incessant bitching between him and Mick. What next? "You'd better ask the bitch," Keith replied.

The bitch himself already gave HIS answer in the form of a second solo album: *Primitive Cool*, another collaboration with guitarist Jeff Beck, this time with the production and songwriting help of Dave Stewart of the Eurythmics. Jagger sang of low-down dirty juke joints ('Peace For The Wicked'), the international arms race ('War Baby') and the Protestant work ethic ('Let's Work') with typical gusto. But while the music behind him was admittedly *moderne,* it lacked the energy and danger of his work with the Rolling Stones. It was just another well-played, middling collection of contemporary rock.

During recording sessions in Holland and Barbados, guitarist Jim Barber remembers rumours of real or imagined threats from Keith. "I've seen all of them throw tantrums at one time or another, so I just presumed it was rock legends letting off steam," says Barber, who played guitar on *Primitive Cool* and served as Richards' guitar technician during the making of *Undercover*. "It was more like two lovers quarrelling, and just being extreme with their words."

She's the Boss ultimately sold two million copies in the US alone, but *Primitive Cool* failed to crack the American top 40. Although it fared better in the UK, where it reached No. 18 on the chart, the figures were nonetheless disappointing. But Jagger wasn't about to abandon this solo career first promised to him in the Stones multi-million-dollar contract with CBS. "I don't wanna be a dinosaur, stuck in one era," Jagger told *Musician* magazine in late 1987. "I don't want to be in 1969, because we're not living in 1969. I did some great things then, there was a great movie. But you can't recreate that. I don't want to recycle those memories."

The other Stones managed to keep busy after *Dirty Work*. In 1986, Ron Wood reunited with Rod Stewart and the Faces at Wembley Stadium, where Bill Wyman filled in for the ailing Ronnie Lane. Wood then embarked on an extensive tour with Bo Diddley, dubbed "The Gunslingers Tour". In London, Wyman opened his *Sticky Fingers* restaurant, while Charlie Watts fulfilled his jazzman dreams with his own 33-man big band and the release of their *Live At The Fulham Town Hall* album.

No point in waiting for Mick. His return was not guaranteed. Richards spent these first days away

> "I love Keith... but I don't think we can really work together anymore"
> — Mick Jagger

steel wheels

from the Stones co-producing and playing guitars on Aretha Franklin's recording of 'Jumpin' Jack Flash', later a top-30 hit in the US. And in October 1986, Richards acted as musical director for Chuck Berry's 60th birthday celebration concerts, which were filmed for the documentary Hail! Hail! Rock 'N' Roll. But the main focus of Richards' energies by 1987 was the recording of his first solo album, a project he had avoided for more than a decade.

"Having to make a record without the Stones was a failure in itself to me," Keith told Stanley Booth in 1989. "It meant I couldn't keep my band together. But when you start making it, you realize how much room there is to grow."

Instead of gathering whatever Stones he could, Richards created a new band. His key collaborator was dreadlocked drummer Steve Jordan, who had been part of those recent Berry and Franklin projects. At New York's cosy Studio 900, they gathered guitarist Waddy Wachtel, bassist Charley Drayton and keyboardist Ivan Neville to work up some new songs. Sessions were soon moved to Toronto, and vocals recorded in Bermuda. "Keith wanted it to be anti-formula, anti-commercial," Wachtel told Mojo in 1997. "He wanted it to be art."

> **"Even if the Stones never played another note... Mick and I still have to deal with each other for the rest of our lives with the business of the last 25 years"**
>
> Keith Richards

The result was Talk Is Cheap, an album more consistently enjoyable than anything Richards had done since Tattoo You – and certainly more memorable than either of Jagger's solo discs. Across 11 tracks, Richards and his band – the X-Pensive Winos – travelled from Stones-style rock to reggae to Al Green-style soul to Chuck Berry riffing. Richards sang in a low growl, the rough edges within his pipes adding a layer of rugged authenticity. Richards was finally fulfilling his dream to take rock and roll to a new place: if not respectability, at least somewhere potentially as meaningful to adults as to the demanding adolescent boys and girls.

Most attention was given to the song 'You Don't Move Me', which seemed to be an attack aimed at Jagger and his solo career ("You've already crapped out twice"). Beneath the rancour, though, Keith just wanted to reunite the Rolling Stones. And by middle of 1988, Jagger was feeling the same way.

"Even if the Stones never played another note in their lives, Mick and I still have to deal with each other for the rest of our lives with the business of the

last 25 years," Keith told journalist Lisa Robinson in 1988. "We can't even get divorced; it would be easier to do that with an old lady than to do with Mick, but we can't get out of it so we might as well learn to live with each other. We've just got to. I see it as growing pains. Whereas Mick was afraid the Rolling Stones could turn into some sort of nostalgia dead end, I see the Rolling Stones on the cutting edge of growing this music up and the only band in this position to do it. Listen darlin', this thing is bigger than both of us."

In January 1989, the Glimmer Twins agreed to meet in Barbados to work out their differences and write songs for an upcoming album. As he left for the islands, Richards told the wife he'd be back either in two weeks or two days. But he needn't have worried. Within 48 hours of arriving, they had five or six songs in the works. They sat on the

Charlie Watts showed his true colours with the formation of a 33-piece big band.

steel wheels

balcony of their hotel, with guitars, a keyboard, drinks and a tape-recorder. Except for a break to attend the Rolling Stones' induction into the *Rock And Roll Hall Of Fame*, Mick and Keith were still writing well into February.

"We didn't bother with anything else," Richards told *Rolling Stone* in 1989. "I did have to take Mick to a few discos – which are not my favourite places in the world – because Mick likes to go out and dance at night. So I did that. That was my sacrifice. I humoured him. And that's when I knew we could work together."

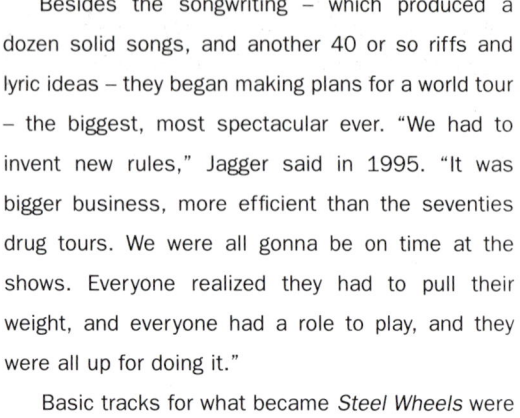

A generation apart: Mick Jagger shares the stage with Little Richard.

Besides the songwriting – which produced a dozen solid songs, and another 40 or so riffs and lyric ideas – they began making plans for a world tour – the biggest, most spectacular ever. "We had to invent new rules," Jagger said in 1995. "It was bigger business, more efficient than the seventies drug tours. We were all gonna be on time at the shows. Everyone realized they had to pull their weight, and everyone had a role to play, and they were all up for doing it."

Basic tracks for what became *Steel Wheels* were recorded during five fast weeks at AIR Studios in Montserrat, and then mixed in the basement Studio 2 of Olympic in London. A cover of Jimmy Butler's 'For Your Precious Love' was recorded, but failed to make it to the final album. Chris Kimsey, who had first worked with the Stones on 1971's *Sticky Fingers*, again co-produced with the Glimmer Twins. "It's definitely one of the most exciting albums I've worked on since *Some Girls*," Kimsey told *Musician* magazine.

Steel Wheels was largely greeted in 1989 as the Stones' long-awaited return to greatness. There seemed to be an excitement again within the band. And the Stones were exploring new (and old) ideas freely: the stirring trance rhythms from Joujouka on 'Continental Drift', Jagger singing with new subtlety on 'Terrifying', Keith's heart-wrenching balladry on 'Slipping Away'. But in the end, *Steel Wheels* was more a triumph of craftsmanship than inspiration. The edge of *Dirty Work* was gone, and except for the occasional balls-out rocker ('Hold On To Your Hat'), the Stones never broke a sweat. The reunion was encouraging though, demonstrating a willingness by the band to once again act with seriousness and resolve. Good things could still come of it.

sad sad sad

Two chords and a furious beat. Keith Richards didn't need much to set a mood, not after waiting three years for the return of Mick Jagger. The opening riff pattern on 'Sad Sad Sad' may be unspectacular in the context of the band's rich history, but there was no mistaking the rhythm and roll in these first moments of *Steel Wheels*. The Rolling Stones were back in business, and playing with renewed energy.

Like the coming world tour, the new album was made with a new sense of professionalism. The Stones were finally a band for the eighties, present here with every lick and beat in place. But something was inevitably lost within the flawless grooves of 'Sad Sad Sad', something reckless and free that had made the band's early seventies work so stirring. *Dirty Work* hadn't recaptured it either, for all its tense, edgy guitar work. *Steel Wheels* at least enjoyed a warmer sound, but much of the album ultimately falters from its own slickness and conventionality.

Keith grinds out a charged, rugged lead passage late in the song, as Jagger sings of finding comfort even amid the chaos of life. "You're going to be fine," Jagger insists, perhaps as much to the band as to anyone else. Ron Wood plays bass as the singer rushes past the brawling electric guitars with a sense of euphoria, as if the band were happy just to be making music again. If the Stones were playing it safe on *Steel Wheels*, the band could still be satisfied at having survived the recent past.

"There's a part of you that feels the Stones will be here forever, but you know that can't be," Richards said in 1994. "The truth is, things were a lot more fragile for us during the eighties than anyone realized, including the band. It's only now that I can look back and see how close it came to coming apart."

The reasons for a breakup were not nearly as simple as was depicted in the press. Mick and Keith's feud made for entertaining reading, but the truth was that Wyman had already talked of retiring after the 1981 tour. During the same period, the historically temperate and utterly sensible Charlie Watts finally succumbed to a life of drink and drugs. "I was pretty ill – for me, very ill," Watts told the *Los Angeles Times*. "I nearly lost everything. I nearly lost my marriage and the band as well through it." Sad, sad, sad.

So while the Glimmer Twins had patched up their differences within hours of their songwriting reunion, it wasn't until the arrival of Watts in Barbados that Richards was convinced that the Stones had a future. "I drove up to the rehearsal space and I heard him playing," the guitarist told *Rolling Stone*. "I just sat in the car for five minutes and listened, and I said, 'Yeah, no problem. This year's made'."

> **" The truth is, things were a lot more fragile for us during the eighties than anyone realized, including the band. It's only now that I can look back and see how close it came to coming apart "**
>
> Keith Richards

mixed emotions

Keith Richards jokingly refers to this track as 'Mick's Emotions', sharing the view of many that the song was a response to all of Keith's nagging over the last few years – "Let's bury the hatchet, wipe out the past". Jagger insists it has nothing to do with Richards at all, and was inspired by a girl he knows. Either way, the song is another forceful exercise in modern rock, an assault on the senses with a flood of guitars awash in production syrup.

steel wheels

Respectable job: Bill Wyman opens the *Sticky Fingers* restaurant in Kensington.

The guitars do swing convincingly, and the chorus of voices chanting "You're not the only one!" effectively add a layer of human melodrama. Even within the album's crisp soundscape, the song undoubtedly benefited from their thankfully archaic recording technique, unchanged from the days of *Exile On Main Street*. Once again, the band gathered together around their microphones for the basic track. "To me, it's the only way," Richards told *Bam* magazine in 1989. "If you want the group to sound like a group, then you have to be able to look at the guy in the eyes."

terrifying

Guitars are mere support players here as the Stones dive into a frenetic funk groove, finding more speed but less warmth than on the measured funk of 1976's 'Hot Stuff'. This shouldn't, however, suggest the song is without its pleasures. It's more inoffensive modern rock, but it's kept afloat by Jagger's taunting love confession ("I got these strange, strange, strange desires!") and a stirring trumpet solo from Roddy Corimer. Most crucial is the relentless rhythm of Watts and Wyman, sending the band on a brisk, heady spin.

'Terrifying' would mark one of Wyman's final trips as a Stone. "His bass playing was so lively yet steady, and it just pounds you away," Chris Kimsey said in 1989. "I think the bass on this album is even louder than on most of the other ones."

hold on to your hat

xperience counts for something in rock and roll. And proof enough emerges within the explosive rock of 'Hold On To Your Hat', which at least demonstrates the Stones' continued knack for pacing. By the time this rip-roaring jam erupts from *Steel Wheels*, it comes as a relief – a moment of raw, boundless elation to counteract the slicked-up sounds that precede it.

The intense guitar riffing is clearly inspired by Keith's beloved Chuck Berry, but it was Jagger who already had this song in the works when the Glimmer Twins arrived in Barbados. He sings here like a man on fire, barking something about tearing the mad house down, which one interviewer actually suggested was about the British Parliament. Not likely. Not with nonsense asides like "You had a fair whack, hold on to your butt!" It's just another fight song from Jagger, and would have fitted comfortably within the agitated grooves of *Dirty Work*.

Jagger seems to be spitting mad at someone. More importantly, though, 'Hold On To Your Hat' proves that Jagger could still rock and roll convincingly in 1989. Jagger even plays some of the slashing guitar parts himself, not exactly the act of a fading rock aristocrat. "It's very nice if people think I'm a country gentleman or something," Jagger told *20/20* magazine in 1989. That same year, Richards said, "Mick's playing quite a lot of guitar on this album. He's a good rhythm player…he sings more rhythmically when he's playing, kind of like Aretha Franklin."

hearts for sale

uring the Rolling Stones' golden age at the end of the 1960s, the years that produced *Beggars Banquet*, *Let It Bleed* and *Sticky Fingers*, the band stuck to a solid formula – no more than 10 tracks per album. With the exception of the epic *Exile On Main Street*, that formula held all the way up through *Dirty Work* in 1986. But when the band reunited after its period of public self-loathing, that policy was inexplicably left behind. The Stones were not the only band to buckle to temptation now that CDs allowed for much longer albums, but no act has suffered more as a result. A tighter edit would have benefited *Steel Wheels* and the overlong *Voodoo Lounge*, with its 15

inconsistent songs. 'Hearts For Sale' falls into this category. It's by no means an embarrassment, just filler that normally should not have survived the Stones editing process. Jagger proclaims himself "the voice of conscience, the voice of reason" here across a slinky R&B groove. The underlying rhythm begins promisingly, with a grinding guitar riff, and delicate funk flourishes at the margins. There's also a frustratingly brief flash of fiery harmonica from Jagger. But the song finally leads nowhere in particular as the singer rambles inconclusively on love and lust one more time.

blinded by love

Not everything on *Steel Wheels* is constructed with a cool precision. And the album's most satisfying moments are not limited to the handful of rockers scattered amid the middling pop-rock. 'Blinded By Love' is a charming acoustic ballad, a construct of country and island rhythms unique to the Glimmer Twins. It stands as one of the album's most relaxed performances, mixing delicate guitar picking, fiddle and a tastefully restrained vocal from Jagger. The singer is at his most approachable here, preaching a sermon on historical and mythical figures ruined by love, from Samson and Mark Anthony to King Edward, who abdicated the British throne for the companionship of an American divorcee.

'Blinded By Love' – on which Jagger's younger brother, Chris, is credited as "literary editor" – miraculously escapes the modern production sheen that numbs so much of *Steel Wheels*, and displays the warmth that was still within their reach.

King Edward gave up the British throne for the love of a US divorcee, Wallis Simpson.

rock and a hard place

s one of the singles released from *Steel Wheels*, 'Rock And A Hard Place' is best measured as a statement on where the Stones saw themselves in 1989. The song was originally called 'Steel Wheels', a title chosen for the album and coming American tour for its suggestion of motion and power. (In Europe, the name would be changed to the Urban Jungle Tour.)

As ever, Richards and Wood combine forces for a striking opening shot of guitars, but the sound is strangely bright and airy for the big, bad Stones. As Jagger sings of the downtrodden living under the rule of dubious foreign governments, the music is left without any sense of danger, or the notion that something surprising might occur.

Of course, in a year that saw the rise of such featherweight pop acts as Milli Vanilli and New Kids On The Block, a song like 'Rock And A Hard Place' might sound truly substantial. Yet for anyone who paid attention to the legacy of the Stones, the song had little to offer. It was well-played, crisply recorded, and yet it somehow lacked the reckless essence of Keith Richards, and what he hoped to accomplish with the band as it drifted into middle age. For all the emotional investment here, the Stones might as well have been session players.

can't be seen

isten to the panicked beat, the edge in Keith's voice. 'Can't Be Seen' is a story of forbidden love, made real by the guitarist's agitated rasp. Though some of the rougher musical edges are buffed away, Keith's ragged vocals slice through rich layers of organ, drums and guitar: "Yeah, I've got to chill this thing with you." Though played by the Stones, the song sounds like it could be a leftover track from Richards' solo album. It's a standard Richards outlaw anthem, even if the guitarist was by now living in toddler splendor, raising small children with the help of wife and an ocean of stuffed animals.

Keith sings here in a panic about an adulterous relationship, but the overall sentiment suggested by the song's title had special relevance to Bill Wyman. In 1986, British tabloids published revelations that the bassist had just ended a three-year relationship with Mandy Smith – begun when she was just 13. Now Wild Bill Wyman was the outlaw, in the cradle-robbing tradition of Chuck Berry and Jerry Lee Lewis, who had created a scandal in 1957 when he married his 13-year-old cousin: "JAIL THIS WORM WYMAN FOR LOVING MANDY 13", read a typical headline.

Until then, Wyman had been able to keep the relationship secret, managing to avoid probing photographers during their nights on the town. As young Mandy later told *Vanity Fair* in 1987: "There was always the, you know, LEGAL side to think about." And her mother was always there to help, telling her daughter, "He's got the choice of any woman he wants in the world. He's a Rolling Stone, and he's picked you!" Now that he'd been discovered, Wyman fled to France, until assured that police had questioned the Smith family and decided not to arrest him.

During the making of *Steel Wheels*, Wild Bill announced that he and Mandy Smith, now 19, were to be married – his relationship with Astrid Lundstrom had ended in 1983. The ceremony took place in England during mixing sessions for the new album, and was attended by all of the Stones. But when the impending marriage was first discovered by the press, Wyman quickly travelled to Antigua for a press conference, leaving Wood to handle bass on four songs. Thus, Wyman's final appearance on a Stones album was abbreviated.

steel wheels

almost hear you sigh

Chris Jagger, "literary editor" to elder brother Mick.

ick Jagger describes a miserable breakup on 'Almost Hear You Sigh', contrasting his memories of warmth and romance with the cold voice telling him goodbye. The mid-tempo lament is also one album track where the blend of production and performance finds a balance true to the song's emotion. Richards plucks at an acoustic guitar as Jagger gives a moving, lovelorn performance. And yet 'Almost Hear You Sigh' actually began as a Richards song co-authored by drummer Steve Jordan – Keith's main collaborator for his solo work. Richards brought the song to Barbados, where Jagger re-wrote many of the lyrics with the help of brother Chris, again credited as "literary editor".

The overlapping between Keith's solo work and his role with the Stones presented a potential conflict that had long concerned the guitarist. "In 1985 we started getting into solo shit, and it's a whole new can of worms. I told him I didn't want to be put into that position after all these years, because I knew it would be a conflict of interests," Richards told *Guitar Player* in 1992. "I knew then that I'm gonna write songs and I'm gonna go 'That's mine. Stones can't have that. Oh, the Stones can have this'. What do I do? Give 'em the best I got? The second best?"

continental drift

elcome back Brian Jones, or at least his lingering influence on the band he founded at the beginning of the 1960s. *Steel Wheels* was designed to be an epic return to form for the Rolling Stones, an album that took the band into new, expanded territory. So Jagger and Richards decided on a return to Tangier in Morocco, the North African playground of their youth, to tap into the local trance rhythms of Joujouka that Jones first recorded back in 1968.

For Jagger, 'Continental Drift' was a chance to resurrect the band's experimental mindset of the late sixties. "A lot of that had gone by the boards in the last few years. Not necessarily this particular kind of sound, but the whole idea of pushing the envelope open a little bit," Jagger told *Rolling Stone*. "We became a hard rock band, and we became very content with it. The ballads got left a little behind as well. The hard rock thing just took over, and we lost a little bit of sensitivity and adventure."

On 'Continental Drift', the Stones experimented with a cross-cultural blend perfected long before by Led Zeppelin and others. More recently, Peter Gabriel and the Talking Heads had injected the exotic beats and rhythms of world music into their pop recordings. The idea to collaborate with the Master Musicians of Joujouka came to Jagger as he wrote 'Continental Drift', a strangely spiritual tract on the power of love.

Coincidentally, he received a letter from Bachir Attar, who had met Jones in the hills of Joujouka as a seven-year-old when the blonde Stone was there to record the group. Now, many years later, Attar was chief of the musical tribe. He invited Jagger for a visit.

"I was writing this song and remembering their harmonics and thinking wouldn't it be great to have them on the track and this letter arrived," Jagger told *20/20* magazine. "Amazing, eh?"

The singer visited the Joujouka village, which was about two hours away from Tangier by donkey. Ultimately, the Glimmer Twins had to bring the group to Tangier, where there was electricity for recording equipment. The musicians arrived in yellow turbans and hooded brown robes, and performed their soulful, rollicking rhythms to a pre-recorded track made during sessions at AIR Studios in Montserrat. Not everything was quite so exotic on 'Continental Drift' – the shrill metallic noise at the song's beginning was made by Keith, scraping a knife against a bicycle wheel.

> **"We lost a little bit of sensitivity and adventure"**
> Mick Jagger

break the spell

If the return to Joujouka was a musical nod to the Stones' youth, nothing could touch the soul of the band more deeply than the blues of the Mississippi Delta. Jagger sings vaguely here of witchcraft and bad love as Keith picks at a guitar and Ronnie plucks a dobro. The song's defining element emerges in the blues harp blowing of Jagger himself, wheezing up a hailstorm. It's an effective exercise, conjuring up an appropriate chill, but with none of the pathos of 'No Expectations'. As a singer, Jagger expresses little of emotional resonance here, but it hardly seems to matter amid the scratching and wailing. Sometimes it is enough to just go through the motions.

slipping away

By 1989, listeners had learned to appreciate another side of Keith Richards. Not simply the human riff or the groaning, croaking "singer" of 'Happy'. As an interpreter of ballads, Richards was now as capable and interesting as the immortal Mick himself. As the years progressed, Keith's voice grew more able to carry a tune, even if it still sounded like maybe it shouldn't. Which only added to its ragged charm. On 'Slipping Away', Keith again sings under his breath in a voice weathered from decades of inhaling Marlboro Reds, this time to examine mortality over a quiet layer of horns. "Well, it's just another song," he sings, "but it's slipping away."

As *Steel Wheels* closed, it appeared that another era had begun for Stones, one with a winking tolerance for the solo careers of its fabulous Glimmer Twins. The coming world tour would fill stadiums and confirm the Stones' position as the "World's Greatest Rock And Roll Band", at least in terms of drawing power. The Rolling Stones were at peace, at last, and seemed to be headed for another busy period. But that momentum was somehow lost. Most traumatically, Bill Wyman finally made good on his threats and quit the band for good. Mick entered a studio with producer Rick Rubin for his next solo record. And the Stones did not return to recording for another five years.

chapter twenty

1994 voodoo lounge

No expense spared: the *Voodoo Lounge* tour is one of the most spectacular ever staged by a rock band.

Love Is Strong
You Got Me Rocking
Sparks Will Fly
The Worst
News Faces
Moon Is Up
Out Of Tears
I Go Wild

Brand New Car
Sweethearts Together
Suck On The Jugular
Blinded By Rainbows
Baby Break It Down
Thru And Thru
Mean Disposition

aybe it's best to forget the eighties altogether. Things began well enough with *Tattoo You*, that miraculous album of outtakes, lost ideas and utter rejects, and one of the best-selling discs of the Rolling Stones' career. The decade even ended with the momentous *Steel Wheels* album and subsequent worldwide tour. But in between were the lost years, and a band grounded by hate, disarray and irrelevance. The nineties were supposed to be different. The Stones looked ready for a new assault on the charts, riding the unholy momentum of their *Steel Wheels* reunion toward an era of dedication and action. Not bloody likely. Another studio album would not emerge for nearly five years, their longest stretch of silence in three decades.

Times were different now. Nobody realistically expected the Rolling Stones to go back to the relentless pace of their youth, when the creepy quintet spent its days endlessly on the road, taking breaks only to enter a studio for all-night hit-making sessions. That's a fine lifestyle for young men, not millionaire rock elders. The Stones had now adopted the bad habits of later pop generations, allowing the drifting years to accumulate between albums. Not that the Stones had nothing else to do. There were long vacations in Jamaica and the Far East, house-hunting in Ireland, solo careers to pursue, children to raise, a divorce for Wyman, marriage for Jagger – to longtime companion Jerry Hall – a hospital stay for Woody after breaking both legs in a car crash. Mick also had a daughter about to graduate from Yale, another ready to give birth – Satan's own messenger was about to become a GRANDFATHER.

The Stones went their separate ways in 1991, but not before finishing the largest music tour in history, grossing more than $200 million. While passing through Prague the band stopped for dinner and drinks at the presidential palace with Vaclav Havel before their local sold-out gig, which attracted fans from all over Eastern Europe.

The band also entered the Hit Factory in London to record two new songs as bonus tracks to their upcoming Flashpoint live album. Among those was 'Highwire', a critique of the international arms trade. It was an unspectacular piece of music, but unusually timely given the Persian Gulf War, which ended just as the record hit the streets. So the Stones were still able to generate some controversy, leading the BBC-TV's *Top of the Pops* to censor 'Highwire's' offending first line: "We sell them missiles, we sell them tanks, we give them credit, you can call up the bank". "It's not about the war *per se*," Keith explained at the time. "It's about how such things start in the first place. You get various governments building up the army of some tin-pot dictator like Saddam Hussein and letting him get away with murder for years. Many of those same companies were actively trading with him when the UN were delivering their ultimatum. He's probably still wondering what he did wrong."

These grand old men of rock were soon signing a new contract with Virgin Records worth £25 million. But Wyman refused to sign the document. It was immediately clear to the band that the bassist was making good on his threats of the last decade and retiring from the Stones for good. From then on he would only occasionally appear on stage with Willy and the Poor Boys and at various charity events. "He was always the first one there and first one to leave," remembers engineer Andy Johns, who worked regularly with the Stones during the early seventies, and considered Wyman a friend and hero. Johns even named his first son after the poker-faced bassist. "Bill's pretty straight. He's a homebody. It was work. He got there and played bass, and when it was time to go, he would go home." Now it was time for Wyman to retire and bask in the riches he'd accumulated.

There was also the matter of *Stone Alone*, Wyman's autobiography co-written with journalist Ray Coleman. An epic of almost 600 pages, the book recounted the Stones' career in great detail, from the death of Brian Jones to every contested nickel in the band's financial history. It also allowed

> **"It was work. He got there and played bass, and when it was time to go, he would go home"**
>
> Andy Johns, engineer, on Bill Wyman

voodoo lounge

Wyman to voice his every long-held resentment against the Glimmer Twins. His verdicts on Mick and Keith were sometimes harsh, but never cruel. Writing the book may have been his way of saying goodbye.

For the moment, at least, it mattered little, since the band was drifting into a mode of permanent vacation. Keith kept busy producing and appearing on tracks for albums by John Lee Hooker and Johnnie Johnson. In 1992, Richards and his X-Pensive Winos travelled to San Rafael, California, to work on his second solo album, *Main Offender* – a much less satisfying effort than his debut. The future of the Stones was still in doubt then. Now that the Stones were officially a functioning unit again, it was as if the fire had gone out of his solo career.

Wood released *Slide On This*, his first solo album in a decade. And the Charlie Watts Quintet began a non-stop world tour of clubs across the globe, from London to Tokyo. Charlie was a real jazzman at last.

Unexpectedly, Jagger released what was easily the best of his three solo albums during this same period. With the help of producer Rick Rubin (of Run DMC and Beastie Boys fame), Jagger's *Wandering Spirit* was a dynamic, memorable collection of songs which succeeded because, in no small irony, it sounded like the Stones. Jagger also recorded a spirited album of blues standards with a Los Angeles band called the Red Devils, though it was only released as a bootleg. And Jagger still made time to co-star in his worst film, *Freejack*, a vehicle

Jagger's take on the Gulf war proves the Stones still have the capacity to shock.

for Emilio Estevez that Jagger had expected to be like the sci-fi cult flick *Blade Runner*. It wasn't. More cartoon than drama, *Freejack* disappeared from screens quickly, Mick's dreams of movie stardom foiled again.

By the middle of 1993, Jagger, Richards and Watts were down in Barbados working up material for a new Stones project, this time to be produced by Don Was. Mr Was had once been a part of the band Was (Not Was), known for an aggressively eclectic mix of funk, rock and the occasional avant-garde monkeyshine. After leaving that unit, Was launched a successful career as a producer of artists ranging from Bonnie Raitt to Brian Wilson. Now it was the turn of the Stones.

"These guys are masters of what they do," Was told *Goldmine* magazine in 1995. "It's really like, what Muddy Waters is to blues, these guys are to rock and roll. They are so good. I can go through, man by man. Jagger, the way his vocals leap off the tape. That's something that's just supernatural… and his harp playing is superlative."

The Stones recorded 30 songs in Ireland with Was, finishing with overdubs at A&M Studios in Hollywood. Playing bass was Darryl Jones, a veteran of Miles Davis and Sting. The final result was *Voodoo Lounge*, an album that rocked convincingly in the styles that had always been at their disposal. But although the album was full of energy it had little in the way of ideas. *Voodoo Lounge* was something of an improvement on *Steel Wheels*, with a handful of truly exciting tracks, but a tighter edit might have left a stronger impact on listeners in the era of Kurt Cobain and Snoop Doggy Dogg.

Jagger claimed to have sensed a greater group vibe on *Voodoo Lounge*, even with the absence of Bill Wyman. He was happy with the sound of the ballads and the rockers, he told *Rolling Stone* in 1995, but was ultimately unsatisfied with the album as a whole. "It's very much a kind of time and place album," Jagger said. "In that way I was quite pleased with the results. But there were a lot of things that we wrote for *Voodoo Lounge* that Don steered us away from – groove songs, African influences and things like that – and he steered us very clear of all that. And I think it was a mistake."

> **"These guys are masters of what they do…what Muddy Waters is to blues, these guys are to rock and roll. They are so good"**
>
> Don Was, producer

love is strong

Voodoo Lounge begins on an encouraging note: all heavy breathing and jagged guitars, shooting fireballs of lust and danger. 'Love Is Strong' is the modern Stones at their sophisticated best, not blazing new trails, just kicking out the jams as only they can. Mick Jagger seethes with the usual *double entendres* while Keith Richards and Ronnie Wood chop out archetypal Stones riffs against the muscular restraint of Watts' steady thumping.

"There are things, or at least textures, that are evocative of songs they've done in the past," producer Was said of the music on *Voodoo Lounge*. If so, 'Love Is Strong' argued that the classic Stones groove somehow still had room for growth.

This wasn't a band of sixties survivors going through the motions for a fast buck. Even if Jagger's lyrics offered little more than cheap lust, his searing harp playing suggested that the man still had something to say as a musician. And this time the main engine driving the works was not Keith, but the beloved Charlie Watts, a drummer Was has compared to jazz deity Art Blakey.

"He sits like him – he plays from the waist down," Was said later. "And yet, he sounds so powerful, you can't believe that it's not some weight-lifting maniac

voodoo lounge

Mick Jagger: destined to carry on while he's still got the energy and spirit.

sitting on the kit... He is such an integral part of what they do, that everything that's in that band kind of emanates from his drumming."

Fittingly, 'Love Is Strong' was chosen as the first single released off of *Voodoo Lounge*. Mixmaster Teddy Riley found enough inspiration within the grooves here (or within his pay cheque) to craft six different dance remixes for a CD single. Bob Clearmountain did another. But the best version remains the original, the most focussed piece of pop music the Stones had recorded in a decade. In the stylish black and white video directed by David Fincher, the four remaining Rolling Stones are depicted stomping through Manhattan as giants, which may be the only justification for an quartet of aging rockers to be competing with fiery new voices like Nirvana and Pearl Jam. This many years down the road, what could the Stones have to say to the *Woodstock II* generation?

Their answer is maybe heard within the soothing, masculine background vocals singing behind Jagger. The blend of Wood, Richards, Ivan Neville and Bernard Fowler suggest the Stones have soul after all, with the sound of a 30-year brotherhood, determined to push themselves ever forward.

"People say 'How long are they gonna do it?' I say 'Why should they not?'" says Bobby Womack, a longtime Stones friend who sang backup elsewhere on *Voodoo Lounge*. "They got the energy, they got the spirit. You grow together, you live together, you go through ups and downs together. That's what makes the Stones the Stones."

you got me rocking

If the looseness of *Exile On Main Street* was a long way behind them, the Rolling Stones could still conjure up a reasonable facsimile when the mood was right. But Keith Richards was not interested in holding back, as if the band's reputation rested solely on their ability to rock as hard as the youngsters. So too often the emotional subtlety of the blues was simply abandoned. That explains the increasingly hard rocking sound of the band since *Dirty Work*. And that forced hardness at times resulted in some awkwardness, as if the brutal thrust of the band's delivery prevented them from finding a balance among all the colliding guitars.

'You Got Me Rocking' is crowded with exciting bits and pieces that add up to an unsatisfying whole. Jagger sings of finding renewed faith and inspiration, with images of blood and meat, sex and fear. The guitars of Richards and Wood are propelled with undeniable enthusiasm, and yet it's all grounded by uncertain melodies and a clumsy arrangement. 'You Got Me Rocking' moves like a locomotive, but there's little here to remember once it's over.

The band and crew of *Voodoo Lounge* were perhaps trying too hard to recreate past glories, Jagger said later – the final album was "too retro". He told Jann Wenner in 1995 that both he and Watts were opposed to the nostalgia he sensed in the mix. Not that he's ready to abandon rock and roll. "I still love performing it, but it's no longer a new, evangelical form," Jagger said. "It's still capable of expression, and it's still capable of change and novelty. But it's not as exciting for me. It's not a perfect medium for someone my age, given the rebelliousness of the whole thing, the angst and youth of it. In some ways it's foolish to try and re-create that."

sparks will fly

In the eighties and nineties, Stones albums were made by appointment. The Stones juggernaut ran on a schedule or not at all. And *Voodoo Lounge* was no different. First, the Glimmer Twins would reunite for several weeks of intense songwriting sessions on some island paradise. Then the Stones gathered for several more weeks of recording. Then maybe a tour. Then nothing, until it was time for another album years hence.

The days of obsession for Mick and Keith were years behind them now. No more were they in near-constant contact, bouncing around ideas, working together over long, fruitful periods. What a drag it is growing old.

Voodoo Lounge was fuelled by 15 new Jagger/Richards originals, written under the gun in Barbados. The Glimmer Twins left the islands with 75 songs and fragments, testifying to Keith's remarkable ability to craft an endless supply of rock riffs. "Keith's playing is so intuitive, and it's also really generous," said Was. "He processes information really quickly."

Even so, the busy fingers of Richards have their limitations. Revolutionary sounds on the scale of 'Gimme Shelter' were not likely to emerge amid the sun and surf of some brief island confab with his songwriting partner. So there is an unavoidable sameness to many of the rockers on *Voodoo Lounge*. Not that Keith's playing is ever less than evocative of power and attitude. But what exactly is the difference between the tough riffing and nasty lyrics of 'Sparks Will Fly' and 'You Got Me Rocking' and 'I Go Wild'? Virtually nothing at all.

'Sparks Will Fly' has Jagger promising to set his lover aflame with his lust. He resorts to the empty shock value of occasional explicitness, but it has no particular message, and none of the suggestive undercurrent of such earlier songs as 'Brown Sugar', which seemed to hint at darker themes, whether Jagger meant to or not. Literature, the blues and life experience were once Jagger's source of inspiration. The rockers on *Voodoo Lounge* seemed to emerge from X-rated comic books.

The new-look "clean" Keith Richards.

voodoo lounge

Jimmie Rodgers: Keith Richards has retained a love for country and western music.

the worst

Young Mick's earliest memories of Keith are of a boy with a passion for singing cowboys – Roy Rogers, Gene Autry and a thousand other forgotten yodellers. It wasn't the singing that fascinated little Keith. It was the guitar. He eventually graduated to real country and western, plugging into the white blues of Jimmie Rodgers, Hank Williams and the Carter Family. And it's stayed with him ever since. Keith's love for country music emerged on *Beggars Banquet* and *Exile On Main Street*, and was the original inspiration for 'Honky Tonk Women'. The same sound provided one of the most heartfelt moments on *Voodoo Lounge*.

'The Worst' is guided along by Ron Wood's pedal steel and a plaintive fiddle passage by Frankie Gavin. Keith picks softly at an acoustic guitar as he sings a loser's love lament in a voice that, although rough and thin, is capable of emotional revelation. There is vulnerability within those gravelly pipes. And 'The Worst' is the album's most natural moment.

new faces

How strange that Mick Jagger would even consent to sing the likes of 'New Faces', let alone write the thing. Witness the harpsichord, the prickly, sweet guitars, and Jagger straining for the sound of innocence. 'New Faces' is the resurrection of the Rolling Stones circa 1965, the era of pop and childlike wonder. For all his complaints of being hounded by the past, Jagger here offers a sound that is beyond retro, singing of his broken heart and the girl who strayed into the arms of a bad, bad boy. It's all sugary sweet, even with the hint of trouble within the lyrics, and Jagger sounds like he's reading a fairy tale. From a man who had spent the last three decades fleeing from nostalgia, 'New Faces' made no sense at all.

moon is up

Jagger's got love on his mind. It's everywhere on *Voodoo Lounge*. And that's not exactly good news for the Stones. With few exceptions, Jagger's songwriting repertoire in 1994 was inexplicably limited to love and sex. Despite the occasional explicit line, even Jagger's legendary misogyny was largely missing. Instead, the songs document the machinations of men and women, without much in the way of wisdom or revelation. 'Moon Is Up' is no different, telling much the same old story.

Like much of the album, 'Moon Is Up' is at least partly redeemed by Jagger's vocal performance. The singer was now fully at one with the Stones, unlike the dark days of *Dirty Work*, when his solo career seemed more important to him.

out of tears

As with Keith Richards groaning through 'The Worst', the performance of Mick Jagger on 'Out Of Tears' is a welcome moment of emotional release and clarity. Jagger sings here of the inevitable end of a relationship with a real quiver in his voice, spread across the emotive solo piano work of Chuck Leavell. David Campbell's rich string arrangement swells at the chorus to great, melodramatic effect. Jagger hadn't sounded this emotionally naked since 'Angie' or 'Fool To Cry'. Even within this torch song, Jagger was tapping into the depths of the blues once again.

i go wild

'I Go Wild' is launched with a sudden burst of electric guitars before falling into a measured groove of riffing and Mick Jagger's words of desperate love. "Without you I'm dead meat," he sings, rapping through a list of nightmarish scenes of sex, violence, sickness and masochism. He sounds comfortably nasty here, reciting the song title with raw, lascivious glee. The tune's three-chord approach keeps this rocker simple and direct, but the bridge of big beats and scattered guitar is a lumbering misstep. Better to keep it wild.

brand new car

Why 15 tracks on *Voodoo Lounge*? The empty funk of 'Brand New Car' begs the question. A blend of new funk and Chuck Berry, the song never erupts beyond its simple, thumping rhythm. The horns of saxophonist David McMurray and trumpeter Mark Isham send a brief moment of warmth across the track, but nothing uplift's Jagger's seedy tale, which uses a car as yet another convenient metaphor for his woman. *Voodoo Lounge* would have survived without it.

sweethearts together

'Sweethearts Together' was another unexpected blast from the early Stones. It's the kind of song that manager Andrew Loog Oldham used to peddle to unsuspecting pop singers. The Rolling Stones rarely performed such songs themselves, but left them to singers like Gene Pitney and Cliff Richard, who enjoyed hits with the Glimmer Twins' discards. 'Sweethearts Together' is mildly diverting, a mid-tempo ballad with a tropical vibe. Mick is feeling romantic, pledging himself to his love forever, while acknowledging "there's always something tempting in the wilderness of youth." Tex-Mex accordion master Flaco Jimenez adds another layer of gentle melody. The recording's lethargic shuffle is not unlike the Beach Boys' syrupy 'Kokomo', which miraculously returned that band to the top of the US singles chart at the end of the eighties. Listeners might expect more angst from the makers of 'Paint It Black', and a band that's been loving and leaving since the early sixties. Now if only Merv Griffin and Anthony Newly were available to sing it...

suck on the jugular

The Rolling Stones mastered the funk decades ago. They experimented with the hard stuff on 'Hot Stuff' in 1976 and went on successfully to create their own blend with 'Miss You' two years later. Mick Jagger also spent half that decade on the dance floor. All of which makes 'Suck On The Jugular' hard to explain.

The bass lines of Darryl Jones roll convincingly, and the guitars find a fitting funk riff. But somehow the end result is bloodless bar-band funk, more flat groove than anything resembling a song. The call and response chorus doesn't help either. And his lyrics add up to nothing. Only Jagger's own ragged harp playing rescues the song momentarily from complete listlessness.

blinded by rainbows

Northern Ireland, an unlikely source of inspiration for Mick Jagger.

Another moving performance by Mick Jagger. 'Blinded By Rainbows' is a haunted ballad, built on a simple blend of light instrumentation from the Stones, joined by percussionist Lenny Castro and Benmont Tench on organ. An edgy guitar passage emerges memorably at the bridge, but it's Jagger who makes the track breathe, drawing on what are without doubt the most meaningful lyrics on *Voodoo Lounge*.

The song recounts scenes of real horror: fatherless children, neighbourhood bombs exploding indiscriminately, an endless religious war in the streets. Recorded in Dublin, Jagger was undoubtedly inspired by the hopeless battles over Northern Ireland. The song was the Stones' most overtly political statement since 1991's 'Highwire', their critique of the international arms trade. 'Blinded By Rainbows' hit closer to home, and was inevitably more emotionally genuine.

voodoo lounge

baby break it down

The makings of a fine album were buried within the grooves of *Voodoo Lounge*. Jagger sang well and the Stones played with real energy during the sessions at Windmill Lane Studios in Dublin. Worthy musical ideas were scattered across its 15 tracks, but too many songs lacked enough focus to coalesce into truly memorable moments. It doesn't help that the lyrics of 'Baby Break It Down' tell the story of a couple at loggerheads, a concept dealt with far more effectively by others – for example, the Beatles' 'We Can Work It Out'. 'Baby Break It Down' has some worthwhile elements: the slow, moody riffing, the chorus that finally brings the song to life with the help of singers Ivan Neville and Bernard Fowler. But ultimately its just more middling funk, and not a track destined to join the Stones immortal hit parade.

voodoo lounge

thru and thru

Keith Richards is just not interested in your help. Particularly not in the midst of an early morning session for a track like 'Thru And Thru' – an edgy, darkly contemplative song the guitarist had made into a personal project, and one not to be taken lightly. That's a hard lesson even fellow rock stars must understand.

By now, Richards had become a supremely confident vocal presence, with two solo albums and the making of *Dirty Work* – with an infuriatingly distracted and absent Mick Jagger – already behind him. Keith's days of croaking shyly and awkwardly through the likes of 'Salt Of The Earth' were a distant memory by 1994. All of which brought him well-prepared to tackle the nearly epic 'Thru And Thru', a tortured declaration of love with the rough edges of Richards' voice exposed against a mostly barren guitar track before kicking into a tough rock groove. "Keith is at a real creative peak in his life right now," producer Don Was told *Goldmine* magazine in 1995. "He's writing some songs that are really different."

For 'Thru And Thru', Richards had his own specific plans for the song, and not even Ronnie Wood was invited to play on it – although, oddly, crew member Pierre de Beauport provided a layer of acoustic guitar. All of this somehow managed to escape the notice of Slash, guitarist with Guns N' Roses, who was then visiting the studio and sharing a couch at the back with the amiable Wood.

Slash's mistake was perhaps in liking too much of what he heard in 'Thru And Thru', and imagining his own hot blues licks somewhere in the mix, which is a reasonable notion to explore if you're the famous lead guitarist for one of the world's thousand greatest (and most dysfunctional) rock and roll bands, and have been a welcome guest performer on albums by artists ranging from Michael Jackson to Iggy Pop.

"Yeah," Slash told Richards enthusiastically, "if you just let me get set up with an amp out there, I hear these blues licks that I could really play on the end of the thing."

Don Was remembers the moment. The pregnant pause. The eyes of Keith seeming, somehow, to turn black. "Look, I like ya, kid, but don't press your luck," Richards said. "You're not coming anywhere near my fuckin' track."

There was another acidic comment or two about a "guitar apprentice" in the room from Richards before the Rolling Stone continued alone with his dirty work. "Keith's not a guy to hide his feelings," Was said. "He left no doubt that he didn't appreciate the suggestion. He knew very clearly what he wanted to do on the record."

Still wet behind the ears: Slash's offer of assistance went unappreciated.

mean disposition

Is rock and roll a young man's game? The late Muddy Waters was no child by the time the Rollin' Stones first heard the man. And Chuck Berry is certainly not a youngster today, spending his golden years night after night on the road playing a tight set of oldies. Yet so many of the Stones' contemporaries lost touch in the eighties and nineties (if not sooner) with whatever focus and energy that had once made their early work worthwhile, leaving behind a small crowd of veteran rockers still making music of power and consequence (Neil Young and Lou Reed among them). Mick Jagger may forever regret abandoning the more primitive elements and ideas he and Richards first brought to the *Voodoo Lounge* sessions, but tracks like 'Mean Disposition' at least demonstrated the Rolling Stones could play straight-ahead rock and roll with true, wild-eyed conviction.

"If I'm going to go, I'm going to go in a blaze of lights!" sings Jagger on 'Mean Disposition', closing *Voodoo Lounge* with an explosion of fragmenting Chuck Berry riffs, some euphoric boogie-woogie piano by Chuck Leavell and the snarling basslines of Darryl Jones.

"The kind of sparks that fly between Charlie and Keith, I don't think that happens in bands that have been together for two years," Don Was told *Goldmine*. "I think it takes decades of playing together to get that kind of rapport happening. I'd liken it more maybe to Duke Ellington's band, or some lifetime aggregation, really. So we're just starting to see how that affects rock and roll music.

"The reality is, you don't compare it to *Beggars Banquet*. That's not what it's about. You're setting the precedent for what happens to a band after 30 years."

So even if the "World's Greatest Rock And Roll Band" was not quite twisting the course of pop music history to their own ends, these survivors of the original British blues movement, and the frenzied days of the British invasion of America, could at least still burn the doors off when the mood was right. Not a bad way to sign off for the Rolling Stones circa 1994, merely three decades after Brian Jones thought it might be nice to play music with Jagger, Richards, Watts and Wyman.

> **" The kind of sparks that fly between Charlie and Keith, I don't think that happens in bands that have been together for two years...it takes decades of playing together to get that kind of rapport "**
>
> Don Was, producer

chapter twenty one

hot stuff
singles, EPs, B-sides and other oddities

Imagine no *Beggars Banquet*. No *Aftermath*. No *Let It Bleed*. Take away ALL of their albums, and the Rolling Stones would still be ranked among the very best in the history of rock and roll. Album artists were an anomaly in 1963, the year the Rollin' Stones first saw the inside of a recording studio. The pop medium of choice was the single, seven inches of lo-fi plastic that opened up a new world for millions of young record buyers. And few singles had greater social impact in those dark days than the latest dispatch of dangerous vinyl from the Stones.

If singles exist at all in the digital age, they're designed mostly to be part of a grander marketing scheme to sell more albums, particularly in the US. When the career of the Stones began, singles were entirely separate from albums. And singles were how most fans got their first dose of the band. Precious coins were spent at neighbourhood record shops or dropped into some glowing juke box, all for the privilege of hearing whatever state-of-the-art music was being offered, whether by the Beatles ('Hey Jude'), the Supremes ('Where Did Our Love Go?'), the Who ('I Can See For Miles'), Bob Dylan ('Like A Rolling Stone'), the list was endless. Each one of these tracks – like the single Brian Wilson once called his little "pocket symphony", the Beach Boys' 'Good Vibrations' – were crowded together on radio playlists of no particular sense or sensibility other than passing fashion and fleeting popularity. Together, they managed to capture the mood of an era. Singles were really an artificially brief format from which complete reputations could emerge among the larger public, if not hardcore listeners. So each release needed to be a singular musical production, one that lived up to the Stones' early boast: "It's the singer, not the song".

For the vast majority of listeners, then, the music of the Stones was best summed up by career-defining songs such as '(I Can't Get No) Satisfaction', 'Jumpin' Jack Flash' and 'Honky Tonk Women', each of which saw life first as a hit single. The brilliant, sprawling rock and blues disasterpiece of *Exile On Main Street* barely even registers on that scale.

The seven-inch disc is extinct now, except as a novelty item. So, too, has gone the four-to-five-song vinyl EP, along with those precious, brooding cover photographs of the young Stones by David Bailey, Gered Mankowitz or Michael Cooper. But for a time, the singles and EPs counted for everything, whether they were cover tunes written by Muddy Waters or Bobby Womack, or original compositions by Jagger and Richards or the mysterious Nanker Phelge. Our concern in this chapter, again, are with those songs written by the Stones themselves. The tracks here never appeared on albums – at least in their native Britain – until compiled on the likes of *Hot Rocks*, *Through The Past Darkly*, *Sucking In The Seventies* and other wayward collections.

Other oddities examined here, such as the impudent *Jamming With Edward* and the horrific *Metamorphosis*, are just small pieces of the Stones puzzle. They are far from essential listening, but at least demonstrate the inclination of the Rolling Stones to have a joke at your expense.

1963
Stoned

'Stoned' may seem a dubious place to begin a chronology of the Stones as songwriters of trend-shattering singles, but history would not have it any other way. The very first original song recorded and released by the young Rolling Stones was built on a standard blues rhythm stolen from Booker T & the MGs' 'Green Onions'. Credited to Nanker Phelge – the fictitious name used for songs jointly written by all of the Stones and manager Andrew Loog Oldham – 'Stoned' was recorded within 30 minutes on October 1963 at Kingsway Sound Studios in London. It was originally released as the B-side to their rendition of Lennon and McCartney's 'I Wanna Be Your Man' and is performed with a charming sloppiness – listen closely, and you might hear another good reason for kicking pianist Ian Stewart from the band. At just over two minutes, the mostly instrumental song offers no lyrical content of any import, just Mick Jagger's breathless cheap thrill at claiming to be stoned "out of my mind". The song was initially banned in the US when it was deemed too suggestive for American kids. Strange when the man doesn't actually SOUND high at all. That kind of authenticity would come with practice.

1964
Good Times, Bad Times

Only a few months after 'Stoned', the band showed a marked improvement as composers with this ringing country-blues track. Heavy slabs of acoustic guitar carry Jagger through this lumbering love plaint. The singer's delivery isn't at all convincing – he hasn't yet learned to express the pain required. But the blend of guitars and harmonica behind him make the point for him. Originally released as the B-side to 'It's All Over Now', the song was recorded during sessions at Chess Studios in Chicago.

Surprise, Surprise

Here is an early example of the classic, bitter Jagger/Richards love song. Mick sings with great urgency to a girl who's "been tellin' lies", and informs her that he doesn't want her around anymore. Recorded at Regent in London, 'Surprise, Surprise' is built on a prominent and frantic drum beat meshed with a lively rock guitar pattern. The expressions of anger and bitterness that Jagger would one day have at his disposal are not yet present. Instead, the singer sounds almost detached. 'Surprise, Surprise' was first released on the US-only album *The Rolling Stones, Now!*, and in the UK on *Fourteen*, a multi-artist charity compilation benefitting the Lord Taverners National Playing Fields Association. Strangely, the track was resurrected as a B-side for 1970's 'Street Fighting Man', as if the early Stones actually had anything to do with the apocalyptic messengers they had become by the end of the decade.

That Girl Belongs To Yesterday

The Rolling Stones never recorded this dubious selection, at least not anywhere it might be ever found. But the song is worth noting here because it became a UK hit single for American pop singer Gene Pitney. 'That Girl Belongs to Yesterday' dates back to the very first Jagger/Richards songwriting sessions, which also spawned the ballad 'As Tears Go By'. Pitney's Spectorish rendition of the song found an audience, but Richards was never convinced of its value. In 1989, Richards pronounced it a "horrible song".

Congratulations

The road to *Some Girls* begins here. Mick Jagger sings bitterly to a girl who is leaving him for the second time, congratulating her for breaking yet another heart. "There'll be no next time," he sings with a slight sneer. 'Congratulations' is a loping love ballad, built on a low thumping guitar melody. Recorded in 1964 at Regent in London, the track first appeared that year on the US-only *12x5* album. It wasn't made available in the UK until 1973's *No Stone Unturned* collection.

FIVE BY FIVE EP

If You Need Me
(Pickett/Bateman/Sanders)
Empty Heart
(Phelge)
2120 South Michigan Avenue
(Phelge)
Confessin' The Blues
(Brown/McShann)
Around And Around
(Berry)

Empty Heart

This Nanker Phelge track is an upbeat tune, but it's ultimately a sloppy mix of vocals, guitar, organ and harmonica that rides a single riff for its entire 2:36 minutes. It's most distinctive element is the shimmering rock guitar of Keith Richards, playing a sharp mix of Chuck Berry and surf sounds. 'Empty Heart' first appeared in the US on the *12x5* album.

2120 Michigan Avenue

Ian Stewart trades organ riffs with Brian Jones' breezy harmonica wheezes on this tribute to Chess Records. The two-minute Nanker Phelge instrumental is named for the address of the famed Chicago studio, where the work of Muddy Waters, Chuck Berry and other blues and rock immortals recorded the music that gave birth to the Rollin' Stones.

1965
The Last Time

Keith now calls 'The Last Time' the very first Jagger/Richards song that could honestly be described as an archetypal Stones number. It was also the first original song the writers actually felt comfortable presenting to the band. Recorded in early 1965 at RCA Studios in Hollywood, with Jack Nitschze on keyboards, it marks a critical accomplishment for the band, who were now making music of real daring and excitement, sounding like no one but themselves. The finished recording was Jagger sounding dangerous and aloof, seething with aimless sexuality and indifference to the needs of the poor girl he's threatening to leave. He's accompanied by a storm of acoustic guitars, welded tightly with a loping electric guitar lead that remains among the most recognizable sounds in the Stones repertoire. Producer/manager Andrew Loog Oldham knew he had something, but he still had some doubts. So he invited Phil Spector to the studio that same night to hear his opinion and chart prediction. When Spector arrived, he listened and told Oldham, "I think you've got a No. 10".

Play With Fire
(B-side of 'The Last Time')

Spector's reaction to 'The Last Time' was reassuring, but the Stones still needed a B-side for the single. The band was set to leave for a tour of Australia the next day, and Charlie and Bill had already passed out. Oldham, Jagger and Richards decided to record another song, 'Play With Fire', with Nitschze on harpsichord and Spector on bass – the first time Wyman was substituted at a session. Joining on background vocals was a portly RCA janitor who had just arrived for work. "Had we been in Chicago he would have been some famous blues singer," said Oldham. "But it was just a studio cleaner who was cleaning the studio up at 8 o'clock in the morning."

The song emerges at a quiet, haunted pace on harpsichord and the delicate plucking of grim melodies on guitar. Jagger shakes the tambourine as he sings in a vaguely threatening tone to a young woman. The single released of 'The Last Time' and 'Play With Fire' made a powerful combination. Together, the songs revealed an early hint of the pop brilliance slowly emerging from these blues fanatics. And Spector's chart prediction wasn't far off. The UK single reached No. 1, and a few weeks later hit No. 9 in America.

(I Can't Get No) Satisfaction

Keith didn't like it. The cat just didn't get it. Too damn simple. He'd awoken in a hotel room on the road one night, heard the thing in his head – that brutal riff and key lyric – and wrote it down. Richards had loved the song then, but by the time the Rolling Stones tried '(I Can't Get No) Satisfaction' in the studio, he was bored with it. And all that fuzz guitar was just nonsense. "It sounded like a folk song when we first started working on it, and Keith didn't like it much, he didn't want it to be a single, he didn't think it would do very well," Jagger said in 1968. "That's the only time we have had a disagreement."

The first, acoustic version of the song was recorded at Chicago's Chess Records studios on May 10, 1965, but was attempted again the following day at RCA Studios in Hollywood. The second time had a new tempo from Watts and the charged electric guitar opening, along with Jagger's breathless swagger, combining to express a level of sexual alienation previously unheard of on pop radio. The song's title and key phrase may have been inspired by Chuck Berry's '30 Days' ("I can't get no satisfaction from the judge!"), but the Stones had recast it into an entirely new, and dangerous meaning.

The Rolling Stones were already in the midst of an American tour when the song landed on the radio for the first time, and transformed them instantly from just another faceless British invasion act. Combined with the parallel success in the US of their *Out Of Our Heads* album, '(I Can't Get No) Satisfaction' was the breakthrough that defined the Stones' persona for the rest of their career. Richards, of course, soon learned to love the tune again, without too much urging needed from the band's young manager, Andrew Loog Oldham. "It was the beginning of the period where we were on a roll," Oldham says today, "and nothing could stop us."

The Spider And The Fly

Here's a message for the girls waiting back home. It's a Jimmy Reed-style blues with young Mick describing his lonely life on the road, and the endless temptation he finds there. Not that he's fighting very hard to uphold the notion of fidelity after the shows, at the bars, amid the women who stumble into his web.

Jagger has the role of predator here, but his attitude isn't the usual bitterness that so often emerges in Jagger/Richards love-hate songs. 'The Spider And The Fly' was recorded at Chess during first US tour, along with 'It's All Over Now' and 'Confessin' The Blues'. It appeared on the US version of *Out Of Our Heads* and the UK compilation *Stone Age*. The Stones later reworked the song on 1995's *Stripped*, this time with a more weathered vocal delivery and scalding harmonica solo from Mick. In this later version, the woman who finally approaches the singer is 50, not 30!

Get Off Of My Cloud

Not even Charlie's relentless drumbeat can keep up: Mick Jagger's singing is so rushed that the words overlap into a desperately incoherent demand for satisfaction. He just wants to be left alone ("two's a crowd on my cloud, baby!"), free from the stupidity of a man at his door inquiring about his laundry detergent, and free from the invasion of neighbours intruding on his loud music and good times.

In 1968, Jagger said the lyrics were "crap". Nearly three decades later, he evaluated 'Get Off Of My Cloud' as a post-teenage-alienation song. Inspiration came from the orderly UK society he knew so well, but even more so from his first impressions of the United States, which seemed more restricted in behaviour and dress. "New York was wonderful and so on, and LA was also kind of interesting," Jagger told *Rolling Stone*. "But outside of that we found it the most repressive society, very prejudiced in every way. There was still segregation. And the attitudes were fantastically old-fashioned. Americans shocked me by their behaviour and their narrow-mindedness."

Richards, meanwhile, grumbled endlessly about Oldham's production of 'Get Off Of My Cloud'. The sound was too dense, bleeding everywhere, a horrible sonic mess, and just barely held together by Charlie's martial drumbeats and handclaps. Yet it was a hit single, topping the charts on both sides of the Atlantic. "I never dug it as a record," Keith said in 1971. "The chorus was a nice idea but we rushed it as the follow-up. We were in LA and it was time for another single. But how do you follow 'Satisfaction'? Actually, what I wanted to do was to do it slow like a Lee Dorsey thing. We rocked it up. I thought it was one of Andrew's worst productions."

The Singer, Not The Song *B-side*
(B-side of 'Get Off Of My Cloud')

The title may have been a bold statement, but it was absolutely true for the generation of pop musicians that included the Rolling Stones. The sixties began an era where a single performance of a song, specifically one captured on a record, was viewed as THE definitive interpretation. So what was the need for Sinatra to sing 'Something'? Or Johnny Cash to trivialize the Stones' 'No Expectations'? Or to endure William Shatner convulsing through 'Lucy In The Sky With Diamonds'? Of course, several standards did emerge from the era, but 'The Singer, Not The Song' certainly was not one of them. Is that atonal or just out of tune? Even the most forgiving listeners must have wondered. Jagger manages a slightly diverting vocal melody at the chorus, but the track otherwise falls flat.

One More Try

Come to Mick with all your love problems. On 'One More Try' the singer offers advice to a friend frustrated over some chick who's never happy, even after providing everything she wants. "Sit, down, shut up...things will get better if you really try," Jagger shouts with increasing urgency. His frantic vocal speeds across the sounds of this blues-based rocker, interrupted only by some fluid harmonica passages, most likely played by Brian Jones. Like 'The Spider And The Fly', 'One More Try' first appeared on the US version of *Out Of Our Heads*, and wasn't released in the UK until the 1971 *Stone Age* compilation.

Blue Turns To Grey

Recorded at RCA Studios in Hollywood in 1965, 'Blue Turns To Grey' is a melancholy ballad about a breakup. And Jagger's vocal is unusually warm and soothing here, describing the lingering emotions after a girl has left. The song was a 1966 top-20 hit for Cliff Richard in England. It first appeared in America on the US-only album *December's Children (And Everybody's)*, but did not see release in the UK until 1971's *Stone Age*.

1966

19th Nervous Breakdown

Poor Chrissie Shrimpton is often forgotten in casual Stones remembrances, her time beside young Mick overshadowed by the grim fairy tale of Jagger and Faithfull that followed. And yet her role was significant, though perhaps not in ways Miss Shrimpton would like to remember. She was the young blues-rocker's main squeeze during the years when his wandering eye was just beginning to emerge. '19th Nervous Breakdown' was a cruel dissection of a young woman who some thought resembled Shrimpton a bit too closely. Whatever its core inspiration, the recording marked another dynamic move toward ultimate maturity as songwriters for Jagger and Richards.

The song was recorded in December 1965 during the sessions for *Aftermath*. It's another muddy Oldham production, another would-be Phil Spector epic. But none of that ultimately matters. The Stones poke through that muddle by sheer energy and attitude, led by a brisk guitar intro from Richards. Before closing with a tense, dive bomb bass warble played by Wyman, '19th Nervous Breakdown' dissects the life of a young society girl in the throes of an LSD episode, whose mind is quickly fraying from the pressure.

The song title is said to have started as a wisecrack by Jagger regarding the 1965 tour of the States, which he called his "19th nervous breakdown". Fans debated the supposed drug references, and Jagger told interviewers that, again, it was just another song about a girl.

As Tears Go By *B-side*
(B-side of '19th Nervous Breakdown')

Marianne Faithfull never sang the blues, never jammed with Cream or Mayall or Jimi. She was that "angel with big tits" discovered at a party by Rollin' Stones manager Andrew Loog Oldham in 1964 and transformed into a comely icon of Brit-pop fantasy. She hit the charts via the precocious Jagger/Richards ballad 'As Tears Go By', co-wrote the Stones' 'Sister Morphine' then disappeared into a cloud of drug addiction and self-loathing. Who could have expected anything more out of her? She was just another girl singer, a rock star's concubine.

Faithfull later demonstrated she was much more with *Broken English*, her 1979 album of ferocious punk and disco-addled confession. The voice that had once whispered so sweetly into the ear of beau Jagger was now a raspy, whiskey-soured wail. Ever since, she's remained an adventurous interpreter of the pop-rock-jazz canon, more relevant today than in her forgotten heyday. This was no sixties casualty. And yet by 1997, she was still performing 'As Tears Go By' on stage, mixed among a repertoire heavy with Weill/Brecht tunes, in effect demonstrating that this simple little ballad carried some weight after all.

The Stones never intended to perform the song themselves. It was merely an early attempt at songwriting for the Glimmer Twins, something to peddle to the first ballad singer who passed by (much as Lennon and McCartney had unloaded 'I Wanna Be Your Man' on the Stones). That singer turned out to be Ms. Faithfull, who was summoned to Olympic Studios in London by Oldham for her first recording session without even an audition. Talent was not the issue to the young Stones manager. In Faithfull, he saw an alluring character, a blonde mixture of innocence and sexuality he could sell to the kids, to the young (and not so young) boys especially. If this little girl actually turned out to have a nice voice too, so much the better.

"I thought he was mad, but I liked him," Faithfull says now of her first meeting with Oldham at Olympic.

Mick and Keith were, of course, in attendance, watching grimly from the control booth, but saying nothing. The 17-year-old novice singer barely noticed them. She laughs, "I wasn't at all overwhelmed by the Stones".

Nor was she taken with the first song handed her by Oldham – 'I Don't Know How (To Tell You)' by Lionel Bart, composer of the hit musical *Oliver!* After several failed attempts, the producer-manager had Faithfull try 'As Tears Go By', and something finally gelled: her soft, lilting vocals wrapped themselves around the strangely melancholy words, evoking a lifetime of experience. She sang of watching children playing, of feeling sadly distant from that kind of innocence and happiness, somehow lost on the journey to wealth and wisdom.

"I don't know if I could recognize a great song at that point," says Faithfull, "but I was lucky – I didn't have to. It was decided. It was obvious because we tried another song and it was so inferior. 'As Tears Go By' was the only one that stood up. I can't sing second-rate material really. It doesn't work. I can't make it real."

Her recording of 'As Tears Go By' became a top-10 hit in England, and her career was launched. The song may have been a early bit of hackwork from the baby Glimmer Twins, but their subversively simple tune touched a nerve that would continue to carry emotional weight for decades after.

If the song was a career-defining moment for Faithfull, the Stones reclaimed 'As Tears Go By', at least momentarily, more than a year later. Oldham's simple pop arrangement was replaced by the Stones on their 1966 recording with a low thumping guitar melody, accented with strings. Coming after the shouted conviction of 'Get Off of My Cloud', the almost child-like performance of Jagger here, singing at the softest end of his voice, may have been a surprise to some fans. Even John Lennon suggested that the ballad's delicate strings owed something to the recent example of the Beatles' 'Yesterday'. In the UK, the track was relegated to the B-side of '19th Nervous Breakdown', but 'As Tears Go By' enjoyed a higher profile in the US – where Faithfull's version was virtually unheard – as a top-10 single.

Sad Day

This middling pop tune was first released as the B-side to the American single of '19th Nervous Breakdown', and rightfully remained buried in obscurity in the UK until it was unearthed as an early-seventies single by Decca and later on *The Singles Collection* box in 1989. As recorded at RCA Studios in Hollywood, 'Sad Day' offers a flat mid-tempo throbbing, with light psychedelic flourishes at the margins. Jagger sings here of being let go by his girl, but there's little regret in his voice until the lilting chorus. It's as if for all his study, the blues hadn't taught him anything at all.

Paint It, Black

Behold a new vision for a new age, and for the rock and roll band best suited to document its bleaker moments. Mick Jagger sings here of turning the world BLACK to soothe his own shattered soul in the aftermath of some unspeakable loss. The words are Jagger's, the music Richards', but the success of 'Paint It, Black' owes much to the presence of Brian Jones, who adds a Turkish vibe to the proceedings via excited sitar passages. Jones hadn't mastered the unwieldy instrument overnight, but he had figured out how to make sounds that connected with the dark rhythms the Stones were now exploring. In television performances of the song, Jones was a focal point, sitting cross-legged and balancing the sitar on his lap. The blond bluesboy who had worshipped Elmore James and Muddy Waters (virtually to the exclusion of anything else) was now transformed into a pop adventurer. It was a role well-suited to Jones, who flourished as a member of the Stones in the mid-sixties, even as band control had gone to the Glimmer Twins. His mastery of an ever-widening range of instruments, from marimbas to the Mellotron, would have secured him an important role with the band into the future, if drugs and paranoia hadn't done him in.

The song had somehow begun as a joke, a parody of songs played at Jewish weddings, according to Jagger. "What's amazing about that one for me is the sitar," Richards told *Rolling Stone* in 1971. "Also the fact that we cut it as a comedy track. Bill was playing an organ, doing a takeoff of our first manager who started his career in show business as an organist in a cinema pit. We'd been doing it with funky rhythms and it hadn't worked, and he started playing it like this and everybody got behind it. It's a two-beat, very strange. Brian playing the sitar makes it a whole other thing."

The song title as it appeared on the single – with a comma before "black" – caused some to wonder about the possibility of racial undertones. It was more likely a random quirk of punctuation, and ever since it's appeared in print both with and without the comma. The Stones' own albums and sheet music don't even agree.

Long Long While
B-side
(B-side of 'Paint It Black')

Jagger once jokingly asked Bobby Womack to teach him how to sing soul. "I couldn't teach you how to sing no soul," Womack replied. "If I could teach you to do that in one day, what is the value in it? You sing from the heart." That was a lesson Jagger already seemed to understand on 1966's 'Long Long While', which enjoys the edgy passion of a classic Stax-Volt single. It's also the kind of thing Elvis himself might have sung by the end of that decade, with stylish guitar played by Richards and Jones, and a rare note of regret from Jagger, who begs for forgiveness from a girl he once left behind.

Have You Seen Your Mother, Baby, Standing In The Shadow?

Stand back for an onslaught. 'Have You Seen Your Mother, Baby, Standing In The Shadow?' begins in sonic overdrive, even before the squeaky horn section of Mike Leander breaks in to joust with blasts of frantic piano. Guitars and bass bleed together creating a strange buzzing noise. The track opens and closes with a slow riff of raw, metallic guitar, framing Jagger's taunting lyrics that he once described as the "ultimate freakout".

While the tone and title suggest another anti-female theme, the song is more in the tradition of 'Mother's Little Helper', challenging old societal values with relentless glee. "All these songs were written in America,"

GOT LIVE IF YOU WANT IT EP

We Want The Stones
(Phelge)
Everybody Needs Somebody To Love
(Russell/Burke/Wexler)
Pain In My Heart (Neville)
Route 66 (Troup)
I'm Moving On (Snow)
I'm Alright
(Phelge)

We Want The Stones
Left off the CD reissue of the Stones catalogue, 'We Want the Stones' is not a song really, just a recording of fans at London's Royal Albert Hall chanting their name. The band still earned some publishing royalties from the track by crediting it to Nanker Phelge.

I'm Alright
'I'm Alright' is tuneful Jagger/Richards rocker with a western beat, and is built on a single relentless guitar riff. Its simplicity does not prevent the band from giving it an excited performance, rising above the roar of endless screaming that greeted all the band's shows in the mid-sixties. This same recording also appeared on the US version of *Out Of Our Heads*. If the Stones recorded a studio version of 'I'm Alright' bootleggers have yet to find it.

Jagger said in 1968. "It is a great place to write because all the time you are being bombarded and you can't help but try and put it in some kind of form... As far as I'm concerned those songs just reflect what's going on."

Keith was never happy with the sound of the track, and complained that it was recorded too quickly and poorly mastered, burying the rhythm section in the final mix. "The only reason we were so hot on it was that the track blew our heads off," Richards told *Rolling Stone* in 1971. "Everything else was rushed too quickly... It needed another couple of weeks."

The song is also notable for inspiring the Stones to one of their most infamous photo sessions. One day in New York, the quintet gathered with photographer Jerry Shatzberg, who had them dress as women. They then rolled on to the streets of Manhattan, with Wyman posing in a wheelchair, for some pictures. Afterward, they remained in costume and went into a bar for some beer and TV.

Who's Driving Your Plane
B-side
(B-side of 'Have You Seen Your Mother, Baby, Standing In The Shadow?')

'Who's Driving Your Plane' is three minutes of the most ferocious blues the Stones had mustered in years. It was also a dramatic demonstration that the band wasn't leaving the blues behind as it drifted deeper into pop. The first clue comes from Jack Nitzsche, who pounds the keyboards here alongside Jagger, who's shouting at some girl to escape the dominance of her parents. A tense blues harp wheezes in the distance.

1967
Let's Spend The Night Together

Silly Mick denied it for years, but we knew better, even when there wasn't a video to back it up: in January 1967, on the *Ed Sullivan Show*, Jagger did acquiesce and censor himself. He actually did sing "Let's spend SOME TIME together". How un-rock and roll! How weak! Yes, but the man had little choice – other than to walk off the show, as Dylan had once done, or to sing it anyway, as Jim Morrison once did (to Mr Ed's horror). In any case, it hardly caused permanent damage to the song. Jagger didn't seem to care much about the Sullivan request anyway, then or now. It was just a television show, a fleeting performance that would disappear into the ether, where no one could find it. But a gig on American network television was too good to pass by. So why not change a word or two? There were, of course, appearances to maintain. "I never said 'time', I said 'Let's Spend some mmmmm together, let's spend some mmmmm together,'" Jagger insisted in 1968. "They would have cut it off if I said 'night'."

Which was certainly true of a song of such blatant sexual content. The message here is one of simple lust, with Jagger imploring some woman into bed with him. He sings across a sound of rich, driving force, a blend of excited piano chords and Charlie Watts' forceful drumbeat. The result is a song that's more hopeful than the frazzled boy-man found in 'Satisfaction', as if Jagger only has to ask this time out.

Marianne Faithfull has suggested that the song was written after Jagger spent his first night with her, which is a reasonable claim, given the song's timing. It was recorded in November 1966 during sessions for *Between The Buttons* at Olympic, with Jack Nitzsche on keyboards. The UK single reached No. 2, with 'Ruby Tuesday' as the B-side; in America, the songs were switched, and 'Ruby Tuesday' went to the top.

Ruby Tuesday
B-side
(B-side of 'Let's Spend The Night Together')

"That's a wonderful song," Jagger told Jann Wenner in 1995. "It's just a nice melody, really. And a lovely lyric. Neither of which I wrote, but I always enjoy singing it." Brian Jones blows a charming flute melody, blending into a rich, pure pop sound of acoustic guitar, piano and acoustic bass. Jagger sings with charming softness of a mysterious girl who warns him to "Catch your dreams before they slip away!"

The song began as an instrumental collaboration between Richards and Jones, making 'Ruby Tuesday' one song that apparently deserved a co-writing credit for Brian Jones – a first. "He was a gas," Richards said of Jones. "He was a cat who could play any instrument." Yet when the single was released in January 1967, it was credited to Jagger/Richards.

Ride On, Baby

The harpsichord and marimbas seem so pleasant, the lilting pop melody so warm and upbeat. The music nearly disguises this cruel brush-off directed at some unfortunate party girl Jagger berates as torn and frayed from too much time in the fast lane.

Recorded in December 1965 at RCA Studios, 'Ride On, Baby' was released nearly two years later on the US-only compilation *Flowers* and nowhere else. That album was a collection of UK singles and discarded tracks put together by Andrew Oldham for American fans hungry for product while the Rolling Stones were mired in drug and legal problems at home. It reached No. 3 on the American album charts. "All that stuff had been cut a year or so before and rejected by us as not making it," Richards said in 1971. "I was really surprised when people dug it."

'Ride On, Baby' was also recorded as a single for Oldham's Immediate label by Chris Farlowe, marking the singer's third Jagger/Richards cover, and this time with Jagger himself as producer.

Sittin' On A Fence

'Sittin' On A Fence' is another track exclusive to *Flowers*. It's also a rare song that takes a wistful look at the life Mick Jagger might have led if he hadn't abandoned his economic studies for the Stones. There is no regret in his voice, accompanied here by a pair of folky acoustic guitars and a few moments of harpsichord. He's happily escaped living a normal middle class life, and looks back with some wonder at the friends he left behind at school. They have since grown up and "mortgaged up their lives… they just get married cause there's nothing else to do."

We Love You

That bust at Redlands was no joke. Keith's problems with the law, with drugs and other nasty habits, were just beginning, of course. But Mick understood the ramifications of his hours behind bars: the loss of freedom, the threat to this rock and roll dream on which he and the Stones had somehow stumbled. So with their release on appeal, Jagger and Richards immediately booked themselves some studio time. The result was 'We Love You', a tense, psychedelic loveletter to their fans as thanks for their deathless support during these dark days of 1967.

The track opens with the sound of footsteps echoing down a long corridor, followed by the slamming shut of jailhouse doors. It wasn't meant to be subtle. And neither were the urgent piano chords that launch the song, accompanied by some brilliant flashes of Mellotron by Brian Jones and a rumbling bassline that floats from one channel to the other on the stereo release.

Less a proper song than a slice of psychedelic experimentalism that actually worked, the Rolling Stones here demonstrated a sudden flair for the genre that rivalled the Beatles' *Sgt. Pepper's Lonely Hearts Club Band*. So it's no small irony that both John Lennon and Paul McCartney visited the 'We Love You' session and provided some recognizable background vocals. The final track was both edgy and musically rich. If only *Their Satanic Majesties Request* had been so well-constructed.

"'We Love You' was quite an amazing track, with that Mellotron," remembers tape op/assistant engineer George Chkiantz. "It was just incredible. That was Brian doing one of his numbers."

Another visitor that same day was Beat poet Allen Ginsberg, who was in London that week to attend a pro-marijuana rally in Hyde Park. After presenting the police with flowers, Ginsberg went to McCartney's house, where he met Jagger and was invited to the session. When the poet arrived he found both Lennon and McCartney there, joining the Stones for the background vocals. "It was wonderful. They all looked like little angels," he told friends the next day, according to *Ginsberg*, the 1989 biography by Barry Miles. In a postcard to his lover Peter Orlovsky, Ginsberg wrote: "Last night I spent at recording studio with Mick Jagger, Paul McCartney and John Lennon looking like Botticelli Graces singing together for the first time. I conducted through the window with Shiva Beads and Tibetan oracle ring."

The earliest sessions for the track weren't quite so romantic. Olympic had been warned that the session would begin on time at 2:30 pm, remembers Chkiantz. And it was true: Mick, Keith, Brian and Bill all showed up ready to work. But no Charlie. So they all waited. But in the meantime no one had wanted to broach the uncomfortable subject of the recent arrests, trials and jailtime. "So when Charlie rolls in at around five there's some sigh of relief," says Chkiantz. "Charlie looks up and takes in the scene very quickly. As he came up the steps he had a grin that I can remember to this day. He really looked like a cat that had stolen all the cream. He just looked around, surveyed the scene, and said 'So how are our two jailbirds then?'"

Chkiantz laughs at the memory. Up until that day, the legendary rhythm section of Wyman and Watts seemed to be taken for granted. Their ideas weren't taken so seriously, so they rarely offered any. Watts' irreverent comment seemed to change that. "It was actually from that day that they started taking Charlie seriously. That made all the difference for him," Chkiantz says. "I think that curiously sewed them together in quite a way."

Dandelion
B-side
(B-side of 'We Love You')

More swelling flower-power pop from the Stones, with melodies that are surprisingly sweet from these badass rockers. Some of the vocal harmonies even sound borrowed from the Beach Boys. Dandelion was also the name Keith and Anita later gave their daughter, although she now prefers to be called Angela. The cheery vibes within the track represent the Stones working hard to have a good time at the very moment their world seemed about ready to come crashing down.

"We didn't have a chance to go through too much flower power because of the bust," Keith commented in 1971. "We're outlaws."

1968
Jumpin' Jack Flash

Jumpin' Jack Flash' is what rescued the Rolling Stones from their psychedelic dead-end, and sent them rushing back to a heavy rock and blues base. The cascading riffs at the beginning boil with an urgency that even fellow deviants in the Velvet Underground would have appreciated.

In 1968, Mick Jagger called the track "the most basic thing we have done this time". PRIMAL is more like it. If 'Satisfaction' initially transformed these five London boys from cheap blues copyists, then 'Jumpin' Jack Flash' revealed them at their most dangerous and refined, crafting rock and roll of unstoppable force and utter perfection.

The era of pop was over for Jagger and Richards. 'Jumpin' Jack Flash' was their ultimate musical manifesto on the band's new sound and purpose, setting a standard for rock and roll just as 'Hound Dog' and 'Johnny B. Goode' had done a generation earlier.

"When I play that first riff in 'Jumpin' Jack Flash', something happens in my stomach – a feeling of tremendous exhilaration, an amazing superhuman feeling," Richards once told author Terry Southern. "An explosion is the best way to describe it. You just jump on that riff, and IT plays YOU. It's the one feeling I would say approaches nirvana."

Bill Wyman has always claimed authorship of the song's key riff, created while jamming on an electronic keyboard with Charlie Watts and Brian Jones. Richards has acknowledged as much in later interviews, though the song is credited to Jagger/Richards. "It happened frequently that basic ideas and middle bits by Brian, Charlie and me went into the melting pot during long studio sessions," Wyman wrote in his *Stone Alone* autobiography, "but over a period of hours or days the origins of our suggestions disappeared... I'd dismiss it with a laugh rather than argue at the time – who wants a disagreement in the studio when you are all trying to be creative?"

The recording of 'Jumpin' Jack Flash' emerged during early sessions for *Beggars Banquet* at Olympic Studios in London, and was the first time the Stones worked with producer Jimmy Miller. The result was a track of raw, driving force, propelled by that immortal riff pattern. Lyrically, the structure is not unlike Bo Diddley's 'Who Do You Love?', but Jagger is perfecting a strange and unique persona here, a voice that is powerful, stormy, outrageous. The singer would forever be known to many by that alter-ego, "Mr Jumpin' Jack Flash".

A promotional film by Michael Lindsay-Hogg (later to direct the Stones' *Rock And Roll Circus* and the Beatles' *Let It Be*) presented the Stones to BBC audiences performing the song in war paint and instilled new fears about a Satanic influence on their music. But the kids knew what they were seeing: the Stones reborn, filled with new energy, finally broken free from the passing plastic fashion of Carnaby Street.

Words are few in 'Jumpin' Jack Flash', but they seem to recount a brutal childhood, with grim scenes of poverty and abuse. "But it's all right now, in fact it's a gas, gas, gas," Jagger sings in a leering, haunted tone. For him, the song represented a return to clarity after a long season of acid madness. "It's about having a hard time and getting out," Jagger told *Rolling Stone* in 1995. "Just a metaphor for getting out of all the acid things."

The song is played with even more swagger on the *Get Yer Ya-Ya's Out!* live album from the 1969 tour, but nothing can quite match the impact of the original recording. It was a sound and fury that even such later classic Stones tracks as 'Brown Sugar' could only approximate. That 3:39-minute assault recorded in 1968 stands as the prototype for much of what followed from the "World's Greatest Rock And Roll Band", and remains a crucial, untouchable document. Unless your name is Mick Jagger.

The singer's indifference to the importance of rock in general, and the Rolling Stones' music in particular, is notorious and even bizarre, as engineer Dave Jerden was to discover while working on both *Dirty Work* and Jagger's *She's The Boss*. One day in Paris, Jerden was summoned by Jagger into a studio. The Glimmer Twin was there to record a new vocal of 'Jumpin' Jack Flash' for a Whoopie Goldberg film of the same name (and long since forgotten). Jagger had the original master with him.

"Well, I should make a copy," Jerden said, noting that there were no open tracks left on the tape for a second vocal. "No, I'll just go over the original vocal," Jagger replied. Which he did, meaning the original master performance is now gone forever. So much for history. 'That's the way Mick is," says Jerden now. "To him, all this other stuff about the history just doesn't really mean anything to him. He's got this cavalier attitude about the Stones stuff. Keith is not like that. For him, everything about the Stones is sacred."

Child Of The Moon
(B-side of 'Jumpin' Jack Flash')

In the context of the A-side, the sentimental 'Child Of The Moon' seemed to come from another era entirely. Though it features some vaguely psychedelic pop, the song is uncluttered by excessive experimentation. Jangly guitars and a rattling mid-tempo drumbeat carry the song forward as Jagger performs a restrained, almost Dylanesque vocal. The lyrics offer a parting vision of innocence for the flower power generation, by then marching blindly toward Altamont.

1969
Honky Tonk Women

As originally envisioned by Keith Richards, 'Honky Tonk Women' was just another country and western tune, the sort of thing that could be played by any back-porch jug band. (The Stones explored that vision of the song via 'Country Honk' on *Let It Bleed*.) But it was in the rocked-up 'Honky Tonk Women' that the band created one of its most memorable tracks, while marking the debut of young Mick Taylor.

The song starts off with the muffled clanging of a cowbell, which is played by producer Jimmy Miller, who taps out a spare beat before drummer Charlie Watts steps in to send the song into a lumbering rock and roll groove. It's a rhythm which is particularly well suited for Jagger, who struts happily through this wanton tale of sex and drugs, and sings of his seduction by "a gin-soaked bar-room queen in Memphis" and some Manhattan divorcee.

Slowly chopping out chords is Richards, playing in the open tuning first learned from Ry Cooder. And sitting

---

1972
JAMMING WITH EDWARD

Boudoir Stomp
(Hopkins/Cooder)
It Hurts Me Too (James)
Edward's Thump Up
(Hopkins/Cooder/Watts)
Blow With Ry
(Hopkins/Cooder/Watts)
Interlude A La El Hopo
(Hopkins/Cooder/Watts)
Highland Fling
(Hopkins/Cooder/Watts)

The Rolling Stones work in mysterious ways. But why THIS? No explanation is possible. *Jamming With Edward* is the strangest disc in the Stones catalogue – a collection of rambling jam sessions, poorly miked vocals and idle chatter between the band and control booth. The six tracks here – a mixture that includes Elmore James' 'It Hurts Me Too' and "songs" credited to Hopkins/Cooder/Watts – document an impromptu May 1969 session with Mick Jagger, Bill Wyman, Charlie Watts, guitarist Ry Cooder and pianist Nicky Hopkins. In his original liner notes, Jagger called the subsequent album release "a nice little piece of bullshit...cut one night in London, England while waiting for our guitar player to get out of bed."

According to legend, the jams were built around the playing of Hopkins ("Edward") who also drew the sketchy cover art. But there's little to distinguish one track from another. Certainly any Stones fanatic would be glad to own it, just like any other half-decent bootleg. After all, the sound quality here is sharper than on the typical bootleg. And there are brief moments of inspired playing, particularly from Cooder. But considering the wealth of material languishing in the Stones vaults, the 1972 release of *Jamming With Edward* was a confounding event indeed. The 1997 re-release by Virgin/Point Blank/Rolling Stones Records was equally surprising.

1975

METAMORPHOSIS

Album oddity

Out Of Time
Don't Lie To Me (Berry)
Some Things Just Stick
  In Your Mind
Each And Every Day Of
  The Year
Heart Of Stone
I'd Much Rather Be With
  The Boys
  (Oldham/Richards)
(Walkin' Thru The)
  Sleepy City
We're Wasting Time
Try A Little Harder
I Don't Know Why
  (Wonder/Riser/Hunter)
If You Let Me
Jiving Sister Fanny
Downtown Suzie
  (Wyman)
Family
Memo From Turner
I'm Going Down
  (Jagger/Richards/Taylor)

The Kafka-esque cover art would certainly seem to be appropriate. Dark, insidious, it's a drawing of the band pulling away their masks to reveal that Jagger, Richards, Wyman, Watts, Jones and Taylor are really insects underneath. Suspicions confirmed! Indeed, *Metamorphosis* is a cretinous batch of dubious outtakes, demos and outright rejects from the Stones' Decca/London years. And a great embarrassment was had by all.

"It's just a lot of junk really," Charlie Watts later said of the album, which was released by Klein after he had rejected Bill Wyman's own retrospective – *The Black Box*.

Klein and the Stones had clearly not parted on good terms. Much of the earliest material on *Metamorphosis* comprises demos left over from the days when Jagger and Richards were hawking their dopiest songs to would-be pop stars. Many of the tracks are not even played by the Stones, but session players hired to back up Jagger. So there's a version of 'Heart Of Stone' that sounds as if it were done by the Righteous Brothers. Further indication of this collection's quality is the sloppiness regarding songwriting credits: Jagger and Richards are credited in the album with writing Chuck Berry's 'Don't Lie to Me' and Stevie Wonder's 'I Don't Know Why'.

There are a few worthwhile curiosities recorded during some of the band's best years, but much of the rest is worthless and virtually unlistenable, making *Metamorphosis* little better than one of the numerous botched Rolling Stones bootlegs.

Each And Every Day Of The Year

The teen dream melodrama of 'Each And Every Day of the Year' is the kind of laughable torch song that made the Stones' blues-based work so necessary at the beginning of the sixties. Jagger sings dreamily against layers of strings, French horn, acoustic guitar and harp. This is not the Stones, but a demo, designed to help other singers learn these putrid lyrics.

I'd Much Rather Be With The Boys

Sounds like Jagger would much rather be with the Beatles. The perky handclaps and earnest singing have little in common with the Stones oeuvre. 'I'd Much Rather Be With The Boys' is another example of Jagger, Richards and Oldham aiming for the most commercial songcraft within their reach. If the Stones had always sounded like this, no one would be writing books about them today.

(Walkin' Thru The) Sleepy City

This is the sound of a would-be hit factory, not a rock and roll band. This tune was for sale, not for the Stones. '(Walkin' Thru The) Sleepy City' is a dumb romance song, light years away from the agitated love-hate girls-against-boys diatribes the Stones would find so inspiring. Bring back the bad vibes PLEASE.

Try a little harder

'Try A Little Harder' is a perky little throwaway fit for a toothpaste commercial – it's a gross misrepresentation to label this the Rolling Stones. Just another reason why your copy of *Metamorphosis* should be melted immediately.

If You Let Me

'If You Let Me' is a middling, up-beat folk tune, all *faux* innocence and earnestness, with the added *moderne* element of electric piano for a strange, low rumble underneath. Although it's not a particularly memorable track, at least it sounds like the Rolling Stones at work, and is therefore far less offensive than the majority of *Metamorphosis*.

Jiving Sister Fanny

Along with the Stones' version of Stevie Wonder's love lament 'I Don't Know Why', the rock strut of 'Jiving Sister Fanny' is one of the very few tracks on *Metamorphosis* that deserves to live another day. The tune doesn't lead anywhere, but it captures the band in the summer of 1969, still very much at their peak. It's carried by Keef's tough-as-nails driving riff, along with some typically exciting blues lead work from Mick Taylor. An organ hums along as Jagger slurs toward mush-mouthed nirvana. ABKCO released 'Jiving Sister Fanny' as the B-side to the 1975 single 'Out Of Time', also culled from *Metamorphosis*.

Downtown Suzie

Recorded during sessions for *Beggars Banquet*, 'Downtown Suzie' is only the second song written by Bill Wyman to appear on a Stones album. The song has little in common with the psychedelia of his 'In Another Land' from *Their Satanic Majesties Request*. It's a droning country blues, with strangely moaning background vocals, until it kicks in during a tuneful hootenanny chorus.

Family

'Family' is another reject from the *Beggars Banquet* sessions. It's a simple blend of acoustic guitar and the piano of Nicky Hopkins that bounds into a playful vaudevillian chorus. Jagger seems to be mocking Dylan in this performance, singing in a strangely understated mode.

I'm Going Down

Metamorphosis at least closes on a high note, with a song of some relevance to where the Stones were at the time of the album's 1975 release. 'I'm Going Down' opens with another of Keith's dynamic riff patterns. It's a sound that would be welcome on any new Stones project, but it was hardly a standout in the context of other work emerging. The track features an early appearance by Bobby Keys, here playing a restrained solo against a driving conga beat. Although Jagger's vocal sounds unfinished, 'I'm Going Down' undeniably finds the Stones during their period of greatest inspiration, when even a throwaway like this has some allure and value. Nothing to be embarrassed about here.

beside him for the first time is Taylor, who Richards later credited as being instrumental in transforming the song from its original 'Country Honk' vision. In 1969, Taylor was barely 21. His soft, smooth features (with just a hint of acne) did not immediately fit in visually with these rock degenerates, but beneath that quiet, angelic exterior burned a serious bluesman.

Taylor's expressive slide guitar playing never threatens to overtake 'Honky Tonk Women', and yet it's an important flavour here. His true showcase would not arrive until 1971's *Sticky Fingers*, which would recast the Stones sound to include epic musical passages now made possible by the presence of Taylor. But with 'Honky Tonk Women' the Rolling Stones had already crossed yet another creative threshold, adding to the recent accomplishments 'Jumpin' Jack Flash' and Beggars Banquet, and beginning a period when the Stones could do almost no wrong.

'Honky Tonk Women' was released as a single on July 4, 1969, the day after Brian's death, and the day before the concert in Hyde Park. The massive 1969 world tour was fast approaching. These were clearly monumental days for the band. The song quickly hit No. 1 in the UK. The same happened in America, until it was knocked from the top position by the Archies.

1978
Everything Is Turning To Gold
(Jagger/Richards/Wood)
(B-side of 'Shattered')

Some Girls came just in time for the Rolling Stones, at the end of a discouraging period of lethargy and wasted opportunity. There had been some great tracks during those years, of course, and *Black And Blue* was a hopeful sign. But by the middle of the seventies, the band's hard-won aura of genius and invincibility were deep into a slow fade. As the decade wore on, the title of "World's Greatest Rock And Roll Band" was sounding more and more like sarcasm. What have you done for me lately?

The true believers were rewarded with 1978's *Some Girls*, the band's tightest, smartest, funniest, most exciting collection since the beginning of the decade. At sessions in Paris, new sidekick Ronnie Wood emerged as an energetic force, demonstrating that he would be more than a silent partner. The sound of *Some Girls* owes much to his influence. It was a fruitful period, and leftover tracks from these sessions would continue to appear on albums up through *Tattoo You* in 1981.

Among the tracks recorded in Paris was 'Everything Is Turning To Gold', a shivering, up-tempo ballad. Jagger sings as a man blinded by love, happy for this golden moment even if he knows it will one day fade. Built around Charlie Watts' incessant thumping, the song includes two lengthy instrumental passages, including a bluesy saxophone solo from Mel Collins. 'Everything Is Turning To Gold' first appeared as the B-side on the 'Shattered' single. It re-emerged in 1981 on the *Sucking In The Seventies* collection.

1981
If I Was A Dancer (Dance Pt. 2)
(Jagger/Richards/Wood)

'If I Was A Dancer (Dance Pt. 2)' was first released on the *Sucking In The Seventies* album, but as indicated by the title, the song is a continuation of 'Dance Pt. 1' from 1980's *Emotional Rescue*, and was recorded during the same sessions. Listeners will recognize the same sharp funk riff and disco beat with a few lyrical variations.

1989
Fancy Man Blues
(B-side of 'Mixed Emotions')

Keith Richards has long been an admirer of Mick Jagger's abilities on the blues harp. To Richards, the singer's musical soul is bared whenever he's blowing a harmonica riff. That's how it's been since the early days. 'Fancy Man Blues' is a explosive showcase of Jagger's playing, and sounds more organic than other tracks that also emerged from the *Steel Wheels* sessions. The song appeared as a B-side to the single of 'Mixed Emotions'. According to Richards, even members of the band were moved by the quality of Jagger's playing: "Bill thought it was Jimmy Reed the first time he heard this song".

Cook Cook Blues
(B-side of 'Rock And A Hard Place')

'Cook Cook Blues' can best be described as middling chooglin' from a band that should know better.

1991
Highwire

The 1990s began with a rejuvenated Rolling Stones, who were then riding the momentum of their *Steel Wheels* album and enjoying their first tour in nearly a decade. As usual, plans were to release a live album from the tour. But this time, the Glimmer Twins decided to record a pair of new studio tracks to include on *Flashpoint*. So in January 1991, the Rolling Stones stepped off the road and entered the Hit Factory in London.

It was like a throwback to the early days. The Stones habitually interrupted their first American tours with impromptu recording dates at studios in Chicago and Los Angeles. Thus the band was always fresh from the road and playing at their best. That's how 'Satisfaction' was made, and that's how the Stones found success up through their 1969 tour, when they stopped in Muscle Shoals, Alabama, long enough to record 'Brown Sugar', 'Wild Horses' and 'You Gotta Move'. Now they were hoping to reconnect with that muse.

'Highwire' begins with the usual dual riffing of Richards and Wood, and this time it's notably harder than on *Steel Wheels*. Jagger sings his first pointedly topical lyrics since *Undercover*. His inspiration was the Persian Gulf War. At the time of the 'Highwire'/'Sex Drive' sessions, the forces of the West were preparing to launch a ground assault against Iraq in retaliation for its invasion of the tiny oil-rich nation of Kuwait. An apocalyptic air war was already in progress against Iraq, with nightly attacks on Baghdad and various military targets. The grim irony was that during the eighties Iraq was considered an ally of the US, and thus was sold a broad range of high-tech weaponry. Much of that weaponry was now aimed at the gathered forces of America, England, France and other coalition members. Jagger's response was to condemn the international arms trade – a stance that earned the Stones some criticism amid the post-war hoopla of parades and patriotic speeches. But 'Highwire' was a relevant political statement from the band, although perhaps not in the same league as 'Street Fighting Man'. The main problem was that beyond the opening riff, the tune just wasn't memorable.

Sex Drive
(B-side of 'High Wire')

Marginally more successful as a musical statement was 'Sex Drive'. Built on an edgy funk groove, Jagger seethes as always accompanied by the squealing of saxophone of Bobby Keys.

When these brief 1991 sessions ended, the Stones entered a new and uncertain time. What had appeared to be the beginning of a period of frenzied Stones activity disappeared into a cloud of solo projects and idle time. The Rolling Stones would not be back in a studio for three years, and by then Bill Wyman was gone.

1994
The storm
(B-side of 'Love Is Strong')

The Rolling Stones return again to the Delta blues on 'The Storm', a track that could stand proudly beside all but the very best of their early blues work. Released as the B-side to 'Love Is Strong' from *Voodoo Lounge*, the recording is built on a low, haunted vocal from Jagger, who also provides some fiery harmonica flourishes amid the picking and slidework from Richards and Wood. The result is nearly three minutes of spare, authentic blues. The Stones had clearly regained some of their feel for the genre. Even more of it would have been welcome on *Voodoo Lounge*.

So Young
(Second B-side of 'Love Is Strong')

This blues-based track has Jagger lusting for some young French girl. "God help me!" the singer shouts above the blues-rock bluster. The track was produced by Chris Kimsey and is a likely left-over from the *Steel Wheels* sessions. It's a powerful blend of barrelhouse boogie and edgy guitar work from Richards and Wood, and suggests that three decades after discovering the blues in the clubs of London, the Rolling Stones can still find that timeless groove. Elmo Lewis would be proud.

chapter twenty two

not fade away

1997
the rolling stones in

Age is no enemy to the Rolling Stones. Not anymore. Maybe Bill Wyman saw himself as too feeble, too embarrassed, too rich to carry on, but the rest of the Stones found renewed purpose in the 1990s. For the band to break apart now, this deep into their lives, this close to the new millennium, would merely signal a failure of the imagination. Ringmaster Jagger could never allow anything quite so anticlimactic, anything so utterly BORING to stain his reputation for timing and taste. So Keith had been right. Just like Muddy, the Rolling Stones were here to stay.

The dark days of hate and resentment were somehow behind the Glimmer Twins, who had survived the battlefield of *Dirty Work* to understand that active solo careers could coexist peacefully with the Stones, and Mick had never put his acting hopes ahead of the band, for all his talk of movie projects in the pipeline. But it had been nearly five years between *Steel Wheels* and *Voodoo Lounge*, a silence longer than any other in the band's history. In 1997, the Rolling Stones looked ready to make up for lost time, announcing plans to record a new album before embarking on a fall tour.

"I want to do something that's a bit more groundbreaking," Jagger told journalist David Sinclair of his hopes for the next album. "Producers and engineers always want you to do another *Exile On Main Street*, but I want to move on to something that's different and new and a bit more exciting."

Yet for all his grumbling about the retro sound of *Voodoo Lounge*, Jagger agreed to bring back producer Don Was to oversee the new recording. *Voodoo Lounge* had, after all, sold a respectable 5.5 million worldwide. Similarly, the Was-produced live album, *Stripped*, sold more than 3.5 million. Those are impressive numbers for a quartet of aging hipsters, and Jagger is the last man to argue with success. Diamond Don was back as executive producer.

The Glimmer Twins also brought in a few hired guns to help edge the band toward contemporary nirvana. Their choices were typically extreme. Babyface, who had produced Eric Clapton's Grammy-winning *Change The World*, placed the Stones within his smooooooth, warm groove on at least one ballad. Most alarming, the Stones were also working with the infamous Dust Brothers, the production team that had brought a euphoric mix of crazy beats and intense sampling to genre-breaking albums by Beck – the Grammy-winning *Odelay* – and *Paul's Boutique* by the Beastie Boys. Not exactly the Stones' usual crowd. Welcome to the nineties.

The Stones chose not to journey to some exotic studio in Jamaica or Munich, or even the South of France for the new album. Work began early in the year much closer to home, with a series of songwriting sessions in New York City. One visitor was Marianne Faithfull, then about to embark on another tour singing the Weimar Republic songbook of Brecht and Weill. "Lovely," Faithfull says of the session she witnessed, where time hadn't dramatically altered the work habits of the band she had known for so long. "Maybe a little bit. It comes from the heart, you know?"

not fade away

By spring, the Stones gathered for work in Los Angeles, setting up for the long job ahead at Ocean Way Studios, once known as United Western, in rooms where Louis Armstrong, Ella Fitzgerald, the Beach Boys, Johnny Cash and Frank Sinatra had all recorded. Sessions usually began on time at 7 pm, with a dinner break at 10 pm, and then typically drifted deep into the early morning hours or, as Was said more than once, "Until Keith gets tired".

The usual stream of friends, musicians and other visitors came and went at Ocean Way, which offered valet parking during Stones sessions. One visitor was the young neo-folk singer Jewel, there to talk to Was about an upcoming project. She drank tea with the band and chatted with Jagger about touring Europe. Elsewhere at the Ocean Way complex, located on Sunset Boulevard in the heart of Hollywood, one-time Stones sideman Ry Cooder worked on a movie soundtrack, and Liz Phair, whose acclaimed *Exile In Guyville* was a song-by-song response to a similarly titled album by the Stones, worked on her third album. One evening, B.B. King arrived with producer John Porter to record a track with Watts and Ron Wood for the bluesman's new album.

Another visitor was former Stones engineer Andy Johns, now living in Los Angeles. "They were set up the same ol' way. It looked like it did 30 years ago," says Johns, who chatted amiably with Richards and Watts. "Mick's working in one room with one guy, Keith and Charlie are working in the other room with another guy, and Don Was is executive producer for everything. It looks like absolute chaos. Who knows? They'll pull it off."

As ever, the band had dozens of songs in the works during these early stages. Among the working song titles were 'Ever Changing World' and 'Thief In The Night', both produced by Was. Tracks tended to be recorded live in the studio, with band members standing eye-to-eye, including bassist Darryl Jones and percussionist Jim Keltner. "Was is not in the control room, but actually in the studio behind a keyboard, sort of like an arranger orchestrator, counting off the takes. He's actually in the spread," recounts Harvey Kubernick, an LA-based producer who witnessed several sessions.

According to Kubernick, the April session for 'Thief In The Night' documented a slow blues-based tune. During the recording, Jagger played harmonica, sat on a stool reading lyrics from his notebook.

"It's a pretty, slow song. Keith is playing some pretty guitar, and it's percussion driven a little bit," says Kubernick, guest of Keltner and Watts. "It's a very loose atmosphere. Don Was seems to run a very nice programme, from the meticulous sound design to the food coming at precise times to just a really good vibe. It's not a party. The only woman in the room was Jane Rose, who is Keith's manager. This was all business, but not like some corporate board meeting. Studio time costs money."

Between takes, the conversation tended to remain focused on music. Watts wanted to know where the old LA jazz clubs had once stood. Where was Billy Berg's? The Haig? During one break, the band watched *Lady Sings The Blues* on TV, and Keith noticed that the musical arrangement of one scene was dragging. He snapped at the tube: "Pick it up!" Richards also spoke of Eddie Cochran, whose song 'Something Else' the guitarist had covered on his last solo tour. Cochran, Keith noted, had even played drums on the original track. "Hey mate," Keith said. "you can hear a lot of polka on that stuff, too."

The scene was very different at the Dust Brothers sessions. Most of their work was done at their home studio, PCP Labs, up in the hills of nearby Silver Lake. In 1997, Silver Lake was still in the waning days of an over-hyped rock and pop scene, where clubs like Spaceland and The Garage were host to an endless stream of would-be alternative superstars. But it was also headquarters to the illustrious Dust Brothers,

Don Was makes the transition from avant-garde funkster to top producer.

who transformed an innocuous three-bedroom stucco house into a groundbreaking studio.

Of all the Stones, Jagger was the most frequent visitor to PCP Labs. No doubt the Stones' interest in the postmodern and in passing pop fashion was initiated by Mick, who cooked up a few demos that already sounded as if the Dust Brothers had worked on them. "The very first demo that Mick played for us just had these amazing Dusty drums, just totally bangin' drums that sounded distorted," says Dust Brother Mike Simpson. "It just had a nasty flow, electrofunk kind of sound to it. And it was just right up our alley. I was delighted because I was a little nervous going to meet with them to hear what kind of songs they had in mind. They had obviously done their homework.

> **"They are not interested in recreating the past"**
>
> Mike Simpson, Dust Brothers

"They're very enthusiastic. Before meeting them and getting into it, my one concern was that after all these years how could they still have the passion and the hunger? With all the money and success they've had it seems like it would be real difficult to get them excited. But they're definitely more passionate than most new bands. So far my experience with them is that they don't even need a producer. They have a really strong vision and they know what they're doing, and they know their way around the studio just as well as any producer."

Sessions with the Dust Brothers were far more private than the madness at Ocean Way. Very often it was just Mick, Dust Brothers Mike Simpson and John King, and engineer Charlie Goodan. Jagger typically arrived in his black Lincoln Continental during the afternoon, usually accompanied by his driver and assistant Rowan Blade. PCP Labs has no air conditioning, so the singer was initially bothered by the Southern California heat. He got used to it.

"A couple of weeks ago, all the windows were open while we were recording because it was so hot," says Goodan. "You could hear Mick singing from down the block. There were people outside walking their dog. He sounds just like he does live, and he dances around the living room right in front of you. Amazing! It's not an act on stage. That's just him."

By April, the Dust Brothers had worked on two tracks with the Stones, one a classic Stones rocker, the other something more experimental. Players on the tracks included Me'Shell NdegeOcello on bass, and Billy Preston on piano and organ. The Dust Brothers role was largely centred on the underlying rhythm, mixing drum machines and beat samples with the live drumming of Charlie Watts. "Our focus is always the beat and the rhythm tracks," says Simpson. "Charlie's an amazing drummer, and it's not like he needs our help. But we're just trying to put an extra twist on it."

During one visit to PCP Labs, Watts spent much of his time going through the Dust Brothers' vinyl record collection. "Charlie is great," says Goodan. "He's funny and nice and all he talks about is jazz. He has a heyday every time he comes over, and just goes through records. He pulls them out and goes: 'I met this guy once. I played with him...' and the whole story."

Though the Dust Brothers came down once or twice a week to Ocean Way, where all guitars were recorded, they preferred the homey PCP Labs vibe. "It's such a laid back environment and it doesn't feel like a studio, so it doesn't have this sterile 'Oh my God, the clock's ticking!' kind of vibe to it," says Simpson. "They've all been really comfortable working up there."

The Dust Brothers working relationship with Was on the new Stones album was friendly, and designed mainly to promote a certain level of consistency amid all the tracks and producers. Mick Jagger, Watts and Was once dropped in unannounced to hear the Dust Brother tracks, but Was otherwise focused his attentions on the Ocean Way sessions.

"They are not interested in recreating the past," Simpson says of the Stones. "When we initially met with Mick, I told him straight up: 'I'm definitely a fan of your work, and I've probably heard each of your albums at least once, but I'm in no way a Stones freak. So there may be some things I'm not familiar with.' Mick was 'Oh, I'm so RELIEVED, I've worked with so many producers and engineers over the years, and they all grew up listening to the Stones, and they all have their favourite song off their favourite album, and they always come to the project with this baggage. Their goal is to recreate their favourite Stones song. It's so refreshing to work with someone that doesn't come with that baggage'.

That baggage is heavy enough every time the band hits the road. Old songs. New songs. Old, old songs. The 13-month *Voodoo Lounge* tour was declared the highest-grossing tour of the century when it ended in 1995, outpacing ticket sales by the likes of Michael Jackson and Pink Floyd. And the concert experience is different now, for both band and audience. In the old days, Keith and Woody could decide on a whim to drive all night long up to the next gig, and then stumble on stage in a half-conscious stupor. As they demonstrated with the *Steel Wheels* and *Voodoo Lounge* tours, the Stones are now a reliably tight playing unit. In tune and in sync. This isn't the 1972 tour of wild sex, hard drugs and sloppy rock and roll as seen in *Cocksucker Blues*. Things have simply become more professional.

"Right now it's very easy," says saxman Bobby Keys, who has been a part of most Stones tours since the early 1970s. "They have all the bases covered, man. They've got doctors, lawyers, cooks, maids, hairdressers, physical therapists, anything you need. It's like a self-contained travelling city. It's much different than it was in the seventies. In the seventies it was a little more free-wheeling. Now it's a little bit more corporate business structure. But it has to be, because it's a big operation. And I'm older now. I'm not in my twenties anymore, man, I'm in my fifties. So I dig it now. Most of the places we go now I play golf on the days off, rather than the other activities I used to pursue."

The Rolling Stones have by now taken their music beyond any acceptable standard of age and decorum. Journalists first began asking how long Jagger could play this game as he approached 30. But in any other field, the members of the Rolling Stones would be seen not as old and ruined, but merely as middle-aged journeymen, still virile and capable of good work. Think of Duke Ellington, who wasn't peddling nostalgia even in his final days. Or Thelonious Monk or Frank Sinatra or Merle Haggard. That's a rarefied group of cats, but in the field of rock and roll, few fit that role better than the Rolling Stones.

"It's funny what they say about the Stones: Why don't they retire, these old farts," says Marty Balin of the Jefferson Airplane. "When I was a kid growing up, what if Muddy had retired? Or Willie Dixon? Little Walter? If I had never seen those guys as a kid I wouldn't know a lot of things. It's such a ridiculous question – that you can get too old for music. You just get better and better if you're wise. You can see some real interesting bodies of work now."

For John Mayall, whose career emerged from the British blues scene first popularized by the Stones, "Creating music is an art. Jazz musicians and blues

musicians, their careers do not end except by death. It's something that has a built-in longevity. It's not a flash in the pan thing. The years only make you more mature, you learn more and more as the years go by."

Mick Jagger turned 53 in 1997. For him to continue now is just one more rebellious act against the expectations of society. The Rolling Stones somehow managed to remain more relevant than most artistes from their celebrated decade. If their days of undeniable greatness seem far behind them, the Stones at least continue with a measure of real dignity and occasional flashes of the old brilliance, as a band that for now, at least, is still gathering no moss.

Still crazy after all these years: the Stones take a bow at the end of a show.

chapter twenty three

You got me rocking:
A Rolling Stones Discography

Singles

Come On/I Want To Be Loved
June 1963
No. 20 in the UK
Decca/London Records

I Wanna Be Your Man/Stoned
November 1963
No. 12 in the UK
Decca/London Records

Not FadeAway/ Little By Little
February 1964
No. 3 in the UK, No. 48 in the US
Decca/London Records

It's All Over Now/
Good Times, Bad Times
June 1964
No. 1 in the UK, No. 26 in the US
Decca/London Records

Tell Me (You're Coming Back)/
I Just Wanna Make Love To You
August 1964
No. 24 in the US
Decca/London Records

Time Is On My Side/
Congratulations
November 1964
No. 6 in the US
Decca/London Records

Little Red Rooster/
Off The Hook
November 1964
No. 1 in the UK
Decca/London Records

Heart Of Stone/
What A Shame
January 1965
No. 19 in the US
Decca/London Records

The Last Time/Play With Fire
February 1965
No. 1 in the UK, No. 9 in the US
Decca/London Records

(I Can't Get No) Satisfaction/
Spider And The Fly
August 1965
No 1 in both the US and UK
Decca/London Records

Get Off Of My Cloud/
The Singer Not The Song
October 1965
No 1 in both the US and UK
Decca/London Records

As Tears Go By/Gotta Get Away
January 1966
No. 6 in the US
Decca/London Records

19th Nervous Breakdown/
As Tears Go By
February 1966
No. 1 in the US, No. 2 in the UK
Decca/London Records

Paint It, Black/
Long Long While
May 1966
No. 1 in both the US and UK
Decca/London Records

Have You Seen Your Mother
Baby, Standing In The
Shadow?/Who's Driving
Your Plane
September 1966
No. 5 in the UK, No. 9 in the US
Decca/London Records

Let's Spend The Night
Together/Ruby Tuesday
January 1967
No. 1 in the US, No. 3 in the UK
Decca/London Records

We Love You/Dandelion
August 1967
No. 8 in the UK, No. 14 in the US
Decca/London Records

Jumping Jack Flash/
Child Of The Moon
May 1968
No. 1 in the UK, No. 3 in the US
Decca/London Records

Honky Tonk Women/
You Can't Always Get What
You Want
July 1969
No 1 in both the US and UK
Decca/London Records

Brown Sugar/Bitch/
Let It Rock
April 1971
No. 1 in the US, No. 2 in the UK
Rolling Stones Records

Tumbling Dice/
Sweet Black Angel
April 1972
No. 7 in the US, No. 5 in the UK
Rolling Stones Records

Angie/Silver Train
August 1973
No. 1 in the US, No. 5 in the UK
Rolling Stones Records

It's Only Rock 'N' Roll/
Through The Lonely Nights
July 1974
No. 16 in the US, No. 10 in the UK
Rolling Stones Records

Fool To Cry/Crazy Mama
April 1976
No. 4 in the UK, No. 10 in the US
Rolling Stones Records

Miss You/Far Away Eyes
May 1978
No. 1 in the US, No. 2 in the UK
Rolling Stones Records

Beast Of Burden/
When The Whip Comes Down
August 1978
No. 8 in the US
Rolling Stones Records

**Respectable/
When The Whip Comes Down**
September 1978
No. 7 in the US, No. 23 in the UK
Rolling Stones Records

**Emotional Rescue/
Down In The Hole**
July 1980
No. 3 in the US, No. 9 in the UK
Rolling Stones Records

She's So Cold/Send It To Me
September 1980
No. 26 in the US, No. 33 in the UK
Rolling Stones Records

Start Me Up/No Use In Crying
August 1981
No. 2 in the US, No. 4 in the UK
Rolling Stones Records

**Waiting On A Friend/
Little T & A**
November 1981
No. 13 in the US, No. 50 in the UK
Rolling Stones Records

**Going To A Go-Go/
Beast of Burden**
May 1982
No. 25 in the US, No. 26 in the UK
Rolling Stones Records

**Undercover Of The Night/
All The Way Down**
November 1983
No. 9 in the US, No. 11 in the UK
Rolling Stones Records

**She Was Hot/
Think I'm Going Mad**
February 1984
No. 42 in the UK, No. 44 in the US
Rolling Stones Records

Harlem Shuffle/Had It With You
March 1986
No. 5 in the US, No. 7 in the UK
Rolling Stones Records

One Hit To The Body/Fight
May 1986
No. 28 in the US
Rolling Stones Records

**Mixed Emotions/Fancyman
Blues**
August 1989
No. 5 in the US, No. 33 in the UK
Rolling Stones Records

Rock And A Hard Place
November 1989
No. 23 in the US, No. 63 in the UK
Rolling Stones Records

**Almost Hear You Sigh/
Wish I'd Never Met You**
June 1990
No. 31 in the UK, No. 50 in the US
Rolling Stones Records

**Terrifying/Rock And A
Hard Place**
July 1990
Rolling Stones Records

**Highwire/2000 Light Years
From Home (live)**
February 1991
No. 29 in the UK, No. 57 in the US
Rolling Stones Records

Ruby Tuesday (live)
June 1991
Rolling Stones Records

Love Is Strong/The Storm
July 1994
No. 14 in the UK, No. 88 in the US
Rolling Stones Records/Virgin

Out Of Tears
October 1994
Rolling Stones Records/Virgin

**You Got Me Rocking/
Jump On Top Of Me**
October 1994
Rolling Stones Records/Virgin

Albums

Note that up until 1967's *Between The Buttons*, track listings varied greatly between the UK and the US. For more details see the chapters on individual albums.

The Rolling Stones
(*England's Newest Hitmakers* in the US)
April 1964
Route 66, I Just Want To Make Love To You, Honest I Do, I Need You Baby, Now I've Got A Witness, Little By Little, I'm A King Bee, Carol, Tell Me (You're Coming Back), Can I Get A Witness, You Can Make It If You Try, Walking The Dog
US 11, UK 1
ABCKO Records

12x5
(US-only release)
October 1964
Around And Around, Confessin' The Blues, Empty Heart, Time Is On My Side, Good Times, Bad Times, It's All Over Now, 2120 South Michigan Avenue, Under the Boardwalk, Congratulations, Grown Up Wrong, If You Need Me, Susie Q
US 3
London/ABKCO

The Rolling Stones No. 2
(UK-only release)
January 1965
Everybody Needs Somebody to Love, Down Home Girl, You Can't Catch Me, Time Is On My Side, What A Shame, Grown Up Wrong, Down The Road Apiece, Under the Boardwalk, I Can't Be Satisfied, Pain In My Heart, Off The Hook, Susie Q
UK 1
ABCKO Records

The Rolling Stones Now
(US-only release)
February 1965
Everybody Needs Somebody to Love, Down Home Girl, You Can't Catch Me, Heart Of Stone, What A Shame, I Need You Baby, Down The Road Apiece, Off The Hook, Pain In My Heart, Oh Baby (We Got A Good Thing Goin'), Little Red Rooster, Surprise, Surpise
US 5
London/ABKCO

Out Of Our Heads
September 1965
She Said Yeah, Mercy, Mercy, Hitch Hike, That's How Strong My Love Is, Good Times, Gotta Get Away, Talkin Bout You, Cry To Me, Oh Baby (We Got A Good Thing Goin'), Heart Of Stone,The Under Assistant West Coast Promotion Man, I'm Free
US 1, UK 2
ABCKO Records

Aftermath
April 1966
Mother's Little Helper, Stupid Girl, Lady Jane, Under My Thumb, Doncha Bother Me, Goin' Home, Flight 505, High And Dry, Out Of Time, It's Not Easy, I Am Waiting, Take It Or Leave It, Think, What To Do
US 1, UK 1
ABCKO Records

Between The Buttons
January 1967
Yesterday's Papers, My Obsession, Back Street Girl, Connection, She Smiled Sweetly, Cool, Calm And Collected, All Sold Out, Please Go Home, Who's Been Sleeping Here?, Complicated, Miss Amanda Jones, Something Happened To Me Yesterday
US 2, UK 3
ABCKO Records

Flowers
(US-only release)
June 1967
Ruby Tuesday, Have You Seen Your Mother, Baby, Standing in the Shadow?, Let's Spend The Night Together, Lady Jane, Out Of Time, My Girl, Back Street Girl, Please Go Home, Mother's Little Helper, Take It Or Leave It, Ride On Baby, Sittin' On A Fence
US 2
London/ABKCO

**Their Satanic Majesties
Request**
December 1967
Sing This All Together, Citadel, In Another Land, 2000 Man, Sing This All Together (See What Happens), She's A Rainbow, The Lantern, Gomper, 2000 Light Years From Home, On With the Show
US 2, UK 3
ABCKO Records

Beggars Banquet
December 1968
Sympathy For The Devil, No Expectations, Dear Doctor, Parachute Woman, Jig-Saw Puzzle, Street Fighting Man, Prodigal Son, Stray Cat Blues, Factory Girl, Salt Of The Earth
US 2, UK 3
ABCKO Records

Let It Bleed
December 1969
Gimme Shelter, Love In Vain, Country Honk, Live With Me, Let It Bleed, Midnight Rambler, You Got the Silver, Monkey Man, You Can't Always Get What You Want
US 2, UK 1
ABCKO Records

Get Yer Ya Ya's Out
(Live from the 1969 tour)
September 1970
US 5, UK 1
ABCKO Records

Sticky Fingers
April 1971
Brown Sugar, Sway, Wild Horses, Can't You Hear Me Knocking, You Gotta Move, Bitch, I Got the Blues, Sister Morphine, Dead Flowers, Moonlight Mile
US 1, UK 1
Rolling Stones Records/Virgin

Exile On Main Street
May 1972
Rocks Off, Rip This Joint, Hip Shake, Casino Boogie, Tumbling Dice, Sweet Virginia, Torn And Frayed, Sweet Black Angel, Loving Cup, Happy, Turd On the Run, Ventilator Blues, Just Wanna See His Face, Let It Loose, All Down The Line, Stop Breaking Down, Shine A Light, Soul Survivor
US 1, UK 1
Rolling Stones Records/Virgin

Goats Head Soup
August 1973
Dancing With Mr D, 100 Years Ago, Coming Down Again, Doo Doo Doo Doo Doo (Heartbreaker), Angie, Silver Train, Hide Your Love, Winter, Can You Hear the Music, Star Star
US 1, UK 1
Rolling Stones Records/Virgin

It's Only Rock 'N' Roll
October 1974
If You Can't Rock Me, Ain't Too Proud To Beg, It's Only Rock 'N' Roll (But I Like It), Till The Next Goodbye, Time Waits For No One, Luxury, Dance Little Sister, If You Really Want To Be My Friend, Short And Curlies, Fingerprint File
US 1, UK 4
Rolling Stones Records/Virgin

Metamorphosis
June 1975
Out Of Time, Don't Lie To Me, Some Things Just Stick In Your Mind, Each And Every Day Of The Year, Heart Of Stone, I'd Much Rather Be With The Boys, (Walkin Thru The) Sleepy City, We're Wastin' Time, Try A Little Harder, I Don't Know Why, If You Let Me, Jiving Sister Fanny, Downtown Suzie, Family, Memo From Turner, I'm Going Down
(US version deletes Some Things Just Stick In Your Mind and We're Wastin Time)
US 8
ABKCO

Black And Blue
April 1976
Hot Stuff, Hand Of Fate, Cherry Oh Baby, Memory Motel, Hey Negrita, Melody, Fool To Cry, Crazy Mama
US 1, UK 2
Rolling Stones Records/Virgin

Love You Live
September 1977
US 5, UK 3
Rolling Stones Records/Virgin

Some Girls
June 1978
Miss You, When The Whip Comes Down, Just My Imagination, Some Girls, Lies, Far Away Eyes, Respectable, Before They Make Me Run, Beast Of Burden, Shattered
US 1, UK 2
Rolling Stones Records/Virgin

Emotional Rescue
June 1980
Dance (Pt. 1), Summer Romance, Send It To Me, Let Me Go, Indian Girl, Where The Boys Go, Down In The Hole, Emotional Rescue, She's So Cold, All About You
US 1, UK 1
Rolling Stones Records/Virgin

Tattoo You
September 1981
Start Me Up, Hang Fire, Slave, Little T&A, Black Limousine, Neighbors, Worried About You, Tops, Heaven, No Use In Crying, Waiting On A Friend
US 1, UK 1
Rolling Stones Records/Virgin

Still Life
(1981 US Concert)
June 1982
UK 2, US 20
Rolling Stones Records/Virgin

Undercover
November 1983
Undercover Of The Night, She Was Hot, Tie You Up (The Pain Of Love), Wanna Hold You, Feel On Baby, Too Much Blood, Pretty Beat Up, Too Tough, All The Way Down, It Must Be Hell
UK 1, US 4
Rolling Stones Records/Virgin

Dirty Work
April 1986
One Hit (To The Body), Fight, Harlem Shuffle, Hold Back, Too Rude, Winning Ugly, Back To Zero, Dirty Work, Had It With You, Sleep Tonight
US 4, UK 3
Rolling Stones Records/Virgin

Steel Wheels
September 1989
Sad Sad Sad, Mixed Emotions, Terrifying, Hold On To Your Hat, Hearts For Sale, Blinded By Love, Rock And A Hard Place, Can't Be Seen, Almost Hear You Sigh, Continental Drift, Break The Spell, Slipping Away
US 3, UK 2
Rolling Stones Records/Virgin

Flashpoint
April 1991
UK 6
Rolling Stones Records/Virgin

Voodoo Lounge
August 1994
Love Is Strong, You Got Me Rocking, Sparks Will Fly, The Worst, News Faces, Moon Is Up, Out Of Tears, I Go Wild, Brand New Car, Sweethearts Together, Suck On The Jugular, Blinded By Rainbows, Baby Break It Down, Thru And Thru, Mean Disposition
US 2, UK 2
Rolling Stones Records/Virgin

Stripped
(May 1995)
Street Fighting Man, Like A Rolling Stone, Not Fade Away, Shine A Light, The Spider And The Fly, I'm Free, Wild Horses, Let It Bleed, Dead Flowers, Slipping Away, Angie, Love In Vain, Sweet Virginia, Little Baby
Rolling Stones Records/Virgin

The Rolling Stones Rock And Roll Circus
October 1995
1968 film Including performances of Jumping Jack Flash, Parachute Woman, No Expectations, You Can't Always Get What You Want, Sympathy For The Devil, Salt Of The Earth
ABKCO Records

New release (as yet untitled)
(October 1997)
Thief In The Night, Out of Control, Juiced, Saint, Already Over Me, Always Suffering, Nobody's Seen My Baby, Gin Face, Too Tight, You Don't Have to Mean It, How Can I Stop, Flip The Switch, Anyway You Look At It
Rolling Stones Records/Virgin

EPs

The Rolling Stones
January 1964
Bye Bye Johnny, Money, You Better Move On, Poison Ivy
Decca/London

Five By Five
August 1964
If You Need Me, Empty Heart, 2120 South Michigan Avenue, Confessin' The Blues, Around And Around
Decca/London

Got Live If You Want It
June 1965
We Want the Stones, Everybody Needs Somebody To Love, Pain In My Heart, (Get Your Kicks On) Route 66, I'm Moving On, I'm Alright
ABKCO Records

Compilations

Big Hits (High Tide And Green Grass)
November 1966
US 2, UK 4
ABKCO Records

Through The Past Darkly (Big Hits Volume 2)
September 1969
US 2, UK 1
ABKCO Records

Stone Age
April 1971
UK 5
ABKCO Records

Made In The Shade
June 1975
US 6, UK 10
Rolling Stones Records

Sucking In The Seventies
May 1981
Shattered, Everything Is Turning To Gold, Hot Stuff, Time Waits For No One, Fool To Cry, Mannish Boy, When The Whip Comes Down, If I Was A Dancer (Dance Pt. 2), Crazy Mama, Beast of Burden
US 17
Rolling Stones Records

Singles Collection: The London Years
September 1989
ABKCO Records

Rewind (1971–1984)
November 1989
Rolling Stones Records/Virgin

Jump Back (The Best Of…)
November 1993
ABKCO Records

Selected Solo Releases

MICK JAGGER

Memo From Turner/ Natural Magic
(single from the soundtrack to the film *Performance*)
November 1970
Decca/London/ABKCO

She's The Boss
(album)
March 1984
No. 6 in the UK, No. 8 in the US
Columbia Records

Lucky In Love
(single)
April 1985
No. 38 in US
Columbia Records

Dancing In The Street
(single – duet with David Bowie)
August 1985
No. 1 in the UK, No. 7 in the US
EMI Records

Ruthless People/I'm Raining
(single from the soundtrack to the film *Ruthless People*)
July 1986
No. 51 in US
Columbia Records

Let's Work/ Catch As Catch Can
(single)
August 1987
No. 39 in the UK, No. 35 in the US
Columbia Records

Primitive Cool
(album)
September 1987
No. 18 in the UK, No. 41 in the US
Columbia Records

**Throw Away/
Peace Of The Wicked**
(single)
November 1987
Columbia Records

Wandering Spirit
(album)
February 1993
Atlantic Records

KEITH RICHARDS

**Run Rudolph Run/
The Harder They Fall**
(single)
December 1978
Rolling Stones Records

**Take It So Hard/
I Could Have Stood You Up**
(single)
September 1988
Virgin Records

Talk is Cheap
(album)
October 1988
No. 24 in the US
Virgin Records

Make No Mistake
(single)
April 1989
Virgin Records

**Keith Richards And The
X-pensive Winos Live At The
Hollywood Paladium,
December 15, 1988**
(November 1991)
Virgin Records

Main Offender
(album)
October 1992
Virgin Records

BILL WYMAN

Monkey Grip
(album)
May 1974
Rolling Stones Records

White Lightnin'
(single)
November 1974
Rolling Stones Records

Stone Alone
(album)
February 1976
Rolling Stones Records

**Quarter To Three/
Soul Satisfying**
(single)
April 1976
Rolling Stones Records

Green Ice
(film soundtrack)
February 1981
EMI Records

(Si Si) Je Sui Un Rock Star
(single)
July 1981
No. 13 in the UK
Ripple/A&M

Come Back Suzanne
(single)
October 1981
Ripple/A&M

A New Fashion
(single)
March 1982
Ripple/A&M

Willie And The Poorboys
(album – band features Wyman, Jimmy Page
and Paul Rodgers)
April 1985
Ripple Records

CHARLIE WATTS

Live At The Fullham Town Hall
(album by the Charlie Watts Orchestra)
December 1986
Columbia Records

**A Tribute To Charlie Parker,
With Strings**
(album by the Charlie Watts Quintet)
May 1992
Virgin Records

RON WOOD

(Also see albums by the Faces, Jeff Beck
Group and Rod Stewart)

**I've Got My Own Album
To Do**
1974
Warner Bros.

Now Look
1975
Warner Bros.

Mahoney's Last Stand
(album with Ronnie Lane)
1976
Atco Records

Gimme Some Neck
1979
Columbia Records

1234
August 1981
Columbia Records

Slide On This
1992
Continuum Records

MICK TAYLOR

(Also see albums by John Mayall's
Bluesbreakers)

Mick Taylor
1979
Columbia

Stranger In This Town
1980
Maze Music

Too Hot For Snakes
(album with Carla Olson)
1991
Razor Edge Records

Once In A Blue Moon
(album with Gerry Groom)
1996
Shattered Music

Miscellany

**Brian Jones Presents The
Pipes Of Pan At JouJouka**
(album recorded in Morocco by Jones with
engineer George Chkiantz in 1968)
October 1971
Rolling Stones Records

Jamming With Edward
(jam session with Jagger, Wyman, Watts, Ry
Cooder and Nicky Hopkins)
1972/1997
Rolling Stones Records/Pointblank/Virgin

Don't Look Back
(single by Peter Tosh featuring guest vocal by
Mick Jagger)
November 1978
Rolling Stones Records/Virgin

Holdin' Out My Love To You
(album by reggae singer Max Romeo, featuring
playing by Keith Richards)
Summer 1981
Shannachie Records

Silver and Gold
(track featuring Richards, Wood and U2's Bono
from *Artists United Against Apartheid*)
October 1985
EMI Records

**The Symphonic Music Of The
Rolling Stones**
(album featuring performances by Jagger,
Marianne Faithfull, Michael Hutchence,
Maire Brennan, Jerry Hadley and the London
Symphony Orchestral produced by
Chris Kimsey)
1994
RCA Victor

**Shared Vision II: The Songs
Of The Rolling Stones**
(Songs of the Rolling Stones performed by
Johnny Cash, Rod Stewart, Marianne Faithfull,
Joe Cocker, The Pogues, Tom Jones, The
Feelies and others)
October 1996
Mercury Records

index

100 Years Ago 130
19th Nervous Breakdown 35
2000 Light Years From Home 59, 66
2000 Man 62-3

a
Ain't Too Proud To Beg 138
All About You 173
All Down The Line 123-4
All Sold Out 50
All The Way Down 199
Almost Hear You Sigh 266
Angie 49, 128, 131-2
As Tears Go By 38, 49

b
Baby Break It Down 237
Back Street Girl 45, 48
Back To Zero 211
Beast Of Burden 164
Before They Make Me Run 6, 162-3
Bitch 104
Black Limousine 180
Blinded By Love 224
Blinded By Rainbows 236
Brand New Car 235
Break The Spell 227
Brown Sugar 9, 98, 100-1

c
Can You Hear The Music 134
Can't Be Seen 225
Can't You Hear Me Knocking 103-4
Casino Boogie 111
Citadel 60
Coming Down Again 128, 130
Complicated 52
Connection 49
Continental Drift 75, 226-7
Cool, Calm And Collected 50
Country Honk 88
Crazy Mama 153

d
Dance Little Sister 143-4
Dance (Pt. 1) 167, 168-9
Dancing In The Street 29
Dancing With Mr D 127, 129-30
Dead Flowers 107
Dear Doctor 76-7
Dirty Work 212
Doncha Bother Me 39
Doo Doo Doo Doo Doo (Heartbreaker) 131, 137
Down In The Hole 172

e
Emotional Rescue 167, 172

f
Factory Girl 81
Far Away Eyes 161
Feel On Baby 195
Fight 209
Fingerprint File 145
Flight 505 40
Fool To Cry 153

g
Get Off Of My Cloud 35
Gimme Shelter 86-7
Goin' Home 39-40
Gomper 66
Gotta Get Away 31
Grown Up Wrong 26

h
Had It With You 213
Happy 119-20
Hand Of Fate 150
Hang Fire 179
Harlem Shuffle 205
Have Mercy 30
Have You Seen Your Mother, Baby, Standing In The Shadow? 45
Heart Of Stone 25, 32
Hearts For Sale 223-4
Heaven 185
Hey Negrita 151-2
Hide Your Love 132
High And Dry 40
Hold Back 209
Hold On To Your Hat 223
Honest I Do 18
Honky Tonk Women 11, 84, 95
Hot Stuff 149-50, 168

i
I Am Waiting 42
(I Can't Get No) Satisfaction 6, 29, 33
I Go Wild 235
I Got The Blues 105
I Just Want To Make Love To You 18, 23
I Wanna Be Your Man 11, 18-19
If I Was A Dancer (Dance Pt. 2) 169
If You Can't Rock Me 139
If You Really Want To Be My Friend 144
I'm A King Bee 17
I'm Free 33
In Another Land 61
Indian Girl 171
It Must Be Hell 201
It's All Over Now 17-18, 24
It's Not Easy 41
It's Only Rock And Roll (But I Like It) 139-40, 147

j
Jigsaw Puzzle 78
Jumpin' Jack Flash 70, 84, 103
Just Wanna See His Face 121

l
Lady Jane 38
Lantern, The 65
Let It Bleed 11, 91
Let It Loose 122-3, 125
Let Me Go 170
Let's Spend The Night Together 45
Lies 160, 161
Little By Little 21
Little Red Rooster 26
Little T & A 180
Live With Me 88, 91
Love Is Strong 231-2
Loving Cup 119
Luxury 142

m
Mean Disposition 239
Melody 153
Memory Motel 151
Midnight Rambler 93
Miss Amanda Jones 52
Miss You 156-7, 169
Mixed Emotions 221-2
Monkey Man 94-5
Moon Is Up 235
Moonlight Mile 107
Mother's Little Helper 35, 36, 41
My Obsession 47

n
Neighbors 180, 182-3
New Faces 234
No Expectations 69, 75
No Use In Crying 185
Now I've Got A Witness (Like Uncle Phil And Uncle Gene) 19

o
Off The Hook 26
On With The Show 50, 67
One Hit (To The Body) 207-8
Out Of Tears 235
Out Of Time 41, 43, 45

p
Paint It, Black 35, 45, 59
Parachute Woman 77
Play With Fire 30
Please Go Home 45, 50
Pretty Beat Up 198-9
Prodigal Son 69

r
Respectable 161, 162
Rip This Joint 111
Rock And A Hard Place 225
Rocks Off 110-11
Ruby Tuesday 45

s
Sad Sad Sad 221
Salt Of The Earth 81, 125
Send It To Me 170
Shattered 165
She Smiled Sweetly 49
She Was Hot 192-3
She's A Rainbow 59, 65
She's So Cold 173
Shine A Light 125
Short And Curlies 144
Silver Train 132
Sing This All Together (See What Happens) 59-60, 63
Sister Morphine 105-7
Slave 179
Sleep Tonight 213-15
Slipping Away 227
Some Girls 117, 159-60
Something Happened To Me Yesterday 53
Soul Survivor 125
Sparks Will Fly 233
Star Star 128, 134-5
Start Me Up 175, 177, 179
Stop Breaking Down 124
Stray Cat Blues 80
Street Fighting Man 78-9
Stupid Girl 37, 104
Suck On The Jugular 236
Summer Romance 169-70
Sway 101
Sweet Black Angel 116-17
Sweet Virginia 114
Sweethearts Together 236
Sympathy For The Devil 71-3, 129

t
Take It Or Leave It 43
Tell Me You're Coming Back 21
Terrifying 223
That's How Strong My Love Is 30
Think 43
Thru And Thru 238-9
Tie You Up (The Pain Of Love) 195
Till The Next Goodbye 140
Time Is On My Side 24, 26
Time Waits For No One 140-2, 143
Too Much Blood 196-7
Too Tough 198
Tops 183, 185
Torn And Frayed 114-16
Tumbling Dice 109, 113
Turd On The Run 120

u
Under Assistant West Coast Promotion Man, The 30, 32
Under My Thumb 35, 38-9, 43, 97, 104
Undercover Of The Night 191-2

v
Ventilator Blues 121

w
Waiting On A Friend 128, 186-7
Wanna Hold You 195
What A Shame 25
What To Do 43
When The Whip Comes Down 159, 161
Where The Boys Go 171
Who's Been Sleeping Here? 51-2
Wild Horses 11, 98, 102-3
Winning Ugly 211
Winter 133
Worried About You 183
Worst, The 234

y
Yesterday's Papers 46-7
You Can't Always Get What You Want 95, 125
You Don't Move Me 218
You Got Me Rocking 232-3
You Got The Silver 94
You Gotta Move 98, 99

picture credits

The publishers would like to thank the following sources for their kind permission to reproduce the pictures in this book:

All Action Pictures: /Dave Hogan 228; **Jim Barber:** 196/7; **Corbis:** 70 /Morton Beebe 40 - Bettmann/Reuters 220 -Bettmann/UPI 3, 4c, 5cb, 16, 22, 25, 28, 44, 48, 54, 82, 92, 106, 117, 118, 120, 126, 160, 164, 166, 178, 181, 190/1, 224, 232, 234 /Howard Davies 237 /Henry Diltz 171 /Hulton Deutsch Collection 37, 67, 79, 102, 108, 158 /Kurt Krieger 238 /U.S. Department of Defence 230; **London Features International Ltd.:** 4br, 30/1, 33, 62, 105, 112, 122, 130, 135, 157, 194, 210, 252 Anton Corbijn 186/7 /Frank Griffin 193 /Kevin Mazur 5cl, 216 /Michael Putland 136, 145, 152 /Ken Regan 5tr, 188, 206, 218/9 /Herb Snitzer 182; **Pictorial Press Limited:** 6, 18, 27, 41, 42, 51, 53, 58, 60, 68, 72/3, 76, 78, 80, 89, 94, 96, 98, 100, 119, 125, 131, 133, 138/9, 149, 151, 176/7, 200/1, 226 /Tony Gale 34, 74 /Jordan 222 /Jeffrey Mayer 10 /Martin Norris 85 /Ebet Roberts 90 /Sunstills 173 /Vinyl Experience LT 8; **Redferns:** /Richie Aaron 142 /Dick Barnatt 64 /Fin Costello 50 /Gems 115 /Michael Ochs Archives 20 /David Redfern 56/7, 169, 198/Ebet Roberts 202, 208, 211 /Brian Shuel 9 /G. Wiltshire 214/5; **Retna Pictures Ltd.:** /Gary Gershoff 174 /G. Hanekroot/Sunshine 143, 146 / Michael Putland 1, 87, 154, 204 /Pete Tangen 249; **Rex Features Ltd.:** 163 /Stills/Phillipe Hanon 184; **S.I.N.:** 2 /Tony Mott 233, 251.

Every effort has been made to acknowledge correctly and contact the source and/or copyright holder of each picture, and Carlton Books Limited apologises for any unintentional errors or omissions which will be corrected in future editions of this book.